Small Stories, Great People

- Portuguese Pioneers in Canada -

José Mário Coelho

Preserve the past
to have a better future

JMC

Translation:
Ana Fernandes-Iria
Revised:
Ana Sofia Costa

ISBN
0-9735743-1-3

Publisher:
Creative 7 inc.
1166A Dundas St. W.. Toronto ON M6J 1X4
416-530-0273
Designer:
Jamie Iria

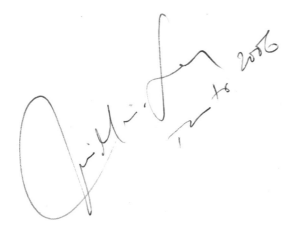

Author's note

I publish this book with two regrets: not being able to write about many others who deserve to be part of this work and my inability to write better. I am not a writer. I am not a journalist. I am simply someone who is interested in everything that surrounds me, particularly, in those who, with much sacrifice and audacity, knew how to open the door to this huge and cold country we call Canada. They were the ones who allowed us to have access to a better future and a better quality of life. Even after hearing these stories in the first person, looking into our pioneers' eyes, I was not able to describe the profound odyssey of pain and sorrow they lived in the first years of Canada. Alone, not understanding the language of the country, and surviving cold temperatures and hunger, these people suffered many setbacks. The only thing that stopped them from returning home was the shame of meeting with failure. We thank them for being so brave.

THANK YOU, PIONEERS!

I would like to take this opportunity to also thank those who – pioneers or not – positively contributed to the development of the Portuguese community in this country. I admire those who, far from their homeland, built a "small Portugal" in Canada. These people did not want to be just one more person among many…

Finally, my eternal gratitude goes to those who, in many different ways, made the publishing of this book possible. bcpbank, Manuel da Costa (Viana Roofing), Frank Sestelo Alvarez (CIRV), Tony Melo (Starlight), Virgílio Pires (Merit Metal), Teacher Ana Fernandes-Iria, José Melo (Melo Landscaping) and José Cesário, Portugal's Secretary of State for the Portuguese Communities.

I would also like to thank consul general of Portugal Artur de Magalhães, Bernardete Gouveia, Raimundo Favas, John Dias and Augusto Pires for their consideration and hard work.

All the best!

José Mário Coelho

Preface

I first met José Mário Coelho almost two decades ago. I had arrived in Toronto fresh from Montreal - where I had spent my first years in this country as a student - to undertake my doctoral studies at York University. At that time I was still an "unknown" in Toronto's Portuguese community and, as my doctoral dissertation would deal with the Portuguese presence in this city, I needed to contact as many "key" people in the community as possible. It was in the course of this research that I first heard the name of a well known and respected "voice" of the Portuguese media in Toronto – J.M.C. – as being an individual whose knowledge about the community might prove invaluable to my work.

My first encounter with J.M.C. was a brief telephone call, during which he graciously granted me – then a total "stranger" to Toronto's Portuguese community – an interview. During this meeting J.M.C. not only provided me with valuable information about the structure and evolution of our community – including some particularly important material about the lives of its "pioneers" – but he also granted me access to his remarkable collection of publications. This included some of his best articles from the "Revista Imagens"; a magazine in Portuguese that he founded with the intention of promoting and informing our community. Although this information was to prove invaluable to my work, J.M.C. also came to play an important role in my personal life in my new city – putting me in touch with many "key" figures in Toronto's Portuguese community – and, in essence, making me feel "at home" in Toronto. Thus, this represents for me an opportunity to remember this first encounter, and to say . . . "Obrigado".

My initial impression of J.M.C. was that he was a man of passion and commitment to his community. As time passed, I came to realize how accurate was this impression. After almost two decades, his persistence and hard work have led to his publication of this remarkable book: "Pequenas Histórias de Gente Grande" (Short Stories of Great People). The range and detail of his in-depth interviews with more than two hundred Portuguese immigrants – including "pioneers" of the Portuguese immigration to Canada – are complemented by the accompanying beautiful pictures, and render this work an important history of our presence and contribution to this great country – Canada. Thus, it represents an important ethno-cultural source of information – a true "cultural bridge" between generations – and a valuable resource not only for the new generations of Portuguese in Canada, but also for academics and scholars researching the Portuguese immigration and settlement in this land. J.M.C.'s passion for both his journalism and our community and its people is evident in his writing – clear and concise, yet sometimes resonant of poetic and nostalgic sense of "saudade"! This is a book that allows us to reflect on our past and our present – who we "were" and who we "are" – as Luso-Canadians.

This book is in large part the compilation of a number of articles published by J.M.C. in the magazine "Revista Imagens" as well as from his newspaper "O Milénio". It is the result of hundreds of hours of interviewing (and re-interviewing, in some cases) the people who have, over the last 50 years, built this great community. As one of the best Portuguese journalists of the portuguese diaspora – himself an "islander," from Madeira, who always "carries" the islands in his heart – J.M.C. collected more than 200 "autobiographies" of our people. These "histories" – whether they focus on the pioneers, the first business entrepreneurs, doctors, priests and teachers, or on the community as a whole with its distinctive cultural and religious practices – are not only stories of struggle but also inspirational accounts of the successes of our people. The book's "autobiographies" are organized in alphabetical order to facilitate access to this significant source of information about not only the "who's who" of the Portuguese community, but also its rich cultural and organizational life. Their stories will allow the new generations of Luso-Canadians to better understand their heritage – when, why and by whom gradually…stone by stone…our community was built.

While the majority of the accounts in this book are stories of success, it should not be forgotten that there are also stories of hardship, great struggle and determination. In many ways J.M.C.'s record of the lives of people who struggled against adversity in this new land, and left us without being "recognized" for what they did for our community, is one of the most important features of this book. Thus, this book fills a major gap in the history of the Portuguese presence in Canada by giving these people a "voice". In sum, this book – with its 333 pages and 670 photos about the "life" of our community – represents a wonderful gift to Luso-Canadians on the 50th anniversary of their immigration to Canada. I would like to express my thanks to JMC for the time and effort . . . for the "life" . . . he has spent creating this remarkable book. Writing from Canada's Pacific coast – in the Okanagan Valley of British Columbia – I would like to add one last word – "até breve" – and my best wishes for this and future publications!

José Carlos Teixeira, Ph.D.
Okanaga Valley, B.C.
January - 2004

Almeida, Maurício Luís de

Town of Sines, Province of Alentejo

Maurício Luís de Almeida was born with a unique ability for the arts. As a young self-taught person, he used to work as a blacksmith just for the pleasure of creating works of art. Maurício de Almeida was born in the small town of Sines, in the province of Alentejo, on February 15, 1933. He is married to Maria Luísa Velhinha Almeida who was born in the city of Beja, Alentejo, on March 21, 1934. From the couple, three sons were born: Luís

Maria Luísa and Maurício Almeida, a truly happy couple.

Manuel (in Beja), Maurício dos Santos (in Barreiro) and Paulo Jorge (in Barreiro).

Maurício Luís de Almeida arrived in Canada on June 7, 1966 and his wife on September 1st of the same year. Soon after their arrival, Maurício began his career as a mechanic working at Rosário Diesel, later on at Quintal Garage and, finally, after 1967, at the Canadian Pacific. He retired in 1992. Maurício de Almeida is a man who is dedicated with all his heart and soul to the arts and, obviously, to the cultural associations where he has demonstrated his abilities in many shapes and forms. Maurício and his wife are co-founders of the Grupo Coral da Casa do Alentejo – a traditional musical group who represents the songs from the province of Alentejo –, a group founded by the couple Bia and Raúl Raposo. They are still active members of the group, which is now divided into Grupo Masculino (male) and Grupo Feminino (female).

Maurício de Almeida is also one of the founders of the association Casa do Alentejo, in Toronto, and is proud to be member number 5. Maurício was also member of the now extinguished associations Nazaré Club and Imbondeiro. The couple Almeida is involved in many activities, from the kitchen to the administration, including the Grupo Coral. From the first Cultural Week of Alentejo, Maurício has been recording on his camera all the remarkable events of Casa do Alentejo. With the purpose of having art exhibitions about Alentejo on the Cultural Weeks, created in Toronto, Maurício "forgot" his wrought iron and dedicated himself to painting and sculpture. Since then, he has been the sensation of all art exhibitions. Maurício Luís de Almeida is, in the true sense of the word, an artist. His works in wood – of ducks and eagles –, his portraits and busts of famous people, among others, have made him one of the most charismatic people of Casa do

May 10, 2003. Maurício Almeida describing to the Portuguese Minister of Foreign Affairs, Martins da Cruz, and the Portuguese Ambassador in Ottawa, José Luiz Gomes, his commemorative panel of the 50th anniversary of the arrival of the Portuguese in Canada, in the Saudade Museum, in Halifax.

Alentejo and even in the community. He has successfully presented his work in many exhibitions in Toronto, Halifax and Portugal.

Maurício is the author of a beautiful panel that preserves the memory of the Portuguese pioneers, at the Saudade Museum, in Halifax. The panel is commemorative of the fifty years of the official arrival of Portuguese in Canada, which was unveiled in May of 2003. Much more is awaited from Maurício Luís de Almeida: a family man, an artist and a friend. All the best, compadre!

JMC - 2003

Alvarez, Francisco Sestelo

Arbo, Spain

Francisco Sestelo Alvarez was born to be a businessman and to triumph. He is bold and ambicioús. When he enters a game, he expects to win and usually, he succeeds.

Francisco Sestelo Alvarez was born in April of 1944, in Arbo, in the province of Galicia, in Spain, close to the river Lima, which borders with the province of Minho, in Portugal. At the age of eight, he emigrated with his parents to Portugal where he began his education. The young Alvarez followed the normal routine of an immigrant: school and work. He eventually became a Portuguese citizen. He began succeeding in life at the cost of his hard work and knowledge. After completing grade 6 – the compulsory

Family picture: Carmen, Frank Sestelo Alvarez, Frank Jr. and Dolores Alvarez.

school years – he dedicated himself to restoration, a profession he embraced at a very young age.

At the age of 20, with his entrepreneurial spirit, he opened a restaurant, D. Henriques, in Cova

At the beginning of his career, Frank Alvarez meets with prime minister Pierre Trudeau and wife Margarette.

Frank Alvarez and singer Jorge Ferreira at Portuguese Day, Canada's Wonderland, after receiving the key of city of Toronto, from the hands of Mayor Mel Lastman, in front of a crowd of thousands.

da Piedade, near Lisbon. Influenced by one of his clients, he went into a partnership in selling women's purses, a enterprise that was not successful. Meanwhile, Francisco Alvarez got married to Dolores Maria, from Brescos, Santo André, in the province of Alentejo. With his wife pregnant of three months and a failed business, he sold the restaurant and ventured in a trip to Canada. He arrived on June 26, 1967, stopping first in Montreal and then in Toronto.

At Toronto's Pearson International airport, he heard a group of people speaking Portuguese and went towards them. Luckily – luck seems to follow those who are bold – one of them was Frank Silva, owner of Império Travel Agency and Imperio Restaurant. Of course, Alvarez began working immediately in a profession he knew very well. From that moment on, everything went smoothly. Among the accomplishments that marked the first years were the remodelling of Imperio Restaurant, which included variety shows and a liquor licence. The then manager of Imperio Travel Agency, Adelino Loureiro Sales, tried to expand his business by opening Sagres Travel Agency. In 1971, Adelino married

Eulália Sales. Adelino Sales joined Frank Alvarez in the restaurant and wedding services partnership, ending the triumvirate with Frank Silva. In 1974, they formed Salva Organizations, a successful partnership for many years. At the same time, Dolores Alvarez opened "A Casa das Noivas" (The Bridal's Home), in 1969 and would manage it until 1984, when she sold it to Hilário Coelho.

Frank Alvarez, a man who knows the power of advertising in the marketing world, began taking some steps within the broadcasting world. From 1972 to 1974, he hosted some television shows

Frank Alvarez, Prof. David Higgs, Ernesto Feu, José Lello, Fernão Perestrelo and Marisol Santos (widow of the economist Humberto Santos), at the Portuguese Embassy in Ottawa, with their badges of merit.

at Metro Cable, York Cable and Rogers Cable, with the artistic support of Mariano Rego. His restaurant business, the wedding services, and the bridal house were very successful. Salva Organizations purchased a building with three halls, known as Lisbon Place, which became "the Portuguese events' house" until October of 1985. On April 25, 1975, Frank Alvarez began hosting a half-hour television show on Global Television Network, which aired every Sunday, right after another Portuguese show hosted by Father Alberto Cunha. When the latter gave up his show, Frank Alvarez acquired his half hour to be able to present the show "Portuguese Festival".

Due to a natural course of events, the show began being hosted on Channel 11, from Hamilton, and finally, on channel 20, the New VR, from Barrie. Back in the 70's, Frank Alvarez invited the already known radio announcer, José Mário Coelho, to work beside him, a duo that remains active until the present time. José Mario Coelho was the producer and host of the radio show "Vozes de Portugal", on CHIN, since 1970, and he counterinvited Frank Alvarez to work with him on CHIN. Due to this experience, Frank Alvarez decided to acquire "Rádio Clube Português" from the late Mário Tomás, in 1982. Later, in 1984-1985, Frank Alvarez, together with a group of ethnic journalists, officially requested from CRTC, the opening of a multicultural radio station, which was granted on June 1st, 1986. It was the birth of CIRV-Fm, a radio station that became the bulwark of the Portuguese community in Southern Ontario.

With the expansion of his business in the broadcasting world, Frank Alvarez and Adelino Sales decided on October 31st, 1985, to sell both Imperio Restaurant and Lisbon Place. After producing and editing, together with Daniel Fernandes, the monthly magazine "Imagens", for two years, Frank Alvarez decided to launch a weekly newspaper. His newspaper Milénio had its first edition published

Frank Alvarez, in Ottawa, surrounded by former Ambassador Duarte de Jesus and former consul of Portugal in Toronto, António Montenegro.

on November 20, 1998. Taking advantage of the new digital cable system approved by CRTC, Frank Alvarez, joined by his minority partners in the company – José Mário Coelho and Alberto Elmir – obtained the licence to open Festival Portugues TV (FPtv), in September of 2001. This channel broadcasts in Portuguese 24 hours a day, seven days a week, with the collaboration of the Portuguese Channel Sic International.

Left behind are other successful initiatives: with TIST, Frank Alvarez began the International Soccer Tournament of Toronto, in 1978, which was responsible for bringing to Toronto, many important Portuguese teams, such as S.L. e

Benfica, to compete with the local ones. He was also a pioneer in organizing concerts with renown artists from Portugal and Brazil, namely Roberto Carlos, Amália Rodrigues, Balett Carmen Mota, Marco Paulo, José Cid, and many others. He created "Summerfest", "Winterfest", and "Portuguese Day", festivals for the Portuguese community. On the day he was able to organize a show to commemorate Amália's 50th anniversary as a fado singer, Frank Alvarez opened up his heart: - "Now and only now, I feel like a businessman".

On his journey to the top, Frank Alvarez never forgot those in need. He organized radiothons, telethons for the poor children in Brazil, Angola and Mozambique, and for Toronto's own Doctor's Hospital. He was the creator of "Cabaz de Natal" (Christmas Basket) which he organized for many years and held the "Miss Portuguese Festival" beauty contest.

All this work did not go unnoticed. Frank Alvarez has been recognized by the Canadian government with the Medallion of the Confederation of Canada, 1876-1992, when Canada celebrated 125 years; the Certificate of Merit from the Canadian Ethnic Journalists' & Writers' Club, in 1999; the Golden Medallion commemorating the Queen's Jubilee, in 2003; Toronto's Key, given by the former Mayor Mel Lastman, in 1999; and the Insignia of National Merit, granted by Portugal's President Jorge Sampaio, in June of 1998, and handed over, in Ottawa, by the Secretary of State of the Portuguese Communities, José Lello.

Frank Alvarez has always dedicated himself to community causes. He was one of the founders of Casa do Benfica (Benfica House of Toronto), and of the Federation of Portuguese Canadian Business and Professionals, serving as its vice-president, interim president and president respectively, between 1985 and 1990. A life full of accomplishments, a journey complete by merit, a world full of colour and fantasy. In the middle of all this work, Frank Alvarez was always a committed family man. His children, Carmen and Frank Jr., are university graduates and with a brilliant future ahead of them. His daughter Carmen Falcone has given him two grandsons: Ryan and Brandon.

However, the Alvarez clan still has a long way to walk.

JMC - February of 2004

Alves, Gilberto

Island of S. Miguel, Azores

I do not recall ever seeing Gilberto in a bad mood, he was always a cheerful individual. He is a man happy with life, with himself and with those who surround him. Gilberto Alves was born on April 22, 1932, in the beautiful town of Sete Cidades, on the island of São Miguel, in the Azores, on April 22, 1932. From a very young age, he dedicated himself to business; agriculture, transport and back home he was the only one with enough courage to buy bulls to organize

Maria Leonilde and Gilberto Alves, a happy couple.

bullfights using a rope.

In S. Miguel, he met Maria Leonilde Torres Pereira, from the town of São José, in Ponta Delgada, S. Miguel, who was born on December 11, 1935. They got married on July 3rd, 1960, at the church of Ponta Delgada. The couple had two children: Ana Paula, born on May 6, 1961 whom is now married and a mother of three girls; and Carlos Eduardo, born on June 15, 1963, whom too is married and is the father of a beautiful girl.

Family B.B.Q.: Carlos, Leonilde, Carli, Gilberto and his brother Nicolau Alves.

Gilberto Alves finished his military service on the island of Terceira where he developed a passion for bullfights. Naturally, with a vocation for business, he bought bulls in Terceira from Diamantino Viseu and organized the first fights, which were not very successful. People from Terceira like bullfights, but the same cannot be said about people from S. Miguel. Always thinking business and thinking big, Gilberto emigrated to Canada, on May 11, 1965, as a tourist. Not long after, he became a landed immigrant.

In Canada, Gilberto Alves lived here and there, between Kitchener, Thompson and Toronto, working in landscape and in the nickel mines. In Toronto, on March 28, 1969, he bought Iberica Fish Store from Correia & Sousa. In 1977, he opened a furniture store named "Sonho do Lar", which he managed for ten years, until 1987, when he decided to leave the furniture business to open the fish and grocery store "Lota", on Dundas, close to Dufferin, which is still run by the family to this day.

Back home, Gilberto kept the "Sociedade Açoriana de Bacalhau" (the Azorean Codfish Society), now inactive, due to the death of the managers.

For a short time, he was a partner in the company Portuguese United Wholesale, a wholesale-retailer company, which began with 28 partners, but nowadays only has 14. Together with his son Carlos, Gilberto Alves established the North Atlantic Fisheries firm, in Toronto, in 1984, and bought a codfish factory, in Nova Scotia, back in 1989. These two firms have grown due to the knowledge of those running them, and the excellent service to the public.

Gilberto Alves on the day he was awarded a certificate of honour by the Federation of Portuguese Canadian Business and Professionals.

The couple Maria Leonilde and Gilberto Alves maintained their joy of life throughout life, maintained their joy of life by travelling between Canada, the Azores and mainland Portugal, even when experiencing some health problems.

Gilberto Alves passed away in 2000.

JMC - 1999

Alves, Teresa de Fátima Teixeira de Sousa Lopes

Arrifes, São Miguel, Azores

Teresa Alves possesses the most beautiful burst of sound of laughter that I know. She is, by nature, a happy person with an immense love for life. However, before we describe Teresa, we shall take a moment to look at the story of her family.

Her father, José dos Santos Sousa Lopes, was born on November 7, 1920, in São João da Pesqueira. He completed his military service in the island of São Miguel, in the Azores, where he met Aldina Teixeira de Sousa, a native of Porto Formoso, with whom he married on June 9, 1945, at Nossa Senhora da Saúde's church, in the small village of Arrifes. From this marriage, four children were born: Aldina Maria, in Lamego, in the continent, José Rui, Teresa Alves and Meno, in Arrifes. José Lopes came to Canada in 1965 and his wife and children arrived two years later. They first decided to live in Oakville, but later on, moved to Brampton. Back in the Azores, the entire family used to gather daily around the piano and other musical instruments just to amuse themselves. Every member of the family played and sang, each one his own way.

Teresa Sousa Lopes loved singing and playing the piano. Together with her sister Aldina, Teresa formed a respectable duo. Teresa de Fátima Teixeira de Sousa Lopes was born in Arrifes, on October 16, 1951. She arrived in Canada when she was only 14 years old. In Brampton, he began attending St. Francis Xavier elementary school. She then went to Centennial High School and finished her high school years at Central Peel. She then went to Ryerson Polythecnical Institute – now a university – in Toronto, where she studied economics and took her Real Estate licence, at Oakville's Sheridan College. At Central Peel High School, she met the young Ermídio Fortunato Alves, who was born on September 18, 1954, in Almada, Lisbon, but then moved with his family to S. Miguel when he was only two years old.

The high school sweet hearts, Teresa and Ermídio, got married on July 28, 1973. The couple had four children, all born in Brampton: Marcel (a model and a piloting student); Clyde (a

Ermídio and Teresa Alves.

professional ballet dancer, now living in New York); Crystal (a professional dancer, choreographer and model); and Tessa (a professional dancer, singer, model and a student of Drama and Martial Arts). For some years, these four children were the members of the artistic dance group "Children of Tomorrow". It is a family marked by talent in many different levels, from dance to painting, to photography and music. Teresa Alves, who has loved music, dance and cinema from a very young age, encouraged her children to enter the world of arts. Her daughter Crystal asked her, when

Clyde Alves

she was only 3, to become a bailarina. After seeing the movie "White Nights", Clyde fell in love with the art of dance and decided that it was what he wanted to do professionally. Young Tessa was admitted into the school of dance even before she qualified for admittance due to her age. They have all accomplished their dreams.

The Alves' children studied dance at the Lynn Morrison School of Ballet, in Brampton, then at Joanne Chapman School of Dance, in Mississauga, and at the Performing Dance Arts, in Woodbridge.

In the middle of all this artistic haste, the Alves' couple acquired a Piper Aztec plane to be able to accompany their children. Ermídio sold the Aztec when his children became independent, but he still holds the pilote's brevet. Teresa Alves has a Solo Pilot Brevet, which only allows her to fly alone.

Together with their children, Teresa and Ermídio flew the skies of the United States and Canada. They are also the owners of Prudential Alfa Realty, in Brampton, with branches in Calgary and Florida. Besides being a full time mother, Teresa helped her husband in the real estate business.

The Alves' children recorded a CD with music and lyrics of their own. At Midi-tech Studio, owned by Hernani Raposo, everyone told Teresa that she also had a beautiful voice to record an album. She used to laugh at the idea. Although she had never thought about recording, she was invited by Nelson Câmara to record the song "Crazy", in 1998. When she heard the song on the radio, she thought it was someone else. Her effort to teach Tessa Portuguese songs paid off because she learned many songs. She returned to the piano and began composing her own songs. Thus, with the support of her family, of Nelson and her own will, Teresa, known as Misty, recorded an album in memory of her parents.

Teresa Alves is full of energy. She still has time to be a director at the Portuguese Heritage Committee, in Brampton, at Brampton Performing Arts Showcase, at Odyssey Committee and practices many forms of Tai Chi. She will continue to be a happy individual, unique in her laughter.

JMC - 1999

Crystal Alves

Alves, Virgínio Elias

Rabo de Peixe,

island of São Miguel, Azores

Virgínio Elias Alves was born in the village of Rabo de Peixe, in the island of S. Miguel, on March 12, 1932. He arrived in Quebec, on April 11, 1956, aboard Columbia, with a group of 109 Azoreans.

In Quebec, they took the train to Montreal where they were separated according to their assignment on the cattle-raising farms. Virgínio Alves did not stay

Virgínio Elias Alves

in Quebec for too long. He moved to Kingston, where he stayed for two months because the farm owner would not give him any food. Unwilling to starve to death, Virgínio went to the Portuguese Consulate to complain about his situation to the vice-consul, Aristides – who is the father-in-law of Carlos Cesar, President of the self-governed region of the Azores – and to the consulate civil servant, Tavares Bello. Once the case was solved, Virgínio went back to Montreal to work in a restaurant where he washed dishes. In 1956, the vice-consul and Tavares Bello founded the Portuguese Association in Montreal, located at the corner of Sherbourne and St. Lawrence. A carpenter by profession, Virginio obtained a part-time job in the Association, while accepting other tasks that were offered to him.

Six months after his arrival, his wife Maria dos Anjos Amaral da Estrela Alves, came to join him. She was nine months pregnant and gave birth to a beautiful girl, Guilhermina, just two weeks after arriving in Canada. Guilhermina was the third child of the couple. José Domingos was born in 1953 and Alzira in 1954, both in Rabo de Peixe.

At the time, it was said that Guilhermina was the first Portuguese-Canadian to be born in Canada. However, other people claim that a woman from the island of Madeira had already given birth. The doubt persists until this day. Virgínio Alves and Maria dos Anjos got married on February 23, 1950. After living three years in Montreal and with the crisis of 1959, Virgínio decided to move to Toronto, on December 24, 1960. His first job was to restore the house of a jewish man which had burnt down. Seeing how professional Virgínio was, this jewish man assigned him other tasks and recommended his work to other fellow jewish men. Two years later, Virgínio began working for himself, never forgetting his jewish friend.

His social life was also very successful and remarkable in the Portuguese community.

In 1966, the late João de Sousa, owner of "Casa das Prendas", formed in his basement, a musical band with six or seven members. At that time, Virgínio was an active parishioner at Santa Maria's church, helping father Lourenço. At the same time, father Antero arrived in Toronto, but personal disputes between them led to the separation of both priests to different churches.

The bishop sent father Antero to

First procession in honour of Senhor da Pedra

Nossa Senhora do Carmo's church, in McCaul. At the same time, father Lourenço, together with father Camacho, decided to purchase a house that would be transformed into a hall for religious celebrations. Due to that purchase, considered illegal, father Lourenço was sent to the United States and was replaced by father Alberto Cunha, the same year Mariano Rego offered

Virgínio and Maria dos Anjos Alves standing proudly among their children and grandchildren.

the image of Senhor Santo Cristo to Santa Maria's church, as part of a promise. Almost simultaneously, João de Sousa asked Virgínio Alves to help the band because the neighbours had complained about the noise level that was coming from his basement. Virgínio spoke to father Cunha who offered the church's hall for the band to rehearse.

In 1969, he sold his house and bought tobacco farms in Mountbridges, between Strathroy and London, in part, to be able to bring his five brothers to Canada. All five came to live in this country where they still dwell. In September of 1962, Virgínio Alves went to the Azores, for the first time after having emigrated, to carry out a religious promise. One very cold winter, Virgínio Alves almost went bankrupt due to the freezing of his tobacco farms. Without giving up all hope, Virgínio came to Toronto where he purchased four old houses, on Dundas, close to Augusta Avenue. After repairing them, he put them up for rent and slowly recuperated all the money he had lost before. Some time after, Toronto's City Hall decided to create Alexander Park on that area and proceeded with the eviction of the area in order to demolish the houses. The resolution created a very chaotic situation and the only person, of seven families, that suffered

another financial loss was Virgínio Alves. Due to that decision taken by City Hall, Virgínio went to court to press charges against the municipality. He won the case and received an indemnity of $60,000 dollars. With that money he went again to buy old houses, and rented them after having them fixed.

In 1980, he decided to go back to S. Miguel, where he stayed for five years. When he decided to come back to Toronto, in 1985, he formed, together with his sons, the firm AMJJ Constructions Ltd., a very successful enterprise until the present day. As part of the business, he moved to Mississauga, where he began buying land to build and sell homes. In 1997, Virgínio decided to retire.

The band grew into 29 members, without a conductor, under the responsibility of João and Virgínio. Father Cunha became interested in the band and suggested each member should buy his own instrument.

First procession in honour of Senhor Santo Cristo, in 1967.

At the same time, the band acquired a conductor, José Brasil, and José Janeiro, brother of father Janeiro. Due to internal disputes, some musicians left the band. Thus, with division among them, half of the members remained at Santa Maria's church connected to Senhor Santo Cristo's band, conducted by José Brasil. The other half went to McCaul to form the band Lira Nossa Senhora de Fátima, best known as the band from Saint Agnes' Church, conducted by José Janeiro and administered by Maria José Pereira. On June 10, 1966, Santo Cristo's band performed for the first time, under the supervision of Virgínio Alves and Juvenal de Freitas, in order to raise funds, by participating in the first communion of Portuguese children. Only in May of 1967, in the very first celebration of Senhor Santo Cristo dos Milagres, at Santa Maria's church, did the band – the first local one – participate in the procession conducted by José Brasil and managed by José Borges, Manuel Sousa, José Brasil and Virgínio Alves.

Once again due to internal problems and lack of money, Virgínio Alves left the band for two years. In 1969, with Mrs. Mercês, he went back to McCaul's church and father Antero to recuperate the band Lira de Nossa Senhora de Fátima. At that time, the only thing left were the instruments. Thus, José de Sousa, Manuel Moniz, Daniel, José Borges and Virgínio Alves worked very hard to prepare the band in order for it to be

First performance of Senhor Santo Cristo's band, on June 10, 1966. In the front row, we can see Virgínio Alves, Manuel Matos, Orlando Kilberg, Juvenal de Freitas and Artur Barrão.

able to perform to the public. That day came on Trinity Sunday, in 1969, at the very first celebration in honour of the Holy Spirit, in Toronto. In 1970, the band went to Saint Agnes' Church with father Antero, which explains the reason why the band is most commonly known by the church's name. In 1970, they ordered the image of Senhor da Pedra and began celebrating this saint at the church and Bellwoods Park.

When he moved to Mississauga, Virgínio Alves decided to help Monsignor Eduardo Resendes, in the construction of two churches: São Salvador do Mundo and Christ the King. He was also one of the founding members of the Portuguese Club of Mississauga, now known as Portuguese Cultural Centre of Mississauga, where he is still a member and serves as chair of the seniors' group. He is still a member of Santo Cristo's and Lira de Nossa Senhora de Fátima's bands. Virgínio Alves is father of eight children, two of them born in Rabo de Peixe – José Domingos Alves and Alzira Alves - and the remaining six in Canada: Guilhermina (Toronto), Virgínia (Toronto), João (Toronto), Linda (Strathroy), Manuel (Toronto) and Daniel (Toronto). So far, he has fourteen grandchildren. He still has many friends, but has decided to leave the clubs and bands. As we all know, a person's lineage never stops. In spite of his advanced age, the community still needs Virgínio Elias Alves.

Amador, Laurindo Rodrigues

Pardilhó, Aveiro

Laurindo Amador shows his medal in Honour of Portuguese Pioneers.

He has a fine figure and a happy face. He is known by the nickname "Créto", but his name is Laurindo Rodrigues Amador.

Laurindo was born in the small village of Pardilhó, in the region of Estarreja, district of Aveiro, on October 14, 1925. Soon after finishing primary school (the first four mandatory years of schooling in Salazar's Portugal), he became a carpenter's apprentice, at the shipyard of António Mónica, in Aveiro. Already as a professional carpenter, with twelve years experience, the firm closed down and Laurindo Amador became a civil carpenter in his homeland. At the same time, he was a musician. He used to play trumpet and saxophone in the band "Nova de Pardilhó". His father, Alfredo Rodrigues Amador – Créto – was also a musician and "injected" in him the love for music. In February of 1955, he found out that Canada was opening the door for men with skills in construction and agriculture. He filled out an application and was chosen to work in agriculture.

Images of the hardships Portuguese immigrants lived, in the cold and snow, at the beginning of Portuguese emigration to Canada.

Laurindo arrived in Montreal, on April 19, 1955. He began working right away at a farm in Ste. Rose de Wafford, in Quebec, carrying stones by hand to build hedges. Soon after, he came back to Montreal where he found a job in masonry, working for Mr. Martérre, fixing miniature boats and caravels. By 1965, together with David Gasena, a fellow countryman, he went to Michipicoten Bay, on Lake Superior, where he worked on the shipyards loading ships with wood cut in the nearby forests. They used to sleep in the company's dormitory, surrounded by local natives. That same year, he went to Hearst to work at the sawmill. Tired of so many sacrifices and low gainings, he decided to

Laurindo Rodrigues Amador in Pardilhó's band.

leave his job and took the train to Toronto.

He travelled with his friend from Pardilhó, Joaquim Pinta. At the train station in Kapuskasing, they signed with Spruce Falls company and tried their luck again. They were immediately hired. Joaquim Pinta still lives there. Years later, Laurindo Amador left for Toronto to fulfill his dream of working as a carpenter. He arrived at Union Station at night. Not knowing where to go, he decided to stay their until the following morning, playing trumpet to distract himself and hide his loneliness. Curiously, he got 25 cents for playing so well... Amused, he wrote:

I arrived in Toronto without any money,
In my torned suitcase, I carried my trumpet
I played a song to give me happiness!...

In Toronto, he began working as a carpenter in small construction companies and at times of crisis he would wander the corner of Spadina and Queen, a common meeting place for contractors. Back then, the few Portuguese people living in Toronto would gather together to ease their homesickness. They decided to create the First Portuguese Club, to meet, to talk about their problems and to have fun. Thus, Laurindo became, at the time, a founding member number 10 of the First Portuguese Club.

In 1957, Laurindo Amador decided it was time for his wife and daughter to join him. They both arrived in Canada on November 10, 1956. Laurindo Amador married Carmelinda Pereira, also from Padrilhó, where she was born on January 22, 1928. The wedding took place at Padrilhó's church on October 14, 1944. The couple's daughter, Maria do Carmo, was also born in Padrilhó, on May 26, 1945. She is now married and goes by the surname of Lions. Maria do Carmo also had a daughter, Ema, who is now 25 years old, has a post-secundary education and is about to be married. Laurindo Amador, after moving from one company to another, established himself at MG Wilson Contractors, and later on, at Ellis Don Construction Ltd., where he worked for more

Carmelinda and Laurindo Amador, proud of their daughter, on the day of her graduation.

than 20 years, only leaving it to retire, in 1991. Laurindo became a member of Union United Brotherhood of Carpenters & Joiners of America Local 27, on March 17, 1958.

Laurindo, together with his wife and daughter, became Canadian citizens on February 22, 1963. Laurindo received from the Secretary of State for Emigration in Portugal the commemorative medal in honour of the Pioneers of Portuguese Emigration (1955-1985). Carmelinda retired in 1998, after working for more than 20 years at Iron Burger Clothing Store. The Amadors go very often on holidays to Portugal, where they have a house. Spain, USA and Canada from coast to coast have also been chosen vacation places for Carmelinda and Laurindo Amador. His favourite hobby is still working on small works of carpentry and taking care of his home and garden. He is leading a well deserved tranquil life, after so many years of hardships.

JMC - 2003

Amorim, Avelino Gomes de

Village of Monte Redondo, town of Arcos de Valdevez

The journey of an emigrant encounters many challenges on its way. This can be proven by some of the stories told to us by our pioneer Avelino Gomes de Amorim, a native of the province of Minho. He was born on April 4, 1927 in the small village of Monte Redondo, in the region of Arcos de Valdevez, district of Viana de Castelo.

- I left Lisbon, together with about 150 men from the north of Portugal, on May 16, 1957. From Lisbon, we went to the island of Santa Maria, then we stopped in Newfoundland, and at last we arrived in Montreal, on May 17. We

Grandfather Amorim with his grandchildren Cristina and Frankie.

spent about 17 hours flying… - said our pioneer, beginning the tale of his arrival in Canada.

- Did you stay with your fellow countrymen in Montreal? – We asked.

- No! – He clarified. – At that time, each emigrant had been assigned a specific destination. I, along with four other friends, had an identification card hung around my neck, which indicted that I was to go to work on a farm in Oshawa. The Immigration Services sent us by train to our destination in Oshawa. The train's collector saw our destination in the cards we had and "abandoned us" in the station where we were supposed to go. – Shaking his head with a sad smile, Amorim said: - When we arrived in Oshawa, the group of people that was supposed to be responsible for us took us to an hotel, to sleep, and disappeared. We were left there for three days without eating or drinking anything. We didn't know where to go or how to ask for food… It was a really rough start! It was our first weekend in Canada!

- How did you solve the situation? – We asked with curiousity.

- Well, already in a situation of despair, we left the hotel and went straight to the train station. It was a Monday. We wanted to disappear from there… The man at the station noticed we were Portuguese and called another Portuguese man who had been living in Oshawa for a while. He was a young man from mainland Portugal, whose name I no longer recall… One of my friends in this adventure, Alfredo Vidal, ended up marrying this man's sister-in-law and decided to live there. Excellent person… He got us a job, offered us a home and food to eat! May God help him always for he deserves it.

- Did you stay in Oshawa for a long time?

- No, quite the opposite. The immigration officials transferred us from farm to farm, as if we were a flock that could be sold… - confessed Avenlino, laughing at the memory of those times. He continued: - The first job in Oshawa was given by lot. Our friend could only find a job for one of us and we were five… We drew lots and the lucky devil was Alfredo Vidal… Not too long ago I re-lived this story with him, when coincidentally I met him at a soccer game between Arsenal do Minho of Toronto and the Atlético de Valdevez, the team from my hometown in Portugal. After so many years, we were able to laugh at this story! When you think about it… I found him at a soccer match in Toronto, 30 years later!

- It must have been pleasant to remember those old times?

- Of course! – Having said this, Avelino let a rebel tear roll down his face. Soon after, he said: - My first job was in Simcoe, where I earned twenty dollars in eight days. I felt so nervous that I wasn't even able to sleep… When I was planting tobacco, the farmer's son used to shove me so that I wouldn't fall asleep, even standing up! They were many days of suffering…

- What happened after?

- Since I had one of my cousin's address, Manuel Caldas, who was working in Elliot Lake, I wrote him a letter and, a week later, he came to pick me up. So I went to Elliot Lake to work in the construction of the uranium factories. – After a brief pause, Amorim continued. – By the time winter arrived, I left for a tobacco farm in Delhi. When the tobacco work was over, I returned to Elliot Lake.

- Where did you work during those times?

- Manitoba, Stratford, Sault St. Marie and Kitchener is where I worked for three years as a bricklayer… In 1963, when president Kennedy died in the United States, I came to Toronto to work in construction. My company was responsible for building the bridges on top of highway 401. After this, I worked on the construction of the CN Tower, the banks of Commerce and Montreal…

- How was it to work in the construction of the CN Tower?

- Very hard! Can you imagine what it is like to climb its staircase? Terrible… Look, one day, I was so fed up of the tower that I went to the boss and told him: until we have an elevator, I refuse to work at 250 feet from the ground! And I didn't go. I was afraid to climb all those stairs. I only went back to work on that tower when they assembled the elevator. At that time, I worked at the top, building the rotating restaurant. The men who worked at the very top made eight dollars more a day than we did. When the tower was finished, the owners were very nice: they sent us an invitation for a dinner at the restaurant on top. I was so fed up with that tower that I decided not to go… not even for free!

- Did you always work for the same company?

- I worked for G&H Steel for sixteen years. Then, problems with my back forced me to go to the Worker's Compensation Board. When I recuperated I went back, however they did not rehire me, stating that I was not in condition to work for them. There was a lot of debate between the union and representatives from the Worker's Compensation Board and the union, but I didn't gain anything from that. It was the union that found me another job. Due to my physical problems, mainly my back, feet and arm, I became disabled. For two years, the union paid me 195 dollars a month because the Worker's Compensation Board never gave me a cent. Now, I receive the disability pension, along with the one from the union. – With a very sad look and an expression of outrage, Amorim continued: - When I hear the representatives from WCB, talking on the radio and on TV, I feel like calling in just to call them liars. The

Avelino Amorim and Eduardo Transmontano, on a tobacco plantation, in 1960.

WCB never helped me. I could never understand how a man with a physical disability like myself is not entitled to any benefits. For the past six years, I haven't been able to do anything. I stopped working on August 31, 1981. I went through some really tough times.

A little more serene, Avelino Amorim told us that if the services from WBC had been as functional then as they are now, he would naturally have received some form of benefits. Times have changed and today, fortunately, the Portuguese people are able to receive financial assistance from WBC, in part due to the fact that some of the employees speak our language and are able to understand the problems that are exposed. Perhaps Amorim's case is still one that deserves the attention of those in charge. Who knows if our countrymen are not still entitled to some benefits?

To make the atmosphere a little more pleasant, we took a different approach: as usual we wanted to know more about unusual, and interesting stories. How many amusing incidents did our pioneers experience?

- So many! – he answered. – You know, when I was in Sault St. Marie, in 1959, in the middle of a conversation with Fernando Vilaça and Manuel Gonçalves Pereira, we decided to pluck away to Kitchener. Arriving there, we went to the local union to look for a job. The job they gave us was at the picket line because the little rascals were on strike! At that time, there were only twelve Portuguese people living in Kitchener. We used to spend the weekends talking in the park.

- Do you have more stories to share with us?

- Oh yes, do I! Still in Kitchener, the very first job that I had, after the strike, was to unload cement bricks from the trucks. Since I didn't understand English, I used to do that job with bare hands, without putting on the gloves they were giving me. All the skin from my hands peeled off. The pain I felt was unbearable. At the time, we found a place to live, a small room that an old lady was renting. We paid the rent, but the following day, when we arrived from work, the lady had kicked us out. All our belongings – although we didn't have many – were on the street. Until this day, I was not able to understand the reason behind such a decision. After that, we went to another house where the blankets were attached to each other by pins… my bed was always made. – After, with a loud laugh, Amorim finished the story. – I would sleep on the same bed another guy had used before. That's how it was back then. Things only got better when I went to live at Francisco Silva's house, better known as "Chico Favas". Chico is an old friend of mine. I stayed in his house until I moved to Toronto.

- When you arrived in Toronto, had the First Portuguese Club already been founded?

- Yes, it had! – with a nostalgic smile on his lips, Amorim continued: - I was never a member of First Portuguese because the first time I
went there for a dance, I was thrown out for that specific reason: I was not
a member. I got so upset that I never went there again.

- Are you, now, a member of any community club or association?

- I am just a parishioner at Santa Maria's church and I belong to St.
Vincent de Paul's Conference, to help the poor.

- Are you married?

- Yes, I am. I was single when I came to Canada, but got married
in 1980 with Gisela Machado who is from the Azores. I was a little old
when I got married, but I am happy! – confessed Amorim, with his eyes
shining. – She was a widow, she has two grandchildren whom I adopted
as my own. We have known each other for 20 years… Among so many
misfortunes, this was by far the happiest moment of my life!

In 1973, working on the construction of rides, at Canada's Wonderland. It was at this job site that Avelino began having back problems.

- Do you ever think about returning back to Portugal?

- No. Both my wife and I like living in Toronto. I have been to many
places, I worked in Puerto Rico when I was an employee for G&H, but to take me away from Toronto is to take away everything I cherish! Toronto is where I like the most…

- Have you ever gone back?

- Yes! Every time I have a chance, I go back to visit. I still have a couple of fields in Portugal and my parents' house, but I feel better here.

- Even with so many problems and misfortunes, do you think it was worth coming to Canada?

- Absolutely! – he answered without hesitating. – With so many health problems, how would I survive in Portugal? After all that, everything was worth it!

- Would you still like to see some old fellow travellers and friends?

- Yes, I would, especially Manuel Caldas, Mariano Almeida and José Maria Sousa who worked with me in Puerto Rico, in the construction of a building, in 1964.

January of 1988

Amorim, Fernando Brandão de

Town of Arcos de Valdevez

Family Amorim, at home.

Fernando Brandão de Amorim is a gentleman. An excellent speaker, very charming, and is a true native of the province of Minho.

Fernando Brandão de Amorim was born in the town of Arcos de Valdevez, north of Portugal, on September 30, 1930. After completing the mandatory schooling, Fernando, at the age of 18, took his driver's licence and began working as a taxi-cab driver. He entered military life, serving under Infantry 8, in the city of Braga where he was the personal driver for Commander Armando da Fontoura. After finishing his military service, Fernando Amorim bought from his brother João all the taxi-cabs he had, beginning again his life in that sector.

Coincidentally, one day, in 1953, he went to City Hall to renew the licence plate for one of the cars and was surprised to see a huge line up of people. Curious, he went to inquire about what was going on and found out it was a line up of people who wanted to leave their names as possible candidates to emigrate to Canada. He thought to himself why Canada? He decided to enrol. He ended up being chosen as a farmer! Amorim, together with his fellow travellers – about a thousand of them – left Lisbon on April 8, 1955, aboard Arosa Star ship and arrived in Quebec City, on April 20 of the same year. After a very unpleasant trip by train, Canada's Immigration Services began the "dispatch" of the newly arrived and Fernando Amorim ended up in a farm, in Cornwall. He was left alone in a farm owned by a Scottish family. There he dwelled for six months, ploughing the land with the farmer's tractors and repairing every piece of mechanical equipment, since he had learned a few things back in Portugal. He was always well treated by the Scottish family and, until today, he is friends with the couple's son, Alex McGregor. After six months, he left Cornwall for Toronto where he found fellow travellers and began living at José Meneses' place. He did a bit of everything, from working at restaurants to cutting grass. Towards the end of 1955, the year of his arrival, Fernando Amorim went to Immigration Services of Canada and spoke with an inspector whom then was able to find Fernando a job at St. Michael's College.

Fernando Amorim, by the airplane from Varig airlines, in the first trip to Brazil.

Due to his interest and dedication, the administration of St. Michael's College paid him to study and he was able to finish his diploma on Hotel Management. Thus, he was easily promoted in those services at St. Michael's College, where he served as manager for many years. After 33 years of good service, he retired in 1988, because he "felt tired of travelling North America to attend courses and seminars". Since he was a member of the Canadian Restaurants' Association, College & Universities

Association and Services of Technical Schools in the USA, he used to travel frequently to Chicago, Syracuse, PEI, Vancouver, Windsor, Montreal, Manitoba, Los Angeles, etc. He remembers his time at St. Michael's College and every portuguese person whom he hired. Many of them are still working there. Fernando Amorim served many times as interpreter for the newly arrived immigrants and he helped many people become Canadian citizens.

The industrialist Manuel Mira, who knew Fernando Amorim since his arrival in Canada, invited him to go work with him, as soon as he learned about his retirement. Thus, in 1989, he founded a partnership with Manuel Mira, the FBA Systems Inc. However, when he thought he was going to rest, his new business, kept growing, causing him to work more then he used to at St. Michael's College. He was frequently flying all over Canada and the United

Fernando Amorim, as manager of the Hotel Services at St. Michael's College, with the head cooks, exchanging gifts

States. In a new deal with Manuel Mira, the company Tektone Sound & Signal, from the USA,

Fernando Amorim and his first car: a Morris Minor of good memories.

The beautiful Stephanie Amorim, in 1999, in Montreal, as member of the Skating Club of Burlington, the team that won the Canadian title for three consecutive years.

amalgamated with the Canadian counterpart, and Amorim began serving as vice-president, which allowed him to stop travelling.

Fernando Brandão de Amorim is married to Diane Mary Dawson-Amorim, a school teacher from Hamilton, where she was born on April 23, 1954. She taught for 33 years and has since retired. The couple has a daughter, Stephanie Diane who was born at St. Joseph's Hospital, in Hamilton, on March 25, 1983. She is still a student and a Canadian champion in ice skating. Fernando Amorim participated in some community activities, and helped establish some clubs, even though he never accepted any administration role… where "everyone fought to be president".

Presently, he is a member of the Federation of Portuguese Canadian Business and Professionals. He loves water skiing, a passion that makes him travel very often to Florida, and he loves reading. Fernando Amorim knew how to work and he found his happiness. He has worked very hard for it.

JMC - 2001

Andrade, Gervásio Matias de

Town of Vila Franca do Campo, island of S. Miguel, Azores

He has a medium stature and an intelligent look. He is a happy, charming and extroverted individual. He is Gervásio Matias de Andrade, a native of Vila Franca do Campo, a small village in the island of S. Miguel, in the Azores, where he was born on January 21, 1929. From a very early age, he began helping his father, José Matias de Andrade, in the store "Loja Matias" (Matias' shop), where they sold pieces of cloth, groceries and various trinkets.

Gervásio Andrade completed grade 4 – mandatory schooling back then – at the school Colégio Vilafranquense. As a teenager, he began dating his friend Laura de Sousa Cadete, who was also from Vila Franca do Campo, where she was born on August 19, 1929. After a 12 year relationship, Laura and Gervásio got married at Vila Franca do Campo's church,

The famous group "Companheiros da Alegria" (Companions in happiness) where one sees known faces such as Maria Adelaide, Helena Maria, Irene Velez, António Alvarinho, Rui de Mascarenhas, Luiz Horta, Igrejas Caeiro, Guilherme Kjolner, Alberto Ramos, Ferrer Trindade, Martinho D'Assunção and Floriano Silva, among others. Gervásio Andrade is the second one from left to right, in the middle row.

in 1952. The couple had five children: Maria de Jesus born in 1953, José Bernardo in 1954 and Gervásio in 1955, all born in Vila Franca do Campo. Already in Toronto, the couple have two more children: Suzy, born in 1961 and Elizabeth, in 1965. Today, they are very happy grandparents of twelve children and already have a great granddaughter.

Gervásio Matias de Andrade arrived in Halifax, Canada, on April 27, 1957. From Halifax he went straight to Montreal and always travelling by train, he was sent to Alberta. Together with the late José Furtado and Gil Carvalho, Gervásio also worked in Victoria, British Columbia, for three months. He remembers those times with a bitter smile when he had to ask his wife, who was still back in the Azores, for money. After those three harsh months, he went to Blue River to work on the construction of the railroad. He worked for CNR for three years. In 1960, Gervásio went to Kitimat, but again due to lack of money, he

When Gervásio performed in "Companheiros da Alegria", in S. Miguel.

moved to Toronto.

In Toronto, Gervásio began singing at the First Portuguese Community Club, with Nunes and Isabel Santos, when António Sousa was president. He was usually accompanied by Mariano Rego and by Orlando Ferreira, from the island of Madeira, most commonly known as "o Estragado" (the Wasted). Around 1970, Gervásio joined the folklore group from Nazaré where he played guitar.

Gervásio in the revue "Louça de Vila Franca" (China from Vila Franca), in 1954.

He was able to find a job at Upholstery Services, where he would remain for 25 years. After that time and having acquired sufficient knowledge, he moved to Body Guard Upholstery where he worked for another eight years. He retired beforehand, in 1987, due to an accident at work and which unabled him to continue his profession.

Joe, Maria, Elizabeth (standing), Suzy and Gervásio around their parents, Gervásio and Laura Andrade, in a family picture in 1998.

As a young person, Gervásio Matias de Andrade began singing fado from Lisbon and from Coimbra, with the well-known Victor Cruz, with José Cabral Rasquinha and Bento Lima on the guitar. He sang with the diva Amália Rodrigues in Solar da Graça. Amália liked his performance and invited him to go to Lisbon. In 1952, the play "Companheiros da Alegria" (Companions in happiness), toured Azores with Igrejas Caeiro as the stage manager, Gervásio won a singing contest and, as a prize, was able to tour with them to Madeira Island. In Madeira, the singing contest was won by the known "cop" João Fernandes.

Gervásio's mother cried so much for her son that, instead of Gervásio going to mainland Portugal, he returned to São Miguel. His grandson Steven, who was very talented as an actor, also gave up his career in the movie industry because of his mother's tears. Today, Steven is the chair of Synergy Entertainment.

Back in the Azores, Gervásio took part in revues and operettas. The couple Andrade has been living in Lake Simcoe since 1974, even though they still keep their house in Toronto. To travel, to live life to its fullest and be together with their numerous family members is their favourite hobbies. Obviously, Gervásio never forgets his songs, even if they are only sang when he is in the shower.

JMC - 1999

Aragão, João Pacheco

Town of Ribeira Funda, island of S. Miguel, Azores

João Pacheco Aragão

João Pacheco Aragão was born on September 11, 1922 in the town of Ribeira Funda, situated in a small place called Fenais da Ajuda, in the island of São Miguel. He is a very simple, honest, and hardworking man. When he found out that many of his friends had emigrated to a strange country by the name Canada, João felt the same desire to begin the same adventure.

At that time he was already married to Isaura Pacheco de Melo, also a native of Ribeira Funda, where she was born on February 7, 1925. In Fenais da Ajuda, two of his children were born: David, now 50 years old, and Maria Angelina, who is now 46. Isaura, with her two children, joined João in Canada in 1956.

João Pacheco travelled by boat, aboard the Homeland, until Halifax, where he arrived on March 26, 1954. From there, he went to Montreal and, later on, to Ottawa-Hull, where he lives. In Hull, two more children were born: John and Suzana. A life of work in construction allowed the Aragão couple Aragão to live a good life, own a house, help their children and helped them prepare for their retirement. Even working so hard, João still found time to dedicate to the Portuguese Centre Band of Hull. Among other positions, João Pacheco Aragão was in charge of the band between 1982 and 1984.

A life dedicated to work, family and the portuguese community of Hull. João Pacheco Aragão is a man who did not accept the idea of being just another person in life.

JMC - 1999

Arruda, Manuel de Sousa

Town of Remédios de Bretanha, island of S. Miguel, Azores

Manuel de Sousa Arruda, a native of the small town Remédios de Bretanha, in the island of S. Miguel, Azores, can be proud of being a portuguese pioneer in Canada and also a pioneer of many initiatives in the community.

Manuel Arruda embarked for Canada from Lisbon, May 8, 1953, with eighteen other friends, all from S. Miguel, and he arrived in Halifax on May 13, 1953. This was the first official group of immigrant azoreans coming to Canada.

Manuel Arruda was born on February 17, 1929.

The couple Manuel and Odília Arruda, at home, in Toronto. A very happy couple.

He got married, to Odília Vicente Arruda, first by proxy, in January of 1956, and then, on July 29, of the same year, at Nossa Senhora dos Remédios' Church, in S. Miguel. After the honeymoon, he returned to Canada, on September 15. From the marriage, five children were born. With a beautiful smile appearing on his face, Manuel tells us about the many different branches his family tree has:

- Just my mother alone had 15 children! And my father died at a very young age… Fortunately, my mother is still alive, she lives with us in Canada and is turning 86 this year.

- What is your mother's name?

- Silvana Arruda. She has 39 grandchildren and 17 great grandchildren.

- If Canada's survival depended on the Arruda's, there would not be any problems! – we said, sharing a moment of laughter with him.

- Yes, we have fulfilled our part. – he concluded, still laughing.

- When you arrived in Canada, what was your first job?

- Well, I went to a farm to milk cows… At that time, I did not even know how to say "yes" in English. I used to work 16 hours a day and ate very little. I remember making $30 dollars, but five days later, I moved to Sherbourne, in Quebec, where I worked for fifteen days. At that time, a friend from Feteiras, back home, José Martins, called me and I took off to Montreal, where he was living. Once there, we went to see the Consul General of Portugal, Father Almeida, the only portuguese person in Canada who spoke English at that time. He found us a job.

- Did you suffer a lot?

- If I did! You know, just to go to church, I walked four hours each way. Since I did not know how to speak my boss's language, and I remembered having seen a church when I was traveling by car to the farm, I decided to walk there… Only by miracle was I able to return home after going to mass. I was fortunate enough to mark the way with crosses, otherwise I would not have returned home. I went through some really tough times.

- How did you end up in Toronto? – We asked.

- It was a long journey… My friend José Martins went to the States with an aunt of his. In Reviera Prairie, where we worked, the salaries were miserable and I decided, with Manuel Vieira, from the town Água de Pau, to look for work in Montreal. We didn't find anything. I called my uncle João Vicente, in the States, who called my wife's uncle, António Vieira, to ask him to help me. António Vieira knew Manuel Cabral, in Galt, Ontario, and asked him to give me a hand. António Vieira went to Montreal to get me. From December of 1953 to August of 1954, I lived at Manuel

First group of azoreans from the island of S. Miguel who emigrated to Canada. Top row: Evaristo Almeida, José Botelho, José Bento, António Couto, Agostinho Martins, Manuel Machado, Guilherme Cabral and Jaime Cardoso. Middle row: Armando Vieira, Afonso Maria Tavares, Eugénio Sousa, João Martins, Manuel Arruda and Manuel Vieira. Bottom row: Vasco Oliveira, Victinho Martins, inspector Ferreira da Costa, Manuel Pavão and José Martins.

First president and second board of directors of First Portuguese Canadian Association, the very first portuguese club in Canada. Standing: Ângelo Bacalhau, José Pacheco, Norberto Rebelo, Manuel Medeiros and Manuel Vieira. Sitting: Gil Maiato, José Meneses (first president) and Manuel Arruda.

Cabral's place, and my job was to kill horses, to skin them and then sell the skins to the company Mink's. Disgusting job!

- What happened after? – we insisted.

- I found out that Manuel Vieira and José Marques, from the island of Terceira, were already living in Toronto, and I decided to go meet them. The Consul General of Portugal in Toronto, Mr. V.R. Williams, and his secretary, Mrs. Galaka, who spoke Portuguese, helped me find a job at St. Joseph's College, where I worked for three years. I was the first one to get a job as an interpreter at Immigration Canada for a portuguese lady.

- As a pioneer of this community, you must have been the first one to organize many initiatives.

- Yes! I was part of the foundation of the First Portuguese Canadian Association, the first musical band, the first religious celebrations in honour of Santo Cristo dos Milagres…

- Start with the First Portuguese… - I interrupted with interest.

- Well, at that time, the first president of the club, José Meneses, had some problems with the other members of the administration and he asked me to serve as vice-president, to see if we could put the club up and running. I accepted and organized the very first "cantorias ao desafio" (a traditional singsong made up as the singer is interpreting it)…

- I made so many broad bean platefuls to sell there! – remembered Odília Arruda, with a loud laugh, mixed with a sentiment of satisfaction and longing.

- It's true! – continued her husband. – This way, we were able to make the club successful. Like that and selling beer without a licence, obviously! Because of that, one day I had to go to jail to get my brother, because the authorities had been at the First Portuguese… Anyways, adventures of life. I remember that at that time I already spoke English and was able to help with the situation. I was invited by the city councillor of my area to serve as interpreter, but because they only paid one dollar and fifty cents, I didn't accept the offer and decided to go work at Nielson's chocolate factory, where I have been working for 29 years. Marcelino Moniz went to work at the Portuguese Consulate through us.

- Do you regret anything?

- No, not at all. I do not regret coming to Canada or doing what I did.

- After your wedding, did you go back to visit the Azores?

- Yes, I did… When we celebrated the 25th anniversary of the arrival of the Portuguese to Canada, I went to the islands of S. Miguel and Terceira. I took with me the Santo Cristo's band from Toronto, the first portuguese band in Canada, because I was the president. When we landed in the Azores, we went straight to Santo Cristo's church, in the city of Ponta Delgada, island of S. Miguel, where we performed our first concert. It was 10 p.m.

- When was the first religious celebration of "Santo Cristo dos Milagres" in Toronto? – We asked, convinced that Manuel Arruda has a great memory for these important facts from those times.

- It was in May of 1966! Before that, Mariano Rego had offered the image of Senhor Santo Cristo dos Milagres to Father Esteves Lourenço, for worship at Santa Maria's church. When Father Alberto Cunha came to Santa Maria's church, we began the celebrations. I still remember that the music of the procession was recorded and played on tape recorder lent to us… Obviously, I was the one carrying it.

- Have you always organized of the celebrations?

- Always! Right now I am the Treasurer of the Commission at Santa Maria's church.

- And I – continued Odília – have been singing in the choir for ten years.

Here, I would like to mention the family's skills for singing. Johnny, the eldest son, is the vocalist of the musical group Capas Negras and his youngest sister, Diana, is taking the first steps as performer and, we are convinced, if she studies and works hard at it, she will be successful.

- Would you like to return to the Azores? – we asked.

- Forever? No, I wouldn't. I have all my family here and I have planted my roots here. However, I have a dream that I would love see accomplished: I would love to take all my children to the place where I was born. God willing, I will be able to.

We wish you all the best in that endeavour. Manuel Arruda, first among the pioneers, deserves being helped due to his courage and tenacity. Manuel Arruda is a pioneer who deserves our respect for what he has done and still does for the portuguese community. Thanks to his sacrifice, and that of many others like him, the journey became easier for those who arrived after.

It is with his story – and others – that we will be able to write our community's history.

JMC - May 1986

Aurélio, Maria Lucinda Sias

Town of Crato, Province of Alentejo

As a child, she dreamt about being a hair dresser and the dream has come true. Maria Lucinda Sias Aurélio was born on September 26, 1948, in the town of Crato, in the province of Alentejo. She completed her primary years of school – up to grade 4 – in Crato. From a very young age, the beautiful and restless Lucinda began her "training" in the art of hairdos, using her father's head, Nicolau Sias, as her model. At the same time, she was learning the art at a hair salon in Crato.

Her boyfriend left with his family to

Lucinda, at her salon, doing what she always wanted.

Canada on April 25, 1965. António Fernando Aurélio, also a native of Crato, where he was born on April, 1946, decided to marry his girlfriend whom he missed deeply. The dream was accomplished. They married by proxy in June of 1967. In Toronto, they decided to have a real wedding, at Santa Maria's church, blessed by the late Father Cândido Nogueira, on March 2, 1968. Maria Lucinda's professional journey was easy. She had hardly arrived and began working at Tony & Martins Beauty Salon.

Tony was from the island of Madeira and Martins was from Lisbon. At the time, as she recalls it, there was only another portuguese salon: Fernanda & Lima. Her husband, an electrician by profession, began working in factories, and ended up opening his own hardware store, in partnership with his brother. Things did not go as well as planned. Unfortunately, a long fatal disease took his life on October 23, 1984, when he was only 37. Maria Lucinda did not give up all hope. Before her husband's death, the couple had already bought the building, located on 1466 Dundas Street West, where she still has her Lucinda Beauty Salon. They lived there for two years, before buying their own house.

The couple António and Maria Lucinda Aurélio, the day of their wedding.

The couple had a beautiful daughter, Filomena, who "saw the first light of day" on March 5, 1973. Filomena has an Honours Bachelor of Science from the University of Toronto, in psychology and anthropology, as well as a Bachelor of Education. She is a certified teacher for the Dufferin Peel Catholic District School Board. Today, still single, she teaches in Brampton. Filomena also went to the Transmontano Portuguese School, where she fluently learned how to read and write in Portuguese. Maria Lucinda lives with her daughter.

The Aurélios, when they began their life in Toronto.

At Lucinda Beauty Salon, Lucinda has an amazing team working with her, where her sister Carolina, is a friend, a helper and a beautician. Lucinda's favourite hobbies are reading and shopping. If she decided to retire one day – though she only feels at home when she is in her salon – she plans to help her daughter and grandchildren (if she ever has them, as he hopes), and will continue to be a hairdresser, doing volunteer work at the hospitals and nursing homes, to help those less fortunate. She feels a special tenderness for seniors and the ill. She wants, through volunteer work, to thank God for all He has given

Lucinda's daughter baptism

Young Lucinda, in her fields of Alentejo.

her. She has a house in Crato, back home, where she plans to, one day, spend some time and catch up on her reading.

Maria Lucinda Sias Aurélio, a woman who always knew what she wanted and who will always follow her heart. May the remaining journey be one of happiness and self-fulfilment.

JMC - 2001

A very happy day. At the University of Toronto, Maria Lucinda congratulates her daughter the day of her graduation.

Lucinda with her sister Carolina Martins.

Barbosa, António da Silva

Village of Abraveses, town of Tondela

When we were young, serving in the Portuguese Air Force, we never imagined that we would meet again, in Toronto, Canada. Every time I get together with Ferreira, Zé Henriques, Heitor Morais and many others whose names I do not remember now, we always have fun, even though it is not important for our story. António da Silva Barbosa was born in the village of Abraveses, in the town of Tondela, on April 30, 1939. He was brought up in the city of Viseu. At Viseu's Cathedral, he married Maria Carlota da Costa, who was born in the village of Asseisseira, on January 18, 1941. The wedding took place on October 22, 1962. From this union, Dulce was born on September 11, 1963, in Viseu. Dulce Barbosa is a successful artistic agent in Toronto. António da Silva Barbosa com-

Maria Carlota and daughter Dulce, together with António. A family picture.

António Barbosa displaying some medals he has won.

pleted his course in Radar Operations at FAP and, in September of 1966, emigrated to Canada. His wife and daughter came to live with him in 1967. Before emigrating to Canada, António Barbosa, he left the Air Force and joined the Portuguese Airline, Tap Air

Portugal, to work as a mechanic.

In Toronto, he began his career as a watchmaker at Milano Jewellers. He then became a partner with Chris Shinohar, at Time Craft, located at Yorkdale Shopping Centre, in Toronto, a company that he ended up buying. In 1971, with his brother Júlio, he obtained the repairs' section of Time Craft, and, in 1973, they bought the entire firm. The company grew through various franchises located in Pickering, Steeles and 404, Wardenwoods Mall, etc... In 1985, António Barbosa founded a firm, Barcan Agencies, responsible for importing portuguese wines. Since 1998, António Barbosa has expanded the firm to export products to Brazil, Portugal, Spain, and beginning soon, he will be exporting to China a special Canadian lubricant, which transforms any car oil, lowering the level of consumption, protecting the motor and the oil itself. This lubricant, as well as all the companies of the group, is under Blue Bay International Group Inc., of which António Barbosa is the chair.

António Barbosa running a marathon in the USA.

António Barbosa was always fond of sports. He was a soccer player for both the junior and senior teams of Académico de Viseu. In Toronto, he played for the First Portuguese team, together

Virgílio Pires, Leo Pereira and Engineer Sarmento, surround António Barbosa after he had finished running a marathon in New York.

Rosa Mota and António Barbosa, after running Rosa Mota's Marathon, to raise funds for Doctor's Hospital.

with Waldemar, Rilhas, Daniel, Martelo, Vicente, and many others. They were champions of the National Soccer League, in 1969, trained by coach Artur Rodrigues.

His dedication and long hours of work caused him a lot of stress and order to fight this stress, he began running a couple of kilometres at the Colombus Centre and around his neighbourhood. Three years later, already in his forties, he began participating in fund raising marathons, just for fun, such as Terry Fox, Diabetes, Doctor's Hospital... Always for fun and pleasure, he has made it through 21 marathons: six in Toronto, six in Ottawa, two in New York, two in Boston, one in Hamilton, two in Chicago and two in Montreal. The best timing he accomplished was 3 hours, 14 minutes and 18 seconds, in New York, when he was 53. He stopped a few months ago due to an operation to one of his knees. However, he says he will be back... He is a member and sits on the board of directors at the Columbus Centre, in charge of the sports section. António da Silva Barbosa is a friend who never turns away a friend.

JMC - 1999

Barros, Maria José Correia Carreiro

Village of Lomba da Maia, island of S. Miguel, Azores

The years go by, but the beautiful and tender smile stays in her face. Maria José Correia Carreiro Barros was born on August 22, 1921, in the village of Lomba da Maia, in the island of S. Miguel, Azores. In S. Miguel, she met a young military man, António Rodrigues

Maria José Barros with her son Eduardo at Lagoa Azul.

Barros, a native of Braga, in mainland Portugal, where he was born on October 3, 1923. António Barros, integrated in the Marines, did part of his military service in the Azores and decided to stay there.

Maria José and António Barros married on February 2, 1946, at São José's Church, in the city of Ponta Delgada, S. Miguel. Unlike most Portuguese families at that time, the couple only emigrated to Canada, after their children. In 1965, their son Eduardo Manuel, born in S. Miguel, emigrated to Canada. Custódio António, also born in S. Miguel, went to the Netherlands, but ended up in Canada, a few months later. Only in 1966, do we see António coming to Canada, and Maria José the year after. The Barros couple, also had two daughters, Helena and Maria Manuela, who were born in the island of Santa Maria. Soon after arriving, in 1970, António opened the first Portuguese homeopathy store "Lagoa Azul", on Dundas and Bellwoods, moving in 1977 to the location where it still is today, on Dundas, before Ossington.

António Barros had taken the homeopathic course at "Gabinete Botânico Diedético", in Lisbon. António Rodrigues Barros passed away on May 3, 1987, in Toronto. Maria José did not give up all hope

António Rodrigues Barros (1923 - 1987).

and decided to run "Lagoa Azul" with the same enthusiasm and with the knowledge acquired throughout the years. Today, with a special smile, Maria José continues to serve her numerous clients and friends. By her side, and after a successful period working for real estate, she has her son Eduardo who, just like his late father, studied homeopathy and natural products, having finished the courses "Dispensing Nutritional Supplements and Herbal Remedies", at the Canadian Health Food Association, and the "Nutrition and Certification Homeopathy Certificate of Recognition". He is now taking "The Certified Natural Products Advisor Education Program".

The two sisters: Maria Manuela and Helena Barros.

All the products at Lagoa Azul are imported from Portugal, with a few exceptions, which are obtained in Canada. We hope that Maria José's simple smile continues to charm everyone for many years to come.

JMC -2001

Maria José Barros with her son Custódio and one of her grandsons, in a family reunion.

Barroso, José de Amaral

Town of Rabo de Peixe, island of S. Miguel

He still keeps his pleasant and honest look. Emigration to Canada gave him a new profession, one that made him and many others happy. José de Amaral Barroso was born in the town of Rabo de Peixe, in the island of S. Miguel, on September 5, 1925.

After completing the mandatory grade 4, he went to work in the fields with his father Francisco. He was always involved in agriculture until the day he finished his military service in the city of Ponta Delgada and the town of Arrifes, in 1945. When he left the army, he went back to agriculture, but on his own. José Barroso met Maria do Espírito Santo Silva, also from Rabo de Peixe, where she was born on December 29, 1927, marrying her exactly 25 years later, on December 29, 1952. In Rabo de Peixe, the couple had two daughters: Ana Maria and Maria. With the hardships of life in his native island, he decided to go away. He left the city of Ponta Delgada, boarding the Homeland ship, on April 23 and arrived in Halifax, on April 29, 1954. His wife arrived in Toronto, with the couple's daughters, on November 5, 1957. In Toronto,

Chef Barroso displaying a fish course for which he got a first prize.

the Barrosos had two more children: Dora and José. Today, they are all married, and the Barrosos are the proud grandparents of nine grandchildren. However, life in Canada was not a bed of roses. José de Amaral Barroso, as soon as he arrived in Halifax, was transferred to Quebec City, with a group of 70 other fellow travellers. They remained there for three weeks without any work.

The Barrosos greeting with a Port Wine the success of their restaurant L'Étude.

Mr. Romano, a Portuguese inspector, brought them to Montreal. A farmer liked José Barroso and offered him a job on his farm to take care of the cows, even knowing that José had no experience. He was offered $55 dollars a month. At the end of the month, he only received $45 dollars. Upset, he went to the Department of Immigration, where he found a brazilian assistant who helped him. His complaint had good results. The farmer gave him the $10 dollars that were owed to him.

A few more weeks went by, in St. Ramires, Montreal, where he worked in a vegetable farm. There he had a good boss and good food at the table, as he remembered many years later. A group of friends from his homeland incited him to go work with them cutting down trees in North Quebec. Since it was very hard work to do, they decided to buy a power saw to facilitate their life. They ended up not making enough money to pay for the machine... They gave up and sold the power saw. Disappointed, José Barroso went back to Montreal.

Liberace greets Chef Barroso.

The brazilian civil servant at the Department of Immigration got him a job at a restaurant washing dishes. George, the head cook, liked José and became his "godfather". From washing dishes he became a kitchen boy. When George was invited to manage Park Plaza Hotel, in Toronto, he brought with him José Barroso. Slowly, with his rare intuition for gastronomy, José Barroso was promoted, ending up as second head cook. At Park Plaza Hotel, where he worked for almost nine years, Barroso received a certificate of honour for serving the Queen of England with rigour. In 1964, José Barroso went to the Celebrity Club as Head Cook, where he served the biggest canadian and american celebrities. In 1974, José Barroso bought the restaurant L'Étude, on Dundas and Kipling. This was a very successful enterprise. He still remembers the visits from Father Lima and the couple Rosa and António Barros who used to stay at the restaurant till all hours....

In 1981, he sold the restaurant to a fellow Greek. However, before that, in 1977, he was hired as Head of the Banquets Section at Inn On The Park. At the Inn, he served the famous american pianist Liberace who, happy with the service, gave him one of his pictures autographed. In 1980, Chef Barroso went to inaugurate Pier 4, from the Whaler's group. When he was head cook at Pier 4, he used to love fishing on his boss' private boat, on Lake Ontario. Feeling the weight of his years, José de Amaral Barroso, decided to work at smaller places and finished his functions at the Grace Restaurant. At the age of 70, in 1995, he retired after suffering a stroke. As he confessed, he never thought he could be a cook. However, he was happy to have found his new profession, one he practised with passion until the end. He built a beautiful career and a good life for his family. He specialized in banquets and cakes for important occasions.

The last time he worked as head cook was at the fund raising event, in Brampton, organized by his friend Afonso Tavares for East Timor. He obviously did it for free! José de Amaral Barroso was always by the side of those in need… and always had his nice, tender smile.

JMC - 2001

Belém, Vasco Furtado de Simas
Town of Lajes das Flores, island of Flores, Azores

He has a very strong personality. Vasco Furtado de Simas Belém was born on the town of Lajes das Flores, on the island of Flores, Azores, on January 14, 1935. He studied at the Liceu Nacional de Angra do Heroísmo, completing the old grade 7 (equivalent today to grade 12). He began his professional career as First Civil Officer of the American Air Force and Officer of telecommunications.

In high school, he met Maria Lígia da Silva Gregório, from the island of Graciosa, where she was born on December 29, 1940. After high school, Maria Lígia continued her studies and became an elementary teacher. Vasco and Maria Lígia got married on September 28, 1960, at Nossa Senhora da Conceição's church, in the city of Angra do Heroísmo, in the island of Terceira. After a brief stay – of 13 months – in Salvador da Bahia, in Brazil, Vasco Belém

Maria Lígia and Vasco Belém, a happy couple, in one of the community events.

moved to Canada, where he arrived on April 4, 1966. He began his career working for CP Telecommunications, and later on in life, transferred to Douglas Aircraft Canada.

The Beléms have three children: Renato, born in Angra do Heroísmo, on August 5, 1962, Rui, also born in Angra do Heroísmo, on January 11, 1964, and Robin, who was born in Mississauga, Ontario, on June 28, 1977. Robin, the youngest, is now attending McMaster University, in Hamilton, where she is studying sciences. Slowly, Vasco began losing interest in telecommunications. He

At Belém Travel, Vasco Belém and his secretary Lídia.

decided to switch to communications... where he could work directly with the public and with the islands of his native Azores: he opened a travel agency – named after his last name. Belém Travel opened, in Mississauga, on May 1, 1974.

Just a few months later, on July 7, he decided to move Belém Travel to Toronto, where it still operates, on Dundas and Brock. Besides the normal business of the agency, Vasco specialized in the organization of excursions to Our Lady of Fatima, Santo Cristo, Jerusalem, among other destinations. Vasco is a benefactor member of the Sport Club Angrense of Toronto, where, in the past, he served as president

Belém's children: Renato, Robin and Rui.

of the general assembly. As a family man, his favourite hobbies are going out with his family, camping, reading, traveling and sports. He practices swimming, plays soccer and baseball. We have had the pleasure of travelling withVasco. You may not notice it, but he is a fun person to travel with: extremely correct, well-mannered and diligent. A true fellow traveller!

JMC - 1999

Belo, António Fernandes

Town of Santa Cruz, Madeira Island

To socialize with the couple Belo, at their upscale house, in one of Toronto's richest areas, is to feel the joy of life and the pleasure of talking to happy people.

António Fernandes Belo was born in the town of Santa Cruz, Madeira island, on October 31, 1915. The 71 years that have already gone by go unnoticed when you look at the happy António Belo. He loves talking, especially to tell stories about himself and those close to him.

Father Carlos and António Belo, in 1960, surrounded by members of the Conference of St. Vincent de Paul, in Toronto.

António Belo married Lurdes Teixeira, also from Santa Cruz, where she was born on December 28, 1918.

The couple has six children, all born in Madeira Island. The oldest is António who joined his father in Canada, in 1957; José, who came to Canada in 1958; and Juvenal, who arrived in 1959. The three youngest ones, Maria José, Duarte and Ernesto, all came with their mother on April 6, 1962.

- My story began well before

coming to Canada – António Belo began telling his story, with a tender look in his eyes. – Can you believe that on the ship, the famous Olympia, I sat at a table with six people: a couple from Green Cape and another couple form the United States, who had a daughter. During the trip, we always sat together and spoke about everything. When I told them who I was, the American couple laughed and asked me if I were related to the family Belo who lived in Witica, close to New York. I nodded yes with my head and explained to them that some of my brothers and relatives were already living in the States. Then, the man told me that his daughter had been a school mate of my niece. You know, we became friends at that moment…

- Were they going to Canada?

- No, they stayed in New York… The ship docked at the port there. – Belo explained. – They were exceptional with me. Because they were Americans, they left the ship earlier than I. It took so long for me to leave the ship that I thought I would never see them again. But the truth was: they were waiting for me and showed me New York. It was wonderful! I will never forget the experience. Before I boarded the train, he explained the situation to the agent and gave a paper with directions of whatever was necessary. When the train stopped in Albania, the agent asked me for the paper, which had all the information about my relatives, and contacted them. When I arrived in Witica, there were more than thirty people waiting for me! What a wonderful reception! We didn't stay there for too long. One of my brother's brother-in-law came with me to Canada.

Samuel Shopsysweet (Mr. Shopsy's) and wife, with Bob Hope and the pioneer António Belo. Because it was a Chinese dinner, Bob Hope decided to use the tress braid as a moustache.

- So you had your brother in the US, but you decided to come to Canada?

- No, I had brothers in the States and here! – he explained immediately. – I came to Canada with a contract on my brother's name – Fernando Fernandes Belo. But, going back, when I saw all the family in Witica – brothers, brothers-in-law, nephews and nieces – I even cried with all the commotion… - a little light showing in his eyes, as he remembered that moment. – I immediately told my niece Maria Luísa the story of the American couple who knew her…

- So, when did you leave Madeira and when did you arrive in Canada?

- I left Funchal on May 5, 1955, stopping in Lisbon for three days. After, it was the trip to New York. I arrived in Halifax on May 18 and in Toronto on May 22.

- How many people from Madeira travelled with you?

- From Madeira? I was the only one. Over all, we were 52 Portuguese men going to Canada, all the other ones were from mainland Portugal.

- What was your profession in Madeira?

- I was a waiter at the Ritz Hotel. When I got to Canada, I found a job in a restaurant as a busboy. I was making $23 dollars a week. My first day at work was May 28, 1955.

- Did you stay there for a long time?

- No! Only three months. Right after that, I went to work at Shopsy's where I stayed for 25 years. – he answered in a very proud manner.

- Really?

- Yes! But, before that, I remember very well complaining to my brother that I was not making enough money, besides having a worthless job. In Madeira, at the Ritz, during the high season of tourism I was making a lot more than in Canada. I remember my brother telling me: Be patient! We will find something better! Thank God, it ended up happening.

- What was your first task at Shopsy's?

- Counter-helper. From there, I was transferred to the confectionery section and ended up being the manager of the Shopsy's Catering Department.

- How did that happen?

- Well, I was always a perfectionist and very hospitable. Although I was at the counter, making salads, I always noticed that the confectionery section was not in good hands. Maliciously, but with good intentions, I used to go there every so often to decorate the cakes. One day, Mr. Shopsysweet, the owner, noticing what was going on and liking my work, sent the manager to the deli section and moved me to the cakes department. The person in charge of the catering department – continued Mr. Belo – was a young man who, due to his age, wanted to have fun and spend the night out. As a consequence, he was always asking me to take care of things while he was sleeping, hiding from everybody. Obviously, the other employees began noticing it... Mr Shopsy, one day, decided he had enough and transferred me to the catering department and promoted me to manager. I never left that place.

- Did you help many portuguese people?

- Did I ever! To this day, there are portuguese people still working there who were hired and taught by me. Every time someone was hired, Mr. Shopsy would send that person to me to be trained. He was a wonderful man.

- My husband was the 'godfather' of many portuguese people – Lurdes Belo interrupted as she was listening to our conversation while serving us passion fruit liquor and honey cake.

- But, thank God, I have friends! – said António, adding to his wife's remark. – Shopsy's was the king of hot-dogs and corn beef and he had all the means to help the Portuguese.

- Where did you cater?

- At Shopsy's or in the halls chosen by the clients. For example, the artists would be served at their own dressing room, at the theatre.

- Did you serve many artists?

- Yes, many! – he answered with a sigh of happiness and longing. I have the best memories from the time I spent with the pianist Victor Burg, the comedians Danny Kaye, the Three Stooges and Bob Hope... - After a burst of laughter, he continued. – Bob Hope was a good friend! I served politicians, millionaires, industrialists, businessmen and athletes.

Lurdes and António Belo, showing their diplomas from Brian Mulroney, David Peterson and Alan Tonks, when they celebrated their wedding 50th anniversary.

- Speaking of athletes, I know you served a big banquet at Maple Leaf Gardens, right?

- Yes! It was the banquet to commemorate the 25th anniversary of Shopsy's. What a party! Mr. Shopsysweet and Mr. Ballard were very good friends. Mr. Ballard allowed the Maple Leaf Gardens to be the place for the banquet... You know, I did my service so well that Mr. Shopsysweet gave me a $1200 bonus!

Proud of this bonus for serving the banquet so well, we changed the direction of our conversation and went back to the early years.

- We know that you came to Canada alone in 1955. Why?

- Because back then we were not allowed to travel with our families. – he clarified. – My wife only came in 1962.

- On April 6. I will never forget! – explained Lurdes.

- Actually, something funny happened at that time. My three youngest children came with my wife and they brought her grandmother, a 96 year old lady! Her picture came on the newspaper for being the oldest lady to arrive at Toronto's International Airport. At least, at that time. Poor lady… she died eight months later!

- I loved my grandmother! – said Lurdes with consternation.

- With all your life dedicated to helping those next to you, and at the same time catering to big personalities, do you remember any episode, one that you will never forget?

At the restaurant "The Boat", Lurdes and António Belo, surrounded by their children, sons and daughters-in-law. A happy family. Just grandchildren, the Belos have 17.

- Oh yes! I will never forget Mr. Churchill, whom I helped serve at the Ritz, when he went to Madeira. He was a true gentleman and loved Madeira wine! – almost dreaming, António finished saying: - Mr. Churchill, at his farewell, gave me one of his famous cigars. I kept it religiously for years…

- What happened to it?

- You know, with so many trips, with the adventures of emigration, I lost the cigar! It's one of the few sorrows I have in my life.

- Actually, since we began our conversation, we've noticed an atmosphere of happiness in your house. You are really happy, aren't you?

- Yes, we really are! – answered António immediately, echoed by his wife.

- We are very happy. I don't think there is a happier family. Thank God, we are very close…

- Especially at Christmas. We all get together. There is nothing in this world that can break us apart.

- Before, I used to have Christmas supper at our house, but now it is at one of our children's place because our house became too small and, at the same time, I am getting too old to do all the work.

- Fortunately, all my children are doing well. We all go to their place. They have bigger houses, modern and we feel more calm there! – finished António, reinforcing his wife's words.

A few weeks ago, the Belos celebrated their 50th anniversary. It was a grand party, offered by the couple's children at the restaurant "The Boat", in Toronto. It was a wonderful surprise for the happy couple, to have on that special day the entire family reunited. It was a day to be forever remembered…

- It was a wonderful day! – Belo said, moved by the thought. – I was not expecting so much love around us. I have a great family! – he finished with great joy.

- Now that you are retired, would you go back to Madeira island?

- Don't even think about it!

- Just grandchildren, we have 17. – Lurdes confirmed, interrupting her husband.

- We have everything here: both our families, our grandchildren. Look, my eldest grandson just finished his bachelor of education at the University of Toronto. I am very proud of them. The little we have in Madeira doesn't interest us anymore. It can stay there.

Still going back to their 50th anniversary, António Belo showed us the diplomas congratulating him sent by politicians from both the federal and provincial governments, as well as from the municipality of York where they live. Some of these are signed by Prime Minister Brian Mulroney, Premier David Peterson and councillor Allan Tonks.

- I have worked very hard and, thus, feel like I have been compensated for everything. May God bless everyone for everything given to us! – he said. – June 30th was well remembered!

António Fernandes Belo, as a pioneer of the Portuguese community, was also a very active member in the activities that began taking place throughout the years.

- I am one of the founding members of the Canadian Madeira Club. The first religious celebrations were cater by me. I was vice-president and director for many years. When we organized the first excursion to Madeira, I was the vice-president and Juvenal de Freitas was the president.

- Have you only been involved with Madeira Club or were there other initiatives?

- No, there were more. For ten years, I was president of St. Vince de Paul's Conference for the portuguese community in Toronto. This conference was organized in 1960, by Father Carlos, from Philadelphia, and later by Father Antero de Melo, at St. Agnes' Church. After so much volunteer work, now I have decided to just spend time with my family.

Before leaving their house, we went to check another passion that keeps António Belo busy: his garden. We found many different types of fruit on the same tree! It's true! All of them are a result from many grafts done on the same tree.

JMC - August of 1988

Belo, Juvenal Fernandes
Town of Santa Cruz, Madeira Island

He is a happy citizen living in this country. Juvenal Fernandes Belo was born in the town of Santa Cruz, from the Autonomous Region of Madeira, on November 8, 1943. At the age of 16, he left Madeira, with his mother Lurdes Teixeira Belo, who was also from Santa Cruz, to come live with his father who was already in Canada from 1955.

The jovial Juvenal Fernandes Belo arrived in Toronto on August 9, 1960. In 1961, at the gathering of people from Madeira – Festa dos Madeirenses –, he met Diana Alves who had already been born in New Bedford, on November 10, 1948. Diana and Juvenal were married on July 30, 1966, in Harthford,

Juvenal Belo besides his aunt Maria Alves, a Portuguese-american singer.

Conneniticut, but moved to Toronto, afterwards. Now, they live in Brampton. Diana Alves Belo has a degree in Business Management and Juvenal holds a diploma in Electronics, taken at George Brown College. The Belos have 3 children: Nancy, 30, a nurse; Richard, an accountant and Michelle, a secretary, all born in Toronto. Juvenal Belo began his career at the State Contractors, where he was the supervisor of the Services Division, from 1967 to 1985.

Portuguese United Team where we see, among the players, Juvenal Belo and, on the left, standingue, goalie Rodrigues who, later on, became the coach for First Portuguese Soccer Club.

In 1985, he decided to found his own company "Future-Tec" and took charge of all the electronic services, Data and Communications, of major companies such as Eaton Centre and Money Life Centre, as well as of public services such as those at the Queen's Park, in Toronto. Juvenal Fernandes Belo has his friend David Restrick as a partner in Future-Tec, a friend

The Belos at a family gathering.

he had known from the time he worked at the State Contractors.

Juvenal Fernandes Belo has also been a sports person throughout his life, being dedicated mainly to soccer. Still back home, he played for the junior section of Nacional da Madeira, in 1958-1959, although he was a fan of the club Marítimo. In Toronto, in 1962, Juvenal was one of the founding members of the Portuguese United, which, later on, changed its name to First Portuguese Canadian Club Soccer Team, together with the brothers Bacalhau, Artur Rodrigues,

The couple Diana and Juvenal Belo, in fraternization with friends.

Albuquerque, brothers Silva and many others. She played soccer along side Rilhas and Valdemar, among others from his time. He was also a director at the First Portuguese soccer club. Juvenal, as a player for the Portuguese United, was punished for five years for playing a little joke on the referee. It was one of those days where even a person like Juvenal looses his joviality.

Juvenal Belo is also a founding member of Canadian Madeira Club, an association that saw the light of day in 1963, now celebrating its 36th anniversary.

Life has been good to the Belo's family. However, they have strived to be successful in life. Juvenal Fernandes

Belo deserves what he has for his charm, knowledge and dedication to work, love of family and wife next to him. Not to mention his irradiating joviality.

JMC - 1999

Botelho, António Arruda

Town of Ribeirinha, Island of S. Miguel, Azores

António e Maria Manuela Botelho, a very happy couple.

António Arruda Botelho is from the town of Ribeirinha, in the island of S. Miguel, in the Autonomous Region of the Azores, where he was born on July 27, 1929. He is a very calm, modest and kind man. He was unable to finish the mandatory school years due to the work he had to do in agriculture, helping his family. When he found out that many of his friends were going to Canada, he decided to fill out an application and try his luck in a different place.

He was chosen and arrived in Montreal on May 12, 1956. Advised by his friends to go to the Canadian Department of Immigration from where he would be sent to a farm to take care of cows and pigs, António decided to come to Toronto, after staying for two days at Guilherme Padeira place. Taking the train to Toronto, he was hoping to find in this city a chance to be hired to work at the construction of the railroads. His dream did not come true. Without solutions and without money, he decided to call the late José Medeiros Janeiro – who would become his brother-in-law, who at the time worked on mushroom farm, on Dufferin and highway 401. Janeiro got him a job at the farm for eight months. In January of 1957, António Botelho came back to Toronto and in March of the same year decided to move to Elliot Lake, where he began working in construction. After two years, when worked finished, he came to Toronto, taking advantage of this interval in his life to go visit his island of S. Miguel

The sisters Estrela and Maria, with the brother Clemente, the groom António and bride Tracy, the parents Botelho and grandson Joshua.

and get married. He married Maria Manuela Medeiros Janeiro, born in Ribeirinha on October 25, 1934. The wedding took place at Ribeirinha's church, on January 3, 1959. In June of that year, he came back to Canada, leaving behind Maria Manuela who was pregnant with their first child, Maria José, who was born in Ribeirinha, on November 17, 1959. Maria José finished her studies, is married and the mother of one boy. Curiously, the second child, António Francisco, was also born in Ribeirinha, on August 16, 1962, after António's second visit to S. Miguel.

Maria Manuela only came to Toronto on October 24, 1965. In this city, two other children were born: Clemente, on January 19, 1967, who has a degree in Arts, married and has a son, and Estrela, born October 6, 1972, single and a nurse. The Botelho's saga continued. Maria Manuela was always a dedicated mother, but when she had a chance, he began working to help her husband. She worked until her retirement in the priests home, at St. Michael's College, in the University of Toronto. At the same time, António went back to work on a mushroom farm and, in 1960, he went to Manitoba where he stayed for two years building a nickel mine.

Botelhos continuity is well established with their children, sons and daughters-in-law, and the grandchildren who became the happiness of their home.

He finished his work in 1976, the year he made a third visit to S. Miguel. On his return, and already with his family in Canada, he went back to work in construction until 1976. In 1977, he was hired by the University of Toronto to work in the cleaning and maintenance department, where he stayed until his retirement on January 31, 1996. António Arruda Botelho, Father Francisco Medeiros Janeiro's brother-in-law, now responsible for Santa Maria's church in Hamilton, was always an active member in the

Maria Manuela serving soup to her brother, Father Janeiro, under António Botelho's look.

religious and social life of the catholic church, together with his wife Manuela, Father Janeiro's sister. The couple were always involved in the church's choir, both back home and in Toronto, at Santa Maria's church, at the time of Father Lourenço, and at St. Peter's church with Fathers Amadeu Pereira and Francisco Janeiro. António Botelho was a member of the Holy Spirit's and Fatima's Commissions for 17 years at St. Peter's church, in Toronto.

Today, retired and happy with life, António and Manuela take care of their grandchildren. António Botelho also takes time to do small things at home. They often visit the Azores and love taking trips to Our Lady of Fatima Shrine in Midland and in Buffalo. A good deserved life.

JMC - 2002

Branco, José Abel de Freitas

Village of São Gonçalo, City of Funchal, Madeira Island

There are people in life who, very easily, have the ability to turn certain events on 180° degree and become very successful. José Branco is one of them. José Abel de Freitas Branco is from the village of São Gonçalo, district of Funchal, in Madeira Island. He was born on the beautiful island of scented flowers, on August 13, 1922.

He completed the first four years of school and about two years in the Business Institute of Funchal. He began his professional career in the Travel and Passport Agency, where he worked until 1947, when the government decided to shut down the agency. He then transferred to the Agency of Air Transportation, the first company to have flights between Madeira Island and the Continent with hydroplanes. For eight years he worked at the company as 2nd Officer of Administrative Services for the merchant navy,

At their home, for many years, José and Maria Noémia Branco, living in harmony.

aircrafts and fisheries. José Branco married his childhood friend and neighbour, Maria Noémia Correia, who was also from São Gonçalo, where she was born on July 29, 1926. They got married at São Gonçalo's church on April 13, 1947. Maria Noémia Correia de Freitas Branco was and still is an excellent web embroiderer, a traditional style from Madeira. A daughter was born to the Branco couple in Funchal named Dília de Freitas Branco.

Irreverent but conscious of his skills, José decided to emigrate to Canada. He left with his wife and daughter, on July 17, 1957. Dília was only nine years old. In Toronto, through his friend Silva, he went to work at Park Plaza Hotel. Silva went to work on a tabacco farm, a very popular profession at that time, and Branco went to replace him temporarily at Park Plaza Hotel. When Silva returned, the manager did not allow him to take his former place, choosing Branco over him. Silva decided, then, to go work as a plumber and Branco stayed at the kitchen of Park Plaza. Curiously, he ended up with a brilliant career in this new phase of his life. He worked at Park Plaza Hotel for 14 years. He was promoted many times and was able to help many Portuguese who knocked at his door. In 1967, the year Canada turned 100 years, José Branco won the first prize – the Golden Chef Award - for his Ville Reine, in the category of Cold Hors d'Oeuvres, at the Centennial Culinary Arts Competition. A dis-

Chef José Branco by his hors d'oeuvres at Park Plaza Hotel.

The hors d'oeuvres that won first prize at the celebration of the first centenary of Canada.

José Abel de Freitas Branco, wearing his uni-form, as Officer of Administrative Services for the merchant navy, aircrafts and fisheries.

A happy family celebrating 75 years of José's life. Wife, daughter, son-in-law, as well as his grandson and girlfriend.

tinction won only by a few.

Through the medium of a German friend, José Branco left Park Plaza Hotel, in 1971, to go work at the Hilton Hotel, by the airport, as Chef Steward. The distance and lack of transportation did not help José Branco keep his job for more than 9 months. Unhappy with the fact that he had been working for so many years outside his field, he decided to go the Canadian Office of Unemployment Services to explain his situation. He was advised to call an insurance company who was looking for an agent. José Branco filled an application and was hired.

Pilot Insurance Company gave him six months to learn their system and two years to prove himself. José Branco felt like "fish in water". After so many years, he was finally working in a field he understood. He stayed 15 years at Pilot Insurance, in charge of the mail services and material supply for other branches. Fifteen years of good service, compensated by prizes and high estimation. He retired in 1988, but still has the same benefits from the company, which he deeply misses. His wife worked at the Park Plaza Hotel for 22 years. She retired the same year as her husband. They still feel the same love they first felt for each other in their youth years. A kidney failure, in 1988, sent José to the hospital. Although feeling better, he still has to go to the hospital three times a week to undergo treatment.

José Abel de Freitas Branco is one of the founding members of Madeira Park and of Canadian Madeira Club. He was never a director, but always helped as a member. He remembers the enthusiast Angelo Bacalhau who, together with a group of other people from Madeira, decided to get the park and found the club. The couple know Madeira Island and the Continent very well, and they have travelled to Brazil, Venezuela and the USA. Their daughter Dilia finished a business course. She married Fernando Confraria and has given her parents a beautiful grandson, Christopher. Today, José's favourite hobby is to read the community newspapers. He loves reading and watching television. A life full of surprises and turns, but one he knew how to live without hurting himself and his family. Whoever knows what to look for, always end up accomplishing it.

JMC - 2001

Branco, Tibério Augusto Furtado
City of Ponta Delgada, island of S. Miguel, Azores

Tibério Augusto Furtado Branco and Maria Rosa Borges de Lima Branco make up a happy and enjoyable couple. Tibério Augusto was born in the city of Ponta Delgada, in the island of S. Miguel, Azores, on December 20, 1943. He took a business course at Ponta Delgada's Industrial and Commercial School of the time. He began his professional career as a civil servant for the ministry of justice – the property and auto registry office – in Ponta Delgada. Between 1965 and 1969, he did his

Audrey and Brenda Branco by their parents side.

military service, first in the continent and then in Guinea, leaving as a quartermaster servant.

On June 17, 1971, he arrived in Canada, establishing himself in Toronto. Maria Rosa Borges de Lima was born in the town of Povoação, in the island of S. Miguel, Azores, on July 28, 1942. Rosa and Tibério are high school sweethearts. The civil wedding took place in Ponta Delgada, in February of 1971, and on September 4, 1971, already in Toronto, the religious wedding took place at Santa Maria's church. The couple has two daughters, both born in Toronto: Brenda, born on August 11, 1975 and Audrey, born September 2, 1977. Both beautiful and single. Tibério took an accounting course at Seneca College, in Toronto, and began working at Sagres' Travel Agency. In 1975, Tibério decided to open his own travel agency, the ABC Travel and, today, he owns Alfa Mar Travel.

His involvement with travel and tourism made him become a member of the company Accord Travel, since 1994, where he has served twice as president, between 1995 and 1997. Today, Rosa is a Real Estate agent. For many years, Tibério has been an active member of the community, he is a member of Casa dos Açores community centre, he has been president of the Cultural Department, and an active member of the Portuguese club of Mississauga. He is a member, and now serves as president, of the Boddy & Soul Portugal Wine Club, a group of people dedicated to Portuguese wine tasting in Canada.

His favourite hobbies are reading, watching television and practising sports. Lately he loves playing golf, but he was for a long time a practitioner of diving. Rosa and Tibério Branco are often seen in Portuguese events. Rosa loves dancing. Rosa and Tibério Branco, an enjoyable couple, always standing by their friends.

JMC - 1999

Rosa and Tibério surrounded by Dolores and Maria Scott at a New Year's Party, at the Mississauga Convention Centre.

Cabral, Paulo da Silva

Town of Rabo de Peixe, Island of S. Miguel, Azores

Even living in Canada for many years, Paulo da Silva Cabral is a young man who knows the ground he is walking. Paulo da Silva Cabral was born in the town of Rabo de Peixe, in the island of S. Miguel, Azores, on April 9, 1953. His parents, Cândida and Manuel Cabral, emigrated to Canada in April of 1956, bringing their children, Paulo, José, Dora and Conceição. They later got married and went to back to S. Miguel. In Toronto, Paulo da Silva Cabral

Paulo and Adelaide Cabral in a visit to S. Miguel.

studied at S. Francis, St. Lucy's and Central Tech High School, on Bathurst and Harbord. While he was taking his cooking course, Paulo was working, in part-time, at the Silver Real Restaurant and, later on, moved to Celebrity Club. When he finished his course, the Chef went to work at Casa Loma, where he stayed for 26 years.

In Toronto, he met his compatriot Adelaide Ventura, born in the village of Arrifes, in the island of S. Miguel, on April 26, 1955. Paulo and Adelaide married at St. Agnes' church on September 4, 1976. Adelaide is a bank clerk in Toronto. The couple has one son, Randy, who was born on February 28, 1979. Randy specialized in parabolic aerials and works for Orbit Satellite Systems. Paulo opened his own catering company, Cabral Catering, in 1996, in Mississauga.

From a very young age, Paulo has been a sympathizer of soccer. Skilful, he played soccer for many years. Between 1968 and 1970, he played for Benfica Açoriano. Then, he transferred to the Ungarian Club where he was a valuable player conquering the Metro Cup, the Championship and the Ontario Cup for his team. He was played for the Sub-21 team of the First Portuguese Canadian Club, in 1971, and finished his soccer career in the Micaelense Soccer Club, in 1983.

Paulo Cabral, in 1972, when he participated in the religious ceremonies of the Holy Spirit, in the town of Rabo de Peixe.

Adelaide and Paulo Cabral, with their son Randy, in one visit to the Azores.

Aside from his catering company, Paulo is the manager of some singers and often organizes shows for the Portuguese community. The singer Fernando Correia Marques and his son Axel, from Portugal, Henrik Cipriano, from Montreal, and Nélia, from the USA, are some of the names that have marked his shows. He has also been able to reunite old bands to perform at New Year's parties. He has been successful in reuniting the group Capas Negras, in 1999/2000, who played along the "old friends" from Boa Esperança. Paulo Cabral is a young Chef-businessman with talent and initiative. He knows what he wants and where he wants to go.

JMC - 1999

Chef Paulo Cabral, after being complimented by the musical star Bryan Adams, in a dinner offered at Casa Loma, in Toronto, in 1985.

Caires, Maria das Mercês Camacho

Town of Santo António do Funchal, Madeira Island

In our first year of contact with the Portuguese emigrants, we had a main objective in mind from the beginning: to highlight the life of the main characters of our story: the pioneers. However, after 13 issues of the magazine Imagens, we had not yet found a female pioneer. This female pioneer, perhaps the most sacrificed and always forgotten, of our emigration process. It took some time, but we succeeded!

Her name is Maria das Mercês Camacho Caires and she was born in the town of Santo António do Funchal, in Madeira Island. She is blonde and still has the features of a beautiful woman that she must have been in her youth. She still had a nice, gentle look to her face.

The pioneer immigrant, Maria das Mercês Caires, the year she arrived in Canada.

- When were you born? – we asked to begin our conversation.

- That's the type of question you should never ask a lady! – he answered with a burst of laughter.

That's right! We forgot that we were interviewing a lady for our Archive of the Past. Thinking to ourselves, but sharing her good disposition, we mumbled: "Women".

-When did you arrive in Canada?

- I left Funchal by a TWA airplane, on January 23, 1954. We landed in New York and arrived in Toronto, the next day, January 24.

- Were you sponsored by someone? – we tried to find out.

- Yes! My husband sponsored me.

Besides Maria, there was João Alberto Rodrigues de Caires who, hearing the word "sponsorship", he began laughing.

- My wife was arriving in Toronto – he said, still laughing – and I was in the hospital with a fractured finger. At that time, I was working at Dr. Ballard's factory.

- It's true! – Maria continued. – It was a problem the minute I arrived because I didn't know anybody and didn't speak English...

- The person who went to pick her up was the landlord of the house where I was living, a Czechoslovak! – João remembered.

- Just think about it: I arrived in Canada to find my husband in the hospital where he stayed for 15 days. Everything was in a muddle!

- You know, at that time I received a proposal – continued João. – To cut my finger and receive five hundred dollars in compensation or remain in the hospital for treatment. Obviously, I stayed in the hospital...

- As we say in Portuguese, we lose the rings, but we keep the fingers – Maria said.

We took this moment to also find out about João's arrival and first steps in Canada.

- I took the Neo Hellas ship, on May 27 and arrived in Halifax on June 4, 1953 – he answered.

- How did you meet your wife?

- We were born in the same town, Santo António do Funchal, where we dated and got married.

We turned again to Maria.

- It's always difficult to begin a new life, especially so far away from our homeland. How were your first years in Canada?

- Very sad... - she said with her eyes fixed in the horizon, as if searching for her own past. – My first job was at a screw factory... I didn't go back to Madeira because I was embarrassed. I cried a river... My mother died not very long after from missing me. It was all very hard...

- Did you stay long at the factory? – We asked to interrupt all the lamentations.

- No. Because I spoke French, Mrs Galaka who worked at the Portuguese consulate of Toronto, found me a job at a daycare on Sherbourne, in Toronto. Meanwhile, I became pregnant and moved to the factory of cleaning carpets because it wasn't as heavy and was closer to home.

- Being a pioneer of the Portuguese emigration in Canada, it makes sense to think that your son is a "pioneer" born in Canada. Is he the first Portuguese-Canadian?

- In Canada, I am not sure, but in Toronto he was the first one for sure! Maria answered immediately, with a gleam in her eyes. – My son Alberto Magno was born on November 15, 1954, in Toronto.

- Was there ever a reference to him being the first one? – we asked with a great deal of interest.

- Yes! – João answered very proud of the fact. – It was during the celebration of the 25th anniversary of our community in Canada.

- Yes, it is true! – Maria confirmed and continued. – At the ceremony, where he was one of the honour guests, the president of the Regional Government of Madeira, Alberto João Jardim, gave us a medal and my son a silver tray for being the first Portuguese-Canadian in Toronto. Probably in Canada! It was a wonderful day, one we will never forget!

- What does your son do?

- He is a gymnastics instructor at Super Fitness.

We decided to allow them to remember the 25th anniversary of the community in

Canada, a celebration organized to honour the Portuguese pioneers who worked so hard and suffered so much to survive in this country and to pave the way for those who came after. It is never in excess to honour those who deserve to be honoured.

- At a certain point in your lives, you became business people. How did that start? – we asked, changing the course of Maria's thoughts.

- It all started during a trip to Madeira. We brought chairs and osier baskets from there to put in our veranda, in Toronto. The experience had a great result.

- Because of that – her husband continued – we decided to open a store, on 213 Augusta Avenue, in May of 1960. It was the first gift store, where we also sold shoes and records. It was called "Casa da Madeira".

- We also were – Maria continued – the first ones to open a store at the CNE in Toronto

The couple Maria and João Caires, in Toronto.

with handicrafts from Madeira and the Continent. We organized there many different exhibitions between 1962 and 1978. Thus, in a very simple way, this couple of pioneers became a very successful business couple.

- Life didn't stop and if we remember well, you remodelled and made some transformations at the store, didn't you?

-Unfortunately, it is true. – Maria said with some sadness. – In 1975, we transformed the basement into a bar, the Tropical Paradise, managed by our son. The bar didn't work out, for many reasons, among them, the invasion of young people from other ethnic groups, the so-called Punks, who transformed the bar in a place of drugs and prostitution.

- To avoid problems with the justice system – João continued – we closed both stores.

- And now?

- Well, now we are going to sell the building and rest! – she opened up, full of energy. – It's about time…

For a moment, the couple fell in silence. The good and bad moments clashed. To appease the thoughts, we asked:

- We would like to know about a good, funny moment of your life as business people.

- Well – began João spied by his wife's look. – I was one of the founding members of the Canadian Madeira Club. One day, during a party there, I was not allowed to sell hats there and decided to go there again. Things that happen at certain times in our lives that cut deep. I never went there again… - then, with a smile, he said: - because I never paid attention to the subscription dues, I lost my affiliation of the Canadian Madeira Club.

The minute the atmosphere became more pleasant, we turned our attention to Maria.

- Do you still remember any pioneer women?

- Yes – she immediately confirmed. – When I arrived, I didn't meet any Portuguese women right away. But from those times, I remember Agostinha de Freitas, the wives of José and João Camarata, the wife of Ângelo Bacalhau, Guiomar…

- Would you still like to see some of them or one in particular?

- Yes, yes… I would love to see Guiomar Plácido, from Funchal.

For a few minutes, Maria and João tried to remember some more names. The images came very vividly to their minds, but the names were lost along the way of emigration...
- It seems like I have their names on the tip of my tongue – Maria said very sadly.
- Would you like to go back to Madeira?
- To go and come back, until I can. – João said with a dreamer's look.

Through Maria das Mercês Camacho Caires, we wish every pioneer woman a happy and easy 1987, because they deserve it for the sacrifices they all did for us. It is not easy to be a woman and a mother. It is every harder to be a woman, a mother and an immigrant! God bless.

JMC - January of 1987

Camacho, Manuel Gomes
Town of São Roque, Madeira island

"**D**estiny marks each moment" was the title of a movie and a fado song, interpreted by Tony de Matos. Do you remember? When I wrote the Camacho's biography, this title came to my mind...

Manuel Gomes Camacho was born in the town of São Roque, Madeira Island, on the distant January 6, 1919. After finishing school, Manuel Camacho began his life working at the counter of a grocery store, but soon changing to the services of annotator of loads and unloads, at the Pontinha's quay, in Funchal.

Manuel and Maria Ângela.

Moved by his dreams, Manuel Gomes Camacho emigrated to Canada, as part of the first group of people from Madeira to officially go to that country. He arrived with his fellow travellers in Halifax, on June 2, 1953. Unlike the majority, Camacho was sent to Vancouver where, in a cattle breed farm, he worked for two years. After those two years, he moved to Toronto.

In Toronto, in 1955, he found a job in a restaurant to wash dishes, but because he "was breaking too many dishes", he left to go work at the Toronto docks, where he was Longshoreman. There he remained until his retirement in 1988. The year he retired, he fell ill. Suffering from severe pain on his legs and poor circulation sent him to the hospital, where he had his left leg amputated. For eight years, Manuel Camacho lived with an artificial limb, which allowed him to walk and drive his car. He died in 1992, when he was 71.

Maria Ângela Xavier Abreu was also born in the town of São Roque, in Madeira island, on January 27, 1923. She knew Manuel since childhood. They were

Maria Ângela Xavier Abreu, at the old quay of Funchal, before leaving for Canada.

schoolmates, never dated, never even thought about it. Time went by… In 1959, Manuel Gomes Camacho went to Madeira, in attempt to find a woman to marry, because he was feeling tired from living alone in Canada. Manuel and Maria ran into each other. They began seeing each other more often, and ended up getting married within the same month of his arrival. They married at São Roque's church, on March 24, 1959. Maria Ângela only arrived in Toronto, months after, on September

Maria Ângela Camacho.

17, 1959. She came by ship, from Funchal to the island of Santa Maria, in the Azores,

where she stayed for four days, at a friends' house, and from their taking the plane to Toronto. The first son, Emanuel, was born in Toronto, on December 22, 1960, but dying two days later, due to natural deficiencies.

Michael was born after, on April 13, 1967. He got a Business Administration degree from the University of Toronto, in 1992. He now has his own office. Maria Angela lives alone in her house. She worked for about four months, after her son's death, to try to forget the blow in her life given by destiny. She spent her life being the wife, the mother and the housewife. Due to her arthritis, Ângela Camacho underwent surgery on both knees. Due to the success of the operations, she has been able to walk,

Manuel Camacho, already using a cain, was able to see his son's graduation from the University of Toronto.

without having to depend on a wheel chair.

Since she still has family in Madeira, she goes back every two years, besides spending some time in Florida, every year. She travels a lot in Canada and the USA. Manuel Gomes Camacho, in the first years of Canada, was of the founding members of the Canadian Madeira Club and Madeira Park. Maria Ângela Xavier Abreu Camacho, after so many vicissitudes, tries to enjoy life to the fullest, dreaming about the day she is going to see the birth of a grandchild.

JMC - October of 2000

Michael Camacho, the day of his graduation of the University of Toronto.

Camarata,

Maria Luísa Bernardete Gouveia

Island of Porto Santo, Archipelago of Madeira

The charming Maria Luísa Bernardete Gouveia Camarata, of thin stature, but stiff as an apple, did not have an easy life. Death knocked at her door, taking away her son, in 1984, and her husband, in 1985. She did not lose hope. Whoever stays behind needs to continue the journey. Maria Luísa Bernardete Gouveia was born in the golden island of Porto Santo, in the Autonomous Region of Madeira, on October 14, 1924.

She married José Garcês Teixeira Camarata, born in the town of Ribeira Brava, Madeira island, on December 1, 1923. Luísa and José married on May 5, 1946, at São Pedro's church, in the city of Funchal. José Garcês Teixeira Camarata emigrated to Canada in 1953, among the first group to come, in 1953. He arrived in Halifax, on June 2, 1953. His first job was in St. Catherines, at a cherry farm, where he worked with other fellow travellers. Just a bit over a month, José moved to Toronto where he found a job in a restaurant, first in the cleaning and then in the kitchen. By this time, around January of 1954, Maria Luísa arrived in Toronto with their daughter, Maria Luísa, who was only 6 years old. The daughter Maria Luísa was born in Funchal on

Maria Luísa Bernardete Gouveia Camarata

José Camarata, his children, Maria Luísa and José Luís, and Maria Luísa Camarata at home.

June 28, 1947. She studied and got married in Toronto. He is a happy mother of five children and a teacher at St. Florence School, in Scarborough. The second son of the couple, José Luís, was already born in Toronto, in 1959, with a cardiac deficiency which victimized him in 1984. Meanwhile, in 1954, José Camarata found a job at the Toronto Abattoir, a company in charge of slaughtering cattle, where he was promoted to manager and worked there for more than 30 years. It was José who found a job for many Portuguese men at the Toronto Abattoir, among them, his brothers-in-law: the late Francisco and Manuel José who is still working there. A very rare disease forced José to leave his job and caused his death on November 27, 1985.

Due to the small salary her husband was getting at the beginning, Maria Luísa looked for work with great difficulty because of the language barrier. She learned how

The family Camarata at a party.

First group of men from Madeira, in St. Catherines, in 1953. Standing up, Ângelo Bacalhau, José Camarata and Belo, among others. Bottom row: Jordão do Faial, Quintal, Plácido and others.

to say "work" and began "knocking" the Unemployment's door until she was received by an agent, one day. She got a job at a leather sandals factory, where she worked for seven years, sewing the sandals on a professional machine. The factory closed down and, soon after, she found a job as a housekeeper at the Priests' Congregation – The Basilian Fathers –, in Toronto. For Maria Luísa, that job was paradise, because she stayed there for 27 years, until the day she retired in 1988. She was always cared for by the Basilian Fathers who gave a party the day she completed 25 years at their service. The

The couple Camarata with their daughter, before leaving for Canada.

sadness of a life, at times very dramatic, compensated with a job where she was respected. José and Luísa Camarata participated in the group that bought the Madeira Park, in 1963.

After the death of both her son and husband, Maria Luísa Bernardete Gouveia Camarata sold her house, in 1986, and went to live with her daughter Maria Luísa McCormick, taking care of the house and her five grandchildren. She is a very active woman and a believer. "To stop is to die" is the motto she will live by until the end of her days. All the best!

JMC - 2000

Carneiro, Isaura Maria dos Santos
Town of Ribeira Quente, island of São Miguel, Azores

Her constant smile is an unchanging challenge to the fate that launched her to a wheel chair. Yet nothing or anybody makes her give up. She lives by the motto "better to break than to distort". Isaura Maria dos Santos Carneiro was born in the town of Ribeira Quente, in the island of S. Miguel, Azores, on February 20, 1948.

She finished primary school (grade 4) and began dedicating herself to sewing. In July of 1969, she came to Toronto to visit her aunt Libânia Cardoso. What started as a simple holiday trip for a young girl, at the age of 21, ended up as the beginning of a new life, settling down in Toronto, Ontário, and choosing Canada as her new country.

Isaura Maria dos Santos Carneiro

In Toronto, Isaura Carneiro began working in her field, sewing at private houses. After, as she studied English at Seneca College, she had some part-time jobs, first at a supermarket and then at a plastic factory.

Isaura Carneiro was definitely marked by fate. From an early age, an illness was digging inside her body. She was suffering from scoliosis, a disease that affects the spinal column. The doctor who was looking after her, advised her to undergo a very delicate surgery to try to avoid ending up on a wheel chair. Thus, in 1979, at Sunnybrook Hospital, she was operated to her spine. The doctor was not successful and made her condition worse. She was taken in emergency to Western Hospital where she underwent another surgery. What they were fearing, ended up happening. Isaura Maria dos Santos Carneiro, as a result of her operations, ended up on a wheel chair. There was a group of people in the community who tried to fight for the damage caused by the surgeries in order to try and get a good thing out of it. However, the lawyer who took the case did not go ahead because Isaura had assigned a consent paper for the surgery.

Isaura Carneiro among her friends and members of the Society, showing her beautiful smile.

Isaura Carneiro, alone in the world and living with a small grant from the government, did not become discouraged. She began dedicating herself with her heart and soul to the cause of handicapped people. She accepted the challenge presented by her companion in misfortune, António Fraga, who, making use of Father Cunha's idea, formed the Society of Disabled Persons, a group of twelve people, in 1987, which was officially incorporated on January 29, 1989. From that moment, Isaura Maria dos Santos Carneiro was always a member of the board of directors. She became a true activist for their cause, full of energy and compassion, always giving out a smile that never ceases to surprise people on every situation.

Annual picnic of the Society of Portuguese Disabled People in High Park.

Isaura Carneiro served as president of the Society for four years, another two as secretary and now she is member of the board, in charge of organizing the dinner celebrating their existence. Isaura never stops! She does a little of everything: she helps feed her friends, who are in a worse situation. As seamstress, Isaura organized, a successful a fashion show with her disabled friends in wheel chairs, with clothes designed by them, and it was described by those who had the privileged of assisting it that it was truly incredible. Lamentably,

Isaura Carneiro and António Fraga receive a $10,000 cheque from the hands of António Dionisio, representing Local 183.

the Portuguese Society of Disabled Persons does not receive any grant from the Portuguese Government. Isaura Carneiro, besides her daily effort in favour of the Society, is also a member of other boards, namely the committee at St. Christopher's House, Access Alliance, Health Association, Women Health and Women Hands, and the Canadian Paraplegic Association.

The Society of Portuguese Disabled Persons survives with the generous subscription dues of the members, yard sales, gifts from other institutions and friends, banquets and picnics. Recently, on July 10, 2001, the Society welcomed a very practical bus for disabled people, given by the Local Union 183. Isaura Maria dos Santos Carneiro has as her ultimate goal fighting for the disabled people, showing society that, in spite of their disabilities, they are able to think and accomplish great things, within their limits, and their own talents. Isaura Carneiro wants to finish a video to show the community the value of disabled people. Isaura Carneiro keeps religiously many tapes done throughout the years with all the initiatives and parties organized by the Society, so that they will be used to make one film to be distributed by other institutions, clubs and among friends. Only if we see her activity and that of her fellow companions in misfortune can we believe her skills. And after so much work and so many sacrifices, seeing her always smiling, it is astonishing! We should keep the images of the smiles of the individuals in our memories and not their disability!

JMC - 2001

Carreira, António Jacinto

City of Nazaré

The couple António and Rosária Carreira.

Inever met a person from Nazaré who did not know how to dance the folkloric songs of his homeland. António Jacinto Carreira is not exception to the rule. Just like his wife and children, António Jacinto Carreira is from the city of Nazaré, where he was born on November 11, 1929. As soon as he finished the four mandatory years of school, he began learning carpentry. From here, he went on to learn printing and composition. Later on, borrowing a bike, he went to the nearby town of Caldas da Rainha, to work as a printer. He came back to Nazaré to work as an apprentice of electrician in the building industry, where the manager was his uncle Evangelino Borges Jacinto. Three years later, at the final stage of the building, the main electrician, Ribeiro, promised him the professional certificate, if he went to Lisbon to work for him. António accepted the offer and worked in Lisbon between 1947 and 1949. He also worked at CIBRA, a cement factory, in the village of Pataias, city of Alcobaça.

Family gathering where we can see Adriano Codinha (second from the left), today a successful ship owner in Ontario.

When he was still in school, he met Rosária da Silva Águeda with whom he married on September 3, 1950, at Nossa Senhora da Nazaré's church. The couple had two children, both born in Nazaré: António José, born on July 22, 1951, and Maria João, on July 10, 1957. In 1955, António found out about the emigration movement to Canada. He decided to give his name. Due to the excessive number of applications and the distress of local contractor, the minister responsible for the Department of Emigration in Portugal, forbade the departure of people from the district of Leiria. Advised by a friend, António went to Lisbon to ask inspector São Romão to help him go to Canada. This one did not want to interfere in the minister's business, but told him to write a letter to the government of Ottawa, explaining he was a professional electrician willing to emigrate to Canada. The answer from Ottawa was positive. António left for Canada on June 18, 1958, the same day of a small rebellion in Lisbon because of General Humberto Delgado's political campaign.

António left by plane from Lisbon to the island of Santa Maria, from there to Montreal and his final destination was Toronto, where he arrived June 19, 1958. Just like every pioneer, he "went through hell", working on landscaping, as

a painter and in the maintenance section of a fur coat factory, on Spadina Avenue, in Toronto. At his factory, he was laid off and, through a friend, he went to work as an electrician to a Jewish contractor. Meanwhile, on December 29, 1958, his wife Rosário and the two children arrived in Toronto. In spite of her children being small, the difficulties of life forced Rosário to look for a job. She found one in the field she knew well: sewing. However, despite her knowledge of the profession, she suffered a lot due to her lack of knowledge of the English language. She would cry from morning to night...

The desire to be involved in the social life of his community, and special in folklore, was always glowing inside him. In 1959, António Carreira and

Premier Bill Davis, besides Alan Grossman, getting a basquet with Madeira wine, given by Maria João, dressed as "Nazarena".

Isabel Santos were approached by Lourenço Gonçalves, a member of the committee responsible for organizing the religious celebrations of St. Vincent de Paul of Santa Maria's church, in Toronto, to form a dancing group to perform at every benefit event organized by them. This way, the folklore group, Rancho Folclórico da Nazaré, was born with three couples: António and Rosária Carreira, Isabel Santos and her brother António, José Santos, António Batalha, Grace and Madalena Moreira. A success! At the first celebrations of St. Vincent de Paul, Raúl Costa would

be in charge of every aspect of the show. For this, he earned the nickname "Ánhuca". In 1964, the Rancho da Nazaré participated in the International Festival of Folklore of Canada, with the presence of 37 folkloric groups, at the O'Keefe Centre. It had to be presented by stages of elimination. For the big final, the groups that were chosen were those from Portugal, the Ukraine and Russia. At the final show, they performed for a huge crowd, among them, the Prime Minister Lester B. Pearson, and presented by MC Al Baliska. The charming Al, at one moment, said to the prime minister: "We need more groups like this one from Nazaré, but we need to raise funds to buy them shoes!" We

The first folklore group representing the city of Nazaré, in 1959, in action. Dancing, António Batalha, Grace Moreira, José Santos, Isabel Santos and her brother Tony, António Carreira and Rosária, and Madalena Moreira.

know, but he did not know that people from Nazaré (Nazarenos) do not use shoes! They dance barefoot. A pride for every Portuguese, Racho da Nazaré won the Festival. The Telegram newspaper (today, The Toronto Sun) published a report about the Festival and an interview with Rosaria Carreira, admiring the fact that she worked, found time to dance, and still taught her children how to dance so that they could one day continue the tradition. How can a person find time to do so much? "With love and willingly, one can accomplish anything" was Rosaria's answer.

António Carreira, after six years of working for the friendly employer, went to another company where he was earning more money. At that time, the Electricians Union was undergoing some changes. They were accepting 75 percent of the employees that applied for membership. António was part of that percentage, but lost his job due to lack of work. He went to the Union to complain about his situation, and the Union accepted him as an associated member of two years. In 1976, he became an effective member of the Union IEBW. From that moment, Antócio Jacinto Carreira always worked as an electrician. He finished his long career at the company Future-Tec, owned by Juvenal Belo, from Madeira Island. He retired in 1994.

With irony and longing, António Carreira told us that, at the beginning, the only one who owned a house was Lourenço Gonçalves. For that

Picture from the newspaper Telegram (today the Toronto Sun) with Rosária Carreira and her children António and Maria João.

reason, the rehearsals were done at his place, more particularly, in the basement, with an old furnace that looked like an octopus and took up a lot of space. For that reason, they had to squat to be able to dance. The first day of the presentation of

the group, they used a record player and records to accompany them. Each time they jumped, the record player would skip and the dance stopped... You can imagine, can't you? They ended up relying on the sound of their own voices singing each song they danced. When, in 1962, they decided to make the Rancho official, in Galt, the first president was António Sousa, also a native of Nazaré. Rancho da Nazaré was chosen to be the opening act for the late fado diva Amália Rodrigues, at Massey Hall, in 1964. Besides being a member, António Carreira was also one of the founding people and the choreographer of the Infantile Group of Nazaré, from the First Portuguese Canadian Club.

In the USA, in 1962, Maria João kisses Matateu, when the soccer team of Belenenses visited that country.

According to António, his son António José must have been the first Portuguese-Canadian to get a degree in electronic engineering, at the University of Waterloo, in Canada. He finished his course in 1977.

The Carreira's already have two grandchildren, one from each child. The Carreira family has achieved a brilliant career among us. In the dance of life, they knew how to move. Today, António and Rosária dance peacefully with their grandchildren and with the memories of the past.

JMC - 2000

Carreira, Manuel

Town of Reguengo

To be an emigrant is to be an adventurer, either by nature or by necessity. To be an emigrant is also to be courageous and strong to face the obstacles and difficulties of life. Every emigrant has his or her own story, sprinkled with tears, sorrows and successes. A native of Reguengo, a small town between the towns of Fatima and Batalha, Manuel Carreira arrived in Halifax in 1955, after a trip of seven days and seven nights.

- It was a good trip. I had never been in a boat before, only in Nazaré. But it was good – he told us.

After arriving in Halifax, he went to Windsor and, since there were no jobs in that city, he was taken to Harrow. Manuel Carreira was the first Portuguese to arrive in Harrow, a small community 35 kilometres from the city of Windsor, and mainly populated by farmers. His first job was in a farm planting melons.

- The work was very hard and the boss was very mean. We

Pioneer Manuel Carreira in conversation with Eduarda Matos.

worked seven days a week in the summer, only stopping if it rained. I still don't know where I got so much energy. Besides the hard work, the conditions under which I was living were deplorable – Manuel explained.

At his first job, he worked with a contract that forced his boss to provide him a home and food, even though that never happened.

- We lived in a small shack. The nights were cold and we slept with our clothes on because we didn't have any blankets. Some time after, we were able to contact the Portuguese inspector who was passing by Windsor and things got a little better for us.

Still taking about his boss, he said:

- He, together with his family, used to upset us, honestly, because they never treated us well. We did not understand them and later on when I began understanding some English, I realized what they were telling us. The worst you can think of.

It was this suffering that gave Manuel the courage to get another job, months later. The new boss was better, but Manuel Carreira was still facing many burdens, the biggest one not knowing English. In 1956, his wife and two children joined him and that was his first joy in Canada. He remembers with a smile:

- My wife, Edgar and Amilcar came in 1956.

As a family, they worked very hard in agriculture, and besides that job, Manuel still worked in a factory in Windsor.

- I was going to Windsor and coming back every day. It was very hard, but it was also worth it.

Meanwhile, the children gained admission to a school. – Amílcar failed grade 1 because he didn't speak English. I was upset, of course and transferred him to a catholic school.

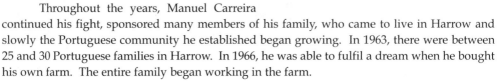

Amílcar's story, just like his father's, had a happy ending. With a proud smile, Carreira continued: - After elementary school, he went to high school with good grades and then decided to go to College, in London, without any problems.

- What happened to your other son?

- Edgar was always very clever. One day, the principal called me to his office. I was worried, but when I arrived there, the principal told me to be proud of Edgar because he was very smart. I felt very relieved.

Throughout the years, Manuel Carreira continued his fight, sponsored many members of his family, who came to live in Harrow and slowly the Portuguese community he established began growing. In 1963, there were between 25 and 30 Portuguese families in Harrow. In 1966, he was able to fulfil a dream when he bought his own farm. The entire family began working in the farm.

- My girlfriend...

- Your girlfriend? – we asked very surprised. With a burst of laughter, he continued:

- Yes! My girlfriend worked very hard. She carried, by herself, 100 pound bags to the wheelbarrow, and Amílcar, who was only 12, would place them in order on top of the truck. During the tomato harvest time, Amílcar would load the tractor with 400 baskets of tomatoes.

Camões Club, the centre where the Portuguese community of Harrow gathers.

Edgar was the driver: he was like a monkey, driving with his feet! I can still see them! – giving us a longing smile, our pioneer continued his tale:

- It was hard because we were only four working in the farm, taking care of all the tasks. It was hard, but we were able to accomplish our goals. I would not have done it if it weren't for my wife and my children. I was working two jobs: the farm and in a factory, as I said before. I was what you can call a slave, but I don't regret it.

As the Portuguese community was growing, the need to have a club or a sports centre for everyone to meet on weekends became a reality. In 1968, the Portuguese Soccer Team of Harrow was born. In 1970, they founded the Camões Portuguese Club of Harrow and Manuel Carreira was one of the key players of this club.

- At that time, we began slowly getting together, each one giving a small contribution – what we really could give – and we founded the club, which, thank God, still exists.

Camões Portuguese Club of Harrow is an important centre of the Portuguese people of Harrow and neighbouring communities. Every month they organize a dance and celebrate annually the feast of Our Lady of Fatima. In 1974, a Portuguese school was started in the premises, even though the Carreiras lamented the fact that it had come to late for their children.

- Neither one of my children went to Portuguese school. It didn't exist. Amilcar speaks the language very well, but Edgar struggles a little bit.

- Do you still work at the factory? – we asked.

- Unfortunately, no, I don't. I suffered a car accident three years ago and am now disabled from that accident. I can no longer work, but I still have my farm.

This accident was another misfortune in the life of this pioneer, but his courage and determination that helped face the hardships of his life as an immigrant, still live in him. Manuel Carreira is very optimistic about the future.

- I will probably move back to Portugal in two years and buy an apartment in the Algarve...

- Won't you miss your children, who will stay here?

- No, I won't. I mean, they are living their own lives. Edgar married a Canadian woman, he has a good job and Amílcar has been promoted at his job. He is now one of the bosses. I can't do anything else. When I came to Canada, nobody gave me anything. So, everything is paid for!

JMC - August of 1987

Carreiro, José Teixeira

Village of Lomba do Pomar, town of Povoação,

Island of S. Miguel, Azores

José Teixeira Carreiro was born in the village of Lomba do Pomar, the town of Povoação in the island of S. Miguel, Azores, on July 5, 1933. He began working in agriculture, with his father and when he finished his military service, began working as taxi driver in Povoação. There, in the town of Povoação, he met Ângela de Fátima Lopes, who was also from the village Lomba do Pomar, where she was born on May 31, 1938, and with whom he married on January 11, 1958, at Nossa Senhora da Mãe de Deus' church. José Teixeira Carreiro arrived in Canada on April 11, 1957 and his wife came the following year on July 26. As soon as he arrived in Montreal, José was transferred to the railroad services – CNR –, in Ontario, where he worked in the towns of Markham, Lindsey, Beavertown, among others.

A salutation between José and Ângela Carreiro, in one of the many trips they have done together.

To the young couple, two children were born, already in Toronto: Joseph, who has given them a granddaughter, and Gina, who is also the mother of two girls. José, after leaving the CNR, came to Toronto where he began working in building demolition. In the summer, he would work in the farm, in the tobacco harvest. With all his simplicity, José told us that during those hard times, moving from one house to another meant taking one suitcase with you. In 1960, José went to work for the Foundation Co., the construction company responsible for building Terminal 1 at Pearson Airport, a job that lasted three years.

In 1964, he switched companies, and began working for Pirini Construction, the company in charge of building the Constelation Hotel and many roads in the city. In 1965, he got a job at Ford, in Oakville, as a painter, a job he kept until his retirement, in July of 1997. José Carreiro moved to Mississauga in 1972. There, with his family, he was always involved in church events. In 1977, he butler for the Holy Spirit Comission, at that time Father Sá was the Portuguese priest in Mississauga. Father Sá, lacking a church for the Portuguese community, would celebrate mass in schools and halls, wherever he could. Due to that difficulty, they had the idea of forming a Club and it was the genesis of the Portuguese Club of Mississauga.

From left to right: Frank, Gina, Kim, Joseph, Ângela and José Carreiro, with the little ones: Daniela, Megan and Zoe, during Megan's baptism. A big happy family.

José Carreiro is member #2 of the Club. At the same time, José Rafael inaugurated the "Casa de Portugal" (Portugal's House), in Mississauga. Things did not go well, and the Portuguese Club moved to the hall that had been rented by José Rafael, the same they still have today. Now, the members are collecting funds to buy their own house. José Carreiro was also a member of the commission that raised funds for the construction of São Salvador do Mundo's church, in Mississauga, built in 1997, under Monsignor Eduardo Resendes' supervision.

The Carreiros and their neighbour Noemia, in one of many picnics they organized.

For seven straight years, José was director at the Portuguese Club of Mississauga and now he sits in the treasure board for the seniors group of the Club. Long ago, he was also a member of the Portuguese Club of College, between the streets Augusta and Spadina, where he paid $5 annually to be able to watch black and white television.

The shock of seeing recently his native Povoação almost demolished by floods brought out in him the desire to go back and visit the place where he was born. Thus, Ângela and José visited São Miguel and were surprised to see the progress in the island, particularly, in Povoação. The Carreiros love to travel. Besides visiting the Azores, they have been to Punta Cana, Bahamas, Portuguese continent, Brazil, Mexico, Bermuda, and many other places. And they promise to continue. We hope they can happily continue travelling for many more years.

JMC - 2000

José Careirro with his wife, mother-in-law, Maria Lopes, and children.

Carrusca, Luís de Sousa

Town of Quinta da Cancela, city of Faro, province of Algarve

To chat with Luís Carrusca is very nice and pleasant. His life is a rosary of adventures, all with a happy ending. We could spend hours listening to Luís Carrusca, as he unfolded his tales with a big smile on his face. He always shows a very natural look and wears an unusual hat...

Luís de Sousa Carrusca was born in the small village of Estói, in the district of Faro, in the Algarve. He was born on January 28, 1923. With the usual life difficulties generated by the laws of that time, he was able to obtain his passport, which he so much longed for, to be able to leave Portugal.

- I came to Canada as a tourist with António Custodinho, more commonly known as "Taranta" – Luís began telling us his story. We arrived in Montreal on April 4, 1954.

Luís Carrusca stopped his tale and began laughing, at the same time as he was shaking his head.

From left to right: Luís Carrusca, Frederico, António Martins Alcaria, Martins from the province of Trás-os-Montes, the "Loulé", Joaquim Frade and Franklim António Rosa (who went back to Portugal). They formed the band "Copos" (cups). After a few beers, they would play without any compassion.

– At that time, everything was so much harder... Imagine that the airplane was stopped for four hours, at the Gander's airport, in Newfoundland, because of us. We were carrying with us about $1200 american and our passport was valid for four months. Still, it was really hard to convince the officials to let us stay.

By our side, Luís' son, Jack, was also handling his head, as if in agreement with his father's words. Then, he said, almost as a criticism:

- Now a days, anyone who claims to be persecuted because of his religious or political views stays right away...

We let things calmed down and continued:

- Where did you first work?

- It was cutting down firewood, for two months, in Anticosti Island, in Québec. After, I went to Seven Islands to work at the building of the railroad, where I was making .75 cents an hour. Later on, I went to work at Baie-Comeau, the homeland of Bryan Mulroney, again to work in the cutting down of firewood. I spent two years at this job...

- Was it hard?

- Oh was it ever! – Carrusca answered. – It was hard, it was difficult, everything was different... Look, I spent four days with my friends eating pig's feet with white beans because it was the only food we knew at the place where we were staying! – a beautiful smile showed up on Carrusca's face as he was remembering this episode.

- The language barrier just made things worse! – said Carrusca's son, ending our burst of laughter due to the gastronomical joke.

- What did you do after? Did you come to Toronto?

- No! – he answered in a very mysterious tone. – I still had to walk many kilometres before getting to Toronto.

- How did it happen?

- In 1965, I decided, together with Armando Pedro da Marcelina, to go try the USA. We paid $500 to cross the border. At the end of three months, the American Immigration Officer caught me working illegally and I was sent to prison. I left it on a $2,000 bail. I was also paying a lawyer $100 a month to see if I could get my legal status in the country. Unable to accomplish my dream, in 1966, around Christmas time, I went back to Lisbon.

- You didn't have any problems in Lisbon?

- Oh yes I did! PIDE (the Portuguese Secret Police from Salazar's time) arrested me, but I knew Mr. Matos Parreira, the president of the party National Union, in the Algarve, and I was able to get a hearing at the court of Vila Real de Santo António, a town in the Algarve, which borders with Spain. The judge was Mr. Parreira's son, and I was set free.

Amid so many setbacks, he was lucky to have a "godfather". Besides, the only thing that actually works among Portuguese people is the "patronage" and the "recommendation". A person without godfathers is unable to survive...

- Even so, I still wanted to leave, but was always refused a passport – Carrusca continued.

- So you came to Toronto!

- No! I decided to go to Luanda, the capital city of Angola. – he explained. – I arrived in Luanda in May of 1958. In Luanda, I was able to get a passport and then, in August, took off to Canada.

- It must have been a very long trip! – we said, astonished with the revelation.

- Oh yes! – he answered with a smile. – I left Angola straight to Brasaville, then to Rome, from Rome to Paris, then London and finally arrived in Montreal.

Inside their furniture store, Jack and Luís Carrusca with one of his famous hats.

- So – we interrupted him – we are now in Montreal, and what happens on your journey to Toronto?

Luís Carrusca laughed, before continuing his tale.

- It still takes a few years... When I arrived in Montreal, the second time, I bought, together with Franklim António Rosa, a car for $300 and went to Eliot Lake. We worked at the Aldoden Hotel. At the end of six months, I bought a taxi-car and began working by myself.

- What happened to the family? – we wanted to know.

- In 1961, my wife Maria Clementina, came to live with me, bringing with her our daughters Maria Marta and Maria Odete. The following year, my son Joaquim arrived. In 1963, I bought the Luigi Restaurant which I managed until 1965.

- Why did you sell the restaurant?

- Because the uranium mines began closing down on Eliot Lake and businesses were no longer profitable. There were no jobs, and people began leaving the town to go somewhere else. I did the same! – concluded Luís Carrusca.

- So, we will now get to Toronto, right? – we maliciously asked.

- It happened in May of 1965… I was in Toronto for seven months, without any work. It was the first time that such a thing happened to me.

- After so many adventures, you deserved some peace. – we said.

- It's not good to stop. I went to drive a truck for the Canterbury Foods Café and, years later, I got a job at the CNE, as a painter. Not happy, I went back to driving a truck, for a paper company, while working a second job at the Newport fish, owned by Dias.

- How did you get involved in second hand furniture and appliances' business?

- You know, I decided to open a store on Beatrice and College – he answered calmly. – I sold many second hand items. I would buy and resell, fix things… I was the first Portuguese person to have such a business in Toronto. My son, after coming home from his job, used to come to the store to help me. He was a welder.

Luís Carrusca, receiving his medal in honour of the pioneers, in 1985, from the hands of Consul General of Portugal, Dr. Tânger Correia.

- After coming home from work, I used to help my father welding items, fixing ranges, irons… - Jack told us.

- The first year was working to pay the rent. We had to be courageous…

- Courage is something a person like you will never lack. After so many adventures, everywhere in the world, struggling and suffering, you still had the courage to open a store?

- It wasn't easy, but we were able to carry it out. The business began being profitable and we decided to move here, at 409 College, where we plan to stay.

Today, Europa Furniture has just as many second hand as brand new items. Nowadays, father and son work together, in perfect harmony and without thinking in any more adventures. Now, adventures? Only when they go on holidays.

- Would you like to see any of your fellow companions from the past?

- Yes, I would! – Luís answered with a longing look in his face. – I would like to meet, specially, Moisés, from Carrazeda de Anciães, who came to Canada in 1953. I never saw him again.

- As a pioneer, you must have seen the birth of many clubs… Were you a member of any of them?

- Yes, I was. I am founding member and hold the member card #2 of Casa do Algarve in Toronto. The association Casa do Algarve was founded on March 12, 1972. I was the president for one year and director for four years in a row… I was in charge of the kitchen! – he finalized with a burst of laughter.

- I am member #19 – Jack said.

The Carruscas were being constantly interrupted by their clients. We felt it was time to leave them because their obligations should come before the adventures. Adventures that had a happy ending, but left some signs. We hope his fight has been worth every drop of sweat and that he has the chance of living a happy life when he retires. We hope that the tale of this pioneer serves as a lesson for the younger ones.

JMC - December of 1986

Carvalho, Américo Henriques

Neighbourhood of Alto Pina, Lisbon

Now that the First Portuguese Canadian Club woke up from a sound sleep and got back to its mission of representative of the community at the National Soccer League, we went searching for a pioneer who was, at the same time, a pioneer of soccer team of the club. We found Américo Henriques Carvalho, the perfect person for our story…

Américo Henriques Carvalho was born at Alto Pina, in Lisbon, on January 9, 1926. He is married to Isabel Batalha Carvalho, who is from the town of Nazaré. They got married in 1960 and had a son, Nelson,

Nowadays, Isabel and Américo Carvalho, in their living room, at the house they own in Toronto.

who, today, is the manager, with his father, of King Shell, in Toronto, a job that Américo has had since 1959. From his first marriage, he had another son, Eduardo, who is a civil engineer.

Américo disembarked from the Olympia ship, in Halifax, in May of 1955. Not long after arriving in Canada, he was sent to Hamilton where, for two days, he had to weed beets. Soon after, he decided to leave Hamilton to come to Toronto. His first job in Ontario's capital city was to wash dishes in the known – but already closed down – Bassley's restaurant. Do you remember it?

- After – he said – I went to work at Hertz to wash cars and later on to the garage where I worked as a mechanic for more than a year. Due to economical reasons, I left in 1957 to go work at the uranium mines, on Eliot Lake, where I spent about six months. Then, I went back to Portugal on holidays.

After his well worked and deserved holidays, Américo came back to Toronto finding a job right away in what he knew how to do. He went to work at Texaco, on Cherry Street, that went bankrupted later on. The owners of Texaco, recognizing Américo's merit, invited him to reopen the gas station. From 1959, Américo became the first Portuguese citizen to own a gas station with mechanical services, in Toronto.

For reasons not important for our story, he decided to leave this gas station, and went to manage another one, the Esso gas station, on Linppincot and College, where he stayed for 13 years.

- Let's leave oil, which is undergoing a crisis, for a while and remember how the first club, and as a consequence, the first soccer team in the Portuguese community came to existence. – we asked with an enormous curiosity.

- Wow… that is a little bit more complicated – he said, unable to hide a longing smile. – The club was founded at the time Jordão arrived from Montreal… Jordão spoke about the need to found a club, just like the ones back home, where we could spend our time. So, Jordão, Amadeu Vaz, the old Alves, Alzirinho, Chico Alentejano, António Alentejano and myself…, and some others whose names I do not recall right now, got together at the Sousa's restaurant and decided to bring back to life the First Portuguese Canadian Club…

- Where was the first headquarters? – we asked.

- It was the same place where the Portuguese Book Store is now, on Nassau Street… - he explained.

- What happened after?

- After… the usual routine. Mário Tomás let us use his typewriter…, Alves and Alzirinho built the tables and a ping pong table... Well, the club that was supposed to be a place of gathering where everyone could have a good time, for the founders it became a place of work and worries, just like it happens today in any club, right?

- So, when do we see soccer coming into the picture? – we insisted.

- Wait! – he said, laughing. – Let me tell you the rest of the story, at least the rest that I remember. For reasons I don't recall anymore, the club at Nassau closed. When I came back from holidays, I decided, together with Amadeu and the old Alves, to rent a house in Augusta Avenue, to make the Portuguese Canadian Club there. In Augusta, during many years, we organized dances, auctions, theatre...

- And soccer?!

- Oh yes! Soccer... - he said, always smiling. After reflecting for a little while. – We still did not have shoes, or jerseys and we decided to represent the club, anyway. It was more of beating a game!

- Why?

- Why?... Because of stupid rivalries and to open up. In a worthless soccer game, kind of married guys against single guys, we would alleviate our stress, we would forget the longing for our homeland, our family, our wives and children... Believe it or not, it was also to defend our flag.

- Who were your biggest rivals?

- Italians and Greeks. With the Greeks, hardly any games would go into second half... we always ended up fighting.

Américo stopped his tale for a moment. We respected his silence. During this volunteer pause, his subconscious was working arduously, trying to remember old stories, stored for many years. Smiling, he went back to his tale.

- At the beginning, when we arrived, our team would lead until summer time. Then, some of us would find a job at the tabacco farms, other at the carrot farms... and that was the end of our lead. We would play with only seven or eight players. Good old times!

- Do you still remember everyone's names?

- Ah... thirty years have gone by! Chico Alentejano was the masseur; the players were Amadeu, Carlos Madeira, Chico Espanhol, Orlando Estragado, Silva do Arroios, Carlos Moreira, Viegas... and me, obviously! I apologize for not remembering the other ones. When I got married, in 1960, I quit soccer.

- But not the club!?

- No! Don't even think about it. I am member #7, still today.

Many more memories came to this dialogue, always about soccer. The years went by and Américo decided to play a different game, travelling around the world, living life to its fullest. Canada, USA and Portugal are destinations he includes in his annual guidebook.

Standing up: Chico Alentejano, Artur Rodrigues; --; Vilas, Manuel; Chico Gregório; Américo Carvalho; Fernando and Armando. Sitting down: Silva; Albuquerque; Horácio; Mateus; --; Correia Dias; Viegas; Lampreia and Manelinho.

JMC - June of 1986

Codinha, Adriano

City of Nazaré

Always exhibiting a smile, Adriano Codinha in "his" folkloric group Rancho da Nazaré de Leamington.

Adriano Codinha, a 'nazareno' (a native from the city of Nazaré) who placed inside the same bag profit and joy of life to live together. In 1998, we participated in a magnificent party at the Portuguese Club of Leamington, through the courtesy of Adriano Codinha, who reunited all his family – without the family, nothing could be accomplished –, friends and clients from all time to celebrate the 25th anniversary of his company Saco Fisheries. It was an amazing gathering, very easily digestive, just like the dinner that was served. Obviously, the best fish in town was served! The master of ceremonies, Carlos Cavalheiro (another nazareno) made everything run smoothly. It was nice to see old friends again from the past who live in Leamington, Windsor, London and even in Toronto.

Travelling from Toronto to Leamington, I had the pleasant company of António Sousa, a pioneer from Nazaré who made sure, just like his brother Jess, to be in Leamington to greet the Codinha's family. Excluding myself and several Canadians at the party, everyone else was from Nazaré. Ilda and Adriano Codinha, together with their daughter Isabel Maria and their son-in-law Jorge Barbosa, have many reasons to feel happy about the work they have done together and about what the future still holds for them. – I have the sea and fishing in my blood – Adriano Codinha said proudly of his accomplishment. – I began my life as a fisherman in Nazaré, then I went to the cod fishery and,

Three pioneers from Nazaré: António Sousa, Adriano Codinha and Tony Galveias.

one day, I decided to settle in Canada. It was the best decision of my life. In this country, I maintained my passion by dedicating myself to the fish industry and it has been 25 years. Today, Saco Fisheries is an important fish market in the area of southern Ontario. I am happy.

Adriano Codinha arrived in Canada on June 6, 1961. He opened Saco Fisheries in May of 1973. Today, he owns six fishing boats and has seventeen licenses. Adriano Codinha looks very young for his age. There two things he worries about in life: his physical and moral aspect. He is still an active member of the folkloric group Rancho da Nazaré de Leamington, and encourages the younger ones to maintain the tradition. Seeing him dance, and smile, its as if we are watching a 20 year old because the Corridinho da Nazaré dance is not for everyone!

Tony Galveias, who lives in Toronto, and António Forno, from Leamington and Chatham, were both sitting at the table with us, and confessed that just seeing Codinha dance was enough to make them sweat. Adriano Codinha, with his way of being in life, has been able to convince his daughter to be in the Rancho, together with his three granddaughters. His granddaughter Nicole studies at York University,

The couple Ilda and Adriano Codinha surrounded by their family.

Melissa is at Fleming College and Vanessa goes to Cardinal Carter High School. The couple Codinha is worthy of the admiration people feel for them and the luck that has always protected them. However, only those who search for luck can find it. I hope I will be able to participate in many more parties organized by Codinha, in Leamington. Specially if Adriano Codinha keeps on being an active member of the Rancho da Nazaré.

JMC - 2004

Cordeiro, João António Travassos

Town of Santa Cruz da Lagoa, island of S. Miguel, Azores

João Cordeiro was born with the inclination for syndicalism. When he was 17 years old, he was already in charge of registering the companies in their respective union...

João António Travassos Cordeiro was born in the town of Santa Cruz da Lagoa, in the island of S. Miguel, on February 3, 1954.

As a child, while in school, he would

João, holding his sister's hand, beside his grandfather, the day of the religious celebrations in Lagoa.

The couple Esperança and João Cordeiro.

help his family by working on his grandfather's farms. At the age of 11, he emigrated to Canada, sponsored by his father, José Cordeiro, who had arrived in spring of 1957. Accompanied by his mother and brothers, João António Travassos Cordeiro arrived in Toronto in August of 1965. In Toronto, he studied until the age of 16. To help his family through the hardships of life, João went to work in Kopac, the factory responsible for making plastic bottles. A year later, at the age of 17, João and his friend Raul, enrolled in the Kopac's union, which had its headquarters on Adelaide Avenue, west of Spadina. At Kopac, he met and dated Esperança da Liberdade Pereira, who was born in the village of Trovões, a town of São João da Pesqueira, district of Viseu, on January 23, 1952.

Esperança arrived in Canada in August of 1969. They got married on July 26 of 1975, at the church of the Holy Cross, in Toronto. The couple had two children, both born in Toronto: Louise Marie, on November 9, 1976 and Kevin, on November 22, 1992. Soon after having accomplished his dream of seeing Kopac be part of a union, João left in order to have a better life and went to work at AIMCO Canada, a factory that built car breaks. All of this took place in 1973. He then became part of the union United Steel Workers of North America.

João Cordeiro, a member of the pilgrims of S. Miguel, when he was 9 years old.

Wedding day: Esperança and João, in a family picture with their parents, brothers and sisters.

In 1974, he moved again and went to work at Inglis, an appliance factory. Disagreements between the administration and the workers led to a long strike. João and his friend José Realejo, both young and active man, went searching for new paths in their lives. They went to construction, specifically the sector responsible for the construction of highways. He became a member of the laborer's international union of North America, also known as Local 183. In 1976, he became foreman for the company, a position he held until Christmas of 1986. During the winter of 1985 and 1986, he trained workers at local 183.

On December 24 of 1986, Tony Dionísio invited him to be director at Local 183, due to an unexpected vacancy at the office. He was undecided for a while because he wanted to make sure his colleagues would remain in their functions. Don Andrew, the boss at Andrew Paving & Eng. Ltd. made the commitment of keeping everyone if João left. Thus, João began a new career at Local 183, on April 7, 1987, making him the first Portuguese man from the Azores to take such a position at a local union. Just like every representative at Local 183, he suffered six dramatic weeks of suspension, in front of the headquarters, facing his rivals, together with Tony Dionisio and João Dias, among others, in that gloomy March of 1996. Everything went fine, they held new elections, and João Cordeiro, again invited by Tony Dionisio, went to the executive office, a position he still holds today. Since 1991, he has been re-elected at Local 183.

Nowadays, with a stable life, the Cordeiro family lives life to its fullest, having camping as their favourite hobby. He owns a bungalow in Wasaga Beach, where he spends part of the summer. Esperança Cordeiro and daughter Louise Marie are now bank clerks at Scotia Bank, in Brampton.

Their children, Kevin and Luise Marie.

João's son, Kevin, is in Grade 13 at St. Joseph High School, in the Peel Region. The couple Esperança and João are often seen in many events in different clubs of the community. João Cordeiro is a member of the Portuguese Cultural Centre of Mississauga, of Peniche Cultural Club and of Casa dos Açores of Toronto. In different years, they visit the continent and the Azores. It has been a life full of challenges and work, but a happy life.

JMC - 2000

Costa, Damião Patacho

City of Lagos, province of Algarve

Damião Patacho da Costa was born in the city of Lagos, the province of Algarve, on July 4, 1927. It was in the Algarve that he completed his teaching course and, in Lisbon, he passed the National Exam, which is equivalent to a Bachelor of Education. The first school where he taught was in the city of Faro, the Industrial and Commercial School.

In 1954, Damão Costa transferred to the city of Ponta Delgada, São Miguel, Azores, where he taught for 11 years. The administrative office of the Industrial and Commercial School of Ponta Delgada honoured him on October 15, 1965, for his level of professional competence and his dedication to every activity. Still in Faro, Damião met and dated another teacher, Virginia Maria Isabel Cremilde Jacques de Sousa Prazeres Jorge Tricate

Damião Patacho da Costa, showing his insignia from the Order of Merit.

Cerqueira, born in Faro, on May 3, 1925 and with whom he married on April 10, 1954, at the Cathedral of Faro.

Already living in Ponta Delgada, the couple Virginia and Damião were given the happiest moment of their lives: the birth of daughters Ana Maria and Margarida Solange, both born on the Green Island (S. Miguel). The Costa's family emigrated to Canada in 1965 with a temporary permit, on October 10. In Toronto, Damião began working as a technician of cameras and teaching Portuguese, together with his wife, at the First Portuguese. At that

Wedding day: Virginia and Damião, surrounded by family members, in 1954.

time, Damião also met other teachers: Maria José, who later moved to Montreal, Branca Gomes, the first Portuguese teacher in Toronto, and Débora Raposo de Morais, the principal. From March 2, 1972 to June 30, 1980, Damião was in charge of the First Portuguese School. Due to discordances within the school, Damião left and opened his own school at the "Clube Transmontano". The daughters Ana Maria and Margarida are both graduates of the University of Toronto and University of Guelph, respectively, and help their parents with the school.

Ana Maria has also taken a folkloric dance course and, at the Transmontano School, besides teaching Portuguese, she is charge of rehearsing the three folkloric groups: Rancho Infantil (for the little ones), Grupo Estudantil (students' group) and Os Marotos (senior group). They are a team that knows what they want and what they do. From his time as a teacher in Faro, in Ponta Delgada and in Toronto, Damião remembers particularly his most peaceful and calm student, little Aníbal, now Professor Aníbal Cavaco Silva, who was prime minister of Portugal. On June 10, 1991, the President of the Republic, Master of the Honorary Orders of Portugal, bestowed Damião with the insignia from the Order of Merit, given to him by the consul general of Portugal, Pessanha Viegas, in Toronto. Damião and Virginia have dedicated their life to teaching, a life full of sacrifices and rewards. Today, they are both retired, but still work at the school they founded, as volunteers. Always showing a beautiful smile, Damião told us that from now on he is going to be spending five months in the Algarve and the remaining months of the year in Toronto. This division has a simple explanation: their will to go back to their roots, and their will to spend some time with their grandchildren, Andreia and Alexandre. So, until fate allows it, their life will be spent here and there. We hope it will be for many years.

JMC - 2000

Margarida da Costa Pinto, the youngest daughter of the couple.

Virginia and Damião with their granddaughter Andreia.

Damião's grandchildren: Andreia and Alexander.

At a Portuguese Community event, Damião, his wife and daughter Ana Maria.

Costa, Eduardo

Stongton-Massachusetts, USA

Gouveia, Firmino

Town of Serra d'Água,

Madeira island

To know the stories and history of our Portuguese emigrant-pioneers is a pleasure, but also an obligation. This reunion took place at Felizmina and Manuel Firmino de Gouveia's place, where we learned the story of Manuel, but also of his friend Eduardo Costa.

Firmino Gouveia and Eduardo Costa, when they received the "Medal of Merit", at the Portuguese consulate. Behind them, Fernando Nóbrega, another pioneer from Madeira island.

They both emigrated together from Madeira Island, worked together and, now that they are retired, they live very close to each other, in Toronto.

Eduardo Costa considers himself a man with three nationalities. His parents came to the United States of America in 1908 and on September 6, 1917, Eduardo was born in Stongton, Massachussetts.

When he was only two years old, his parents decided to go back to Madeira and the little Eduardo obtained his second nationality. As a grown man, without a glimpse of his future, he decided to come to Canada, together with the first group of people from Madeira, where he got his third "flag" as he calls it. He left from the city of Funchal, on May 26, 1953, on board of Nea Hellas, a Greek ship, and arrived in Halifax, Canada, on June 2, 1953, together with his friend Manuel Gouveia.

Manuel Firmino de Gouveia was born in the town of Serra d'Água, in Madeira island, on March 13, 1919. A cop back home, he decided to become an emigrant. He left behind his island, wife and children.

- I remember leaving Funchal with my eyes swollen from crying – Manuel said, with his eyes lost somewhere in the past.

- Three whistles and we took off! – he continued. He looks at the ceiling of his own house and says: - But it was worth it! We left our beautiful city of Funchal and, after a wonderful trip, we entered Halifax, another place of dazzling beauty. At the time, I remembered Christopher Columbus' voyage to the Americas and said:

Christopher Columbus navigated
Crossing the waves, strong as a fort
He was the first one to enter America
Without a visa or passport.

Everyone began laughing and his present wife (the first one died when their fourth son was only 9 months), Felizmina, joined the group. – I was a widow for seven years, living like a stray dog – continued Manuel. Felizmina showed some surprise at the poetic side of her husband. She is an amazing housewife. Due to the quatrain, we remembered Eduardo Costa's musical side.

- Yes, I love playing and singing, but I am only able to produce lyrics when I feel warm inside. – he explained when we asked him about his music.

We looked at the dainties and drinks at the table, and a little hope was born inside us. Perhaps Eduardo was going to sing for us...

- I remember perfectly well – continued Eduardo. – I was always the clown of the group. At that time, during Christmas, I used to gather a group of friends and go out to sing. on the streets. It helped to kill our feelings of longing and forget the hardships of life. Boy, we made some noise!

- There were times that the cops would stop us – Manuel interrupted, laughing. – But they were nice. They actually admired us for doing that. In those times, we were all living the way we could on Augusta and Spadina.

- We were six in one room! – Eduardo clarified.

- When you were singing on the streets, did you feel cold at all?

- Cold? We drank so much that there was no chance of feeling cold.

The group of men from Madeira who officially emigrated to Canada in 1953.

Another burst of laughter. Then we began our research of the past:

- Mr. Costa, what was your first job in Canada?

- In the farm... I had to milk cows and plant vegetables. I was so lost in time that I used to work on Sundays without knowing it was Sunday.

- Did you ever feel deprived of anything?

- Oh yes! Specially of food. I was working a lot and eating very little. I worked ten to twelve hours a day... It got to a point that I used to steal milk. I had a small container hidden in the grass for the milk. I don't think it was ever washed... - he said, laughing and shaking his head.

- Continue, please!

- This is the type of story no one should share... - he continued, still laughing. – because of the water and milk I was drinking without any hygienic conditions, I got such a bad constipation that forced me to write to my wife, who was still in Madeira, to send me pills. I will never forget the day I received her letter with pills inside. They were yellow. No one can imagine how great I felt!

The language barrier did not help in the situation. We can only imagine the hardships our pioneers had to suffer.

- And you, Mr. Gouveia, how did your life start in Canada?

- In the farm, as well! When I arrived in Halifax, I was sent to London, in Ontario. I travelled in an old train, with wood benches and smoke all over the place. In order to rest a little bit, I had to pay a dollar for a pillow. I went to work at a farm owned by a Jewish man, who was married to a Brazilian lady, in Camoka, near London. I was making .50 cents an hour, working from 7 a.m. to 7 p.m. planting lettuce. I ended up with wounds on my knees. – A painful grimace was seen in his face, as he was remembering those hard times. Still a little sad, he continued his tale: - The Jewish man had promised me .60 cents an hour, but never kept his promise. So, I went to work at another farm, in Mt. Bridge, where the conditions were better. Here, I was planting tabacco. The owner has already died, but until this day I still get along with the son.

Remembering every adventure he went through, Manuel continued his rosary of incidents from the time he lived in London.

- Once, in 1953, we had a huge party because we found by chance a group of five or six people who spoke Portugues. It was wonderful! They were Portuguese pilots who had come to London and Winnipeg to get a special license. A little later, we were all pilots... under the knowledge of wine!

After a new burst laughter, we had a new question:
- When did you start working together?
- It was in Kitimate. – Eduardo answered promptly. – We worked for an aluminium company and in a kitchen known to serve meals to the workers. After, we moved to Toronto, where we worked in a restaurant for many years. Later on, we got a job at the maintenance department of the University of Toronto, we stayed until we retired.
- When I retired – Manuel concluded – I was already a boss.
- It's life! – we said. – Do you miss any friends from that time?
- Yes, I do. – Eduardo said. – I would love to see Francisco de Sousa and Álvaro Pinto Reis again. They still live in Kitimat.

- And José Fernandes, who is still living in British Columbia – Manuel remembered.

- Do you have any interesting stories to share with us from that time?

- Well, one day, in 1955, I was walking the streets of Toronto with Mairinho, talking about life, when suddenly a young man came towards us and began crying. – You are Portuguese, please help me! – he said. He was from the Azores, I don't remember his name anymore, and was lost, without money and without a job. Poor fellow! He was

In Kitimat, Eduardo Costa, feeding a bear.

desperate. I took him to my place, where I gave him food and my bed to sleep. After, we took him to the house of a group of men from the Azores whom we knew. It would be nice if he read this story... You know – Manuel continued – I was dating my wife... via satellite! – Laughing at all the memories, he explained. – My late wife used to tell me, every time she wrote me, that she would never see me again. So, I sent her a letter saying: "At four o'clock in the afternoon, in Madeira, look at the sun and think of me. I will do the same at the corresponding time here in Canada. You know, we always had a feeling we could see each other!

- And what about the one from Agostinho? – Manuel asked Eduardo.

- Oh yes! I cry every time I think about it. Agostinho is a friend of ours, from the Azores, who, one day, became desperate. Without a job and without money, he decided to die slowly. He told everyone he was going to go to the lake where he would wait for his death. "I will not kill myself, but I will wait for death to take me!", he said. And he went. A group of children who used to play near the place he chose, called the cops. Agostinho had been there for three days. Those children saved him. I used to tell those who made fun of us: "You can sell all you have. It won't be enough to pay for the longing, the hunger and the anguish I went through to open the door for you!.

- Unwanted tears showed in his face, while Eduardo agreed with him.

- Do you regret anything?

- No, I don't! To the very contrary, I believe it was all worth it. Now, I am retired. My wife sings in the folkloric group Rancho da Madeira and my children are dancers. I have seven children and two grandchildren, all living in Canada. I am trying to get back the house I have in Madeira, which I rented at a bad time, but it has been difficult. If I succeed, I think I want to spend the remaining days of my life in my homeland. If those in power in Madeira read my story, they will probably be able to help me obtain what is mine and help me accomplish my last dream of going back.

- You never know. And you, Mr. Costa, are you planning to go back or stay?

- I will stay. My son is a mechanical engineer and is well in life. My wife and I have nobody else. I will dwell in the land of my third flag.

After so many memories, Mr. Costa ended his story this way:

We both left, side by side
Discovering the unknown
Retired, we end up here
With our mission accomplished.

Congratulations! If fate ever draws you apart, let the good times you spent together be the courage you need to continue your legacy. All the best.

JMC - March of 1986

Manuel Firmino de Gouveia with wife Felizmina Gouveia and children: Elizabeth, Suzan and David, all members of Rancho da Madeira, at the Canadian Madeira Club.

Costa, Helder Reis

Lagoas, village of Febres,

town of Cantanhede

Helder and Lídia Costa at a party.

The world is very small and takes many turns. This is what we feel like saying about the life of the young entrepreneur Helder Reis Costa.

Helder Reis Costa was born in a small place called Lagoas, in the village of Febres, in Cantanhede (a small town close to Lisbon), on December 25, 1959. Immediately after the Carnation Revolution of April 25, 1974, at the age of 13, he left Portugal with his mother and came to live with his father, Amadeu, who has been in Canadá since 1972. He studied at Harbord Collegiate where he completed grade 12. In a trip to Portugal, in August of 1979, Helder met the young Lídia Maria Rodrigues Vinhas, also from Lagoas, where she was born on January 7, 1959, but was living in France with her family. Even with distant residences, in Canada and in France, the young couple fell in love and got married. A wedding with an amusing story! They married in Toronto, at City Hall, on February 16, 1979 and asked the Consulate of Portugal to register and transfer their wedding papers to Portugal to get married there in the church.

Of course! The papers never got to Portugal, and Helder and Lídia had to get married again at City Hall in order to finally get married in church. The religious ceremony took place in Febres, on August 16, 1980. There is a saying that who gets married in August lives a life in sorrow. Not this couple!

Lidia and Helder have three daughters, all born in Toronto. Ângela, 14 years old, Jessica, 12 and Mónica, 9. While a student, Helder had a part-time job at the airport, cleaning airplanes. Subsequently, he left his job at the airport to go work at the Capitan Jones Restaurant, in

Helder and Lídia with their three daughters: Ângela, Jessica and Mónica.

Toronto, as a busboy. By the time he left Captain Jones he was manage of events. Between 1981 and 1983, Helder moved to R.G. Henderson, where he worked in the repairs section, while studying electronics and electricity at night. In 1984, after completing his course, he opened his own company of repairs, the MC Technical Service Ltd, which he kept for 13 years. He also owned 50 percent of Alfa Full Machinery, which he sold in 1995.

In 1995, he decided to become a salesperson of hotel and restaurant equipment, travelling frequently to Portugal, Italy, Mexico and the USA. This phase of his life did not last very long, because it was still in 1995 that he decided to try his luck in the bakery and pastry business, with José Dias, Carlos Dias and his brother José. He is a partner and manager of Caldense Bakery, and had shares in the Nova Era Bakeries until 1999. At the Nova Era in Oakville, Victor Silva has a percentage of the business. Talking with us, Helder confessed that the bakery-pastry business is a sweet job… Thus, business grew. In 2000, the owners of Caldense and Nova Era decided to go their separate ways. Caldense now owns a factory where they make their bread and pastry, on Symington Avenue, in Toronto. Helder has expanded his business to the restaurant sector, opening the restaurant Piripiri with Agnelo Costa.

As an entrepreneur and family man, Helder is a busy man. However, he does not give up his Sunday morning hobby, which is to play soccer at Bellwoods Park, with "old" friends. They meet without calling anybody. Some of them have been at this for more than thirty years.

The addiction is playing soccer and they share it by this friendship of so many years.

We hope Helder continues to play successfully in every endeavour of his life.

JMC - 1999

The Costa brothers at their famous Caldense BBQ, on Symington Avenue. They are being observed by community counsellor Mário Gomes.

Costa, José Manuel Antunes

Town of Arcos de Valdevez

José Manuel Antunes da Costa was born in the town of Arcos de Valdevez, a small green paradise in the North of Portugal. José, son of Albertina Antunes and Silvério da Costa, was born on February 19, 1950, and has a brother and a sister living in Canada – António and Maria – and another brother, José, and sister, Custódia, living in France.

José Manuel arrived in Canada in May of 1969. He went to Givens Public School and Harbord Collegiate, in Toronto. José married Fátima Costa – from the island of S. Miguel. He works in the real estate market, and is the father of Mark, 22 years old, and Tracy, 16 years old, both born in Toronto. José da Costa has an enviable professional career.

Since his youth years, he has dedicated himself to the car industry, more specifically selling cars. In 1974, he began his career at Ford, in Toronto, where he remained until 1980, the year he decided to "drive" himself to Addison on Bay, concessionaire of GM. His personality, know-how and will to sell well got him an extraordinary charm that, throughout the years, has made him the number one sales person in Ontario, possibly in Canada, in respect to serving clients on a one-on-one basis.

As a community individual, he has contributed to Clubs,

José Manuel Antunes da Costa

Associations and Parishes, particularly, to Associação Cultural do Minho, the first association representing his homeland in Toronto, and to the Portuguese Cultural Centre of Mississauga, the club from the area where he lives. In relation to the latter, he has been an active member of the Committee to raise funds for the new headquarters of the club, a dream the Portuguese community of Mississauga has had for many years. When it comes to the "minhotos" (name given to the people who are from the province of Minho, José's homeland), he would like to see the Associação Cultural do Minho, Arsenal do Minho and Associação de Barcelos (also from Minho), get together to form just one big club, so that the celebrations would be better and more beautiful. José da Costa is a man who fights for unity, against any division. As he says, all together, we can only be stronger.

José Manuel Antunes da Costa, a dedicated servant of his friends and clients, 24 hours a day. A profession he holds so dearly that sometimes he forgets about himself and his own family. José is a man who deserves our regard and gratitude.

JMC - 2004

Fátima and José da Costa with son Mark and daughter Tracy.

José da Costa and Horácio Domingues, and other friends, making bbq sardines at the fund raising for the CCPM

Lucília Duarte with daughter Suzana Rita, sharing the joy of life.

Costa (Duarte), Lucília da Conceição Martins

Terceira island, Azores

She is as fragile as she is talented. Lucília da Conceição Martins da Costa was born in the festive island of Terceira, on January 15, 1927. The natural beauty of the island, the blue sky and the green sea gave

A beautiful painting by Lucília.

One of the priceless whale teeth painted by Lucília.

Lucília Duarte, showing, with a beautiful smile, one of her many works of art.

Manuel Duarte in his office.

Lucília and Manuel's son, Emanuel Duarte.

her the notion of colour, and her own sensibility gave her everything else... She is a self-taught person on drawing and painting. Proudly, she owns a very unique and rich collection of whale's teeth, painted by her.

The ivory painted by her hands, changes into a piece of art. As a young girl, Lucília met Manuel Gerardo Duarte, from the town of Monte, in the Madeira Island, where he was born on September 24, 1926. Manuel Duarte went to Terceira Island on a work mission to investigate the military task of ATC. He was "caught" by the military life – Air Force – and by love. Curiously, Lucília was the first young woman Manuel met when he arrived in Terceira. Fate working its own mysterious way! They got married at Santa Luzia's church, on June 29, 1952.

From this couple with a background from Madeira and Azores, two children were born in Terceira: Emanuel Gerardo, born in 1953, who holds now a naval architect and lives in Miami, and Suzana Rita, born in 1957, married to Dr. Jack Sullivan, and mother of two girls. Lucília and Manuel came to Canada on September 12, 1966. Lucília has dedicated most of her life to her home and her paintings where Manuel worked in finances, his speciality, for Gormack Books, an association which assembled many companies. Lucília and Manuel also opened the Universo Travel Agency, in May of 1972. She has successfully exhibited her work many times, at the Terceira's Air Base 4, at the City Hall of Angra do Heroísmo – Terceira's capital city –, at the Almada Negreiros Gallery of the Consulate of Portugal in Toronto, and among other places. Lucília Duarte is a true artist in every aspect. She is fragile, beautiful and full of talent. Congratulations.

JMC - 1999

Costa, Manuel da

Town of Castelo de Neiva, district of Viana do Castelo

Manuel da Costa

Manuel da Costa, with 26 years of experience in his line of business, founded, together with his wife, the company Viana Roofing & Sheet Metal Ltd., twelve years ago. Manuel da Costa does not like to be known as president of his company. He feels like any other worker, believing that "nobody is superior to anybody else", an image he wants to transmit and maintain.

Manuel da Costa dedicates six days a week to his work, 12 to 13 hours daily. He is always available to his clients, getting himself involved in every project of the company. Frequently, he is the one dealing directly with the client. His biggest concern in each project is to make sure it is safe for the employees. According to him, the time when anyone could work on roofing is way past. Nowadays, roofing is a profession, which requires preparation and some experience. Viana Roofing & Sheet Metal Ltd. is a member of the Ontario Industrial Roofing Contractors Association, a group that has as its main purpose the assurance of the employee's benefits and safety in the workplace. Manuel da Costa advises his employees to seek special training, such as in the area of working with chemicals. This type of training and the concern of the company in defence of a safe working environment is what makes Viana Roofing a safe company with credibility, at the same time it gives the clients the confidence they seek.

Viana Roofing and Sheet Metal Ltd. supplies and installs every type of roof. About 30 per cent of the business comes from new contractors especially in the area of condominiums and high-rises. The remaining 70 percent of the work the company does is on repairs and change of roofs. For Manuel da Costa, there is no such thing as a small or a big project, since they all make up the whole. On a daily basis, Manuel da Costa deals with about ten projects, which range from industrial and commercial areas to residential and institutional. Casino Niagara and Swan Lake Retirement Village are among the exciting challenges Manuel took with his team.

A short summary about what can be written about Manuel and Viana Roofing and Sheet Metal Ltd. How did it all start? From the town of Castelo de Neiva, where he is from, the Costa family started for adventure. The father, Manuel, arrived in Sudbury, in

Manuel da Costa and Bernardete Gouveia, two of the founders of the Gallery of the Portuguese Pioneers and members of the 50 Years Committee, at Maurício's place (with his wife Bia), the author of the commemorative panel, which is at Pier 21, in Halifax.

1969. The mother, Leotina, and her sons Manuel, José, Martinho and Antónia came to Canadá in 1970. The youngest one, Linda, was already born in Toronto, on March 3, 1971. Manuel da Costa junior was born on October 2, 1955. At a very early age in his life, he began working, while studying. With a lot of good will and sacrifice, Manuel finished an architectural course at Ryerson University, which enabled him to work and progress in a Canadian company. On the way, there is always a love story...

Manuel met Jacinta, from the town of Arcos de Valdevez, in the north of Portugal, marrying her on May 28, 1977, in Toronto. The couple had two children, both born in Toronto: Michael, who has a bachelor of Arts from the University of Toronto, and Stephany, a graduate from York University.

The knowledge, experience and skills Manuel had did not mix with the slow pace of the company where he was working. Thus, with his wife, he got the company Viana Roofing & Sheet Metal Ltd., in 1987, and, until the present day, the company has had a constant success. His brothers work with him, in many sectors of the company. Manuel is seduced by work. He never stops. With calmness and audacity, he knew how to grow, and how to slowly get into other types of business, all very successful.

Jacinta and Manuel da Costa, a happy couple, at the last dinner of the Federation of Portuguese Canadian Business and Professionals.

Nowadays, Manuel and Jacinta da Costa are in charge of a group of companies in many different areas which give them exceptional comfort and stability in life and, which take up most of their time. A family of workmanship and a family which deserves all the rewards it has received. Manuel bought the building where the First Portuguese Canadian Club used to be providing the club with better conditions, and allowed it to stay where it has been for many years.

In honour of the Portuguese Pioneers, Manuel da Costa offered the installations for the Gallery of the Portuguese Pioneers, inaugurated on May 13, 2000, together with Bernadete Gouveia and José Mário Coelho. In May of 2003, during the commemorations of the 50th anniversary of the official arrival of the Portuguese community to Canada, he raised a monument in honour of the pioneers in the Partkette of the Pioneers, on Crawford and College streets, in Toronto. At the same time, together with the artist-craftsman Maurício Almeida, Manuel

offered the Saudade Museum, in Halifax, a carved wooden panel of the History of the Portuguese people from their first arrival to the present day. Manuel and Jacinta da Costa have not forgotten Portugal or the Portuguese. All the best.

JMC-2004

Manuel da Costa holds Canada's flag, which João Belo and Felizmina Gouveia unveiled from the Commemorative stone.

Costa, Manuel Braga da

Town of Vila do Porto,

Island of Santa Maria, Azores

Manuel Braga da Costa

Manuel Braga da Costa dreamt of being a marine and ended up "navigating" to Canada. Manuel Braga da Costa was born in the town of Vila do Porto, in the island of Santa Maria, Azores, on July 1, 1938. When he finished grade 4 at the school of Vila do Porto, Manuel began working for Pan America, with his uncle Jacinto, cleaning the airplanes. At the same time, he dreamt of becoming a member of the Portuguese Navy, so he decided to get his marine certificate in 1953 and a crew certificate in 1957, the same year the Capelinhos' volcano erupted.

Everything changed in Manuel's life and, obviously, in many people's lives. Thus, he fixed his azimuth to travel to Canada, a country where he arrived on May 20, 1958. Before taking off to Canada, he got married to Maria do Livramento Nunes Ribeiro who was from the island of Pico, where she was born on April 30, 1941. They got married at the Vila do Porto's church, in February of 1958. When he came to Canada, he settled in Hull, Québec. A week later, the Immigration Services of Canada got him a job at a hotel in Québec, washing dishes in the kitchen. A Jewish traveler, who spoke a little Portuguese, saw him and decided to take him to Ottawa, to the house of some Portuguese people he knew. It was the home of the late Altino, who was from the island of S. Miguel, and who got a job for Manuel at 20 City Du Brick, a factory where he worked for six months.

In 1960, Manuel da Costa went to work for a Danish contractor, William Hansen, who owned Nidan, a company specialized in building residential and commercial units. When Nidan closed, in 1966, Manuel went to work for Leader Mansonry & Foreman until 1969. In this company, Manuel was sent to Belleville, for the construction of the Four Season Hotel, as a fore-man in the cement section. At that time, he hired 24 Portuguese men who were illegally living in Canada. The RCMP visited the site many times, but was unable to locate the Portuguese men. In Ontario, Manuel da Costa was in charge of other projects, such as the venture on Martin Groove and highway 27, where they built five high rises. In 1971, he went back to Ottawa to work for Dilvar, which was building the Highland high rise on St. Laurent and Notre Dame Cemetery. In 1974, in partnership with Pierre Ganvin, he opened his own company – Manacont. In 1986, hav-ing left his partnership at Manacont, he went decided to open DaCosta Forming alone.

A heart attack, associated to a serious economical crisis, made him lose about three mil-

Manuel Braga da Costa with his son when they both visited Milenio Newspaper.

lion dollars and give up his company. He sold every-thing he could to be able to recover some of the money lost. Another heart attack weakened him. He was forced to take a long break from work, forced to maintain restricted diet and have a lot of rest. It was not easy for a man used to a working life in construction.

Maria do Livramento and Manuel have two sons, George and Carlos, both born at the old Ottawa General Hospital. They are both carpenters, following their father's footsteps in construction. •

In the social, cultural aspect of life, Manuel Braga

da Costa was a true pioneer. He is one of the founding members of Lusitânia Recreation Centre of Ottawa/Hull, and bought the site where Lusitânia built its own headquarters, in 1977. To recognize his effort, the administration of the club engraved his name on a plate at the center. Manuel was also the foreman in charge of the construction of Nossa Senhora de Fátima's church. He was also one of the founding members of the Amigos Unidos of Hull (Friends United), in 1975, and holds now a commemorative medal of the 25th anniversary of that group. He remembers, with some longing, the old times when Father António Araújo and conductor José formed the committee on Santa Bernardete's church, today a Portuguese church, to form the musical marching band Banda Filarmónica Nossa Senhora de Fátima. "I love musical bands" – he confessed. He also remembers being invited, at José Ferreira's house, to build the church and hall of the Amigos Unidos of Hull.

It has been a life filled with work, drama and happiness. With his wife Maria do Livramento, Manuel has been to every corner of Portugal – continent (from north to south), Azores and Madeira –, Brazil, Cuba, Peru, Argentina, Curaçau, Aruba, Margarita, and many other places. The motto he lives by is "while there is life, one must live it well". This is the philosophy of life of someone who dreamed of being a marine and "navigated" to Canada where he never thought about the sea again.

JMC-1999

Cota, Eliseu Manuel Rocha

Town of Biscoitos, Terceira Island, Azores

He is a highly known and highly regarded person in Montreal. He is an individual dedicated to his family, to music and to his community.

Eliseu Manuel Rocha Cota is from the town of Biscoitos, in the island of Terceira, Azores, where he was born on October 12, 1943. While in school, he dedicated himself to his passion: music. Also from a very young age, he began dating Maria Elsa Nunes da Rocha, from the village of Raminho in the same island, where she was born on June 8, 1946. Maria Elsa emigrated to Canada, with her fam-

Manuel Cota, besides Portuguese-Canadian mayor, Luís Miranda, from Anjou.

ily, in 1964. They kept on dating and got married, by proxy, in 1967. That same year, Eliseu Manuel arrived in Montreal, the same city where, on September 30, 1967, he got married with his lifelong sweetheart, at the Holy Cross church. Someone who adapts easily to new situations, Manuel worked some jobs when he got to Montreal, before forming his own company, Clair-Propre, and later on he was successful in open-

Filarmonic band of N. Srª dos Milagres, marching in one procession.

ing MEC Renovations. He still has the latter.

His wife has been a top clerk at Sears, for more than 25 years. Music and the community were calling him. Manuel Cota, as he is more commonly known, founded a committee to form the Portuguese Association of the Holy Spirit of Hochelaga. After, he formed and founded, in July of 1996, the filarmonic band Nossa Senhora dos Milagres, with the support of his friend Francisco Rocha and others. For this band, the key figure was conductor Leonardo Aguiar. Manuel plays saxofone (his favourite instrument). Besides being a founding member of the Portuguese Society of the Holy Spirit, he served as president, and promoted many initiatives.

Nowadays, Manuel teaches music to young

The president of the Autonomous Region of the Azores, Carlos César, thanking the gift given by Manuel Cota, when César visited the association.

Martin and Orlanda, Henriqueta Resende, Maria Elsa, Manuel Cota and Eduardo Resende.

children, has a beautiful garden on his backyard, all worked by his hands, with a swimming pool, typical springs of water, trees, grass and a lot of flowers. His garden has merited him the City Hall medal of best garden, and has been visited by many people. It is an extraordinary garden. The couple Cota, who lives in Anjou, Montreal, deserves the paradise they have build.

JMC - 2002

Dias, Armando Correia

Campo de Ourique Neighbourhood, Lisbon

His fate was always connected to a leather ball. He kicked his soccer ball with the pleasure of a little boy who never loses sight of his favourite toy. Armando Correia Dias was born in the parish of Santa Isabel, Campo de Ourique, in Lisbon, on January 19, 1935.

Primary school, soccer and learning a profession in the workshop were the main events of his childhood. He began his soccer career in the junior section of Atlético Clube de Portugal, in Alcântara (Lisbon). In this team, Correia Dias was a finalist for the regional division of Lisbon in 1952-53, and in 1953-54 he lost the first round, but won the second against the team Belenenses with a hat-trick scored by himself. At the junior national level, the Atlético was eliminated by CUF. He made his debut in the first

Armando and Rosália Correia Dias.

division when he was 18, under the lead of coach Mário Imbelloni, in 1954. The first game he played was against the rival Marvila, the Oriental Soccer Club, a match he won. At this time, he was almost selected to play in the national team, but due to his age, had to be left out. Castiglia, the coach who replaced Imbelloni, kept him within the first ranks of the Atlético. The last game he played was at the Luz Stadium, against Benfica, when the latter became champion of Portugal in 1955-56, with Otto Glória.

In 1957-58, Correia Dias began representing the Grupo Desportivo Peniche (GDP), where he spent nine professional seasons. The unhappiness of losing a son, on a car accident, in the city of Peniche, changed the course of his life. The traumatic situation forced Correia Dias to contact his friend António Viola, who at that time was already living in Toronto and was the director of the Portuguese United Soccer Team. Thus, Correia Dias was the first professional Portuguese

player to play soccer in Canada. Correia Dias arrived in Toronto on October 22, 1965. His wife Rosália came on January 13, 1966, with their daughter Rosalinda do Rosário (10 years old at the time) and son Armando José (6 months old). When Correia Dias was submitted to the medical inspection in Lisbon, he met with Armando, a player for the club Sporting de Braga, who had been contracted by Father António Cunha, from Hamilton, Ontário, to play for the Portuguese Soccer Team of Hamilton. Correia Dias played one year for the Portuguese United, which then became the First Portuguese Soccer Team) and then was traded to go play for the Croatian Team. In order to avoid tearing his muscles, and because he was feeling a little tired, Correia Dias

Correia Dias, at Tapadinha, wearing the Atlético C. Portugal's shirt.

decided to quit playing and began coaching the Junior team of the First Portuguese until 1974. At the same time, he was assistant coach of the main team.

Peniche's team, champion of the Portuguese League in 1982.

Yet, there is still a lot of soccer being played in the community. When Correia Dias arrived in Toronto, he also began his professional career in the Hertz workshop, for two years. In 1967, he opened his own shop, "Dias Auto Body", on Portland St. in Toronto. Eighteen years later, in 1986, Correia Dias moved locations, to Davenporto Road, where he stayed until 1998.

Correia Dias and Frank Alvarez, with the junior soccer team, at the Festival Portuguese Tv show. It has been more than 20 years.

When Karan, the main coach, decided to leave the team, the president Amadeu Vaz invited Correia Dias to become the coach (1974). Correia Dias still remembers those times and the players, namely Jorge Félix, the goalkeeper Pedro, Walter, Testas, Rilhas, Valemar, Vicente, André, Daniel, and many others, all of them his friends. In 1981, he co-founded the Peniche Community Centre and was invited by the then president Manuel da Silva to coach the team. Because he was told the team was not a serious one, and that soccer was just a hobby, Correia Dias declined the invitation. In his place, Norberto became the coach. From 1972, Correia Dias has been a member of the Committee Pró-Lar de Santa Maria de Peniche, a committee which has as its mission, to raise funds for a seniors home, in the city of Peniche, Portugal. In 1981, the late Cardinal António Ribeiro was in Toronto with Monsignor Bastos to preside the celebrations of the committee.

The committee Pró-Lar de Santa Maria de Toronto, when it participated on the 25th anniversary of the Lar de Santa Maria (senior's home). In this picture, we see Monsignor Bastos, D. António Marcelino, Bishop of Aveiro and Correia Dias among others.

The Picnic organized by this committee took place at Madeira Park. Since the soccer team was there to participate in a tournament, Correia Dias was invited again to become the coach. This time he accepted, and the team won the championship in 1981 and 1983. In 1984, the team was also champion, but this time under the management of José Simões, in virtue of Correia Dias who transfered to the Cultural and Recreation Sector of the club. From 1982 to 1984, Rui Gomes was the president of the club. In 1985, Correia Dias, Rui Gomes and José Simões left Peniche and went to the Niagara Soccer Club, becoming champions in 1985. In 1986, Rui Gomes joined the First Portuguese, José Simões joined Arsenal do Minho and Correia Dias decided it was time to retire. His family needed his attention. However, it is impossible to completely stop what we were born to do. This way, in

1987, Correia Dias, Simões and Rui Gomes got together again, at Arsenal do Minho of Toronto. They conquered the first division, the cup and the super-cup and ended up being champions in Ontário. Representing this province, they played against the National team, in Saskatoon, but were eliminated in the quarter-finals by the British Columbia team. In 1988, Correia Dias came back to Peniche, becoming – yet again – champion in 1988, 1989, 1990 and 1991. At the end of 1991, Armando Correia Dias "retired" from soccer and dedicated himself to his family, to the committee Pró-Lar de Santa Maria and to his workshop. Coincidence or not, the Portuguese Soccer League came to an end in 1992.

Armando José Dias with wife Marylou and daughters Nichole and Amy.

Due to a stroke, Armando Correia Dias sold the business and retired. He dedicated himself more to his family, especially to his grandchildren Brian and Nelson – from his daughter Rosalinda (who is married to Fernando Violante), and Nichole and Amy – from his son Armando (married to Marylou Dias). Correia Dias is still an active member of the committee Pró-Lar de Santa Maria de Peniche. With his wife Rosália, Armando travels all over Canada, the USA and Portugal (the continent). And he still loves to watch soccer games... For Armando Correia Dias, the world is a soccer ball!

JMC - 2000

Dias, João Martins

Village of Monte, Terras de

Bouro, Province of Minho

João Martins Dias is one of those people from the province of Minho who was born to "swim against the tide" to protect his own interests. João Martins Dias was born in the village of Monte, in Terras de Bouro, on April 15, 1944. He left Portugal 37 years ago, beginning a journey through France, Australia and ending up in Canada in 1971. In Terras de Bouro he met and married Felizmina Dias Martins, at the Chamoim's Church, on February 5th, 1972.

João Martins Dias

Soon after arriving in Canada and establishing himself in Montreal, João and his wife decided to move to Ontario, settling in Oakville, the town where his two sons would be born: George, a computer analyst, and John, who is still a student. An active individual by instinct, João Dias began immediately his participation in the local unions, taking the role of the spokesperson for the group. In 1986, João was elected as representantive of the labours for local 183, integrating the team led by António Dionísio. João Dias is a true volunteer for the community. Already in Oakville, when he moved to Ontario, João and other friends, founded the now extinct Oakville Portuguese

The Dias' couple at the early years of their life.

Community Club. From 1983 he has been one of the most active members and administrator of the Associação Cultural do Minho de Toronto, serving as secretary, Public Relations and President. He was very dynamic in the Folkloric Group of the Association and as one of its directors since its foundation. He was also the first one to organize the "First Cultural Week of Minho", on June 13, 1986, and most of the annual picnics organized by the Association.

João Dias before leaving to Canada.

João Dias contributed to the formation of the Alliance of Portuguese Clubs and Associations of Ontario with Martinho Silva and Jack Correia, among others. With the Associação do Minho and other volunteers, João was able to successfully lobby some councils at Toronto's City Hall in order to name one street of the city "Minho Boulevard". João Martins Dias who is always ready to contribute to the community and to the country, is a counsellor for the Council of Portuguese Communities, Vice-President of the Local Council and Treasure of the Toronto's section.

At the moment, João Martins Dias, a dreamer by nature, is fighting to organize a body that will "establish a link among many entities in Minho and the Associations of Emigrants from Minho in the world". A daring initiative, which has already received support from many Clubs and Associations that represent Minho in the Portuguese communities. A dream hard to accomplish, but not impossible. João Dias would also like to organize under one association all the "minhotos" who live in southern Ontario. Union makes everyone strong and João has plenty of energy to dedicate to his dreams and ambitions. Where there is a will, there is power.

JMC - 2001

A beautiful portrait: Felizmina and João Dias, surrounded by sons John and George.

Dionísio, António (Tony) José Rodrigues

Town of Lourinhã

A ntónio José Rodrigues Dionísio, from Pinhoa, in the village of Moita dos Ferreiros, in the town of Lourinhã, where he was born in March of 1949, is a fighter by nature. Leading the destiny of local unions for many years, Tony Dionísio has always been able to carry out his projects.

Tony and Helena Dionísio with daughter Gail and granddaughter Nicole, on her father's lap.

The growth of Local 183 - Universal Workers Union has been mainly related to his perspicacity, ability to speak and sense of responsibility.

Years before, during his childhood and teenage years, António Dionísio suffered the natural consequences common to people of his age in a small, poor country. He went to school, worked in the farms and feed the animals. Tony's father, José António Dionísio, decided to try his luck following the footprints of one of his brother's who had left to Canada in 1957. Soon after arriving, Tony's mother, Maria da

Conceição, came to live with her husband, bringing the children with her.

From Lourinhã to Lisbon, then Montreal, Vancouver, Watson (in the Yukon) to Cassier, in British Columbia, this was Tony's journey when he arrived in Canadá. His father and uncle worked at the asbestos' mine. Tony came in contact with children of different nationalities, giving him what he call a "bath of multiculturalism". In the summer, he used to cut grass and, in the evening, wash dishes in the mine's kitchen. In 1966, the Dionísio family moved to Toronto. In

Tony Dionísio and José Lello giving a certificate to António Fraga, the president of the Portuguese Society of Disabled People.

school, Tony Dionísio studied arts and became a certified welder. He worked for Thames Steel and American Motors, in Brampton. He then moved to the digging of the tunnels for Toronto's subway where he began his journey towards Local 183. He began by defending a case for this own father in the union, and then was "hired" to defend his friends' cases. During the big strike

Tony Dionísio with the insignia given to him by the Secretary of State for the Portuguese Communities José Lello.

of 1978, Tony Dionísio was one of the most active members at the picket line and when the strike was over, he was offered the position of Complaints Officer for Local 183, which he accepted. Soon after, he was named representative of the union for the workers and thanks to his high skills he became president in 1983.

In 1994, during the month of September, when Dionísio was getting ready to replace the then Business Manager J. Reilly, there was a sudden change in the union, due to a strong opposition to Dionísio, which was accused of corruption in many city's newspapers. The board of directors for 183 appealed to the arbitration of the International Union.

Tony Dionísio and his colleagues left victorious, but still today, they face opposition from certain members, an opposition that dates back to 1994. In March of 1996, the powerful chair of the union, Mancinelli, expelled Tony Dionísio, João Dias and João Cordeiro from Local 183. Immediately after, there was a movement, which was made up by the vast majority of members of the union to support Tony Dionísio. After fighting many battles, the general elections were accepted by both parts to be held in July of 1996. Three days before the elections, the Provincial Court Justice Charles Vaillancourt declared Tony Dionísio not guilty in all the accusations made against him. During the polemic elections, Tony Dionísio and his colleagues won with 2568 votes agains 1719. Tony Dionísio is the first Portuguese-Canadian to hold the position of Business Manager of the Universal Workers Union.

The fight has been very sour. Tony Dionísio has worked very hard to enhance all types of services and increase support given to the workers and has created Scholarships to give to the children of the union's members.

At the same time, Tony Dionísio has been an active member in his Portuguese community, supporting many initiatives in clubs and associations. His biggest sports passion, besides soccer, is cycling. Thus, he has participated in races throughout Ontario beside José Calquinhas, João Fonseca, Abílio Lourenço, Ion D'Ornelas, Jocelyn Lovell, António Maria, Aníbal Patrício and Rui Martins and Rui Avelar, who are now family physicians. Inclusively, in 1982, a local cycling team went to Portugal and had good results. Those were good times.

Tony Dionísio has been recognized by thePortuguese and the community politicians. In the Christmas of 1998, he received from the hands of the Portuguese Secretary of State for the Communities, José Lello, the "Gold Medal of the Portuguese Communities" and in October of

2000 he was imposed the Insignia of Merit, granted by the Portuguese President of the Republic. In 2003, the Portuguese Cultural Centre of Mississauga paid a tribute to Tony Dionísio, where he received the "Gold Medal of the Queen's Jubilee", through the hands of the Member of Provincial Parliament, Tony Ruprecht and Tony's friend João Dias. António José Rodriges Dionísio is married to Helena and has a daughter, Gail, who is also married and has given him a granddaughter, Nicole.

With controversies, defeats and victories, life continues for Tony Dionísio.

JMC - February of 2004

At Skydome, Tony Dionísio and the President of the Autonomous Region of the Azores Carlos César at the start of a baseball game with the Blue Jays.

Domingos, Horácio da Cruz

Village of Urros, Province of Trás-os-Montes

Horácio Domingos

The well known businessman and meat industrial Horácio da Cruz Domingos was born in the village of Urros, in the province of Trás-os-Montes, on December 1, 1943. In Portugal, he was a reputed butcher and, in Canadá, after a period of two years where he performed many tasks, including construction– a fate which marks every immigrant – he began his profession. Horácio came to Canada in 1968.

On July 25, 1970, Horácio Domingos married, in Toronto, with Maria Emília, a young girl from the town of Gouveia, near Serra da Estrela

(Estrela's Mountain). Two children were born to the couple: Carlos, who finished his Business Administration degree at Sheridan College, and Nancy, a graduate with an Industrial Relations Degree from the University of Toronto. They both work with their parents.

His experience with cattle and an ambition to triumph in life made him enter the world of business in the cattle industry, soon after marrying Maria Emília. Thus, he began his profession in 1974 and since then he has successfully owned and managed Domingos Wholesale Meats. The company's office is in Toronto, but he

Horácio Domingos with his wife Maria Emília showing the Medal of Merit.

lives with his family in Brampton, between Mississauga Road and Highway 10, north of Steeles Avenue. In a farm that he owns in a small village, between Arthur and Orangeville, Horácio has a slaughterhouse where they breed about 500 pigs.

At the beginning of his career, Horácio Domingos used to breed all types of cattle, but lately he has been concentrated in the breeding of pigs. In his farm in Brampton, Horácio has ten race horses for family and friends. From the beginning, Horácio Domingos has been a friend of the clubs and associations of the community, helping almost all of them. He is also a founding member of the Portuguese Club of Mississauga and of the Portuguese Community Club of Chatham. Horácio was one of the members responsible for the purchase of the headquarters of the Portuguese Club of Mississauga, serving as a member of the committee and "godfather" of the Folkloric Group.

The opening of the magnificent Portuguese Cultural Centre of Mississauga was one of his happiest moments. The effort and the generosity put forward by Horácio in this accomplishment were recognized by the Portuguese government and by the community. Horácio can consider himself a winner. A successful business and a strong united family. How many people can say the same thing? Cardiac problems forced him to slow down, but wherever he is, Horácio does not go by unnoticed, due to his bursts of laughter. All the best.

JMC - 2000

Horácio Domingos receiving from the hands of the Secretary of State of the Portuguese Communities José Lello the diploma of the communities.

Eleutério, Jaime Manuel Moniz

Village of Santa Cruz, Lagoa, S. Miguel, Azores

In the village of Santa Cruz, located in the town of Lagoa, in the island of S. Miguel, Jaime Manuel Moniz Eleutério was born on July 7, 1930. From a very early age, he got used to the smell of the fields, to the dew of the morning. He embraced, without a choice, the farming profession. When he found out that Canada was recruiting people to work on the construction of the railroad (the CNR), Jaime Eleutério did not think twice. He signed a contract and travelled with six hundred fellow travellers abroad the Nea Healls, arriving in Halifax on April 29, 1954. The contract with CNR was valid for one year. In order to take advantage of the long days of the summer time, he worked for CNR for 19 months. As he remembers, with him travelled Mr. Morais, from

Jaime Manuel Moniz Eleutério.

the town of Vila Franca, who was hired to help the Portuguese emigrants from S. Miguel. But they never had his help.

To begin his Canadian adventure, Jaime Eleutério went from Halifax to Montreal, to Barrie and then to Northern Ontario where he began working in the railroad. In November of 1955, Jaime Eleutério decided to settle down in Toronto. For the next five to six years, Eleutério would work in landscaping. In the summer, he would also go to work in the tobacco farms, since it was a very lucrative job. In 1957, Jaime found a job at the Reliable Furs factory, located in the intersection of Richmond and Spadina. He would keep that job for three years. In November of 1959, he decided to go back to S. Miguel where he got married, on January 11, 1960, to Maria da Conceição Freitas de Melo. Maria was also a native of Lagoa, where she was born on February 22, 1938. Jaime came back to Toronto in March, and his wife joined him a year later, in April of 1961.

On June 22, 1962, the couple saw the birth of their daughter Margarida, who is today married and a mother of four children. As soon as he returned

Jaime, Eduardo da Silva, João Luís Moisés and Leonel Mântua. First row: José Rolino, José Maria Pires and António Correia de Melo, in 1954.

to Toronto, Jaime began working at Shopsy's, on Spadina, a job he would keep for six years. From here, and for two years, Jaime worked for Clifside Pipelayers. He left Clifside to go work, after many tries, for the Peel Board of Education where he stayed until his retirement.

Both Jaime and his wife are not very involved in the community's social life. Still, back in the 60s, Jaime was a member of the Portuguese Club, when José Meneses was the president.

The group of men from S. Miguel who left to Canada on April 23, 1954, at the Governor's Palace.

Jaime always had two passions: gardening and music. Back home, he was a trumpet player for the band Estrela D'Alva, from Santa Cruz. In Canada, he tried to be a member of the first Portuguese Band in Toronto, Senhor Santo Cristo's, but due to respiratory problems, Jaime had to give up on his idea. The Eleutério's also like to travel. Before his mother-in-law's illness, they used to go very often to the USA to visit family and friends. They have been a few times to S. Miguel, and Nova Scotia, where their daughter now lives with her husband and children. The Eleutério's are planning to return to Nova Scotia: the grandchildren are a temptation to this couple. Perhaps Jaime still has a bit of energy to teach his grandchildren how to play the trumpet. Why not?

JMC - 1999

Certificate of nationality given to Jaime Eleutério, in Toronto, by Annette Galaka.

Tobacco farm. On top, Jaime Eleutério. Bottom: Floriano Arruda, boss' niece.

The Eleuterio's with their grandchildren: Lans, Joshua, Joseph and Mehgen.

Faria, Augusto Ferrás de

Village of Olival, town of
Vila Nova de Ourém

Maria da Piedade and Augusto de Faria

Meet one of the nicest couples in our community: Maria da Piedade and Augusto de Faria. Augusto was born in Olival, a small town in Vila Nova de Ourém, on July 31st, 1927. His father, a professional carpenter, taught his son the love for the profession. Augusto's father was successful and his son became one of the best in the field. In 1958, Augusto emigrated to France where he worked for seven long years. Unhappy with his situation in France, he began thinking about emigrating again to another country. Canada was the chosen destination where he arrived on April 13, 1965. He began his journey in Winnipeg ending up in Toronto, after four months. He dwells in this latter city since then.

The couple Luísa and Rui Faria, with their sons, just before the accident that took their lives.

Maria Piedade Santos was born in Seiça, another small town in Vila Nova de Ourém, on December 11, 1930. Maria and Augusto were married on Caxarias Church, in Vila Nova de Ourém, on July 22, 1953. Maria da Piedade only came to live with her husband in Toronto, in November of 1965. The couple had three sons, all born in Caxarias, Vila Nova de Ourém. Rui was born on July 22, 1953 and is an architect; Irene was born on February 19, 1955 and is a professional accountant; Tito was born on October 16, 1956 and holds a Bachelor of Education and is the principal at Don Mills High School.

Tragedy hit the Faria's on December 31st, 1989: the eldest son, Rui, died, together with his wife Luisa, in an accident in Bahamas where they were spending holidays. They left behind two sons: Ian and Christopher who were adopted by their uncle Tito. Together with his wife Isabel, who is a psychologist, Tito has dedicated much of his life to the well being of these two boys. Rui Faria, a well-known architecture, was one of the references of the Portuguese community in Toronto, both for his professional and humane skills. His passing was a great loss for everyone.

Back to Maria da Piedade and Augusto, the couple became known for their great sense of unity among their relatives. The tragedy that hit the family in 1989 only helped to bring everyone closer together. Walking the path he had chosen in Canada, Augusto has always worked in this field of specialization. He worked for sev-

The Faria's at a family reunion.

eral companies for many years and in 1983 he decided to found his own carpentry company. Talking about the sacrifices he made, Augusto says they were all worth the pain they caused. He bought his first home in 1966, on Brunswick Avenue, in Toronto, for thirty thousand dollars. At that time, it was a small fortune. However, with the help of his wife and children, Augusto was able to accomplish all his dreams.

Maria da Piedade and Augusto with friends at a picnic on Madeira Park.

Today, they are both retired and living a good life. They are active members at the First Portuguese Canadian Club and at the Canadian Madeira Club. Every year, they visit their homeland, but have elected Toronto as their favorite city to live until the end of their days.

We wish them all the best.

JMC - 1997

Faria, Dr. Carlos (Carl)

Dr. Carlos de Faria

The well known lawyer, Dr. Carlos de Faria, was the first Portuguese-Canadian to be elected Member of the Provincial Parliament, in Ontario, in the ward Mississauga-East, representing the Progressive Conservative Party, in June of 1995. In 1999, he was re-elected, having the honor of becoming as well the first Portuguese-Canadian to be named minister in Ontario by premier Ernie Eves. He took over as Minister

of Citizenship and Minister Responsible for Seniors) on April 15, 2002.

He ran for the third time in 2003, but lost to another Portuguese Canadian

Carl de Faria hands a medal to the substitute member of portuguese parliament Laurentino Esteves, with the applause of consul general, Dr. João Perestrello.

– Peter Fonseca – who was representing the Liberal Party headed by Dalton McGuinty who became premier on October 23.

Carlos de Faria got his Bachelor of Arts in Economics and Finance at the University of Toronto and went on to study Law at Osgoode Hall. As a student, he worked as a Social Assistant for the Peel Children's Aid Society. He is one of the co-founders of Vila Corte Real, a non-profit organization for families with low income. As a minister, Carl de Faria was a delegate of the 38th Canadian Regional Conference of the Commonwealth Parliamentary Association, in Quebec City, held in August of 1999. Also in

Carl de Faria presiding the Canada Day Celebrations in 2002 at Queen's Park.

1999, he was elected director of the Assemblée Parlementaire de la Francophonie, in Ontario. Minister Carl de Faria presided the Canada Day celebrations in 2002, at Queen's Park, an event which gathered thousands of people at the Ontario's legislature.

Carl de Faria is married to the lawyer Riina, who was nominated to represent the Conservative Party in Mississauga East during the Federal Elections of 2004.

Carl de Faria received a badge from the Order of Infante D. Henrique from José Luiz Gomes, ambassador of Portugal in Ottawa, on April 28, 2002.

JMC - February of 2004

At the Portuguese Ambassy, Dr. José Luiz Gomez, ambassador of Portugal, joins, with consul general Dr. João Perestrello, the individuals who received insignias from the Government of Portugal: Father António Araújo, Monsigneur Resendes, Dr. Luís Moura Sobral, Ruy Paes Braga, Maria Odete Nascimento, Iria Fátima Vieira and Dr. Carl de Faria, in May of 2002.

Minister Carl de Faria, presiding the Portugal Day Celebrations by the Portuguese Monument in honor of Portuguese Pioneers in High Park.

Fernandes, José Joaquim

Village of Tângil, town of Monção,

Province of Minho

José Joaquim Fernandes

His face reveals the courage this man has had to make many decisions throughout his life. He is one of those individuals who is not afraid to fight and who never turns his face to sacrifices. José Joaquim Fernandes was born in Tângil, a small village of Monção, in the north of Portugal, on December 12, 1926. At a very early age, he began working in the fields to help his father. As a child, he completed the first mandatory years of schooling and had the cows and the hard work of the fields as his "main toys" to play with.

Also in Tângil, Maria das Dores Teixeira de Sá was born on October 4, 1936. She married José Joaquim in the church of São Salvador de Tângil, on May 7, 1961. They have known each other since they were children and hope to stay together until the end of their days. Still living in Tângil, the couple had two children: José António and Noémia das Dores. Searching for a better life, José Joaquim left Portugal, aboard the Olympia ship, on May 19, 1955. He arrived in Halifax, Canada, on May 23rd. After having spent a night in Halifax, the Immigration Services of Canada decided to send him by train to Hamilton, in Ontario. In Caledonia, Hamilton, José Joaquim began his journey doing what he had done all his life: milking the cows and working on the fields. He lived in Caledonia for one year, making $60.00 a month.

In 1956, his uncle Luís António Fernandes, who was living in California, visited him in Hamilton. Taking a break from his hard life, José Joaquim went for a walk with his uncle. As if fate was taking a different turn on José Joaquim's life, they encountered a group of friends who were cutting the lawn. After a long talk to his friends, José Joaquim decided not to return to the farm where he was working, opting for a landscaping job. At this new job site, José Joaquim could count with the help of his friends Manuel Lima da Rocha (already deceased) and Manuel

Maria das Dores and José Joaquim on the day of their wedding in 1961.

Fernandes Araújo, now owner of Gladstone Motors. He worked in landscaping for eleven years, in Mississauga, where he lived ever since.

In 1966, his wife Maria das Dores and his children José António (4 years old) and Noémia das Dores (2 years old) joined him, in Mississauga. José Joaquim was tired of being alone. The same year his family came to live with him, José Joaquim began working for the firm Scott Jack, a construction company specializing in digging tunnels. Even though his work was much harder, José Joaquim was making more money to provide for his family. Five years later, he began working for the firm McNelly. Beneath the soil, his job was hard, but it paid well. For José Joaquim, working in the tunnels became a job he liked because it

was not too cold and not too hot, in a country where winters are freezing cold and summers are very humid. For him, it was more pleasant than working in the "exterior". His commitment and dedication to his job were noticed by his boss who named José Joaquim "Worker of the Year".

The following eleven years were spent in the construction of the three terminals at Pearson International Airport, in Toronto, for a company owned by a group of Italians, the best bosses José Joaquim has had in his entire life. At the airport, he was responsible for the plumbing. After many years of hard work, in 1992 José Joaquim decided to retire.

Retirement, however, does not mean "stopping" for José Joaquim. He still dedicates part of his life to small works. His busy life never allowed him to dedicate any time to social clubs in the community, but José Joaquim said he would help once in a while whenever he could. He helped build two Portuguese churches in Mississauga and is still part of the Portuguese religious celebrations. Because he still owns some land in Portugal, he often flies to his homeland to take care of his properties.

José Fernandes, José António, Noémia and Maria das Dores Fernandes.

In 1999, while in Portugal, he felt his wife's death. Not capable of explaining what he was feeling, José Joaquim heard a voice whispering the sad news to his ears. Two hours before "hearing" this voice, José Joaquim had spoken with his wife by phone, because Maria das Dores was leaving on that day to Portugal to spend some time with him. As she was leaving her house, she fell down the stairs, hit her head hard and died instantly. It was the worst and saddest moment of his life, one he will never forget. Maria das Dores Fernandes died on May 20, 1999.

Noémia, José Joaquim, Maria das Dores and José António in their house, in Mississauga.

José Joaquim remembers many trips he made with his wife to France, the USA, Brazil and Portugal. Today, with his eyes filled with sadness, José Joaquim lives with his son José António. His daughter Noémia das Dores married and has given him a grandson. Nowadays, José Joaquim lives half of the time in Canada and the other half in Portugal.

José Joaquim is a strong, healthy man; the portrait of faithful Portuguese emigrant.

JMC-1997

Ferreira, Crescêncio José

City of Funchal,
Madeira Island

Who does not know the friendly face of Crescêncio Ferreira who has been working for more than 30 years at

Portugal's secretary of estate, José Lello, implementing Crescêncio Ferreira the badge from the Government of Portugal.

the Portuguese Consulate of Portugal in Toronto? The ever young and smiling Crescêncio José Ferreira was born on September 22, 1936, in the city of Funchal, in Madeira Island.

- How did you decide to leave the beautiful and warm Madeira Island to live in this cold, unknown Canada?

- Well! – Crescêncio began explaining – everything began with a sponsorship letter that my brother José Manuel sent me. He came here on June 2, 1953. He was the only Portuguese from Madeira Island who was part of the first group of people with a contract to work in Canada. They left the city of Funchal on May 26 and arrived in Halifax on June 2, 1953.

- So, when did you and your older brother, Adriano, arrived in Canada? Did you already had the way paved? – We insinuated.

- Oh yes! We were not wondering as two blind men! – He answered, always smiling.

- How was your trip?

- It was pleasant, but long. My brother Adriano and I arrived in Ontario on February 2, 1955, through Fort Erie. We came by train, via New York, where we had arrived the previous day aboard the ship Saturnia. The first Canadian port that I saw was Halifax where the Saturnia touched, on February 31st…

- At that time, was there a lot of snow?

- Snow?! – our pioneer laughed, looking back at that distant, but not forgotten past. – My God, there were mountains of snow everywhere. Halifax and New York were blankets of snow, literally speaking… At that time, I could only think about Madeira…

- Did you regret you had left Madeira?

- No, I don't think so! I would say I felt confused! – Crescêncio answered, still trying to remember those days.

- What about Toronto? Did you find a similar scenario?

- No! In Toronto, there wasn't as much snow and I liked that a lot. A week after arriving in Toronto, I went to the Consulate of Portugal to register myself. At that time, it was an honorary consulate and the serving consul was Verner Willemsen… Due to the number of Portuguese people that were arriving in the country, the consulate needed one more employee. I decided to apply for the job and was hired!

Ferreira brothers, all pioneers, with the consul general of Portugal, the day of the tribute to the pioneers during Christmas of 1985. From left to right: Crescêncio, José Manuel, Dr. Tânger Correia, and Adriano Ferreira.

- And you have worked there until today?

- Yes. I began working at the Consulate on February 21, 1955… A year later, the consulate went from being honorary to a career consulate. – He continued, always revealing a face of genuine happiness. – On February 2, 1968, I was promoted to chanceller, a function I still hold today. I have been witnessing the progress of this community for 31 years…

Crescêncio Ferreira is a pioneer with a different story. He arrived, he saw and he conquered. All the merit to him! During those hard times, he was able to conquer by his own merit the position he so scrupulously keeps at the Consulate of Portugal in Toronto. Did anyone notice his commitment and dedication?

- Well, I fulfill my obligations the best I can and know, without worrying about being noticed or recongnized in any way. Last year, I was very touched by the gesture the consul general, Dr. Tânger Correia, had towards me. Together with my colleagues, he honoured the 30 years of service I have in the Consulate. I was very happy… - Crescêncio admitted, showing a bit of shyness.

Crescêncio José Ferreira is the oldest employee at the Consulate of Portugal in Toronto, having helped, throughout all these years, many diplomats, employees and thousands of Portuguese people in many ways.

- Back then – Crescêncio said – it was very difficult for those who had no knowledge of English to live well in this country. Fortunately, my brothers and I knew a little English, which helped us a lot. José Manuel – the pioneer among us three – has been working for Ford for the past 20 years. Adriano, after some years at Loblaws, has been working at the Royal York where he is the manager of the Convention Floor… We are all well, fortunately!

It is pleasant to hear a pioneer say "we are all well!" It is like going to the theatres to see a drama that has a happy ending.

Crescêncio Ferreira receiving the "Pioneer Medal" from consul general of Portugal in Toronto.

- Do you have any interesting / funny story you would like to share with us from those times?

- Yes! There is always something that happens to you. – he said looking at a distant point as if searching for one particular moment. – The first months we were in Canada, it was a miracle to hear someone speak Portuguese. One day – we lived on Yonge just south of Wellesley – we were walking home, after work, and obviously were speaking Portuguese, I noticed a young lady – who looked about 18 years old – try-

The pioneer of the pioneers: José Manuel at the ceremony in recognition of the pioneers with consul general of Portugal in Toronto.

ing to listen to us. At a certain point, I was very puzzled at her curiosity and asked her if she were Portuguese. To my surprise, she answered in Portuguese that she was not Portuguese but spoke the language because she was born in St. John's where her mother had a bar where many Portuguese fishermen attended. She had learned Portuguese with our "cod sellers"… Interesting!

- And your brothers, do they have any stories they share at family gatherings?

- I cannot think of one, at the moment! – Crescêncio told us. – When we get together, my brother José Manuel usually tells us he remembers the day he arrived in Canada – June 2, 1953 – because they were celebrating the Queen of England's coronation. It was Elizabeth II's coronation.

- As a native from Madeira, were you part of the group, which founded the Canadian

Madeira Club?

- Of course! – he answered right away. – I am a founding member and hold the member-ship card #58. We founded the club on July 4, 1963. It was our escape from the daily problems. Madeira Park is a wonder. Today, I am not nearly as active at the club due to my functions at the Consulate. However, I am proud to be a founding member.

Time flew without us noticing it. Our interviewee could not be with us any longer due to the many calls he was receiving. We left the pleasant Crescêncio José Ferreira with his work at the consulate, lost in the midst of his well organized papers. Crescêncio is a true gentleman. He has spent many decades serving his country and countrymen. Crescêncio José Ferreira is a pioneer who serves as a role model.

JMC - July / August of 1986

Ferreira, Humberto de Brum

Town of Rabo de Peixe,
Island of São Miguel, Azores

Mr. Humberto de Brum Ferreira

Always keeping a low profile, he has done a lot for the community. Humberto de Brum Ferreira was born in Rabo de Peixe, in the island of S. Miguel, on September 10, 1938. He had a normal childhood, always dedicating his time to his studies. He became an elementary school teacher, a degree he earned at Escola do Magistério Primário de Ponta Delgada, in S. Miguel, on July 24, 1957. He began his professional life on August 26, 1960.

Between 1965 and 1969, still in Ponta Delgada, Humberto Ferreira served many organizations in the religious, social, educational and sports sectors. Fate would bring Humberto to Canada. He was the first teacher in Toronto – and maybe in Canada and the USA – to teach elementary Portuguese (grades 5 and 6) from 1970 to 1974. Always teaching at the First Portuguese Canadian Club, Humberto taught for 29 consecutive years, from 1969 to 1998.

His resume also includes teach-

Principal of the First Portuguese School, Celina de Melo, giving Mr. Ferreira the book about emigration, written by deputy Manuela Aguiar, who is signing Mr. Ferreira's book.

ing grades 7,8 and 9 in 1977/78, the same year he taught the course of Heritage Languages. In 1970, the first year the grade 4 exams were held in Toronto, Humberto was member of the examiner's team. For 29 years, at the First Portuguese Canadian Club, he served as member of the school council and secretary of the administrative group.

At the same time, Humberto Ferreira continued his studies at the University of Toronto: after completing grade 13 in French and English, he went on to obtain a degree in international languages, which he finished in 1983. He has participated in many conferences and symposiums, such as the one celebrating 50 years of Portuguese teaching at University of Toronto, in 1997.

Always requested to help his community, Humberto helped many organizations: he was the correspondent for the newspaper "Diário dos Açores", between 1965 and 1969 and columnist in many local newspapers. He published the book "Escola do First Portuguese Canadian Club – 25

Humberto de Brum Ferreira, by the side of Celina Melo and School Trustee Christine Ferreira, at the First Portuguese Canadian Club.

anos de História", in 1989 and was co-writer for "Gente de Rabo de Peixe" with Manuel Falcão Viveiros Estrela, in Fall River, in 1996. He has been the official writer for the First Portuguese, having written three books about the History and Social Events of the Club. He reviewed the books "Quadras de Ternura" by Gabriel Maria de Sousa, in Ponta Delgada, published in 1999, wrote the preface for the book "A História das Medalhas", by Lourenço Rodrigues Gonçalves, in 1985 and reviewed "Os Bastardos da Pátria".

Throughout his career, Humberto Ferreira received many awards for his work: in 1984, the newspaper Correio Português gave him a Merit Award; the medal of the Arts by the minister of heritage and citizenship of Ontario, Bob Wong, in 1989. In 1991, back home, in Ponta Delgada, he received the municipal merit award for contributing to the expansion of the Portuguese culture outside Portugal. Humberto Ferreira was also awarded the Portuguese Communities Merit Medal, given by the secretary Dr. Manuel Filipe Correia de Jesus, on July 13, 1991.

Humberto de Brum Ferreira is a true defendant of the Portuguese language and culture in Canada. It was in the name of this love that he taught portuguese for 41 years; 12 in S. Miguel and 29 in Toronto. Even though he retired, he is still an active member at the school. Humberto Ferreira transformed teaching into "priesthood". Casa dos Açores Community Centre has paid him a homage for all his work. Thank you, Mr. Ferreira.

JMC - 2000

Humberto de Brum Ferreira at a conference at Casa do Alentejo.

Ferreira, João de Jesus

Lapa Neighbourhood, Lisbon

The pioneer João de Jesus Ferreira is such a nice person that his friends call him João Banana! If you do not call him by his nickname among his friends, no one knows who he is. João may have the nickname he does, but let it be said – he is a very clever individual.

João de Jesus Ferreira was born on May 23, 1928, on Lapa, a small district in Lisbon. He is married to the pioneer Celeste Ferreira, who was born on December 11, 1929, in Socorro, Lisbon. They got married on May 31, 1953 at Alcântara's church.

- We have two children. – João began saying. – The eldest, César António, was born in Lisbon, in 1953, and the youngest, Fernando, was already born in Toronto, on June 4, 1966.

- Did you come to Canada with your family?

- I came in 1958! – João continued. – I came by plane – the old propeller ones – from Lisbon on September 9, 1958 and arrived the same day in Canada. We stopped in Montreal and Toronto. It was a 12 hour flight.

- And I arrived on October 11, 1959. César sat on my lap the entire trip! – Celeste concluded with a smile on her lips.

Celeste and João Ferreira with their friend Noémia.

- What was your first job, João?

- Job? The year I arrived, it was hell to find a job. The American factories had closed down. No jobs and no money! Only six months after arriving I was able to find a job. I went to Bradford, to harvest potatoes and carrots.

- How did you survive the first six months?

- I slept at a friend's house – we called him Bolas. He went back to the Algarve, where he now has a laundry and works at a hotel. Not too long ago, I met him in Lisbon and was able to remember the good old days. I am sure I still owe him some rents! – After laughing at this last comment, he said: - I used to have a coffee and a donut the whole day. I had another friend – Vilarinho's brother – who was getting $30 from the unemployment, give me half so that I could survive. They were a really nice group. I still miss them. Sometimes, I would eat at Sousa's Restaurant and pay whenever I could...

- Why don't you tell us about your first Christmas in Canada? – Celeste asked him.

- Don't even mention that! – he said, but continued: - Without a job and without money, all I had was the extreme cold weather to keep me company... That day, I received a letter from my father with $5 inside. I cried like a baby! I don't know how he guessed my situation.

- It was really sad! – Celeste whispered.

- After this first job in Bradford, what did you do?

- Canada's Immigration sent me to the Uranium mines, in Eliot Lake. Before that though, I worked for a little while at the railroad.

- How were things at Eliot Lake?

- So, so. I was only there for three months. I came back to Toronto and because there were no jobs to be found, I decided to go to Halifax, where I began working as an "engine driver" for the Seafood Co. From here, I moved to Gibson Co., a firm with long voyage boats. I still have my driver's licence.

- How did you return to Toronto?

- Well, during this time, my wife and son arrived in Toronto.

A typical party at Benfica House of Toronto with "O meu barbeiro", João Ferreira and Artur Ferreira.

- As soon as I got here, I found a job immediately – Celeste said. – João had no job, but I was working at a shoe factory. Only God knows how much I cried for not being able to understand what people were telling me. Coming from Lisbon and starting to work in Canada, without understanding the language, in a very cold environment, was very hard. I shed many tears.

- How long were you at the factory?

- Quite a long time. I was making 25 cents an hour. I am now working at Leslie Metrics, on the assembly line. I like what I do. I have been there for 20 years.

- João, how were things with you?

- João could not find a job, but he was always happy! – Celeste provoked him and continued: - João, João Nunes – the fado singer – António Paradas and some others whose names I no longer remember, decided to drive up to Simcoe to work in the tabbaco fields. They brought with them a guitar, an accordion and some other instruments. They were partying everyday,

Homage to fado singer Fernando Farinha, in Toronto. In the picture we see João Ferreira, F. Farinha, Chico Alentejano (deceased) and local fado singer João Nunes.

until very late at night! Some days later, they were kicked out of the farm and came back to Toronto the same way they left – empty handed, without anything.

With this story, João could not resist laughing. That is the way João Ferreira is: to live the easiest life.

Our conversation took place at the Nazaré Recreative Club, in Toronto, a club the couple liked particularly. We wanted to know the reason for this preferance.

- Here, at the Nazaré, we spend some good moments. These people from Nazaré like to dance and to have fun. They don't need a lot to make a big party. – Celeste said.

Larry Grossman receiving the Merit Diploma from the First Portuguese Canadian Club. From left to right: António Vicente, C. Custódio, M. Grossman, João Ferreira, Marcelino Moniz, and a couple of young people from Nazaré.

- We are members of this club and have here many friends! – João Ferreira continued. – We like the club and the folkloric group. Last year, the club closed down for a few months for lack of directors. It would be a shame if it had come to an end. Amadeu Vaz, Zé Vão, Mário, Zé da Florência, Silvino and myself decided to form a commission to run the club. We were able to accomplish our goal. We ran the club from October of 1987 to April of 1988. The club is now running well again.

João Ferreira is a man who likes, by nature, to help everyone. From his first day in Canada, he has joined many groups and helped found many clubs. Was it worth it?

- Oh boy! All I had were problems and headaches! – João answered. – I was one of the founding members of the First Portuguese Canadian Club. Paixão, Custódio, Artur Rodrigues and myself were the responsible group for the soccer activities of the club. The First Portuguese player "imported" to Canada was Matateu. I dedicated so much time to the club that my son began playing accordion there, when he was 15 years old...

- It was there that he found his first musical group Estrela Azul (Blue Star). – Celeste remembered, showing a glimpse of homesickness. – My César used a blue suit all the time and decided, because of that, to name the group Estrela Azul.

- At the time, there were already two musical groups – Boa Esperança and Sombras – if I am not mistaken. – João Ferreira said.

- Besides organizing the soccer section, what other responsibilities did the group have?

- We requested and were able to open the Portuguese School, in 1964. the pioneers of this school were Custódio, Paixão, Gonçalves, Pedradas' brother-in-law, and myself. The first teacher was Dona Branca Gomes and the first director was Débora Raposo!

- Weren't there any problems at that time?

- Were there?! – João said. – My wife was very ill at the hospital. I was the treasurer of the club. I used to pay the bills without passing any receipts, lacking time and experience in these things... I was called a thief! Had it not been for the deceased Chico Alentejano, who had seen me paying some of those bills, I don't know what would have happened. I worked very hard, paid many bills from my own pocket and I was still called a thief! When I left I said I would not be involved in anything else ever again!

- If it were up to me, João would never have been involved in anything. But that's the way he is. At that time, I remember him paying $400 from his own pocket. – Celeste opened her heart.

After this confidence, João said:

- I didn't found the Benfica House of Toronto, but was very close to it. I was a member during the time the Ferreira brothers were directors. The Benfica House of Toronto was born in the Império Restaurant.

- Many associations were born at Império...

- That's right. – He agreed. – It was at Império that Lino, António Vicente, Alvarez and the Ferreira Brothers decided to found the House, almost as a joke!

- It was also at Império that the organization of events, such as weddings, special banquets, musical tours, among others, began taking place in our community.

Having diverted from our main topic of conversation, we went back to the time when João arrived in Canada and had such a hard time finding a job...

- Oh yeah! At that time, I decided to work in construction, a job that lasted until about 1965. that year, I applied for a job at Douglas, a company responsible for the manufacturing of airplane wings, and I was hired. I have been there since 1965. My son Fernando also works there. If I don't die until then, I will retire in 1990.

- And you, Mrs. Celeste, When do you plan to retire?

- When I turn 65! I still have a few years to go...

- Oh, you wish! – João retaliated. – when I retire you will also retire! We will go

First team of the First Portuguese C.C. Standing up: Telmo Vilazinho, Ricardo Fereira (deceased), F. Ramalho, Benjamim, the Azorean, Zé Alentejano, Zeca Algarvio, Viegas; Pequenino, Chico Espanhol, João and Manozinho Madeirense. Second row: António Silva, João Silva and the Alentejano (deceased).

camping in the summer and in the remaining months we'll go to Florida.

- Sure, sure...

- Do you ever think of going back to Portugal?

- João thought about that a few years ago. – Celeste said. – But he has forgotten about it... I must confess that I like Canada and I don't even feel like going to Portugal on holidays.

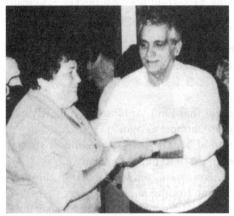

João Ferreira dancing with Celeste.

- We have everything here: our house, our children...

Debating the advantages and disadvantages of returning to Portugal, our conversation shifted to another topic: community events.

- It is with great honor that I participate in social events, specially the end of the year celebrations and tours with artists... I loved being with Carmen Mota and her ballet group, who was brought to Canada by Frank Alvarez. It was the first tour Alvarez organized with artists from Portugal. From that moment on, it was a never ending story. I loved interacting with Marco Paulo, Nilton César, Roberto Leal, Carmen Silva...

- After so many years, do you feel fortunate that you came to Canada?

- Without any doubt. We forgot the hard times, which contributed to the happy moments we now live. – João said, backed by his wife's compliments to Canada.

- We have everything we need to live well, as long as we stay healthy.

- Mrs. Celeste, do you still speak to anyone you met when you arrived in Canada?

- Yes, I do. I still go out with Noémia and Domingos Campos.

It was, for us, a rewarding experience interviewing our pioneers João and Celeste Ferreira at the Nazaré Recreative Club.

We hope João and Celeste continue to enjoy the life's delights in common with the happiness they have always had. May life continue to be sweet – just like a good banana from tropical countries.

JMC - December of 1988

Ferreira, Orlando dos Reis

Sítio do Ilhéu, Câmara de Lobos, Madeira Island

Our pioneer is one of relevance for us. He was the first one to play accordion and viola in the Portuguese community, melodies that brought great memories to many people. Orlando dos Reis Ferreira was born in the village of Sítio do Ilhéu, in Câmara de Lobos, Madeira Island, on January 6, 1929. From a very early age, he began selling fish at Câmara de Lobos' fish market, with his father and brothers. He was also a soccer player for the Club Sports Madeira, a player who achieved such a level of success that an unknown fan wrote the following verse about him:

Orlando, Filomena Celeste and their colleagues Zita and Óscar Pereira with son José António.

This is the new player
With a promising future
Among the 11 players
From the fishermen's town.

He played at Club Sports Madeira until 1953, the year he decided to emigrate to Canada. He still jokes about the fact of being the first Portuguese player to perform in Canada, in the White Eagles, making more in one game ($75) than in one entire season back in Madeira, where he would earn 29 escudos (about 20 cents) a game... Orlando dos Reis Ferreira was a child from a family of musicians and was also the first Portuguese to play accordion and viola in the community. He used to play to cheer up the parties at Bellwood's Park, when the few Portuguese living here used to get together to remember the good old times. At that time, José Mourinho (already deceased) joined him on the viola.

Around 1957, when Mariano Rego arrived in Canada, they got together to accompany the fado singers. Mariano Rego used to play the Portuguese guitar, Orlando on the viola, and sometimes the accordion, and would play for João Nunes, Rui de Mascarenhas and Maria de Lurdes Resende.

Mariano Rego, João Nunes and Orlando Ferreira.

With the latter, they went on a tour to Ottawa, Montreal Galt, London, Hamilton and Newark (USA). In 1964, Mariano and Orlando founded the first musical group, together with Felix Trindade and Carlos Pombo. Some time after, Pombo left and was replaced by Augusto Santos.

In 1966, Orlando decided to quit the group and began playing just to entertain friends and family, on weddings and baptisms, with Abel from Nazaré, Mourinho and Manolo.

In 1956, a group of men from the mainland and the islands decided to get together to form a club. The group from the Azores wanted to name it Lusitânia, the ones from Madeira island wanted Marítimo, and the group from the mainland was divided between Benfica and Sporting... After many discussions, the group from Madeira Island joined the one from the mainland and decided to name the club First Portuguese

Canadian Club. Thus, in 1956, Orlando Ferreira began playing soccer for the First Portuguese. He was a founding member and athlete.

Orlando is best known among friends by the nickname "Estragado", a nickname he explains the following way: His father – Francisco – was a strong man who used to leave the house dressed properly and return looking like a pauper! Orlando's grandfather used to tell him: "You are a waste (estragado)". At that time, another man from Madeira Island, also by name Francisco had returned to the island from Brazil. To avoid any confusion at the financial department, one was named Francisco

The four brothers: Ângelo (who arrived in Canada in 1960), João Ferreira (1956), Orlando (sponsored all his brothers), and Francisco (1959). A family of musicians.

Ferreira – The Brazilian, and the other Francisco Ferreira – Estragado. This way the entire family became known as the Estragados.

Life in Canada was not always a sweet melody. Orlando – who got married shortly before emigrating to Canada to Filomena Celeste Sousa Ferreira, at Câmara de Lobos Church, on April 30, 1953, began working on a farm in Milton picking mushrooms. Sometime after, he moved to another farm where he would take care of the cows and pigs. From here, he moved to Toronto where he began working in construction with his cousin João Pestana, digging and building the subway system. They both used a crucifix hanging on a necklace and their boss told them to get rid of it.

Being very religious, they refused to do it and were fired for not obeying the orders. So, they moved again to another job site, this time to work at Bussels Restaurant for three months. To help the other fellow friends who did not have a job, they used to steal chickens, hide them in the coat pockets and bring them home. The chef used to have the habit of pushing people around by grabbing their arms. Orlando did not like that and the second time the chef did that to him, Orlando threw him against a wall and

went home: he had been fired again. On March 19, 1956, his wife, Filomena Celeste, arrived in Toronto. Here, the couple had six children: Orlando José, Filomena Maria, Dolores Olina, Ângela David, Lúcia and Luis. The latter one died in 1998 when he was swimming in Muskoka, when he was only 31 years old. His mother Filomena had died on July 26, 1976, also at a very young age.

Orlando married a second time with Maria Eugénia Faria, from Câmara de Lobos, on June 30, at St. Lawrence church, in Scarborough, where they

Orlando with his grandchildren.

still live. He continued his work in construction, first in Sarnia, where the company was building tunnels and then in London, going back to the farm. Tired of this job, Orlando came back to Toronto to begin working for the Ontario Seeds, where he was with José de Freitas, Sabino Gonçalves, Juvenal de Freitas, Juvenal Gomes, and Manuel Gomes. At this factory, he suffered an accident that forced him to undergo surgery. When he recuperated from the operation, he was told to find another job because the factory had nothing else for him. Accepting his fate, Orlando got a new job at Honfield Bros, a doll factory, for a very short time, and then moved on to Presswood Bros, a factory for processing pork meat, which was sold to Swift in 1962. Orlando worked for this company for more than 30 years. He got early retirement and WCB, due to job injuries. He stopped working in 1986.

Back in 1963, the Portuguese from Madeira Island got together at Carlos da Atouguia's farm

Orlando and second wife Filomena, with their children and children-in-law.

and founded the commission that got the money to buy the Madeira Park, which is still today the pride and joy of those who come from the island. After buying the park, they decided to found the Canadian Madeira Club, which had the first hall on Adelaide Street, at Santa Maria's church.

Orlando dos Reis Ferreira is proud to be the first to have begun certain initiatives in the Portuguese community. He is also very proud of his big family: they are so many that sometimes he does not remember their names. One of his grandsons plays soccer and two of his granddaughters play piano and trumpet. He may not remember their names, but Orlando is loved by all of them.

JMC - 2000

Fonseca, Peter

Lisbon

Peter Fonseca on campaign.

The Portuguese Canadian Peter Fonseca was born in Lisbon, but grew up in Toronto. He came to Canada, with his parents, in 1968. He was always a very skinny, but healthy boy, with a love for sports. He has won many marathons: both in sports and in politics.

In sports, he was the only Portuguese Canadian to represent Canada in the Olympic Games of 1996, in Atlanta. He was also the best Canadian at the marathon, conquering 21st place in 2 hours, 17 minutes, and 28 seconds.

During his golden period, Peter Fonseca went back to Lisbon to represent the team Sporting Club of Portugal with success. Peter Fonseca won 2nd place in Toronto's marathon, in 1994, the same year he also got 2nd place in Houston. Back in 1990, he finished 3rd in the marathon of Los Angeles and in 1992, he also finished 3rd in New York.

Peter was considered Athlete of the Year when he was attending St. Michael's College School and won the All-American, All-Canadian and Scholar Athlete Awards from the University of Oregon. Peter Fonseca also won the Fred Bagley Memorial Trophy, an award which distinguishes the best Canadian runner.

Peter Fonseca at the 1996 Olympics in Atlanta.

After quitting the competitions, Peter Fonseca – who has a B.A. and B.Ed. – began working as Olympic Advisor and was in charge of the Canadian Olympic Centre for Training Corporate Excellence.

In 2002, Peter Fonseca decided to enter the world of politics. He was elected member of the provincial parliament, in Mississauga East, on October 23, 2003. Young and intelligent, Peter – a man who has Pierre Trudeau as a political reference – is capable of conquering a political career just as fulfilling as the one he has in sports.

JMC - 2004

Joe Pinto and Maggie Unção witness Peter Fonseca giving Manny Coelho a Certificate from the Government of Ontario to Project Diploma.

Fontes, Manuel Bento

Vila Franca do Campo, island of São Miguel, Azores

Manuel Bento Fontes was born in Vila Franca do Campo, in the island of S. Miguel, Azores, on November 26, 1932. He married – first by proxy and then at the church – with Regina Costa Amaral, from the same town, where she was born on May 4, 1958.

Manuel emigrated to Canada, landing on Duval Airport, Quebec, on March 29, 1956, with 200 other companions who went to live in many different places in Canada. Manuel and six other friends went to work at a farm where he had to crop apples and prune fruit trees. Manuel's brother, Ângelo (already deceased)

Manuel Bento Fontes

had arrived in 1954 and was living in Kitimat. He decided to find a job for his brother at the Alcan factory, a company specializing in aluminum. Manuel worked there for about three years. He left Kitimat in 1958 to return to the island of S. Miguel to get married. Coming back to Canada a while after, Manuel settled down in Montreal. His wife only came to Canada in 1961. The couple's children – Cidália, Dino, Natércia and Tommy – were all born in Montreal.

The Fontes with friends at Portuguese events.

Manuel found a job at the Tool Maker, a factory for machinery parts. Disliking the work environment, Manuel transferred to a clothing factory where he worked for ten years. He retired in 1999.

Manuel is a member of the club Casa dos Açores, in Quebec. The couple only went back to visit the Azores in 1996. They rather spend time in Montreal where they have their family and friends. Manuel loves soccer and still remembers the good old times when he used to play soccer for Casa do Povo in Vila Franca do Campo. Now, he does not miss one game on television. He also spends some time reading, a hobby he truly enjoys. To him, a book is a man's best friend.

JMC-1999

Forno, António Joaquim Pereira Alves

Village of Adoufe, city of Vila Real

Antônio Forno and first wife, Rosa, with two of his children.

Antônio Joaquim is a charismatic figure in the Portuguese Community of Chatham and Leamington. He was born in Adoufe, a small village in the northern city of Vila Real, on March 24, 1935. He completed his primary schooling in Peso da Régua and part of High School in the seminary of Santa Clara in Vila Real. After completing the military service, he went to the town of Valpaços where he was treasurer of the Agriculture Club. In Valpaços, he met and fell in love with Rosa Ramos da Costa, from Estorãos, Santiago de Valpaços, with whom he married on April 12, 1952.

The couple was blessed with 8 children, 7 born in Valpaços: Preciosa, Manuel, Domingos, Hernâni, Prazeres, Clara and Luís. In Chatham, the couple had their last son: Paulo. António do Forno came to Canada on May 4, 1966. He worked at a door factory for three months in Toronto and then moved to Chatham, where he has been living since then. In Chatham, he worked on the beet fields, construction and for seven years, at Motor Oil. In 1975, together with his wife, António opened the Portuguese Supermarket of Chatham. In 1977, António do Forno, already an active member of the Portuguese Community in many sectors, was appointed Public Notary by the consul general Dr. Barbosa Ferreira. From 1977 to 1980, António managed Forno's travel, his travel agency, which he moved to Leamington on August 4, 1980.

António has always been a great activist in the community. He joined a group of friends to found the Portuguese Canadian Social Club of Chatham, on March 15, 1971, where he was the first president. Today, he remains an active member. He is also a member of the Portuguese Club of Leamington, but does not hold any administrative position. A militant of the Social Democratic Party (PSD) in Portugal, he was the founder and director for many years of the PSD section of Southern Ontario.

António Forno receiving the FPCBP diploma from Armindo Silva.

He left PSD to be able to be a Delegate for the Council of Portuguese Communities and Treasurer of its Canadian section. He is no longer a delegate.

Nowadays, António do Forno still runs his travel agencies and is, since October of 2003, the honorary consul of Portugal for Southern Ontario, chosen by the Secretary of State, Dr. José Cesário. In 1980, he was awarded for the good services in favour of the community by the Canadian minister, Lily Munro, and in 1991, received the Merit Medal of the Portuguese Communities, from the Portuguese Secretary of State for the Communities, Dr. Correia de Jesus.

António Forno and second wife, Maria de Deus, attending an event in the Portuguese Community.

António do Forno is a member of the Order of the Knights of Columbus, an order for Roman Catholic men founded in 1882 by Father Michael J. McGivney. António do Forno obtained 4th grade in the order.

António's wife, Rosa, died in 1989. He married a second time, in 1993, with Maria de Deus Mota Amaral, from Povoação, in the island of S. Miguel. Maria Amaral has two children: Rick and Carmen. António do Forno lives a happy life in the company of his ten children and seventeen grandchildren.

JMC - 2003

Freitas, José de

Village of Santa Luzia, town of Funchal, Madeira Island

W here you least expect, you find a pioneer... I found this one in the town of Boliqueime, Algarve, the birth place of Prof. Cavaco Silva, former Prime Minister of Portugal. José de Freitas is known as the "Real Estate agent".

- Are you on holidays? – I asked.

- More or less. – José answered with a mysterious smile on his face. – I may end up staying on permanent holidays…

- You are too young to retire... - I insisted.

- It's true, but after 33 years of living in Canada, I believe I deserve to rest...

After the usual salutations, I accepted the invitation to go for a drink at his beautiful place in the Algarve. On the way, we found out a little more about our pioneer.

José de Freitas was born in the small town of Santa Luzia, Funchal, in Madeira Island, on May 27, 1925. He is married to

Conceição and José de Freitas, with grandsons Richard and Jeffrey, at their house, in the Algarve.

Conceição de Freitas. They have a son – Manuel – who lives in Toronto. José emigrated to Canada in 1953, arriving in Halifax on June 2nd. He came as part of a group of 105 people, all from Madeira Island, except one – Rui – who was from the mainland. When we arrived at his place in the Algarve, his wife served us two Canadian whisky's and we began our dialogue.

- My first job in Canada was on a mushroom farm, in Milton... Then, I moved to Toronto where I found a job at a seeds factory, then at a metal factory, a battery factory to end up at a bakery.

- How did you enter the Real Estate business?

- Well – he said, laughing – I was very young, but people used to think I was older because I had white hair. So, I decided to take the Real Estate course, followed by the Broker's license. I was the first Portuguese men in Toronto to have a Broker's license.

- What about agents, were there any in our community?

- Yes! Gaspar Lajes, Meneses and some others whose names I don't remember now, were already working in the Real Estate business.

- Do you remember any particular friend?

At José's house, in Toronto, the deceased Max, nieces Jackie and Landa, wife Conceição and friend Mirandolina.

-At that time, we were all friends, but I remember particularly well Ângelo Bacalhau, who has passed away.

José de Freitas stopped for a moment his narration to remember his friend. His face showed some sadness. How many moments of hope, struggle, happiness and sadness did they live together? I brought him back to reality with another question:

- Did you witness the birth of any clubs?

- Oh yes. The first chance to form a club happened in 1955, through an invitation by the German club, on Jarvis Street, in Toronto. Because the Portuguese men used to frequent that club, the administration invited us to be active members, with our own administrative body. We even chose some directors, but never put our plan to work.

- What happened after?

- Well, after, the people who were from Madeira Island, living in Toronto, decided to buy a park in 1963 to organize their events. The Canadian Madeira Club was also founded around that time. I am still a member of the club.

- Being a native of Madeira Island, why did you choose the Algarve to live? You no longer like the island?! – I asked, mocking him.

- Oh no! I love Madeira. I chose the Algarve to avoid the isolation of the island. This way I go back home every time I miss it.

- At the age of 61, you are still young to retire...

- Don't you think that after so many adventures in Canada I deserve to rest? I still have my broker's license, even though I no longer have an office. If I need to, I can go back and do what I know how to do best. I still haven't forgotten anything.

By our side, always smiling at her husband, there was Conceição. I asked her:

- Do you like Canada?

Father Antero de Melo blessing Conceição and José's rings, at their 25th wedding anniversary.

- I love Canada! – Conceição answered immediately. – I can actually say that Canada is my country.

- If it were up to her, we would move back to Toronto, right away. – José said.

- So, we will see each other soon, on the other side of the Atlantic. – I insisted.

- Probably. – José admitted. – I was not very lucky with some business deals I did recently in Toronto. So, I decided to come to the Algarve to rest. The future?... only God knows what can happen.

Conceição was still hopeful. Even their grandchildren, who were present, felt like their grandparents would go back. I, too, felt the same way. The Portuguese Community of Toronto cannot let go of one of its most precious pioneers. At the end I told him:

- So, see you soon!

José combed his hair using his fingers, looked at his wife, smiling, and asked:

Fraternization dinner. From left to right: Gabriel Freitas, Celina, José de Freitas, two musicians from the band 4 Latinos and Copacabana.

- Here or there?

Here or there, what does it matter? It is our fate to go from here to there, from there to here... Wherever it may be, we wish José and Conceição all the best and a healthy retirement... in the Algarve, where they still live.

September of 1986

Freitas, Juvenal de

Village of São Pedro, town of Funchal, Madeira Island

He is one of those pleasant people to talk to. Juvenal de Freitas was born in the village of S. Pedro, Funchal, on Madeira Island, on January 5, 1920. Juvenal married Agostinha de Freitas and had one son – Hugo – who now lives in Madeira where he runs his own business.

Juvenal completed the 5th year at the Industrial School of Funchal, where he attended evening classes. From 1941 to 1943, he served in the military forces. After the army, he worked for the Fiscal Police until 1953.

- I resigned from the police in order to come to Canada. I left Funchal on May 26, 1953, aboard the Nellas. We touched at the port of Halifax the evening of June 1st, but only disembarked on the 2nd. We were a group of 102 men, all from Madeira Island, except one – Rui Ribeiro – who was from the mainland.

- Where did you first work?

- I began at a fruit farm, in Vineland, near Niagara Falls.

Juvenal de Freitas at his desk at Azores Travel.

- How did you end up in Toronto?

- You know, one day, a group of friends and I decided to visit Toronto, to see the CNE... Obviously, it was nothing like it is today. In Toronto, we ran into José Freitas and Manuel Gomes. They mentioned a few job sites for us to try to find something, but we had no luck and went back to Vineland. Some time after, Álvaro Ferreira came back to Toronto, to see what was available... At that time, in our broken English, we asked the farmer if he had any work for us during the winter... He would not give us a definite answer, so we told him we were going to look for another job. Bad idea! – Juvenal said, laughing. – The following day, an offical from the Immigration Department was knocking at our door.

- What did he want?

- He wanted to know if we had paid for our ticket. Since we had paid for it with our own money, we didn't have any obligation according to the contract. We left to Toronto, trying to prepare for the winter months.

- And in Toronto, was it easier to find a job?

- I can't complain. My first job was at Bassels Restaurant, which no longer exists. From here, I went to a cement factory, and then to the Mount Pleasant Cemetery. – After giving us a malicious smile, he said: - I had to go back to the cement factory. At the same time, I applied for the CP railways and was hired not too long after. I began cleaning and ended up as carman. I was there for 16 years. In 1969, I decided to open a travel agency "Portuguese Travel Services" with my brother, Gastão. He is now living in Madeira.

- Were there any Portuguese travel agencies at that time in Toronto?

- Yes. There were a few. I remember Acadia and Império.

From left to right: Delegate from the USA, Juvenal de Freitas, Canadá; Delegate from Belgium; Dr. João Jardim, President of Madeira; Delegate from South Africa; Dr. Mário Soares, President of the Portuguese Republic; Delegate from the USA; Delegate from Brazil; Delegate from Australia; Delegate from England; Delegate from Uruguai.

Juvenal de Freitas is an extraordinary, active man. He loves the community social life and, above all, loves everything that is related to the people and things from his homeland. He was, without any doubt, one of the biggest pushers for the Canadian Madeira Club.

- After ten years of Canada, we decided to organize a commemorative celebration. It was the base for the birth of the club. It was on June 2nd, 1963 that the Canadian Madeira Club was born. João Camarata, Ângelo Bacalhau, Óscar Pereira, António Freitas, António Plácido, myself and a few others, went knocking from door to door, asking people for $20 to form the club.

- Are you member #1?

- No. To avoid any misunderstandings, everyone who formed the commission was nominated "founding member" and the numbers were given out to the members by alphabetical order. This way I am the founding member #173.

- How did you invest the money you got?

- With the money from the social event gathered from the celebration of our 10th anniversary in Canada as a community, and with the money we got from the door to door campaign, we bought a farm to start doing our outdoor events.

- It is the same place where you now celebrate the festivities of Nossa Senhora do Monte, right?

- Yes. The festivities of our patron saint. - After, remembering those times with nostalgia, he said: - I bought the first image in Montreal. I was told it was the image of Nossa Senhora do Monte, but it wasn't. The bad weather ruined the image because it was made of wood. The second one didn't last very long either. The image we now have is made of metal and it was offered, in 1985, by Virgílio Teixeira, president of the Center for Emigrants from Madeira Island. The cave where the image is, in the Madeira Park, was built and prepared by my father-in-law and I, with the help of some other friends.

- What happens if the members of the Canadian Madeira Club decide to close it down?

- All the patrimony that the club has will go to the Government of Ontario. When I was president, we used to pay $1/year to the government.

Celebrations and festivities are special events for many people, specially if they are immigrants... How many problems and sorrows do we forget at these events? The celebrations are the morphine we take to appease the sad and dramatic moments. It was a beautiful event, the celebration of the 25th anniversary of

25th anniversary of the Portuguese Community. From left to right: Margarida Plácido, first Portuguese woman to arrive in Canada, Juvenal de Freitas, receiving a silver plate. Also in the picture, Ezequiel Silva, José Caires and Oswaldo Santos.

the Portuguese community in Canada. We could not have had better a silver anniversary.

- It was a lot of hard work and money. – Juvenal told us when he continued the narration of his facts. – The chair of the commission, citizenship judge Ezequiel Silva, and myself, gave $2000 each, because others decided, at the last minute, not to contribute...

- Do you remember the names of the members of the commission?

- I was a member with Ezequiel Silva, Clara and Oswaldo Santos, Maria Melo, Maria de Sousa and Captain Venceslau.

- As a native from Madeira Island, you were the one who had the idea to have the Folcklore group from Camacha and the president of the Regional Government, Alberto João Jardim, present at the celebrations...

Image of Nossa Senhora do Monte, patron of Madeira.

- Yes. I had the idea and the commission agreed to it. Dr. Alberto João Jardim loved being here. It was his first official visit outside Portugal.

During the 25th anniversary celebrations of the Portuguese community in Canada, some pioneers were distinguished with some medals, as it usually happens. Juvenal was one of them.

- I am very proud of the distinction. I got a silver plate with an inscription, which read my name as being the first official Portuguese immigrant to get the Canadian citizenship. So, officially, I am the first Portuguese Canadian.

Juvenal's involvement in the community never stopped. He was appointed Permanent Delegate of the Communities, representing Canada in the Madeira's government, from 1985.

- Do those meetings or congresses have any interest?

- Yes. We discuss all the issues that affect our community. We reach many conclusions, even if we cannot accomplish all our goals. The central government has not paid attention to our final reports and to our aspirations.

    - Give us an example.

    - Problems with laws that do not help immigrants solve their issues back home, banking issues...

    - Next year, the community celebrates 35 years and the Canadian Madeira Club its 25th anniversary. Do you have any plans?

    - Of course! When you stop, you die. I am trying to convince the members of the club to organize an event to celebrate the anniversary. It will be the last thing I will do for the club and for the community because I have retired.

    - Are you sure it will be the last one?

    - Well, only God knows what tomorrow brings, but these are my intentions: spend the remaining days of my life with my wife, three months in Canada, another three in Madeira, and so on. Since I have some percentage at Azores Travel, in Toronto, and some things in Madeira, I will divide my time between here and there. I want to die in peace. – Laughing at this last thought, he said: - As you can see, I no longer need to pay my dues at the club because I am a senior.

    We could not help but laugh with him. We had the impression he would not stop so soon, as he said. Whoever was born to do so much, does not stop from one day to another. Usually, people like Juvenal work until they die.

    Unfortunately, that is what happened. He has already left us.

JMC - June of 1987

Furtado, Nelly

Vancouver, Canada

Nelly Furtado's debut album.

The Portuguese Canadian singer, Nelly Furtado, is the pride and joy of all the Portuguese people in North America and a musical reference.

    Born in Victoria, B.C., Nelly is the daughter of immigrants from the island of S. Miguel. She is a beautiful young lady who, from a very early age, was exposed to Portuguese music, "her direct influence". Owner of a beautiful and unique voice, Nelly Furtado, besides singing, has a contagious way of being. She began singing in Portuguese at the age of 4, learned how to play some instruments, and began composing songs in English, her first language.

    Nelly was the revealing artist of 2001 with her debut album "Whoa Nelly". She won four Juno Awards that same year: best single for "I'm like a bird", best new artist, best composer and best album. It was a well deserved recognition. Everyone still

Nelly Furtado, among her people, when she recorded, in Toronto, the video Powerless, from her second album.

remembers Nelly that night at the Copps Coliseum, in Hamilton, when she mentioned Portugal and her grandmother, each time she received a Juno.

She came out with her second album, Folklore, in 2003. For her debut video, Powerless, Nelly invited the local folklore groups of Nazaré, Tricanas, Barcelos and Póvoa do Varzim to participate in the video as a homage to her Portuguese roots. The video was shot in Toronto, on November 25, 2003, two months after Nelly had given birth to a beautiful girl.

Ana Fernandes-Iria interviews Nelly Furtado when she received the Merit Diploma from the FPCBP in 2001.

In Toronto, Nelly Furtado feels at home since part of her family lives in the city and she is welcomed by the entire Portuguese community.

Composing, playing and singing, Nelly Furtado keeps on walking her path to success, both nationally and internationally, specially in Portugal where she is very popular. In April of 2004, Nelly got the Juno Award for Artist of the Year. Thank you, Nelly.

JMC-2004

Nelly Furtado at the Juno Awards in 2001.

Gomes, António

Village of Sítio da Quinta, town of São Roque, Madeira Island

I found António Gomes well installed on a chair, under an umbrella, in the beautiful beach of Cayo Guillermo, in Cuba... It was the well deserved rest after a lifetime of work. He was part of the group of Portuguese people that participates every year in the Winter Get Away, Winterfest, organized by Cirv Fm.

Fernanda and António Gomes.

António Gomes was born in Sítio da Quinta, in the small town of São Roque, in Madeira Island, on July 16, 1923. On July 17, 1950 he married Fernanda Gomes, from Sítio da Terça, also in São Roque, at the town's main church. Two sons were born to the couple: José António Gomes, in 1951, and Fernando Miguel Gomes, in 1952. António Gomes left the city of Funchal on May 26, 1953 adventuring to Canada. He arrived in Halifax on June 2 of the same year. António was part of the very first group of Portuguese men from Madeira Island who immigrated officially to Canada. In Halifax, they reunited with eighteen others, who had come from the Azores. After a brief encounter with an official from the Immigration Department, António Gomes, ignoring completely what the official had told him, left with eight of his companions to Montreal.

Arriving in Montreal, the group was taken to a farm where, for six months, they had to take care of the cows. Confused and tired with the farm's activities, they ran away from the farm, heading to Toronto. In the latter city, António Gomes found a job in a mushroom farm, located in Victoria Park, where he worked for two years. This was a farm where some Portuguese men were already working. Still unhappy with his situation, Manuel Gomes decided to leave the farm and began working at an iron and aluminum foundry where he stayed for two years. However, this would not be his last job opportunity. Always searching for a job he enjoyed doing, Manuel Gomes, after becoming a member of Local Union 1842, found a job at the Docks. This was the place he had been looking for and worked there for 28 years.

While talking to us about his adventures and misfortunes, António Gomes remembered old fellow companions: Juvenal de Freitas, Manuel da Camacha (already deceased), Elias, Carlos Gonçalves from S. Roque, Manuel da Silva – responsible for Madeira Park and "little" Sabino... Time and emo-

tions did not allow him to remember any other name... even though he has not forgotten the faces. In 1986, António Gomes retired. After so much suffering and hard pioneer life in unknown and rustic lands, he is now able to take a well, deserved rest. Their children and grandchildren are now their favourite hobby. Both António and Fernanda also take time to travel. We wish them all the best and still many years to live.

JMC-1999

António and Fernanda Gomes, at their wedding day, in 1950.

Gomes, Francisco Féria

Town of Aljustrel, province of Alentejo

To remember our pioneer Chico Alentejano, we interviewed his widow, fado singer Maria Gomes, who came to live with Chico in Toronto, in 1967. "The good-hearted Chico Alentejano would be 76 years old if he were still among us. He passed away 14 years ago". – Maria said with a tear rolling down her face.

Francisco Féria Gomes was born in the town of Aljustrel, in Alentejo, on May 29, 1926. The calm winds of his native province did not please him and he decided to leave his country, heading to Canada aboard the Saturnia, as part of the first official group of Portuguese men who came in 1953.

Francisco Féria Gomes

His way of being in life earned him the nickname of Chico Alentejano. Ti'Chico, the sweet formula used by many people, was always a dedicated individual to his native Alentejo and to his Portuguese Community. Professionally, as a welder, he had many jobs, not always doing what he could and knew best. He worked at the tunnel excavations, he sold bbq chicken with Armando Albuquerque (businessman already deceased), among other tasks. In the community, he helped everyone. He was part of the group that founded the First Portuguese Canadian Club, where he was member #3, he later on helped with the formation of Casa do Alentejo Community Center and of the Portuguese Canadian Democratic Association. At Casa do Alentejo, he helped with the formation of the singing group. He was the cook, for a long time, at Casa do Alentejo and at the First Portuguese for the soccer teams. With his wife, Fernando Silva and José Gomes, Chico Alentejano founded the fado group "Alegres do Fado", which performed every where in the community. The group had the support of Jaime Aparício and singer Isabel

Fado singers: José Gomes, Maria Gomes and Francisco Silva.

Santos. Some years later, the group Coça-Coça, owned by Diogo Monteiro (already deceased) joined them to help raise funds for charity groups.

Francisco Féria Gomes got married on June 3rd, 1968, in Toronto, to fado singer, Maria Gomes. Chico Alentejano suffered and life was never easy for him. At Toronto's Center Island, where he worked, he suffered an accident that left him with severe back problems. A foot infection devel-

Chico Alentejano among his friends in the Grupo Coral da Casa do Alentejo.

oped into a gangrene. He underwent food surgery 16 times, but due to his diabetic condition was never able to fully recuperate. At the same time, the doctors diagnosed him with a cancer. He was submitted to a medical intervention and cancer treatments, but did not resist so many adversities. He died, in Toronto, on February 20, 1988.

His widow Maria Gomes lives alone, also a victim of many

years of suffering and illness. A platinum knee and a poor heart condition have left her in a wheel chair. A life of suffering has not stopped her from doing well and helping her neighbour. Chico Alentejano is a memory. Maria Gomes is Fado's voice, which is slowly loosing its tune. This is her and our fado!

At the end of his life, Chico Alentejano on a wheel chair.

Francisco and Maria Gomes the day of their wedding in 1968.

JMC-2000

Gomes, Branca Amélia Correia Proença

Town of São Vicente, district of Guarda

It was on October 10, 1964, that a group of about twenty children, between 6 and 15 years old, said "Good morning, Mrs. Gomes!" in Portuguese, at the First Portuguese School, back then located at 244 Augusta Avenue, in Toronto. This was the salutation the first official Portuguese teacher in Canada received at the inauguration of the official Portuguese School of the First Portuguese Canadian Club. This teacher was Mrs. Branca Gomes.

Mrs. Branca Gomes in a social event at the First Portuguese Canadian Club with Arnaldo, Celina and paula Melo, daughter-in-law Emília and Virgílio Gomes.

Branca Amélia Correia Proença, Gomes by marriage, was born in the town of S. Vicente, in the district of Guarda, on July 10, 1914. She got her degree at Escola do Magistério Primário de Braga, on February 20, 1933. She taught in Portugal for 26 years and was president of the school Escola da Caniçada do Distrito Escolar de Braga. In Toronto, where she settled down in January of 1964, Mrs. Branca Gomes was also an elementary teacher at Alexandre Muir School, between 1967 and 1979.

Among other functions, Mrs. Gomes served as member of the school board at the First Portuguese C.C., in 1972, and taught Portuguese for adults at Harbord Collegiate Institute, in 1980. She was also a teacher at St. Luke's Elementary School.

Branca Amélia Correia Proença married José de Oliveira Gomes – born in Leiria on August 4, 1922 – at Santo Ildefonso's church, in Porto, on January 31, 1948. The couple had two sons: Fernando and Vergílio. Mrs. Branca Gomes suffered the heavy hand of destiny when her husband died in 1975 and her son Fernando in 1998.

Mrs. Branca Gomes among friends when her work was recognized by the City of Toronto. Ambassador Luis Navega, Art Egglenton, Consul General Tânger Correia, Armindo Silva, Celina Melo, painter Alberto de Castro and grandson Nuno Miguel, among others.

This teacher was the recipient of many awards from the Portuguese and Canadian Governments, and from individual politicians, among them Américo Tomás – President of the Portuguese Republic (1962), city of Toronto (1962) and First Portuguese (1983), when she celebrated 50 years of her teaching career.

She began the First Portuguese school on October 10, 1964. After more than half a decade teaching, Mrs. Branca Gomes still has a young, care free spirit and a beautiful smile. She also has an outstanding memory. She told us: "In 1950, during the campaign against illiteracy, the government would pay 500 escudos (about $5 cdn.) to every teacher who passed ten students. Back then, it was a fortune! I received the highest pay".

Mrs. Branca Gomes spent 65 years teaching.

The Gomes family arriving in Canada in January of 1964.

Mrs. Branca Gomes with her sons Fernando and Virgílio and daughter-in-law, Emília.

Mrs. Branca Gomes, with former students, when she celebrated her 50 years of teaching.

Mr. Ferreira, Marta Brum, Fernanda, Sílvia, Dr. Ernesto Feu, Celina, Helena Oliveira, Branca Gomes and Mr. Damião.

She definitely deserves a Golden Medal. She stopped teaching two years ago, not due to tiredness, but to her legs that did not want to help her. She lives alone with her memories, the visits she gets from her family, specially from her grandson Nuno Miguel, and from friends. She lives alone, but happy.

After her passing, I say: See you in eternity, Mrs. Branca Gomes!

JMC - 2000

Gomes, Rui Alberto H. Frazão

Town of Bombarral, North of Lisbon

It is hard to talk to Rui Gomes as a pioneer, not because he is one, but because he is very young to be seen as a pioneer. Rui Alberto H. Frazão Gomes was born on March 6, 1952, in Bombarral, a town north of Lisbon. He left Portugal on July 12, 1956, with his mother, Maria dos Remédios, sponsored by his father, Joaquim, who had emigrated to Canada, aboard the Vulcânia, on May 7, 1955.

- I came to Canada when I was only 4 years old. – Our young pioneer began saying with a smile. – I came with my mother aboard the Saturnia. We arrived in New York on July 21, and entered Canada, by bus, through the Niagara Falls border, on the same day. I still remember getting here and not seeing my father. My godfather – Mário Tomás (already deceased) – was waiting for us. My father had had an accident at the tunnels where he was working and was in the hospital with a broken leg.

- Since you remember things so vividly, do you know the name of your first school?

- Of course. It was Ryerson Public School, on Bathurst and Dundas, in Toronto.

- And after this one?

- After elementary school, I went to Harbord Collegiate Institute, on Harbord and Clinton. From 1958 to 1965, I went back to Bombarral and studied at the Externato, until the end of my 3rd year of high school.

- Did you like it there?

Trip to Portugal aboard the Vulcânia, in 1958: Maria dos Remédios, Rui, Joaquim Frazão Gomes (deceased) and Carlos, already born in Toronto.

- It was a good experience. – He said without hesitating. – When I came back to Canada, I took many professional courses. In 1976, I was hired by the federal government to work for the immigration services, where I stayed until 1985. I have a degree in immigration issues. Working for the government allowed me to travel to many places and countries. I am proud to have been recognized by the government of Canada with the Merit Diploma and a Pecuniary award because of a book I wrote about the immigration legislation in Canada. Today, my book is a reference in the government. I am very proud of that.

- Then, why did you leave?

Standing up: Rui Gomes, masseur, Rilhas, Vitorino, Tavares, John, Amorim, Peter, Duque, Alberto, Correia Dias, Arnaldo and Manuel Regado. Kneeling down: Ernesto, Steve, Simões, Coelho, Bolota, Luizinho, Bernardo, Douglas (today playing for Chaves), and Furtado. This is the team from First Portuguese that went on a tour to Portugal, in 1986, playing against Chaves, Alvalade, Bombarral, Faro and Lagos.

- I left because after so many years working for the government, we begin feeling frustrated and apathetic, due to the complexity of the system and lack of administrative competence on the government's part. Our government has a hard time recognizing our competence and dedication to the system, and looking at our political parties – which have very little influence on the daily decisions the government makes – I concluded that I had to do one of the following: show up to work every day, work my 8 hour shift and get paid weekly, just like everybody else, or choose another path.

- So you chose another path...

- Exactly. I quit and opened my own office. At that time, there was no Immigration Consultants in the Portuguese community with my experience and my habilitations.

Rui Gomes still has his office WTC Inc., located on 1201 Dundas Street West, in Toronto.

- Do you have contacts overseas?

Rui Gomes, goaltender for the veteran team of Peniche of Toronto. Soccer is his passion.

- Yes. I have a satellite office in Hong Kong. I believe that until 1997, when Hong Kong will be handed over to the Republic of China, there is a lot of work to do. I have a few Chinese partners working there.

- As a specialist on immigration issues, how do you assess the current polemic situation with some political and religious refugees and with the illegal immigrants in general?

- Everything happens due to the incredible mistakes made by the Canadian legislation! – He answered. – We live in a 'young' country that still has a lot to learn. The way our legislation is, no wonder we have such a chaotic situation. For example, for a mechanic to open a shop, he needs official habilitations and documentation. To solve matters as complicated as immigration issues, anyone can open an office and call himself consultant. It's not right. I will fight to see the new legislation about immigration forcing consultants to present credentials. This way, we will eliminate swindlers getting money from a poor individual, who is trying to legalize his situation in a country he has chosen as a second home. Sometimes, I'm embarassed to say I am an immigration consultant when I hear certain stories.

- Are you going to choose another path, again?

- No, but look: when I was a student and entered the adult world, I worked in the mines, in the construction of tunnels, in construction, in the tobacco fields, I was a waiter, I owned a carpentry shop, I managed the newspaper Globe and Mail, in Sudbury... I did a lot of things and I am not ashamed of any of that. What you see nowadays with immigration cannot even be commented on...

Shifting our conversation from immigration, we decided to find out about Rui's personal life. He is married and is a happy father.

- How did your love story happen?

- Oh, it took place here in Toronto. – He said laughing. – By coincidence, my wife also came to Canada when she was only 4 years old. I met her at a Miss Pageant at the Holiday Inn, organized by the deceased Armando Albuquerque , in April of 1976. Her name is Maria Filomena Santos and she is from Atouguia da Baleia. We got married on April 2, 1977.

- Do you have any children?

- Yes! Two daughters: Tanya is now 9 years old and Chantelle is 2, both born in Toronto. – Then he said: - I also have a brother, born in Toronto, who is already 30 years old. His name is Carlos, also a pioneer.

In Rui's family, everyone is a pioneer. We lament his father's passing, on July 15, 1978. Rui Alberto is a sportsman by nature and loves soccer...

- Oh yes! I love soccer. I have practiced sports all my life, specially athletics, when I was in school. In 1967, at the age of 15, I was Athlete of the Year at King Edward Public School. That year I was particularly good in long jump. However, in 1967, I won every competition on athletics. I was champion in the long jump competition in Toronto and finalist in Ontario.

- What about soccer?

- I was junior for the Bombarralense, in Portugal, when I studied there. I was the goal-keeper. This took place between 1959 and 1965. Rilhas, known by everyone in the Portuguese community, was also playing for Bombarralense at that time. Officially, we never played together, because he is one year older than I.

- Rilhas came to Canada and integrated the First Portuguese Team and you... You simply disappeared?

- No. I began playing on my school's team – Harbord Collegiate. I was actually playing every sport: soccer, basketball, baseball... I continued to be a champion in school in long jump.

Also committed to helping social and community events, Rui is an active member in many clubs, associations and parishes.

- In 1977, I got involved, through my in-laws, on the committee Pró Lar de Santa Maria de Peniche. I did it because I recognized the tremendous work Monsignor Bastos is doing to provide a decent living and better future for poor children and seniors. This home deserves all the support it can get. I left the committee in 1981, but still give my collaboration whenever needed.

- Did you stop you social crusade here?

- No, to the very contrary. – He said smiling at us. – In 1981, I helped the formation of the Peniche Community Club of Toronto. After, I was elected president in 1982-83. Peniche was and still is a club connected to amateur soccer. In 1985, I was the chair of the Niagara Soccer Club and in 1986-87, technical director of the First Portuguese. Right now, I am director of Arsenal do Minho.

- Do you have many titles and championships?

- Yes. Fortunately, I was always a champion. – He answered proudly. – I was champion from 1981 to 1985 – except in 1982, in the Portuguese Canadian Soccer League. The only place where I never conquered any title was at the First Portuguese, I also have many trophies: Taça Camões, Taça Disciplina, Taça Liga Luso-Canadiana, Ontario Cup 1985. In 1986, I went with First Portuguese on a tour to Portugal where we played in Faro, Chaves, Bombarral, Alvalade and Lagos. In Faro, we actually defeated the Farense. It was a compensation for a learning experience that cost a lot of money.

From left to right: Rui Gomes, Cardinal Patriarch António Ribeiro, Monteiro, Mena Gomes, Rosália Dias and Maria José Silva, during the celebrations of the Pró-Lar de Santa Maria de Peniche.

- So it was worth it.

- Yes! – he answered immediately. – Besides the learning experience, it was also a privilege. We learned a lot and made many friends.

After such a journey through clubs, we asked Rui if he still had the interest and energy to continue:

- I must admit I feel tired. It is a big sacrifice for me and my family. I spend a lot of money and energy, without any reward. It is volunteer work, but it tires you after so many years. The lack of support and the unfair criticism we receive is just too cruel... It I did not have this passion for soccer, I would have given up.

- You mentioned your family. How does your wife see your involvement, specially in soccer?

- She has given me all her support. She also demands a lot from me, specially towards our daughters. She has been an amazing companion.

- And the clubs, do they provide the community with what is necessary?

- Considering their natural limitations, I believe so. The clubs' activities – both social and sportive – have served the purpose of fraternizing in order to preserve the culture and to develop the community itself. On the other hand, it has created some divisions in terms of human values. Clubs live based on what humans can give, and our values are changing. With the number of clubs our community has, the few values we still have are very dispersed, thus loosing a lot of what we could do, if we were united. We are in favour of individualism and there is nothing we can do.

Is there really nothing we can do? If we know that as individuals we are not strong, why don't we unite our efforts and ideas? Difficult? Of course! However, with people like Rui Gomes, we can try to go further. We now look at our youth hoping they will build a stronger, more united community.

There is still much more to write about Rui Gomes, but we will stop here. We wish Rui all the best.

JMC - April of 1988

Gonçalves, Emílio Monteiro

Town of Santo André, city of Chaves, province of Trás-os-Montes

When I went to Ottawa to take part in the gathering with the Portuguese minister of Foreign Affairs, Dr. Jaime Gama, at the signing of the convention of the tributary agreement between Portugal and Canada, it ended up being a great occasion to see some old friends and meet new ones. Taking a break from our affairs, we went to a restaurant called Churrasqueira, with our friend José Soares. Churrasqueira is one of those places, which has a Portuguese scent to it. Due to this particular aspect, we did not hesitate and decided to enter to try the exquisite cuisine. Marvelous… The owner was Emílio Monteiro Gonçalves, a Portuguese

man from Santo André, a small village near Chaves, in the northeastern province of Trás-os-Montes. He was born in Santo André on April 13, 1951, the son of António Eanes Gonçaves and Maria Matilde Monteiro.

Back home, Emílio was a farmer and used to sell products at the local markets. When he came to Canada, in July of 1971, he went to work on construction. Tired of this life, he tried his luck on the business sector, in 1980, opening the Sagres Restaurant. After this, and always living in Ottawa, he opened, in 1984, the Café Caco, best known as O Piolho, which

Emílio Gonçalves with parents Maria and António at the Churrasqueira Restaurant.

he still owns. O Piolho is a reference for the Portuguese community in Ottawa. Since 1998, he manages both the Café Caco and the Churrasqueira. His restaurant is known for serving well and cheap. Emílio bets on quality, serving his clientel with simplicity, placing luxury aside.

When he was younger, he used to play soccer for the club Lusitânia of Ottawa, a club where he is still a member. Talking to us, Emílio told us he always had a dream to go back to Portugal, but he is so used to Ottawa

Natália, one of Emílio's employees, at the bar of the Churrasqueira Restaurant.

that it is almost impossible to realize his dream. His parents, Maria and António, do not believe either he will ever move back again.

Wherever he decides to stay, Emílio Monteiro Gonçalves surely deserves to live a good life as a reward for the number of sacrifices he has made, and number of hours he works a day...

JMC - 1999

Gonçalves, Sabino Mendes

Village of Campanário, Town of Ribeira Brava, Madeira Island

Although he already shows his age and even though fate has been cruel to him lately, he still has a great sense of humor!

Sabino Mendes Gonçalves was born on Campanário, a village located in Ribeira Brava, Madeira Island, on May 8, 1928. Very few years of school and a lot of hard work were his fate, something common to most people his age. Working the fields, from a very early age, Sabino had no other opportunities but to help his family. Not seeing a bright future in the farm, he went to the city of Funchal to look for a job. He was hired by Torreão, a sugar factory. The military service, at Quartel 19, in Funchal, forced him to quit his job. When

Sabino Mendes Gonçalves

he finished, Sabino went to work for the famous farmer Miguel Santa Clara, a prestigious individual in the archipelago. It was this farmer who suggested Canada to Sabino.

Sabino arrived in Halifax on June 2, 1953, the same day the first group of Madeirenses arrived in Canada. From Halifax, Sabino was sent to Hamilton, with his brother Elias. In Hamilton, working at a a mushroom farm, his former boss, Miguel Santa Clara, paid him a visit. Feeling sorry for his former employee, Miguel offered to bring Sabino to Toronto where he got him a job at the Ontario Clean Seeds.

Meanwhile, Sabino married by proxy in 1957, with Natividade Lídia, who was still living in Ribeira Brava. Later that year, Natividade came to Toronto and the couple decided to have a religious wedding, which took place at a Hungarian church on Spadina and Dundas, which no longer exists. In Toronto, the couple's four children were born: John, Michael, António and Lídia. Until this day, Sabino already has three grandchildren: Catherine, Matheo and Sarah. A little after his wedding, Sabino found a job at a Gas Company where , with much sacrifice, he would dig holes on the ground and would clean ditches to make way for tubes and cables. In 1958, he began working at Canada Parkers, a company where he would stay for the next 30 years. He left Canada Parkers to retire in 1994.

Sabino with friends and family during a pig's slaughter, Madeira style, in those good old times

Sabino was a member of the group that bought the Madeira Park and formed the Canadian Madeira Club, but he was never a director. With a malicious smile on his face, Sabino told us: "I never went to school to learn those disciplines". Sabino's favourite hobby was and still is to take care of his farm, although he does not have as much energy and strength anymore. Wine, vegetables and flowers were and still are his biggest passion. Now, after his wife's

Natividade Lídia with her two sisters.

passing on November 12, 1999, Sabino lives with his daughter Lídia. The car accident completely changed his life around. He has a lot of difficulty moving his left leg and, as he has told us, sooner or later, he will be dependent on an electric wheel chair. "When I lost my wife, I also lost my life", Sabino said as he remembered and tried to put together the many fragments of his life. Physically thin, but with a strong personality, Sabino does not give up and is willing to accept the challenges life still has for him.

JMC - 2000

The couple's four children, playing outside.

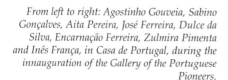

From left to right: Agostinho Gouveia, Sabino Gonçalves, Aita Pereira, José Ferreira, Dulce da Silva, Encarnação Ferreira, Zulmira Pimenta and Inês França, in Casa de Portugal, during the innauguration of the Gallery of the Portuguese Pioneers.

Goulart, Manuel Marcelino da Silveira

São Jorge and

Terceira Islands, Azores

He is nice, kind and someone with whom it is easy to become friends. Since his arrival in Canada, he has successfully dedicated himself, with brothers-in-law Joe and Luís Pimentel, to the catering business. He is Manuel Marcelino da Silveira Goulart. Manuel Silveira was born in the island of S. Jorge, but grew up in the island of Terceira, Azores. In November of 1966, Manuel came to Canada. Among family and friends, he is simply known as Manny Silveira. Both of his brothers-in-law are his business partners and they came to Canada in 1964. Some years later, in 1972, Manny Silveira was married to Maria Pimentel with whom he has two children with – Celina and Clif – both involved in the catering business.

Manny, Joe and Luís created the firm Continental Brothers in 1979, which was a breakthrough in the catering business of the community.

A decade later, they built the Renaissance Hall, in Mississauga, this time with a new partner: Humberto Rebelo, at the time, the owner of Micaelence Bakery. Another decade went by, and Manny opens, in partnership with his family, the spacious and luxurious Mississauga Convention Centre, where he is the manager. Manny still has his partnership with brother-in-law Luís, at the Renaissance Hall, in Mississauga. Joe Pimentel and Humberto Rebelo got together, in 1993, to open the Oasis Convention Centre, in Mississauga. A life connected to banquets and parties.

New Year's Eve Party at the Mississauga Convention Centre: José Mário Coelho, Manny Silveira, Jorge Ferreira and wife and Frank Alvarez.

Couples Manny Silveira and wife and Luís Pimentel and wife at the Mississauga Convention Centre.

Humberto and Lídia Rebelo with Joe Pimentel, standing up, with Hernâni and Edna Raposo, Carmen Silva, Esmeralda Coelho and D. Mota.

Manny is also known for his New Year's Eve parties at the Mississauga Convention Centre. He has had big names of the Portuguese Musical world perform at the hall, such as Roberto Leal and Jorge Ferreira. Actually, the Mississauga Convention Centre, the Oasis Convention Centre, and the Renaissance Hall have been privileged   with the best names in the Portuguese and Brazilian musical scene.

JMC-2004

Manny Silveira, Luís Pimentel and Joe Pimentel at the beginning of their career at the Continental Brothers.

Henriques, Francisco Pestana

Town of Câmara de Lobos, Madeira Island

Francisco Pestana Henriques

The Henriques couple with their two children, in 1983.

Francisco Pestana Henriques is a very dedicated individual of the Portuguese community of Bradford, as well as an active member in provincial and federal politics. He is a candidate in the city council of Bradford.

Francisco was born in Câmara de Lobos, Madeira Island, on April 12, 1943. Still a young man, Francisco left the island to go live in the mainland. Together with his brother, Francisco lived for some time in the city of Porto, and later on moved to the capital, where he finished the second year of university. During the summer holidays, he would return to Madeira to help his mother at the Bakery and Grocery Shop "Viva a Pátria", owned by his parents, Francisco and Gabriela de Jesus.

In 1966, while doing his military service, Francisco went to Angola as the Militia's Second Lieutenant, where he stayed in Nova Lisboa for two year and three months… When he came back to Lisbon, he decided to emigrate to Canada. Boarding an airplane from Lisbon to Toronto, via London, England, Francisco arrived at Ontario's capital on May 16, 1968. In Toronto, he got a job as a life guard at a private condominium building. He had this job for two years and a half, a time he also used to study English and take an accounting (SMA) course. From here, he went to Ryerson to get his CMA.

In Toronto, Frank Henriques met his sweetheart, Celeste, also from Câmara de Lobos, who had come to Toronto in 1965, and they both got married on August 15, 1970. The couple has two children: Denise, born on October 31, 1972, a law and investigation student at York University, and Loyde, born on April 25, 1975, who has a Business Administration degree from Wilfried Laurier University, and is now completing the CMA. For many years, Frank worked as accountant for the firms Stran Stell & West sell Rosco, and for 8 years for Jacob & Thompson and RER International, where he was a manager.

Celeste and Francisco Pestana Henriques.

The Henriques were the first Portuguese family to live in New Market, where they arrived in 1976. A decade later, Frank bought the travel agency Bradford Travel, where he began dedicating himself to booking trips, accounting and financial administration. In 1997, he sold the agency, but kept, in the same building, his office of Financial Services and began working at a representative for the Portuguese bank Sottomayor Bank of Canada.

The founding members of the C.C.P.B.: Domingos Durães, António Guerreiro, Frank Henriques and Gualter Camelo.

In the political field, he ran for city council in Bradford in 1994 and in 1997, but lost, by few votes. In 2001, Frank will be a candidate again, representing Ward 2, and hoping to be elected this time around.

Frank is also an active member in the Portuguese community. The Portuguese Cultural Centre of Bradford, incorporated in 1983, was inaugurated in 1987, by the founders Alfredo Botelho and colleagues. After six months of its inauguration, Frank became member and has since then served in the administration. He has been president of the General Assembly and director many times. He was also president of the Executive for two years, and later on for another year.

Inauguration of the C.C.P.B. In the picture, we can see António Guerreiro, Frank Henriques and Vitor Fernandes.

His life has been very successful in the familiar, professional, political and social spectrum. Frank, a reference in the community and in the social-political life of Bradford, is a man who still has much to give us.

JMC-2000

Jorge, Manuel Dalberto

Pico Island, Azores

Manuel Dalberto Jorge

He is a man of honour and action. Manuel Dalberto Jorge was born in Pico Island, Azores, on July 24, 1927. Unable to stay in small places for too long, he emigrated to Canada in 1965, looking for better opportunities.

A year after his arrival in Canada, Manuel Jorge decided to make his dream a reality. He founded a small cheese factory, although aware of the many difficulties he would have to face. Still, he did not give up. The Portuguese Cheese Co. Ltd. was created and grew up at such a surprising speed for many people, except for its founder who knew exactly how to deal with the business.

From his first marriage, Manuel Dalberto Jorge has a daughter, Maria Humberta, who was also born in Pico, and his business partner from the beginning. He is now married to second wife, Maria José, from the island of S. Miguel, with whom he has a son – Jason, 16 – who was born in Toronto and is still a student. In his active life as a business and industrial man, Manuel created the firm Newfish Import & Export, with stores in Montreal and New York. The non-stopping expansion of the Portuguese Cheese factory did not give him time to dedicate to Newfish Import & Export, which he closed down in 1983. Years went by and the tiredness of a life of work and responsibilities came to an end.

Manuel Jorge with friends, after a soccer game between the teams Santa Clara-Benfica.

Sorrowful for the fact that his children did not want to continue his father's cheese company, Manuel sold his business to António Melo, an immigrant from the island of S. Miguel, who passed the Portuguese Cheese Co. Ltd, to his three children. Manuel helped the new owner continue the business, for a couple of months. Manuel Dalberto Jorge, just like any warrior, is now looking towards having a well deserved calm life. Holidays and more visits to the Azores and the mainland, get to know Canada better and pay for his son's education are among his future plans. All the best, Manuel Jorge.

JMC-1999

Manuel Jorge and Gilberto Alves, two business men and friends.

José, Martinho de São

City of Leiria

Isidro and Martinho São José at their hardware store in Toronto.

Our pioneers' journey was not an easy one. And if we look at the one taken by Martinho de São José, it was perhaps the most painful one.

- Port Colborne marked my life the hard way… - Martinho began his story, with a sad look to his face. – I used to work at a flour factory. I was assigned to do many tasks until the day I burnt myself. I suffered burns in about 66% of my body. I don't even like to remember it. I suffered so much, I was in so much pain that I used to drink more than a bottle of whisky a day to try to fight the unsupportable pain I had. Only those who have suffered some type of burn know what I went through…

Martinho de São José was born on September 27, 1932, in Leiria. On May 11, 1955, he boarded the Olympia, in Lisbon, looking for a better future in a country called Canada. He arrived in Halifax a week later, on May 16.

- Our trip took exactly 120 hours, touching in many ports. – Our pioneer told us. – Do you know who can tell you how the trip went and how many Portuguese came that day? António Vaz who took picture of us when we got here!

- When you arrived, did you stay in Halifax or were you sent to another place?

David, Martinho de São José, Renata and Anita. A happy family!

- No, we stayed in Halifax. About a day later, we took an old steam train to Montreal. From here, we were sent to a farm, in Harrow. I have a few nice stories to share with you about our time in Harrow. Telmo, José, António and I decided to go to the beach in Kingsville. We did not have a car, so we asked for a lift. On the way there, we had no problems. We had a wonderful day. At night… well, that's when our problems arrived. No one would give us a lift and we had to come to Harrow… walking. We spent the whole night walking back home. – Martinho could not continue his story. He was laughing so hard, it took him some time to come back to his narration. – After a short time of living in Harrow, I wanted to go to Ottawa, but the farm owners did not want to allow me to go, saying I had signed a contract with them valid for a year. In my broken English, I told them I had not signed anything, and had no obligation with them. They owed me $80 and if I went, they would not pay me. I got so upset that grabbed a knife and threatened the owner, a guy from the Netherlands. Afraid of my actions, they paid me and I went to Ottawa. At that time, $80 was a fortune… Actually, they still owe me 4 hours of labour that I spent picking up melons. – He finished his narration, laughing again at his own story.

In Ottawa, Martinho de São José worked for a few months in construction and, during the winter months, in a coal company, distributing it in hospitals, universities, and stores… Still unhappy with his life, Martinho left Ottawa to go to Port Colborne, a decision that would tragically mark his life. He was in hospital for many months, where he fought hard for his life, both physically and psychologically. In order to recuperate from the burnings, Martinho moved to Toronto. In this city, Martinho found the strength to go to therapy and to study. He went to Shaw Business College where he got his accounting license. Feeling better from his accident, Martinho went to work for the Maple Leaf Mill Co., the same year he got married – in October of 1960 – to Renata, this one from Prussia. Never giving up on his dreams, Martinho went to the University of Toronto, while working, where he got his RIA. The company where he was working promoted him to Auditor, a position which allowed him to travel from coast to coast in Canada, a job he kept for eight years.

- It was eight wonderful years that made me forget the misfortunes of my life.

- How did you end up owning a business?

- You know, I guess it was destiny. In 1960, I sponsored my brother Isidro and in 1962, I sponsored my other brother Bento. In July of 1971, I decided to open a business with Isidro. That's when we opened the São José Home Hardware, and we are still very successful.

- From those old times, do you remember any friends you haven't seen but would love to encounter one of these days?

- Of course! – he said. – I would love to know where Telmo and José are these days. They were both with me in Harrow.

After telling us some other stories, I asked Martin what he thought about his brother Bento's entry in politics.

- I was very proud of him and helped in his campaign. But I did it for my brother. – he answered without any hesitations. – As a politician representing the Conservative Party, I think my brother still has lot to learn. He is still very new at the political life. A politician needs to be perspicacious, must know how to talk a lot without saying much and without any compromises. And obviously, he needs to do all of this without being dishonest.

Anita São José, playing cow bells at the Austrian Club of Toronto.

- We sense that you would not consider a political career.

- You're right! I am a conservative with a small "c". If I find time, I may get myself involved in politics. Although I am a conservative, I must confess the Liberal Party also has some points I identify with. However, I am not a fanatic about politics. Life has taught me how to be practical and functional.

- After so many years of living in Canada, have you helped form any particular club or association?

- No. I never had the time and life has been pretty hard on me. I had to fight very hard to be able to survive. But I help most Portuguese clubs and also go to many events. I am a member of the Austrian Club because my daughter Anita is the leader of the folkloric group of that club.

- You are really adapted to Canada, then.

- Without any doubt. There are a lot of people who don't like this country… For me, Canada is the best country in the world. Whoever knows Canada the way I do cannot say anything against it. I have political and economical stability. Canada is one of the richest countries in the world. Does anyone know that this country has warm water all year long? I am referring to the Hot Springs of Banff National Park, in the Rocky Mountains, west of Calgary. It is marvelous to be swimming on hot water with snow falling on your head. Please, take time to know this country before you say anything against it.

- What about Portugal, do you still like that country?

- Of course I do! Every time I have a chance, I take the family on holidays to Portugal. But I no longer adapt to that country, neither do my children. At this point, we are trying to sell the business because I need time to rest. At this point, I am thinking of buying a house in Portugal to go on holidays more frequently. But that's about it, holidays.

- So, we will see shortly a Martinho de São José quitting his business to begin a political life...

Martinho could not help but laugh at our question. He stopped for a moment, thinking about our comment, and then said:

- Maybe! I will definitely have more time. I also have some contacts and friends who are willing to help me, and a wife that supports me in every way she can. So why not?

Why not? – we ask. If he has the conditions to dedicate himself to politics, all the merit should be given to him. Our community needs political representatives at all levels of government. With a stable life, the support of his wife and children – Anita and David – we wish Martinho the best in life.

JMC - April of 1987

Lebre, Guilherme Francisco

Village of Santa Catarina da Serra, town of Fátima, district of Leiria

Guilherme and Maria Adelaide Lebre.

Guilherme Francisco Lebre is a very talented man. He taught himself how to paint, to sculpture wood, to make wire figures, etc... Guilherme was born in Santa Catarina da Serra, a village in Fátima, in the district of Leiria, on March 6, 1932. As a child, he attended school and helped his father in the farm. He completed his military service in the cities of Leiria and Coimbra. When he completed the army and not happy with the fact that he was destined to be a farmer, Guilherme decided to leave Portugal. He chose Canada as his new homeland.

Guilherme arrived in Toronto on November 29, 1956, after a long three-day airplane trip.

Guilherme Lebre displaying his hand-made objects.

He had to rely on his brother Joaquim to survive the first months of Canada for he was only able to find a job in February of 1957. His first working place was the Uranium mine of Elliot Lake where he worked for 18 months. The first days on Elliot Lake, Guilherme was forced to rent a car, with three other friends, because he had no place to sleep. Due to the extreme low temperatures, the car had to be running all night long so that they would not freeze to death. At the end of his 18-month contract at Elliot Lake, Guilherme went back to Portugal to get married to Maria Adelaide da Fonseca, a native from the village of Alvares, in the outskirts of the city of Coimbra. Maria Adelaide was born on July 14, 1940. The wedding took place at Fatima's basilica, on January 11, 1958.

Returning to Canada, Guilherme chose Toronto as the place to settle down. Anabela, the couple's daughter, was already born in Toronto: she is now Mrs. Persadle and has two children: Ryan and Jessica. When he moved to Toronto, Guilherme was hired as a mechanic at a bicycle shop, a profession he did not know. So for two years, Guilherme worked at the Duke's shop, learning a trade he would choose as one of his means of earning a living. From Duke's, Guilherme went to Mike Bright Cycle & Sports where he worked for twelve years. By this time, he was already considered one of the best mechanics in town. Due to the death his boss, Mike Bright Cycle closed and Guilherme went to Bloor Cycle, where he was the supervisor for 22 years. This would be Guilherme's last job, before he opened his business. In 1994, Guilherme decided to open his bicycle shop – Queen's Bike Shop – located at 1537-A Queen Street West. Due to his reputation as a great mechanic, Guilherme was visited by many famous cyclists: António Maia, João Fonseca, Dr. Martins, Reinald, Guiana and Fernando Gonçalves. When he retired in 1998, Guilherme decided to close his shop and began dedicating himself to handcrafting.

Guilherme was not expecting to become very successful with the objects he made during his spare time for pleasure. He has organized an exhibit at St. Christopher's house, in Toronto, and sold many to the United States of America, France, Mexico, Italy, Portugal and many regions in Canada. For a very long time, Guilherme could count with his brothers' – Joaquim, António and the late José – help and support.

Guilherme and Maria Adelaide are a happy couple. They like living in Canada with their daughter and grandchildren enjoying their retirement years. They also take time to go back to Portugal on holidays as often as they can. After so many sacrifices, Guilherme is living the life he worked so hard for..

JMC - 2000

The Lebre family.

Guilherme Lebre at his bicycle shop.

Cousins Humberto and Anabela the day of their graduation from the University of Toronto.

1957: Guilherme and colleagues at Elliot Lake. In the picture we still see the car which served as home to Guilherme and a couple of friends in the early days.

Lima, José Henriques Figueiredo de

Socorro neighbourhood, Lisbon

José Henriques Figueiredo de Lima was born in Socorro, a neighbourhood in Lisbon, on December 7, 1930. He has dedicated himself to his profession as auto-body worker, to sports and to politics, never forgetting time to dedicate to his family.

From a very young age, José Lima was a brown belt in judo and took the professional referee's course from the Central Commission of Hockey. As a referee, José Lima worked for ten years and supervised more than five hundred games. Due to his involvement in the attempt to have a coup d'état in Portugal, led by captain Varela, which was aborted at the end, José Lima was forced to leave Portugal. On June 10, 1961, he arrived in Canada.

José Lima at the First Portuguese Canadian Club.

José Lima married on January 24, 1955, at Santa Isabel's church, with Idália Lopes Rodrigues. Idália was born in São Sebastião, another neighbourhood of Lisbon, where she was born on September 7, 1933. The couple has a daughter, Maria Albertina, who was born on February 22, 1957, in Lisbon. Maria Albertina is now married to Carlos Barbosa, a native from the island of São Miguel, and has two children. After teaching for many years, Maria Albertina is now a vice-principal in a school in Markham, Ontário. José's two grandchildren – André, 11, and Simon, 8 – are his favourite hobby, especially Simon who shares José's passion for sports.

When he arrived in Canada, José first worked for Ford for one year, than transferring himself to the Toronto's Transit Commission. He worked at TTC for 22 years. With a group of friends, José also opened the Portugal Auto-Body Shop, which he had for six years. Never forgetting his passion for sports, José went to the Ontario Soccer Referee Association to take the license to be a soccer referee. For 15 years, José refereed more than 600 soccer games for the Portuguese, Italian and Greek leagues. In Toronto, as member and director of the First Portuguese Canadian Club, José administered the soccer section with Vitor Santos and Correia Dias.

Idália and José Lima with grandsons André and Simon.

Nowadays, José Lima and his wife are retired and they divide their time between Florida and Toronto. From January to April, they live in Florida and the other months of the year they are in Toronto. In Florida, José is member of the Portuguese American Fort Lauderdale Club and often visits the Portuguese American West Palm Beach Club, founded by his "old" friend Manuel Mira. He still dedicates himself to sports. José is also an admirer of the "marchas lisboetas", a series of traditional dancing parades, which mark the month of June in Portugal, also known as the month of the Popular Saints St. Anthony, St. John and St. Peter.

JMC - 1999

Grandfather and referee José Lima with grandson and player Simon!

Lima, Juvenal Costa de

Town of Ribeirinha, island of

São Miguel, Azores

He is a happy man always smiling at what life has given him, even though life has not always been pleasant to him. Juvenal Costa de Lima was born in the small town of Ribeirinha, the island of S. Miguel, in the Azores, on April 14, 1923. Shortly after completing his grade school, Juvenal went to work at the dairy factory of Ribeira Grande

The Lima's in the kitchen at the Liver Mushrooms.

where he became, after a few years, the boss responsible for scheduling the employees and their holidays accordingly.

Juvenal married Cláudia da Costa, also from Ribeirinha, on September 17, 1949, at the church of Salvador do Mundo da Ribeirinha. Cláudia da Costa was born in Ribeirinha on April

9, 1921. While doing his military service, Juvenal went on a mission to Angola for two years. He left Portugal when he was 23 years old. In Angola, he had a relatively calm life. Since he was known as an amateur actor , he began organizing shows for the soldiers serving in the Portuguese army. In the Azores, he participated in many plays. He remembers with some longing the famous comedy A Nossa Terra (Our land), where he played a part with his friend Manuel de Almeida, in 1950. There were 25 girls and 13 boys on stage. Always smiling, Juvenal remembered his daughter Esméria de

The brothers Jacinto and Pedro; Esméria and her father Juvenal de Lima.

Lima, who was born on July 11, 1950, who was going to the theatre with her mother in a small basket when she was only six months old. Besides Esméria, the couple had three other children: Francisco, who was born on September 13, 1953, Jacinto Lima born on May 18, 1956, and Pedro, born October 15, 1959.

Juvenal da Costa Lima arrived in Toronto on January 27, 1960, joining his brother Angelo who arrived here in 1957. He got a job right away at the Liver Mushrooms in Mississauga. At the end of three months, Juvenal decided to go work in a restaurant where he was the cook's helper. Only six months after beginning to work at the restaurant, the main chef left and Juvenal was promoted to this posi-

The always smiling Juvenal de Lima at the inauguration of the Portuguese Club of Mississauga with some friends.

tion. Following his boss' advice, Juvenal decided to sponsor his wife and children to Canada, in 1963. As soon as she arrived in Toronto, Cláudia began working with her husband at the restaurant. Juvenal worked at this restaurant for 31 years, only leaving when he decided to retire.

Unfortunately, Cláudia passed away on May 27, 1979. Besides doing his job, Juvenal was also responsible for organizing shows in Mississauga. At one of those events, someone suggested for the creation of a club where they could organize their activities without having to worry about the place where they were going to perform. Thus, Juvenal with Melo Gonçalves, Manuel Raposo, João Silvestre and some others, whose names he did not recall, formed the Portuguese Club of Mississauga. They received the help from a Brazilian priest, Father Kie, and later on from Father Sá, from Goa.

The club was formed in name, but they still had the need for a place where they could put their belongings and organize their events. Thus, with the help of Father Eduardo Resendes,

The Lima's with their children Francisco, Esméria, Jacinto and Pedro.

they were able to find a hall which they rented on Mississauga Road and Britannia, in Streetsville.

Juvenal was always a director and the main chef of the Portuguese Club of Mississauga. Today, he is responsible for the seniors group of that club. Here he still organizes a few plays. Last Halloween, Juvenal decided to organize a play about a wedding where the groom was 80 years old and the bride was 79. Juvenal decided to play the priest's part. The bridesmaids were all in their 80s, dressed in miniskirts, a picture Juvenal will never forget.

When Juvenal does not show up at the club, the other members begin to worry. In 1993, Juvenal – founding member #1 of the Portuguese Club of Mississauga – fell off the stage where he was performing and was paralyzed for some time. Fortunately, he was able to recuperate from the fall and continues to provide everyone in the club with a laugh. Even if life has not always been pleasant to him, Juvenal has always had a smile to give back to life.

In the middle, groom Francisco Lima and bride Lucy Almeida. From left to right: Monsegnor Jacinto Almeida and Daniel (Juvenal's brothers) and Cláudia and Juvenal Lima.

JMC - 2000

Maia, Dalkar Napoleão

Town of Torres Vedras

Dalkar Maia at Pastelaria Ibéria, in Toronto.

How many dreams do you have when you emigrate? How many dreams are destroyed during the trip? To leave one's place to another country is always something new, unknown and adventurous… We try to find something we do not know and we find something we were not looking for! To emigrate is similar to falling in love: it just happens. This was the story of Dalkar Napoleão Maia who, invited by his father and brother, left Portugal on April 10, 1956, boarding the Roma in Lisbon and touching the port of Halifax on April 18. From here, and taking the train, Dalkar arrived in Toronto on April 21st.

Dalkar Napoleão Maia was born on May 18, 1934, in the town of Torres Vedras. In Toronto, when he left, Dalkar had his brother Manuel Augusto –who now lives in British Columbia – waiting for him, while his father Manuel Rodrigues was working in Kitimat. Manuel had arrived in Montreal, in August of 1952, a year after the first official group of Portuguese Immigrants had come to Canada.

The young Dalkar had his first job in the kitchen of a restaurant, washing dishes. The owner of the restaurant – located in Yorkville – was a 105 year old Russian lady. The boss was already 75 years old, and the ugliest woman Dalkar had ever seen. Dalkar was making 45 cents an hour, which at that time was not too bad…

A picture taken in 1956, during the trip to Canada, aboard the Roma. Dalkar is the one sitting on the left.

- In May of 1956, invited by my father, I went to Kitimat with a group of friends. – Dalkar began telling us. – We went on José Azevedo's car. With us was Julio Batalha, a young man from the north of Portugal, and another one from the town of Fátima whose name I don't remember! – After having said this, and always smiling, Dalkar replied: - Since I had been in Canada for just some weeks and had no driver's license, it was dangerous for me to drive. However, the trip was seven days long, and we had to take turns driving: myself included. One time, the cops stopped us when I was driving and to avoid problems, I pretended I was Zé Azevedo. Boy… it was the scare of our lives…

In Kitimat, Dalkar worked in the building of the Aluminum Factory Alcan. Due to the crisis in the aluminum industry, he left the factory and went to the construction site of the Kitimat's hospital. Dalkar, Frank Silva and José Humbria Correia would talk about opening their own business in Toronto.

José Correia was the first one to open up his own business and Frank Silva followed him. In December of 1958, Dalkar left Kitimat to come to Toronto where, in the same month, he began selling bread.

- I began my own business by opening a bakery in March of 1959 with Francisco Silva. We bought a house on Augusta and Oxford, where we opened the Lisbon Bakery. In the Fall of 1961, we decided to end our partnership.- Dalkar elucidated us. – In May of 1962, still wanting to have my own business, I opened the Ibérica Bakery, in partnership with Américo and Fernando José Figueiredo. Due to some misunderstandings, we decided to end the partnership, and I decided to invest, with Correia and Sousa, in another bakery. In 1972, I went on my own.

Dalkar told us this while we were sitting down at his bakery Pastelaria Ibérica and he was taking breaks to talk to his many clients. - So, after so many partnerships, how do you now live your professional life? – we wanted to know.

- I just sold the business to the brothers Tony and Joaquim Araújo. I decided to only keep this bakery for me just to have some form of entertainment. My children all have a business administration course, they worked with me for three years, but didn't like it. They found better jobs and got married. Jimmy and Norman were both born in Toronto and have a different way of living their life. The youngest one has already given me a granddaughter.

Dalkar's eyes showed a special glow when he mentioned his granddaughter. She is definitely the pride and joy of the grandparents, Dalkar and Julieta.

- Which friends, from those times, would you still like to see?

- Many friends! – he said with a certain

Contest "Make cigarettes" at the First Portuguese Canadian Club. By the look of Fernando Ramalho, the MC, Julieta Maia, Antónia Sousa and Teresa Pereira try their luck.

nostalgia. – I would love to see Duro, who was from the province of Minho and decided to live in Vancouver. I have not seen him since our arrival in Canada. This Duro was so desperate, working in a farm, he was so hungry and tired that one day he went to the train station to see if he would have someone pay his ticket to Toronto. He invaded the train and since he only knew how to say Toronto, they actually decided to take him to his destination. He was with me in Kitimat. I would also like to see Algarvio Careca who was the upholster. The Valverde from Nazaré. This João Algarvio married a girl from South America. Last, I would like to see the Madeirense who used to go fishing with me. I had many friends who I have not seen since those times.

As he was remembering his old friends, Dalkar's face got a sad appearance. Even if many names have been forgotten, their images will never disappear from Dalkar's mind. We continued our conversation, between a coffee and a donut.

- When you arrived in 1956, was there a Portuguese club?

- No. I arrived in April and the famous First Portuguese Canadian Club was founded in September of 1956, when I was already living in Kitimat. However, I am now their member #13, a membership I have since 1958.

- How did the club get started?

- It was at the very first Portuguese business establishment in the city: the restaurant owned

The group that traveled to Kitimat: Zé Azevedo, Dalkar Maia, Júlio Batalha, Zé Augusto and Zé de Fátima.

by António Sousa, today known as Brasil Restaurant, on Nassau Street. We used to go there to have our meals, to talk, to write letters to our families and to find jobs. António Sousa - member #1 of the club -, Mário Tomás - who has passed away -, Chico Alentejano, Justino from the town of Bombarral, Luís Francisco and many others whose names I don't remember, decided to open a Portuguese club. The very first "hall" was at Mário Tomás' house with the name "Portuguese Canadian Club"!

- When you came back from Kitimat, in 1958, where was the club's hall?

- It was on Augusta Avenue. – Dalkar said.

- Why did they change its name?

- I am not sure, but I think it was because there was another club, in Montreal by the same name. Thus, since ours had been the first one, they decided to name it First Portuguese Canadian Club.

Dalkar Maia is one of the Portuguese individuals who has worked more at the First Portuguese C.C., where he has twice served as president, president of the soccer department, vice-president of the cultural section, treasurer and vice-president of the fiscal department. What is Dalkar's opinion about the club today?

- When it comes to the person sitting as president – the first woman –, I believe it was a wise choice. Lucy Cardoso is doing a fine job: she knows the club, she is a very pleasant woman and very active in the club. When it comes to the soccer department, I agree with their decision to abandon the professional section, since these are times of crisis, without a group willing to support the soccer. This way the club cannot cope with the expenses.

Having said enough about the First Portuguese Canadian Club, we decided to shift our conversation to Dalkar's personal life: What future plans does he and wife Julieta have: Canada or Portugal?

- I would love to go back to Portugal, but there are two major factors that force us to stay in Canada, perhaps, forever: the really bad social and hospital services we still have in Portugal, and our children and grandchildren. If they are all living here, how can we go back? So I think we are going to be dividing our time from here to there and vice-versa. But you know, the more I travel the world, the more I like the young Canada and the old Portugal.

After this beautiful sentence, we decided to end our conversation. It is nice to publish the successful journey of this Portuguese immigrant in Canada. From the sacrifices of the early years to the sweet refugee he found in his business, Dalkar's journey has not been an easy one, but one that was worth every minute. It is great it has been so. Our pioneers deserve the best for their courage, tenacity and easy adaptation to the country. To end this beautiful story, we did not resist the invitation to have a delicious pastel de nata (Portuguese custard) with Dalkar Maia.

JMC - March of 1987

Matos, António Cardoso Pereira de

City of Guarda,

Province of Beira Alta

The Matos at a community event.

He is an intuitive individual and was born with the skills for mechanics, as well as the ability to invent engines that facilitate and secure one's life. He is António Cardoso Pereira de Matos, born in the city of Guarda, province of Beira Alta, on April 7, 1929. After completing grade school, António decided to take a course to work with machines in the merchant navy. He worked in cargo ships and oil tankers from 1949 to 1956. On October 8, 1956, the war between the French and the English against the Nasser, led to the bombing of the Suez Canal. António's cargo ships was hit. The first bomb that hit the cargo ship almost made it disappear. By pure luck, the pilot of the canal – a Russian who knew the waters well and was aboard the ship – was able to take them to safe waters. When António left the machine room and looked back, he was only able to see smoke and fire, and hear the deafening sound of the bombs. As he recalls, Onasis was the biggest loser in the bombing because he lost 4 oil tankers. Always on the run, they were able to get to one of Iraq's ports. Unfortunately, for them, Iraq had also begun to take part in this war, backing the Egyptian Nasser. They decided to run once again and went to South Africa, where they arrived in December of 1956. Those were hard days of fear at the sea, without any form of communication because the only transmission device had been destroyed during the bombings. They were able to come back to Portugal, where they arrived in January of 1957. Meanwhile,

Urânia and António Matos, on their wedding day, in Lisbon.

when they were coming to Portugal, the boat was approached by another boat. Big surprise! It was António's wife, all dressed in black and grieving, thinking her husband had died. Due to the terrible days at sea and because he had a new family, António decided to try his luck in Canada, known for its maritime system.

He arrived in Canada on May 28, 1957, with Donato Teixeira, who was from Madeira island. They came by plane from Lisbon to Toronto via New York. This trip would also mark António, since his belongings were lost. António did not give up. They took a taxi, which charged them $5.00 to take them from the airport to the intersection of Spadina and College, in Toronto. By chance, Donato saw a man that looked Portuguese. Trying his luck, Donato approached the man and found out he was from the town of Bombarral. This man took them to the only Portuguese restaurant in the city, on Nassau Street, owned by our pioneer António Sousa. António served them a meal for free and gave them the address of Mrs. Isabel, a woman from Madeira who was renting rooms at that time. Without clothes, money and a job, António Matos thought he would not survive in this city. A friend offered his help and went with him back to the airport. After talking to a few people, they were able to locate António's luggage.

Eduardo and Anthony.

António and Donato's next step was to find a job. They went to the department of Immigration where they were sent, like most Portuguese men at that time, to work in the farms. They both refused it. Donato understood the meat business: he was a butcher. António understood boats and cars: he was a mechanic. Vegetables and live cattle were not really what they were looking for. António Sousa told them that every morning, on the corner of Spadina and College, many contractors used to pass by looking for men to work in construction. That is how they found their first job. They used to walk to get there, using the buildings downtown as their reference. Shortly after, they found a job at the slaughterhouse, and rented a flat at a jewish house. Due to lack of money to pay the rent, Donato, one night, jumped from the window of the second floor, using sheets from the bed and disappeared. Two weeks later, António found him living at a place owned by a native. From here they went each other's way. António was able to find a job at a factory, fixing the machines. One day, as he was coming home from work, he found a young man from the island of Terceira, Nuno, who was so desperate with his situation that he wanted to commit suicide. António spoke to him, told him his story to convince the young man that life was too precious to waste like that. António was able to find Nuno a job at the factory where he was working and they both became very good friends. António would later have some problems at the factory when a Greek man, by the name of George, began complaining about António. George

António at the Rogues Restaurant with owner Tony Pereira.

wanted to be the main mechanic and António was the one taking his place. One day, after arguing with George, António lost his patience and gave the Greek a beating that almost left him unconscious. Then, he resigned. From here, António went to work, still as a mechanic, for the company owned by Manuel Rosário.

Eight moths after starting to work for Rosário, António found a job at Liquid Cargo Lines, in Mississauga. In 1964, he moved to Titan Truck Equipment, where he worked until 1966. From here and until 1971, he went to work as contractor for Shell Canada, in Bronty. António was working long hours almost every day of the week. One day, his wife Urânia told him that his son was already shaving. António realized what Urânia was trying to tell him: he had been paying so much attention to his work that his children were growing up without a father. He decided to stop for one year to provide his family with the holidays they had never had. António took them to Portugal, Scotland, Mexico, Argentina, Brazil, Florida and to many other places.

Going back to his younger days, António first met Urânia at a very young age. Urânia da Silva Afonso was born in the town of Santa Maria Maior , in the island of

Rosemary

Madeira, on May 5, 1936. They both got married on September 3, in the Nossa Senhora dos Anjos Church, in Lisbon. The couple's first child – Eduardo António – was born in São João da Pedreira, Lisbon, on September 17, 1957. He is now a mechanic and a pilot for the commercial airlines. Eduardo is married and has two daughters. António and Urânia's second child – Rosemary – was born in Mississauga, on December 10, 1958. She has a university degree, is married and has three children. The youngest child is Anthony, who was born in Oakville, on November 6, 1976, and is now a lawyer.

After that long period of holidays with his family, António in partnership with Andy Caruana, opened the M&A 401 Service Ltd., in Milton, on November 3, 1971. Their company provided services to Shell. António's mechanical services were growing by the day to the point that the company was invited to open a shop in Saudi Arabia. Since Andy spoke the language and was more capable to do business in that country, he was that one who went to develop the project. They only separated in 1977, the same year António passed the business to his son Eduardo, who would keep it until 1999, the year he sold the shop to dedicate himself full time to the commercial aviation.

The Matos in Florida where they have a house.

António Pereira Matos became famous for this invention in transforming car motors with 350 horse power into 450, with less consumption and more resistance. He called it the Mega Motor.

Due to an accident that could have been fatal to his family, António developed a special break system, which sold in high numbers in 1986. From here, and due to his success with the breaks system, António developed a new system based on the car's material and environment temperatures to avoid the tires' explosion. This system gives the drivers more security and provides the dealers with cheaper prices. In the USA, it is known as the Guardian Angel system. António would love to see his "small" invention approved in Portugal and the rest of Europe.

António Pereira de Matos, a sea lover, has had for many years recreational boats. His life at the sea and his passion for mechanics has never left him. Today, he is a "sailor man" without a boat. The inventions, the family, and his age, do not allow him to venture on big adventures. During his first years in Canada, António was one of the founding members of the First Portuguese Canadian Club. Moving away from the city – he has lived on Johnson, east of Meadowood – António eventually stopped coming to the club. From those times, António remembers that his first house was located in the middle of a native tribe. His son, as a child, whose first friends were natives, spoke the dialect. In 1971, a great fire destroyed the whole village.

António Matos, despite his age, still feels like a young man. He now splits his time between Portugal and Florida, where he has a house. After some misadventures, life has given António what he always searched for.

JMC - 2000

Medeiros, António José

Village of Salga, island of São Miguel,

Azores

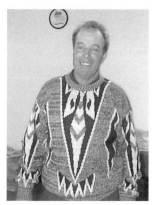

António José Medeiros

António José Medeiros is a kind individual to everyone he knows. He was born on January 3, 1936, in the village of Salga, located in the town of Nordeste, in S. Miguel, Azores. He was one of the very few, who emigrated to Canada at the beginning with his wife and daughter. This was back in 1964. António José got married to Maria Espírito Santo, from the village of Ribeira Funda, in Ribeira Grande, where she was born on April 25, 1936. The couple was married, on February 28, 1962, at the church of Ribeira Funda.

The couple has four daughters; Ana Isabel, born in Salga, Helena, the first one to be born in Toronto, Margareth, also born in Toronto, and Lisa, born in Woodstock. They are all married and have already given the Medeiros six grandchildren.

When António arrived in Montreal with his wife and oldest daughter, on May 28, 1964, they moved immediately to Kingston where António began working as plasterer. He became the manager of the whole section within three years. In 1970, he came with his family to Toronto to visit his brother-in-law Moisés and ended up staying forever! António, member of the local union 183, in Toronto, worked for many years in the construction of bridges and highways.

Margaret, Lisa, Ana and Helena: the couple's four daughters.

In 1974, António sold his house in Toronto and with the money he made decided to move to Woodstock where he still lives with his family. He told us that the decision to move to Woodstock was made to be able to raise his four daughters in a small quite city without any problems. António plans to retire in 2000, the year he plans to take a long holiday with his wife to get to know his homeland better. With a big smile on his face, António José told us that he plans to live in S. Miguel, from May to September, and the remaining months of the year in Woodstock with his daughters, sons-in-law and grandchildren. Since he only knows the islands of S. Miguel – where he was born – and Terceira – where he worked for two years –, António wants to know the remaining islands of the Azores.

That is the way to go. If every Portuguese knew Portugal, there would certainly be more union among us.

JMC-1999

Medeiros, Carlos Manuel Resendes

Village of Lomba do Loução, town of Povoação, island of

S. Miguel, Azores

We have been narrating the stories of our pioneers and of some of their successors. It is about time we begin telling the story of those who came when they were children and have gone through many metamorphoses from the place where they were born, through family separations (caused by immigration) and adaptations to a new land, new values and a new language. Many of these youth are now victims of repatriation in North America because they broke the law. Fortunately, not all of them followed the same path.

The Medeiros with their five children.

Carlos Manuel Resendes Medeiros was born in the village of Lomba do Loução, in Povoação, S. Miguel, on August 22, 1950. He always has a warm, smiling face for everyone. Carlos Manuel arrived in Canada with his mother, Angelina da Ponte, and brothers, on May 10,

A unique picture: Aunt Elvira and daughter Maria José, at the Madeirenses Garden, on Augusta Avenue, the place where many Portuguese used to gather back in the old days. The two boys posing on the picture are the Medeiros brothers.

Top: Carlos Medeiros. To his left: his mother and to his right, uncle António and aunt Maria José, the first ones of the family to arrive in Canada, in 1958.

1961, when he was only 11 years old. They came to live with Carlos Manuel's father, Carlos, who had emigrated to Canada in June of 1959, sponsored by his brother António and sister Maria José, both living in Canada since 1958.

As a child, living in Toronto, Carlos Manuel went to various schools: St. Mary's, St. Patrick, Holy Family and Brockton High School. Always aspiring to follow his vocation, Carlos Manuel went to George Brown College where he completed the professional course of upholsterer. From here, Carlos Manuel found a job in his field, working for a British Company for five years. At the end of this period of time, the factory was sold. Carlos Manuel, after a short time looking for a job, went to work for Mr. Christie, the cookie factory, where he still works today.

Carlos Manuel fell in love with Maria José Campos, also a native from Lomba do Loução, where she was born on March 7, 1953. They got married at Santa Maria Church, in Toronto, a ceremony presided by Father Alberto Cunha. The couple has five children; Francisco Manuel, born on September 12, 1970; Danny, born September 22, 1972; Steve, born on October 11, 1977; Lisa, born January 29, 1982; and Linda, born December 3, 1983.

The girls, the youngest in the family, are still studying

Carlos Manuel Resendes Medeiros

Steve Medeiros

and Francisco, the oldest, has his own landscaping business. Danny also works at Mr. Christie and Steve, the artist of the house, is a musician, now recording his second album.

Maria José, besides taking care of the family and of the house work, has been working at Tip Top Tailors for 26 years, where she is a manager. A true example of a Portuguese woman. Actually, the family is a role model of a united, happy family. The immigration experience, the adaptation to a new city and a new language did not have any negative influence on Maria José and Carlos Manuel.

JMC-1998

Medeiros, Jaime Moniz

Town of Lomba da Maia, island of S. Miguel, Azores

It was in Varadero, Cuba, that we found our pioneer Jaime Moniz Medeiros and wife Maria de Lurdes. Jaime was born in the village of Lomba da Maia, in S. Miguel, on December 3, 1932. He completed his primary schooling in Lomba da Maia. He got his first job as a mason helper with his father. When Jaime turned 19 years old, his father António decided to emigrate to Brazil. Jaime married Maria de Lurdes Sá Ponte, also a native of Lomba da Maia, where she was born on June 22, 1942. The wedding took place at the church of Nossa Senhora do Rosário da Lomba da Maia, on September 26, 1964. Jaime's sister, Maria Augusta had emigrated

The Medeiros, in Varadero, Cuba.

to Canada with husband Arsénio Mota, in 1956 and sponsored her bothers Messias and Jaime. They both arrived in Toronto on June 22, 1959. The same year, his father António came back from Brazil. Jaime sponsores his sister Lília Chaves, in 1961. The same year, António and the remaining children (Mário, Irmete, Manuela and Deodato) joined the rest of the family in Toronto. Maria de Lurdes and Jaime had two children born in Toronto: António, an inspector at Canada's Immigration, and Margareth, an elementary teacher at St. David's School, in Toronto.

When he came to Canada, Jaime lived with his sister Maria Augusta, on 19 Andrews

Street. Two days after arriving, Jaime began working at the construction of highway 401. From here, he went to Strathroy, to work on a tabacco farm. He would also work in Bradford, at a carrot farm, in a bakery, and although he knew nothing about the business, he decided to go try his luck at the railroads. When he got to the railway office, there was such a big line up that he almost gave up, had it not been for a friend of his who had an appointment with the boss and took Jaime with him. It was jaime's lucky day, he was hired. He began working for CN Railways, in Niagara Falls, making $80.00 bi-weekly, with food and housing paid for. Three months later, he was laid-off.

The Medeiros family.

Jaime came back to Toronto to sponsor his sister Lília and saw an ad on the newspaper from CN, looking for men to work in every province. He called in to give his name. When the company called him, he confessed he had been working for CN but had been laid-off. The person on the other side understood him, smiled and offered him a job as welder helper. Sometime after, the boss noticed that Jaime was looking for a promotion and sent him to the company's shop on Keele and Highway 7, which was the biggest one in Canada. Since he could not be in the helper's position for more than two years, according to the company's policy, Jaime – not speak-

Jaime Medeiros at CN Railways.

ing a lot of English but encouraged by the promotion, went to take the welder's course, on Danforth. He was successful. The engineer responsible for the job site had a lot of sympathy for Jaime, unlike the boss who wanted to send him up north. In the middle of this "war", the position for Foreman showed up, in Oakville. He decided to apply and was chosen. At the end of six years, he was called to work at the airport site, in Brampton. Since the company promised to pay him two extra hours a day, without Jaime having to work for them, he accepted. Three weeks later, his former supervisor informed him that there were some positions available to be supervisor's assistant. Jaime did not think twice. He applied and got the job. As a fate's turn, Jaime went to work again for the engineer Bill Harrison who had helped him before. This time, they were both working at Union Station, in Toronto. His dedication and knowledge of the company earned him

Trip to Florida: Tony, Margareth, Lilia. In the middle, Humberto Rebelo, Maria de Lurdes and Jaime Medeiros.

the title of supervisor, in 1980. Jaime was the first Portuguese man, at least in Ontario, to have this position at CN Railways. Jaime was chosen among eleven candidates.

As a supervisor, he began working at the site on Bayview and John Streets. In 1985, the engineer in charge of the job site transferred Jaime to Keele and Highway 7, the site where he first began working as a soldador's helper. Jaime was responsible for budgets of up to five million dollars. He was always able to save money. One time, Jaime finished a job with a surplus of $700,000.

Daughter-in-law Angelee with daughter Taylor, Jaime Medeiros, daughter Margareth and husband John, Maria de Lurdes and son Tony with daughter Mikala.

In 1991, CN Railways enticed the oldest employees to retire. Jaime accepted with special conditions, and retired officially on January 31, when he was 58 years old. However, he only left the company, at the boss' request, on November 30. He received a monetary compensation of $75,000 for the many years of work and dedication to the company, and a monthly pension of $2,443. At CN Railways, Jaime was the Rail Road Union, Local 33, representative, at the beginning of his career at the company. He spent the income he received on properties. Maria de Lurdes and Jaime now travel frequently. They have been to every island in the Azores, to the mainland, Israel, Venezuela, Argentina, Brazil and the USA. Gardening is Jaime's passion. He spends hours around his plants, flowers and cutting grass. The Medeiros couple lives their daily life in harmony with family and friends.

Jaime Moniz Medeiros receiving a plaque of gratitude from CN Railways the day he retired.

JMC-1994

Medeiros, Orlando Manuel Brandão

City of Ponta Delgada, island of S. Miguel, Azores

Orlando Manuel Brandão Medeiros was born in the freguesia of S. José, in the city of Ponta Delgada, S. Miguel. He is the son of Cristóvão de Medeiros and Julieta Maria Borges Brandão. In 1962, he completed the General Business course at the Industrial and Commercial School of Ponta Delgada. A year later, he obtained the certificate at the Business School.

On March 25, 1965, he was hired as assistant of Finances, at the Department of Finance of Pombal, in the district of Leiria. Two years later, on May 6, he was promoted to assistant to the services of Prevention and Tributary Inspection, in the Department of Finances of Ponta Delgada.

Back home, on December 21, 1967, he married Elizabeth Maria Martins Leal Dores. The couple had two children: Patrícia Maria, born in Ponta Delgada, now married with two children, and Orlando, born in Mississauga, who is now 17 years old.

Orlando did his military service in Caldas da Rainha and Santarém, and in October of 1969, he was sent to Guinea, where he stayed for 23 months. On August 31, 1972, he was nominated inspector of the Prevention Services, and Tributary Inspection of the Ministry of Finance in Lisbon. In February of 1976, Orlando

Orlando Manuel Brandão de Medeiros

decided to emigrate with his family to Canada, choosing Toronto as his home.

His first job was in a travel agency in Toronto. Shortly after, Orlando found a job in an accounting firm. At the end of 1977, He decided to open his accounting firm, which he still has today.

On January 3, 1986, the airline Sata Air Azores invited him to represent the airline in Canada. He was the director of the Toronto section (Serviço Açoriano de Transportes Aéreos E.P. Inc.), a position he held until February of 1990. Seven years later, on March 21, SATA would invite him again to be director of SATA Express, a position he has until today. While living in Mississauga, Orlando served in the Portuguese Club of that city as vice-treasurer, member of the Fiscal Council and president of the General Assembly. Even though he still has his office in Toronto, Orlando and family now live in Cambridge.

Orlando is a member of many institutions, among them, the society of Professional Accountants; Canadian Federation of Tax Consultants; Institute of Certified Professional Compilers of Canada; National Society of Public Accountants (USA) and Guild of Institutional, Commercial and Industrial Accountants.

Orlando is catholic and a member of the International Organization of the Knights of Columbus, in Cambridge. Orlando is held in high regard in the Portuguese community, as well as in the Azores.

As a hobby – even though he does not have a lot of free time to spare – Orlando loves playing golf and traveling. This last hobby should not give him any problems.

JMC - 1999

Elizabete and Orlando Medeiros with daughter Patrícia and son Orlando Dores. A happy family.

Melo, José Ferreira de

Town of São Mateus, Terceira Island,

Azores

We have encountered many pioneers who, after thirty years of living in Canada, do not want to go back to Portugal, preferring the country they chose as their second home. However, José Ferreira de Melo is an exception to the rule.

- I went back to Terceira in May of 1979. – José Melo began telling us.

- To suffer, a few months later with the big earthquake of 1980… - his wife interrupted.

José Melo with his famous "red card".

- It's true! Our house after the quake was a pile of stones… - José's voice faded out. After a short pause, he went back to his story. – It wasn't easy. I came back to live in peace and the quake almost destroyed my dreams. It was a disaster. We debated whether or not to go back to Canada or the States, but decided to stay in Terceira to rebuild our house.

Their house now is beautiful. It is big, well decorated and the garden has very north American style. It was at their beautiful place that our dialogue took place.

The old ship Columbia, responsible for the transportation of many Portuguese pioneers.

José Ferreira de Melo was born in the village of São Mateus, in the island of Terceira, on December 16, 1931. On August 30, 1969, he married Maria Isabel Leal Pereira, from Fontinhas, where she was born on March 10, 1947. The couple had a son – Manuel Caetano – who was born in Santa Clara, California, on April 11, 1956. Now, that we know his biography, let's continue with the story.

- I boarded the Columbia, in Ponta Delgada, on April 5, 1956. I arrived in Quebec, on April 11. Taking the train, a group of eleven men from Terceira, myself included, went to Halifax. We were sent to many different places in Nova Scotia with a red card hanging on our necks as an identification form.

- What was your first job in Canada?

- To milk cows on a farm. – He said with a sound laugh. – I was only there for one week. They offered me $50 a month. At the end of one week, I disappeared from there.

Perhaps it was a bad move, but I had to do it. We felt sad and lonely. Had I stayed there for a longer time, I would have been forced to learn the English language properly. I went to look for my fellow Portuguese men and never learned English.

- When you left the farm, where did you go?

- I went to Toronto. I used to write José da Silva, also from Terceira, who was living in Toronto at the time. I began working in landscaping.

Our pioneer is not a physically strong man, he is skinny, a figure which hides his strength to do hard jobs. We asked him how he managed to do these tasks.

When Manuel Melo arrived in 1958, he lived with many pioneers. Standing up: Luciano, Manuel Melo, José Manuel, José Machado, Manuel Bezerra and José Soares. Sitting down: Augusto, António, Ramos and João Pereira.

- You know, it was not easy. – He said with a smile. – But when you leave your country to go work somewhere else, we must do what shows up.

- Did you ever feel hungry? – We interrupted.

- No, food was never a problem, but for a very long time I only had $30 on my pocket. It was very hard.

- Then, did you always have heavy jobs?

- More or less. I went to work for the steal company, Franklim, for about a year, then to Taperman, a demolition company. From there, I went to Permaflex, where I had to roll up paper and plastic...

- Your brother also went to Canada. Did you sponsor him?

- Yes. He arrived in September of 1958. My brother Manuel has also returned to Terceira.

The brothers José and Manuel, in Toronto.

We also had the pleasure of talking with Manuel de Melo, owner of a gas station in S. Mateus, near the city of Angra do Heroísmo.

- I feel great living here, so I don't think I will ever go back to Canada. – Manuel said with a happy face. We hope he is able to carry his plan successfully to the end.

- By the way, say hi to my friends in Toronto. – He said and we could sense he did not miss the country but the friends he had left behind. Going back to José Melo, we asked him if he was working for anybody.

- No. And you know what? I don't plan to work for anybody else ever again. I came back from the USA, in 1979, and since then we have been living from what I make and from what I harvest on my properties, here in Terceira. I still need six more years to receive my pensions from Canada and the USA. I don't regret having returned to Terceira, but if we want to go back to North America, one day, we can because all the documents necessary and up to date. - Taking advantage of her husband's pause, Maria Isabel said:

- I preferred Canada, but I also like it here.

- Did you leave many friends behind?

- Yes, I did. I still remember Jinny, Cândida Dias. Life here is calmer and I'm happy because I'm living with my husband and my son. But I still miss California.

The group from Terceira, in 1956, from left to right: João Leonardo, João Enes, Frank Azevedo, José Homem, José Machado, José Rebelo, José Melo and José Soares.

- I, on the other hand, like Canada better than California. - José interrupted. - Sometimes I miss Toronto.

- Why did you leave Canada to go to the US?

- I left Canada in October of 1961, due to the crisis that hit the country that year. There were no jobs due to the wave of Hungarian refugees that were coming to Canada when Russia invaded their country. I regretted leaving Canada because of my friends and the social life we had. - With a tear showing in his eyes, José remembered his past. - At 75 Bolton Avenue, in Toronto, we were all a family living together.

- In the USA, was it any different?

- You can't even compare. Even though I was living with my uncle and aunt – Francisco and Maria – we were very isolated...

- You've never been back to Toronto again?

- I visited Toronto twice, because of my brother, who always lived there until he decided to return to Terceira.

- What was your job in California?

- I used to work at the Souther Pacific, a company responsible for the construction of communication cables. I was not very lucky there. Due to the extra effort I had to make, I injured my back badly. I had to be operated, but never fully recuperated. I could not work for four years.

- After this period, did you find a better job?

- Yes, at a school, in S. Jose. For eleven years, I worked in the maintenance department of Linebrook High School.

- During that time did you ever visit Terceira?

- For 23 years, I only came to Terceira twice.

In order to forget his sad moments, we asked our pioneer to tell us any funny moments he had at the beginning of his life in Canada.

- Oh, just to think about it... - he began saying, smiling as the thoughts were coming to his mind. – You know, once in Toronto, we got lost. We walked downsome streets back and forth several times, looking for our house, but could not find it. Since it was winter and we were freezing to death, we decided to take a cab. The driver went around the corne, and there we were. Fortunately, the driver was a serious man who felt sorry for us and did not charge much.

- That was it?

- Oh, no! Still in Toronto, in the house where we were living, we all had our own dishes and utensils and each one would cook his own meal, except Manuel Bezerra, who was from the island of Pico. He used my things. One day, by mistake, I broke a plate. I put the two pieces back together and glued them with tape. When Bezerra got home that day, he had the brilliant idea of making soup. We didn't tell him anything. When he poured the soup on the plate, the glue melted and the soup spilled all over his legs. I had never seen Bezerra so upset.

Maria Isabel and José de Melo at their house in Terceira. On the back, we can see the Canadian and American flags.

- Was that the way you found to force him to buy his own things? – We asked still laughing at the story.

- Yes. It was the best solution. – He said laughing at his own story.

- Which friends do you remember the most?

- The Bezerra brothers, from the island of Pico, António Ramos, from Peniche who, unfortunaltely, has passed away. I also remember Frank Azevedo, João Leonardo...

- Do you plan to visit Canada and the USA again?

- I do and will definetly go. – He said with his wife showing a very happy face. – I don't think it will be long before I go back to visit both countries. We haven't done it yet, because the chance has not yet presented itself. But one day...

- And your son?

- Manuel Caetano lives here, in Terceira. He works as an assistant to electricians and plumbers. He is an American citizen, but speaks Portuguese better than English. He is well in life. If one day I open a business, it will be to help him.

- What about you? Are you a citizen of any of those two countries?

- Yes. I am an American citizen, but not my wife. – He suddenly said: - You know, I still have my red card, the one I had to carry on my neck, when I arrived in Canada. It still has the owner's name, the address and the phone number. I'm going to get it.

While José went to pick up the historic card, we spoke with Maria Isabel and waited to photograph the famous card. All the best.

JMC - August of 1988

Melo, José Jacinto de

Town of Candelária, island of

S. Miguel, Azores

José Melo at the University of Waterloo when he placed the biggest granite stone in the country on the University grounds.

There are people who are born under a lucky star. José Jacinto de Melo is one of those people. José was born in the town of Candelária in the island of S. Miguel, Azores, on September 30, 1941. Born to a poor family, José was not able to study as much as he would have liked. However, with the help of his mother and primary school teachers, he was able to complete grade 4. At the same time, the already talented José Jacinto de Melo used to sing songs written by him to raise money for local activities and charities. He did his military service at the Portuguese Air Force for three months. Back in the Azores, he continued to sing whenever he could – from fados to traditional and regional songs – in order to make enough money to study English, twice a week, in a girls' private school. Both teacher and students respected him for his will to learn.

José Jacinto de Melo arrived in Canada in December of 1965. In Canada, José walked the same path. Besides working, he began studying English as soon as he got here. He had problems obtaining his landed immigrant status, however since his teachers wrote many recommendation letters for him, José was seen as a great citizen who could contribute in many ways to the development of this country. José's lucky star never abandoned him. On January 13, 1968, José married Conceição Travassos Costa, in Santa Maria Chuch, in Toronto. The

Conceição and José Melo. Melo's Landscaping anniversary.

ceremony was presided by Father Lima Esteves (already deceased). In a very short time, José Jacinto de Melo, helped by his young wife, dedicated himself to exploring the land around. He would transform a desert into a beautiful garden. He created 30 years ago his own company – Melo's Landscaping – and later on, the Allstone Quarry Products, the first ones among Portuguese Canadians. These firms always had the support of family and close friends.

The couple has three children; Nelson, born in December of 1968; Jim, in July of 1972 and Peter in December of 1977. José Jacinto has always paid a lot of attention to friendships. For an example, when he arrived in Canada and choose Galt as a place to live, he stayed at Manuel da Silva's house, with whom he is still a friend and whom he helps in some jobs. Even his business rivals became his friends. Some people say that José arrived in Canada with little in his pocket, but with his heart filled with ambition for business. He tried the best he could and, as

Conceição and José Melo with friends at a community event.

Tony DiGiovanni – Executive Director of Landscape Ontario – said about him: "he became the best in our industry due to his creativity and natural skills". José de Melo was the pioneer in stone treatment, specially, in granite, for gardens and springs. The big turning point for Melo's Landscaping happened at the 1986 Garden Festival where he got the two most important awards; People's Choice and Professional Award. All the big companies in the landscaping industry were present and both the people and the fifteen-member jury choose José Melo as the big winner.

José Melo at his farm after a horse ride, one of his favourite hobbies.

José's awards were received with pride in the Portuguese community. The Federation of Portuguese Canadian Business and Professionals paid homage to Connie and José Melo. Along with the Federation, the Portuguese Consulate and the Department of Tourism of Portugal also gave them a certificate of recognition. José Melo has inspired many Portuguese people to enter the landscaping business. It was after receiving the awards in 1986 that José Melo opened his first stone quarry in the French River District, in Ontario, and in

Connie and José Melo with their three children and community members when Melo's landscaping received two awards at the 1986 Garden Festival Awards.

1992, the Allstone Quarry Products Inc. His hability to pick up an ordinary stone and transform it into beautiful waterfalls or luminous springs made him a popular individual. DiGiovanni also remembers the famous World Economic Summit of 1988, on Front Street, in Toronto, where José Melo and his team were able to build, in just ten days, the Summit Square which served as stage for the biggest world leaders. José Melo was invited by the premier of Ontario to attend a gala dinner where he received the Medal of the World Economic Summit, given by Toronto's City Hall, and the provincial and the federal governments, in recognition for his project praised internationally.

José Melo, receiving the 1986 Garden Festival Awards form Art Drysdale, radio host and garden specialist.

From a dedicated student, José Melo became a dedicated master, teaching professional courses since 1988. His students are now famous landscaping professionals. José Melo is still known as a professional in his area. Beside his work at Melo Landscaping in the creation of beautiful gardens and springs, José Melo writes articles and teaches courses to the new generation of professionals.

The creativity of José's students has been noticed in the construction of Niagara Butterfly Conservatory and the Science North, in Sudbury. Last year, the biggest granite stone to be extracted in Canada was successfully installed at the University of Waterloo by Melo's Landscaping. At the end of 2003, he built on his garden the biggest Stone Man – Inukshuk – in Canada, which will be sold – or given – to the university's museum.

José Jacinto de Melo, family and friends, continue to create "beauty" with flowers, grass, stones and springs, in a harmony that only the talented can find or those who are born under that lucky star.

JMC - 2003

Melo, Lafaiete Avelino de

Pico Island, Azores

Lafaiete Avelino de Melo was born in the town of Santo António, in Pico island, Azores, on June 18, 1926. He completed his primary schooling in his island. Lafaiete chose his father's profession – sawyer – working for Azorean contractors. Lafaiete married Dulcina Guadalupe de Sousa, from the island of Graciosa, where she was born on October 14, 1930. The ceremony took place at the church of Terra Chã, on the island of Terceira, on October 9, 1949. The Melo couple, with small luggage but a lot of hope, arrived in Halifax, on

Dulcina and Lafaiete de Melo celebrating their 50th wedding anniversary.

March 3, 1959. Lafaiete and Dulcina settled down in Toronto, on April 1 of the same year. In Toronto, Elcie Fátima, the couple's only daughter, was born on January 25, 1962. Elcie is now married with two children: Diedré and Justin. As soon as he arrived in Toronto, Lafaiete found a job as an interior painter. In June of the same year, Lafaiete moved to the Garden Maintenance Works Landscaping, where he worked for two summers.

In 1961, he left Toronto to work in the construction of tunnels, in St. Catherine's. It was a hard work but it paid very well. From here, he went to work as a carpenter's helper for a firm that used to build companies. He was there for eight years. His wife, short after Elcie's birth, began working at the Ocean Fish Store, on Dundas and Manning, which at the time was owned by Correia & Sousa. In 1966, talking to António Sousa, he decided to buy the Ocean Fish Store. Due to the clientele movement in the store, Lafaiete left construction to work with his wife.

In 1982, tired of so much work and no time to rest,

Elcie, husband Ricardo and children Diedré and Justin.

they decided to sell the business, but keep the building. They sold the store to a couple from Pico island. Shortly after, they also sold the building. They were also founding members of the Portuguese Wholesale, in 1971. After so many years of hard work, Lafaiete decided to take a year off to go on holidays, something he was never able to do before. Thus, he retired at the age of 55. However, destiny would change Lafaiete's plans: a blood clot made him loose sight on his left eye. His right eye was also affected by the

Lafaiete de Melo with daughter Elcie and granddaughter Diedré.

Dulcina de Melo and daughter Elcie.

clot, which forced him to stop driving and, thus, delayed his holiday plans.

Today, with the money he was able to save throughout his life and the pension he gets, he lives a good life with wife Dulcina. Their daughter and grandchildren visit him almost everyday. He is proud of the fact that he never received any money from the unemployment center of Canada. Lafaiete did not take part in the foundation of any clubs, but was a member of some of them, in part because they love to dance and take part in the social events of the community. We hope life continues to be like a sweet song to them.

JMC-2000

The Melo's with grandchildren the day of Diedré's first communion.

Melo, Manuel de Almeida

Village of São Vicente de Ferreira, city of Ponta Delgada, island of S. Miguel, Azores

Talking to our pioneer Manuel Melo is like talking to someone who can make you laugh at any sad moment or situation. Manuel de Almeida Melo was born in the village of S. Vicente de Ferreira, in the region of Ponta Delgada, S. Miguel, Azores, on March 5, 1922. For the same reasons that so many others emigrated, Manuel left his island to Santa Maria, on June 11, 1957, where he took the first plane of the Canadian Pacific Airways to fly to Canada. Due to the different time zones and the fact that the flight took twelve hours, Manuel arrived in Montreal on the same day.

- When we told our friends that our trip lasted 12 hours, they would say it was fast compared to theirs by boat. – Manuel said laughing.

When they arrived, the employees from the Canadian Pacific took them to a hotel to eat... - We looked like animals at the market place with a card hanging from our necks so that no one would get lost. – he said, still laughing at his comment. – From here, we went to sleep in the sleeping-cars of the Canadian Pacific. In the morning, after breakfast we took the train to Sudbury. We ate lunch and began to work right away. The day we arrived in Sudbury, we still worked for three hours. – With a proud smile, he said: - The very first day I worked in Canada I made $2.55. I was so happy! You know... in three hours I made the amount money as I would in a week in Portugal.

Manuel de Melo, and other fellow travelers, worked in the railroad, for a long time. From Sudbury and always building the same line, they went to Sault St. Marie. With the arrival of winter, they moved to Galt, after trying their luck at Woodstock and London. At the railroad, through rain or shine, the workers would only get 85 cents.

In the summer of 1958, Manuel de Melo went to Bradford and Strathroy to the tabacco farms, where he got paid $50, with housing and food included.

- This money came from heaven. It helped me so much that I felt I had won the lottery. – Our pioneer told us. – From here, I went back to the railroad, to go back to my 85 cents an hour wage.

Standing up: Joaquim, José and Manuel Arruda. Sitting down: Manuel de Melo, José Soares and Filomeno Cordeiro, in Galt, repairing railroad tracks, in 1957.

Towards the end of 1958, Melo with João Furtado and Miguel, from Vila Franca do Campo, went to Port Arthur to cut wood. Unhappy with the situation, Melo and Miguel decided to go to North Bay, to work in construction. Tired of moving from place to place, in 1959 Manuel decided to come back to settle down in Woodstock. Here, he found the comfort of a home with Manuel Laureano and Elvira.

- Do you know what it is like to work so hard in extreme cold temperatures? Work and work, no wife, no kids, missing everything and everyone back home! On top of that, I didn't speak the language and was humiliated because the so called Canadians gave us the hardest jobs to do and paid us minimum wage. – Manuel opened up his heart, feeling very sadly. – One can only appreciate these things if we go through them.

- When did your wife come to Canada?

- My wife came to live in Woodstock, without the children, in June of 1959.

Ilda da Conceição Miranda, Manuel's wife, is from the island of Terceira. The couple's children only came to live with their parents in 1962.

- In Toronto, the couple had two more children: José Gabriel and Paulo Jorge.

- In Woodstock, what did you do?

- I worked in a Nylon Factory, specializing in lady's pantyhose. In 1960, I went with my wife to Bradford and found a job at the tabacco farms of the Cortez family. From here,

I decided to move to Toronto, where there were more jobs available. I lived at António Ponte's house. I worked for many construction companies.

- You never wanted to change...

- I had the chance to change to a better job in 1968. I went to the Haviland, later on, to Douglas, both companies specializing in the assembly of airplane parts. Due to a cardiac arrest, I had to stop working.

- And you haven't worked ever since?

- No, no. I did work. – he said laughing. – I got into a business with Frank Silva, Radan, and Norberto Rebelo. We used to buy old houses, fix them up and re-sell them for a much higher price. The very first one we sold was the house on 17 Alma Street.

- Was it a good deal?

- You know... When it came to work, I was the only one working and doing the hard job. Then, when we sold the house, the profit had to be divided among three people. I gave up! Today, when I see Norberto, we still laugh about it.

This is the way Manuel de Almeida Melo is: even with drawbacks, he never gets upset at anyone. After this business experience and because he hated to be home without doing anything, he found a cleaning job downtown, but once again his health – or lack of – would force him to stop. He had to retire due to a physical disability. Now, he also receives the old age pension because he is 65 years old.

- After so many years of living in Canada, most of them in Toronto, you must know many things about the Portuguese community. Do you remember the first Portuguese store to open in Toronto?

- Oh yes! It was the store owned by Luis, a guy from S. Miguel. It was on Nassau Street. Then, Sousa opened his place, Norbeto Rebelo followed him, and from here, it was a never ending story.

- Since you laugh at everything in life, do you remember any particular story, a funny one, that happened to you?

- Oh yeah! – he began saying while laughing. – When I was in Bradford, at the Cortez farm, I almost died because I didn't speak English. Cortez made apple wine. He made it on a 40 gallon cask in the garage. When it was ready, he asked us to move it to the basement. I had to be in the front holding the cask by myself as we were going down the stairs. Since it was very heavy, I was yelling at them "push, push". So, instead of pulling, they would push it even more. I don't know how I survived.*

Manuel had to stop his story for a while because he could not speak because he was laughing so hard. Then, he started again:

Father João, the Holy Spirit crowns, and Manuel Melo talking to the parishioners.

Manuel de Melo, washing his clothes, in London, in 1958.

- Another time, in Woodstock, at a demolition site, the Italians had the habit of asking me to do the heaviest jobs. When something required a little more strength, they used to say: "Hey, Portugal!" and would point to the task I had to do. I used to do it and they would laugh at me. When they had something to eat, they would never share it with me. They repeated this so many times that one day, tired of them picking on me, I picked up a beam and went after them. By chance, I missed all of them because they ran away. But do you know what? They never called the "Portugal" again to do anything. They used to say, after the incident: "Portugal, you crazy!" "Yeah! I'm crazy but not stupid", I replied in Portuguese. They left me alone ever since. But you know, all of this happened because I didn't speak English.

This was our pioneer's biggest problem: not speaking English. The language was the obstacle between our pioneers and those already living in Canada. And to think that there still are certain individuals in our community who do not think it is necessary to teach our children and youth to speak Portuguese. What makes them think that just because we speak English and/or French in Canada, Portuguese will not help? Have you stopped to think why some portuguese-Canadians have difficulty communicating with their parents, grandparents at home?

- You participated in many community events, haven't you? – we asked him.

- Yes, I have. In 1972, I got in a commission to create the first Holy Spirit Fraternity of Mississauga. I am a founding member and have been the president from the beginning. Since I was little, I've always liked the Holy Spirit festivities, both in S. Miguel and Terceira.

- Why in Mississauga, in 1972?

- Because there was a big Portuguese community, but there was no church with service in Portuguese. Around 1968, I began helping during mass, at S. Domingos church, on Cawthra and Hotwater. The first mass in Portuguese was celebrated by Father Kea, a German priest who had learned Portuguese in Brazil. He was assigned to say mass in Portuguese, in Mississauga and in Streetsville. From here, and with the bishop's authorization, we began having Portuguese masses in school's and clubs. That's how I began being involved in the Portuguese community of Mississauga. To get the image of Our Lord, Saviour of the World, that we have in Mississauga was our idea. I was the one who ordered it from Lisbon. It is now at the Portuguese church in Mississauga, where Father Eduardo Resendes celebrates mass.

- You are also involved in the Alliance of Portuguese Clubs and Associations...

- Yes! – he said without allowing us to finish the question. – Since I am also the president of the Amor da Pátria Community Centre, we joined the Alliance, a suggestion made by the Consul General, Tânger Correia.

- How many clubs are members?

- Until now, I think we have 15 clubs. At least, that's how many participated in the festivities of Portugal Day. The provisional executive commission was formed by Jack Correia from Casa do Benfica of Toronto, Manuel Caldas from the Nazaré Recreative Club, and Rosa de Sousa from Casa do Alentejo Community Centre.

    - Was there anyone in charge?

    - Yes! The coordinator was Martinho da Silva.

    - How were the celebrations of Portugal Day?

    - I think they were a success. I was told we had some profit. We will see.

    - So, do you agree with the formation of the Alliance?

    - Yes, as long as it is an alliance for everyone. It does not make sense to have so many clubs and associations in Ontario and to organize the events only in Toronto and Mississauga. At the same time, since the majority of the club members represent the region of Azores, I don't agree with the fact that the executive is only made up of individuals from the mainland. Aren't we all Portuguese? Since they are going to create a commission to write the regulations of the alliance, we will see what comes out of it. I think the executive should be made up of members from the mainland, Madeira and Azores. And Portugal Day should be celebrated all over the province where there are Portuguese living.

    It was with this verdict that we ended our conversation with Manuel de Almeida Melo. After laughing so hard at his stories, we decided it was time to let him go. We just hope we can count on him, for many years, to make us laugh with his stories. After all, these are our stories.

* Translator's note: In Portuguese, the verb to push is "empurrar" and to pull is "puxar". Since, "puxa" sounds like "push", it is understandable the confusion created in the above situation.

JMC - November of 1987

Melo, Miguel Machado de

Town of S. António Nordestinho, island of S. Miguel, Azores

When we thought about writing the story of our pioneer Miguel Melo, we could never imagine fate would take him away to a better place before our meeting. Still, we did not give up. Our pioneers deserve all the respect we can give them. Thus, through the kindness of his widow Maria Helena Machado Melo, herself a pioneer, we were able to register his biography.

    Miguel Machado de Melo was born in Santo António Nordestinho, a village in S. Miguel , Azores, on June 10, 1930. He was brought up in a farm where agriculture and cattle breeding was the profession of all his friends and neighbours.

Maria Helena and Miguel de Melo at Melo's Grocery.

Miguel and friends washing their clothes, when they arrived in Canada.

Miguel Melo and companions at the railroad, in Toronto.

Miguel Machado Melo, harbouring many dreams, decided to try his luck in Canada. He left on April 23, 1954, boarding the Homeland, and touched the port of Halifax, on the 29th. Since he already had a contract as a Railway Construction Worker, c/o representative R.F. Welsh Ltd., in Halifax, he took off to Toronto immediately. Thanks to this contract, Miguel worked at the railway for two years. At the end of this contract he found a job at the tabacco farms. Always searching for a better salary, Miguel went back to construction, working in Bront and Hamilton building the drain systems. In the mean time, he decided to get married by proxy to Maria Helena, who was still living in S. António Nordestinho, where she was born on January 1, 1938. Their wedding documents were signed on October 11, 1959. Maria Helena, domestic and embroideress by profession, arrived in Toronto on October 29, 1960. In July of 1961, the couple would open their store – Melo's Grocery – at 47 Denison, in Toronto. Later on, he bought the house on the corner of 41/43 Claremont where he opened his store and had an apartment on the second floor where Helena still lives today.

Maria Helena de Melo with sisters, Maria Lucília Machado and Maria Ribeiro.

The couple has two children; Rosemary, born in Toronto on September 22, 1961, now married and working at Bell Canada. Their son, António José, was born in Toronto, on June 5, 1964. He is still single and works at Pearson International Airport. During his spare time, António José helps his mother at Melo's Grocery. Maria João now enjoys the company of her grandson Joseph Michael, son of his daughter Rosemary.

In 1970, Miguel, with a group of other Portuguese business men, formed the United Portuguese Wholesale Distributors. This was a company who imported, distributed in the warehouse nourishing products; it was a true success in our community.

Miguel passed away on September 2, 2001, after a long battle with cancer, and a cardiac arrest. Miguel was a generous man, very dedicated to his family. At family gatherings, he used to play the

The Melo's with grandson Joseph Michael, daughter Rosemary and son António José.

Portuguese guitar and sing along with everyone. His daughter, Rosemary, also played bass in the school's band. They only visited the Azores a few times and Maria Helena has been to the mainland once.

Miguel and Maria Helena were a very close and happy couple for 42 years. Miguel was never a member of the First Portuguese C.C., but participated in their events and sponsored some of them. Now, Maria Helena is managing the Grocery Store with the help of her son. However, she is beginning to feel tired. Since

Miguel de Melo with daughter Rosemary: the Portuguese guitar and the trombone players.

Maria Helena and Miguel de Melo, when they got married.

both her children are well in life and have no interest in the family business, she is considering transferring or even closing them down. The circle of life is coming to an end for this family.

JMC-2001

Melo, Padre Antero Jacinto de

Town of Ribeira Quente, island of S. Miguel, Azores

Father Antero de Melo is a well respected figure in our community. A serious, humble man, Father Antero is a diligent priest. Antero Jacinto de Melo was born on January 2, 1926, in the village of Ribeira Quente, S. Miguel.

He studied in the Angra Seminary, where he enrolled in 1938. Father Antero was ordained on June 12, 1949. He first celebrated mass at the Church of Covoada, in S. Miguel. In June of 1960, Father Antero left to Canada. He arrived in British Columbia and established his first parish in Castlegara, where, later on, he was appointed bishop Nelson's secretary. Still in B.C., he taught for three years at the Kelowana Seminary.

Father Antero Jacinto de Melo.

In 1966, Father Antero left British Columbia to settle down in Toronto. He spent the first year at Santa Maria church, the historic church that became the first Portuguese church in Toronto. From here he went to St. Joseph's on Leslie Street, for three years. His services were required, even though

The religious festivities of Santo Cristo, at Santa Maria church, in Toronto, the priests Antero de Melo and Eduardo Resendes, listening to Father Libório, in charge of the festivities.

for a short period of time, at the parish of Our Lady of Carmo. From 1970 to 1986, he was in charge of the St. Agnes Parish. From 1986 to 1988, he was at St. Sebastian's church. St. Helen would be Father Antero's last parish, before retiring. At St. Helen, he spent eight years, from 1988 to 1996.

Father Antero de Melo was the initiator of the famous festivities of the Holy Spirit, back in 1968, when he was at the church of Our Lady of Carmo. When he left Our Lady of Carmo parish he had a brotherhood of 30 members. Years later, when he left St. Agnes, the brotherhood was up to three thousand members. Still in 1968, Father Antero got together with master Salgadinho to form the brass band of Our Lady of Fátima, best known as the band of St. Agnes. Three years later, in 1971, he began celebrating the festivities of our Lord, Senhor da Pedra.

Father Antero Jacinto de Melo lives in Toronto with his sisters Maria José Medeiros (married) and Idalina (single). Father Melo has another sister – Salomé Almeida – living in the USA. He had a brother, Mário, who has passed away. Father Melo has dedicated most of his life – 40 years – to the priesthood. In 1982, he decided in conversation with Monsignor Eduardo Resendes, to start organizing pilgrimages to the Holy Land. This first one was done in group. From here, they each decided to organize them individually to give more people the chance to visit the land where Jesus was born. Just out of curiosity, Monsignor Resendes beats Father Antero by three trips: 16 to 19.

Still today, although he has retired, many people still want to speak to him about spiritual and religious advise and to know about the pilgrimages to the Holy Land. Their trips are still a unique opportunity to talk to Father Antero de Melo and hear the story of Jesus as you walk the places he walked two thousand years ago.

Father Antero de Melo is a good man, a believer, a priest dedicated to his mission and an excellent friend.

JMC-1999

Melo, Tony "Starlight"

Town of Ribeira Quente, island of São Miguel, Azores

António Adelino Sousa Melo, from Ribeira Quente, in the island of S. Miguel, Azores, is a popular improviser with plenty of musical intuition. He was born on October 9, 1963. Tony Melo is married to Maria dos Anjos and has two children; Mitchell and Linda, both born in Toronto.

Founder of the musical group Starlight, in 1984, Tony – author, composer and lead singer – has known how to influence his fellow musicians through the musical line he has traced for the band.

Tony and Maria dos Anjos Melo.

In the beginning of the CIRV Song Festival for bands and solo artists, Starlight conquered second place. However, the band – the most famous in our community – has also conquered its way in the Portuguese communities and in Portugal, specially in the mainland. The rhythmic and popular songs: "Viagem aos Açores", "A vida está preta", "Os Tubarões", "Mãe amor", "Elas são assim", "Tia Chica", "É só pedir", "Gente boa", "Pai Santo", "Viva a mulher", "É tudo dela", "Vamos Portugal", "O Reino das Crianças", "Temporal nos Açores", of which the videoclip is a best seller in North America, and many more songs have conquered a legion of fans.

Tony Melo at the newspaper Milénio's editorial office showing the Silver Record from Espacial.

The band's turning point was the song "Canção da Família", by Father Zezinho, was the theme song which launched the band to a bigger scale in Portugal and in the communities around the world. Starlight's popular songs continue to please its numerous fans.

Starlight has won three Gold records from Henda Records USA/Canada, in 1996 for "Canção da Família", in 1998 for "Temporal nos Açores", and in 1999 for "Pai Santo". DataSom and Discossete have also given the band the

Linda and Mitchell Melo.

Gold record, in 1997, for the success obtained with the song "Canção da Família". In 2003, the record company Espacial, in Portugal, gave them the Silver Record for the song "Elas são assim". In February of 2004, the album "Lá diz a Ti'Chica" got Silver from Espacial.

Tony Melo among his fans.

Still, 2004 was a year of successes since Espacial – the band's record label in Portugal – also gave the band the Gold Record. The author, composer and lead singer of Starlight, Tony Melo is also preparing a special show to celebrate the band's 20th anniversary. To celebrate this anniversary, Starlight will launch a CD with the best of the band during the 17th celebration of Portugal Week.

JMC - February of 2004

Menezes, José de Sousa

Town of Ribeirinha, Terceira island, Azores

At the beginning of our communities existence, the biggest problems faced by our pioneers were related to the difference in environment, difficulty in adapting to a new country and new society, and above all, lack of communication due to the lack of knowledge of English and/or French. Our pioneer José de Sousa Menezes actually faced all these problems but because – believe it or not – he spoke and wrote English well. It was at least a different beginning for him...

Pioneer José Menezes at his house.

- That's right! – José Menezes began telling us his story. – When I arrived in Halifax with my fellow travelers, I was in charge of looking after them, since I was the only one in the group who spoke English. I also had to translate for them at Immigration Canada. We came to Montreal where I had to be with the immigration officials distributing everyone to different places and jobs, until I was left alone.

After such a long voyage, to arrive at a country with at least three hundred people and be left alone is a little displeasing, don't you think?

- We left the city of Ponta Delgada, on March 24, 1954, boarding the Homeland. We arrived in Halifax on the 27th of that month. – José Menezes told us. – We were 332 passengers – there was supposed to be 352, but 20 of them dropped out of the list at the last minute. Three hundred were from the island of S. Miguel and thirty from the island of Terceira. I can still see Sebastião Ribeiro, Valdemar Rocha, Avelino Costa – this latter one was from the mainland but was living in Terceira since the time he had gotten married –, Frank Costa, and others on the ship's deck unweaving a rosary of dreams.

José's thoughts also traveled, for a moment, back to that distant, but never forgotten past. How many beads from his rosary did he unweave? José de Sousa Menezes was born in the village of Ribeirinha, in the island of Terceira, on October 24, 1930. He got married at the church of Santo Amaro, to Maria Alice, also born on Ribeirinha, on September 23, 1935. The couple has a son – Victor Manuel – who was born in Ribeirinha, on October 16, 1953.

- We are a family of pioneers, since my wife and my son came to Canada in April of 1955. – José told us with a big smile on his face. – My wife and the late Frank Costa's wife, Maria Noé Terra da Costa, were the first Portuguese women to arrive in Canada.

- Why did you come to Canada?

- You know, I was a mechanic at the Lajes' air base, in Terceira. I used to speak many times to the plane's crew and they all praised Canada. When I found out that many farmers in Canada were looking for workers, I decided to start for the adventure.

- As a farmer? – We asked very surprised.

- Yes! – he said. – It was the only solution back then. We arrived in Halifax at the end of the day. The officials sent us to Montreal in an old train. As I've told you before, I was the translator for all of them

Historic picture. In 1953, from left to right: Manuel Maia, José Menezes, António, Dalkar Maia and Valdemar Rocha.

and ended up alone. Immigration officials decided to send me to Chaval, a small region in Quebec, to work in a cattle-breeding farm. I was never able to milk the cows properly. It was really hard for me to adjust.

- Were you there for a long time?

- No, thank God! Two weeks after arriving there, Frank Costa called me, crying, because he missed his family, and because he was feeling very depressed for not being able to speak or understand English at work. He wanted to live close to his friends. I mentioned Frank's case to my boss and he said he would give him food and a place to live. Frank accepted and came to work with me. After Frank's arrival, five or six others came to work in the farm. Back home, in Terceira, my father was giving out my contact to those who were thinking of emigrating to Canada. These would all come to see me, once in Canada. – José interrupted his story to laugh and continued: - During this time, I read in the newspaper "Diário Insular" that there were two Portuguese men living in Toronto with good professional positions. João da Silveira was apparently a partner at some truck company and Toledo was a hotel manager. I spoke with the gang about this story and we all decided to buy a pick-up truck to come to Toronto to ask these two men for help. It was the first car bought by Portuguese men.

- In Toronto, were you able to find these two famous men?

- Yes! I don't know how, but we ended up on the intersection of Dundas and Jarvis streets. These two "famous" men lived on 33 Euclid. We parked the pick-up and took the streetcar to go to Euclid. We knocked at the door and a lady confirmed that we had the right address.

- So, what happened next?

- Well, they lived there, but were not that famous. I mean, they did not have the jobs mentioned by the newspaper. João da Silveira was indeed working for Rego Truck Manufactors in the cleaning department, but had no partnership. As for Toledo, well... he had been living in Canada for six months and had not even found a job. What a deception!

José Menezes and Maria Alice with grandchildren Linda and Christopher.

- What did you do from here?

- I got together with Sebastião Ribeiro, Frank, Avelino Costa, Agostinho and Aurélio – who now lives in Oshawa – and went to live on 33 Bellview in a house that João Silveira got for us. There we met some individuals from the mainland and Madeira island who informed us about a possible job opportunity at the Canadian National Railways. Since I spoke English, I was in charge of finding everyone a job. At that time, Welsh Co. was in charge of hiring people for the railroad. The foreman was happy to find a Portuguese man who spoke English because he had about 60 men working for him, but none of them able to speak a word of English. I was hired immediately. However, I told him I would only accept the job under the condition that my friends would also be hired. He was nice and hired everyone, but assigned them to different places. I was assigned to the site where the 60 men were working.

So, was this the happy ending for the dramatic adventure? Don't even think about it! In the real world the "they lived happily ever after" does not always apply. Because José spoke English, he suffered more than anybody else. Not only did he have to help everyone with the problems they had to face, he had to witness the abuses and the awful treatment that his Portuguese friends had to suffer from the so-called Canadians. He was outraged.

- Can you believed that they called us D.P.s (Displaced Persons), just like they were doing to the Russians and other war refugees. It was such an atrocious discrimination! I used to tell them that the Portuguese had paid for their fare and were able to go back whenever they felt like it. They used to laugh and make fun of us. I was so upset that decided to quit, shortly after being hired.

- What did you do after?

- João Silveira got me a job at Rego Truck. When I left the railroad, others decided to do the same. I began working the night shift, and during the day, I used to go with them from factory to factory looking for a job and translating. It was hard.

- Was that the end?

- No! I wish it had been. When things started to get better, I began working for a company as maintenance man. I had some letters of recommendation from the air base of

Lajes, where I was a mechanic. Slowly, things began getting better. In 1955, I got a job at The Havilland, an airplane factory where I spent two years working.

- As a translator, you must have funny stories to share with us, even if they were lived during hard time.

- Yes! In 1956, I was the only Portuguese translator for the Canadian government, courts and immigration services. Because of that, I used to travel the country back and forth to translate for many Portuguese men. At the time of the assault to the Santa Maria ship, the consulate general of Portugal – located on Bay St. – appealed to the Portuguese living in Toronto to organize a protest in favour of the Portuguese government and prime minister Salazar. A couple hundred men went to Bay Street with posters and Portuguese flags to support the government. At the same time, a smaller group, which opposed Salazar, went against the manifestation organized by the consulate, which led to some disturbances. The ones in favour of the government outnumbered the group anti-Salazar and began turning their cars upside down. The cops were called and the case was taken to court. Well, guess what? I was the translator in court. Worse: I had friends on both sides. But the truth is the truth and I did my job the best I could. The judge condemned the protestors anti-Salazar, telling them that if they wanted to play politics they had better go back to Portugal. The late Chico Alentejano whose car had been damaged in the confusion was on the side of the anti-Salazar group. He was not very happy with the judge's decision. Again, there was confusion outside the court, this time with José Rafael leading the group. With this second manifestation, they almost ended up in jail. What a disaster!

- Who was the consul general of Portugal at that time?

- It was Dr. Almeida.

Our pioneer, at a certain point in his life, decided to turn his life around, dedicating himself to the real estate business...

- In 1957, I went to work for the Real Estate, since at that time we didn't need to take a course. The first one in the business was José Rafael at the Mann Martel, but he was there for a very short time. I went to J.J. Ellis, located on 1602 Bloor Street West. On a long term, I was the first salesman. I was a

Manuel Fialho, Manuel Menezes, Maria Alice and son Victor Manuel Menezes.

partner and manager at the Bloor Real Estate office. I was there until 1972. The office changed name sometime after to Progress Real Estate.

- Why did you leave?

- At that time, my brother Manuel and I opened the first Portuguese supermarket on Bloor. My brother had come to Canada in 1959. We were there for six years at which point we decided to the sell the business to the Macedo brothers. We also had the Menvar Import & Export which imported canned food, olive oil, cookies, cheese... and I had the Portuguese Bakery, which I had opened in 1958. I have sold everything.

- Were you fed up?

- No! – he said, explaining himself. – I always felt like changing, because I didn't like to be in one place for too long. In 1972, I quit the Real Estate business and began buying old houses, fixing and reselling them. It was different, more active and a lot more labour intensive. Due to my efforts and work stress, I fell ill in 1981. A year later, in July, I underwent heart surgery. I had five bypasses. It was tough, but now I feel better.

- So, you turned your life around...

- Yes! Until 1987, I didn't work. After, I began getting frustrated at being at home without doing anything, something that complicates my system. I found out that a Canadian company was looking for a partner-manager. I applied and got the position.

- Your modesty is impressive. Which company was it?

- Well... the Industrial Spray Painters Ltd., on 140 Rivalda Road, in Weston. We have 136 employees, twenty of which are Portuguese. I'm happy with this company and I don't think I will change again. – He concluded with a sound laugh.

We switched our conversation to another topic. José is such a humble, modest man that he was able to make it in life always helping his neighbours and everyone who required his assistance, specially his linguistic services. José continued his narrative:

- You know, as a child, my parents used to tell me the following; you want to climb higher in life, but should remember that those who climb the highest are the ones falling in the deepest hole. And you know what? Life has taught me this lesson.

Christmas party at the Portuguese Canadian Association. Carlos Ventura (sitting down), José Menezes and Rosinha receiving a gift.

In such a long journey in Canada, many places had José's helping hand in their foundation.

- I was founding member and first president of the first Portuguese Association in Canada. It was the Portuguese Canadian Association, in the beginning of 1957. The headquarters were on 274 College, where the CIBC is now located. I still remember the names of the first executive; I was the president, Gaspar Lages was the vice-president, Valdemar Rocha was the secretary, Manuel Morgado was the treasurer and Romão Graça, António Ramos and Max Caeiros were members of the board. We were the ones who convinced Dr. Almeida to ask the American Embassy to allow the Portuguese living in Toronto to visit their relatives in the United States. At that time, it was really complicated to go to the USA. We also asked the consul to hire Marcelino Moniz, and later on Mário Raposo.

- Were you in charge of the association for a long time?

- I was there for about two years. Life was tough back then, and we didn't have much time to dedicate to an association. I got fed up and decided to quit. José Rafael came in, there immediately were some quarrels and the association closed down, not long after I left. Zé Rafael had this thing to create confusion everywhere he went. – he said laughing.

- Did you get involved in any other association?

- I did some campaigning for the Liberal Party because I was known from my time at the association. However, I was never again involved in a Portuguese association. In 1958, I became a member of the liberal party, by invitation, and supported MPP Andrew Thompson, opposition leader in Ontario. In 1965-66, with the Tory's defeat at the federal level, Andrew Thompson supported Walter Gordon who became minister of finance. During the federal elections I was invited to be the vice-president of the Davenport Liberal Association. The same year, José Martins Aguiar, best known as José Ramalho, from Terceira, ask me to help him become a landed immigrant. Through my contacts in the government, I was able to help him. He was the first Portuguese man to come to Canada as a visitor and become landed immigrant. Through Walter Gordon, I opened the way to legalize many Portuguese who had come to the country as visitors.

- The fact that you are a pioneer and someone involved in the Canadian society, gave you the chance to be the first in many initiatives, right?

- Yes, just like many others in a similar situation. Besides what I told you, I can also say that I was the first Portuguese person to buy a house in Canada. It was in December of 1954, the house on 75 Bolton Avenue.

Thirty four years have gone by since this Portuguese pioneer began his journey, leaving behind the beautiful and celebrated island of Terceira to Canada. Angra do Heroísmo, a patrimony recognized in the world for its beauty and history. Did José ever think of moving back there?

- I would not go back forever, but would like to spend six months there in the Azores, Madeira and the mainland. The remaining six months, I would like to be here. But my wife likes this so much that she doesn't even want to hear me talk about it.

Personally, we understant Alice. They went through some tough times in the beginning, but now they live in a small paradise. The couple's house is a wonder. When we exposed this point to our pioneer, he said:

- Yes, I do agree with you. Besides, we also have our son living here, totally rooted in Canada. He is married, lives in New Market and has already given us two grandchildren. What more can we ask for?

- What does you son do?

- He works for the Nova Scotia bank. He is a supervisor and is doing well in life.

Isn't that every father's dream, to be able to see that his child "is doing well"? It is because of our children that we decide to leave our country and face so many challenges. It is for our children that we work so hard, sometimes more than we should or can. We do not blame them because it is not their fault. We always remember our Portuguese proverb: You are a son now, you will be a father later on! We wish José Menezes all the best. He deserves it.

JMC - July of 1988

Mira, Manuel de Sousa

Town of Carvide,

district of Leiria

Manuel and Maria de Lurdes Mira in the Gallery of Portuguese Pioneers, in Toronto.

Manuel Mira is a man with a successful story. Without any incidents, he was always able to accomplish his dreams. To write his story here is not an easy task. Manuel de Sousa Mira was born in the town of Carvide, in the district of Leiria, on September 16, 1933. Manuel Mira married Maria de Lurdes, born on December 5, 1933. The wedding was on January 10, 1955. The couple has two children; Carlos, born in Rio de Janeiro, Brazil, in 1955, and Teresa, born in Toronto, in 1958. The restless Manuel had however dreamed of other horizons. Thus, in 1952, he went to Brazil. Unhappy with his life, Manuel decided to come to Canada in 1957. Years later, in 1973, with his professional and financial situation stabilized, he decided to move to the USA. His journey was definitely marked by many geographical borders, but with his wisdom, audacity and confidence, Manuel was able to go beyond any obstacle. Manuel Mira has a diploma from the Industrial School Machado Castro, in Lisbon, which he finished in 1952, and an electricians and electronic technicians course from the National Schools, which he got in 1954. In Canada, Manuel Mira took some technical courses and in the USA he got the certificate of electronic engineering, at the Industrial Society of Engineers in the USA.

Lurdes Mira with children Teresa and Carlos, in 1959.

. In 1968, Lurdes and Manuel Mira with children Teresa and Carlos.

In Brazil, he was a technician for many companies, namely Guerin, Chrysler, VW, Porshe, Dito, Cipan and founded the firm Radiomira and systemas Hi-Fi. In Canada, Manuel Mira began his professional career at the Havilland Aircraft of Canada, as a radio and radar technician. In 1959, Manuel Mira founded the company MirTone Communication Systems, a very successful business enterprise.

Socially, Manuel also has an enviable story. From 1971 to 1973, Manuel was secretary and president of the First Portuguese Canadian Club, co-founder and president of the Portuguese Canadian Congress, in Toronto, co-founder and president of the Pro-culture Society of Toronto, vice-president of the International Institute of Metro Toronto, director of the Social Planning Council of Metro Toronto, member of the Federation of Portuguese Canadian Business and Professionals and President of the International Commission of the Rotary Club of Downsview, in Toronto.

In the USA, from 1972, Manuel Mira founded the company TekTone Sound Signal, with factories in Florida and North Carolina, warehouses and distributing stores in Burlington, Ontario, whose management is now under his children. Manuel's grandchildren are also beginning to be successful. For all of this, Manuel Mira is a member of the society of Manufacturer Engineers, of IEEE International Electrical and Electronic Engineers, of the National Electronic Manufacturers Association in Washington and Chair of the Health Care Communication Group, member of the Industrial Advisory Committee for the Underwriters Laboratories, in Chicago.

Always willing to contribute to every initiative in the Portuguese community, wherever he may be, Manuel Mira is co-founder and president of the Portuguese American Cultural Society of Palm Beach County. From 1987 to 1994, he was a Treasurer and Director of the Multi-Cultural Council of Palm Beach County College and co-founder of the Portuguese American Leadership Council of the United States (PALCUS), in Washington. He is also a member of the Macon County Historical Society, of the Portuguese American charities of Portugal, of the Portuguese American Society of Homestead and Portuguese American Historical Society of Fall River, co-founder and director of the

A big happy family. Melissa, Lurdes, Pitalina, Kimberley, Manuel, Teresa, Sheila, Ryan, Michelle, John, Johnny, Carlos and Wesley.

Manuel Mira with grandchildren Ryan, Johnny, Kimberley, Wesley, Michelle and Melissa.

Portuguese American Southeast Chamber of Commerce, honorary member of the Portuguese American Club of Orlando. Manuel Mira is the official correspondent of Lusa – the Portuguese news agency, in the southeast part of the USA and correspondent of the Portuguese American newspaper, in Newark.

Manuel de Sousa Mira is a convinced defender of the Portuguese Language. He is a member of the Portuguese Catholic University. A lover of culture and research, Manuel Mira

In 1998, Manuel Mira with Prime Minister António Guterres.

has dedicated these past years to writing, since his children have taken part in the administration of the business. Thus, and after a profound period of research of the History of America, he published in English and in Portuguese, the book "The Portuguese in the Formation of America – Melungos and the First Pioneers of America", a book which tells the history of the beginnings of America and the collaboration of the Portuguese in the process. A book which also shows the reason why Portuguese people should be proud of their past.

The Portuguese government has recognized Manuel's services by giving him the Merit Medal, among other recognitions. Divided between three passions: Portugal, USA and Canada, happy with his journey in business and community activities, Manuel Mira is living the best days of his life. In 2004 him and his wife Maria de Lurdes celebrate their gold wedding anniversary. He is now studying, traveling and promoting the Portuguese language. Everywhere he goes he makes friends.

Manuel Mira and the president of the self-governed region of Madeira, Alberto João Jardim, in 1999.

Secretary of State for the Portuguese Communities, José Lello, given Manuel Mira de Merit Medal on November 5, 2000

Manuel Mira challenged his fate when he was only 18 years old, going after his dreams. He challenged it and was able to conquer it. Still, he has challenges that go on, even though they are different from the ones he had in his youth.

Manuel Mira is ready for the next battles. For him, there are no boundaries.

JMC - 2001

Miranda, Honourable Luís

Island of S. Miguel, Azores

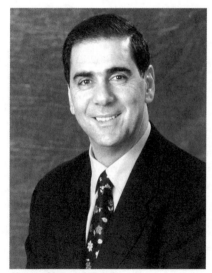

Honourable Luís Miranda

The young Luís Miranda, born in the island of S. Miguel, Azores, dreamt about becoming a firefighter. He made his dream come true. Luís arrived in Canada with his family at the age of 8, in 1963. Due to his dreams, Luis integrated himself in the French-Canadian community, leaving behind for a while his Portuguese counterpart. Years later, in the Ville d'Anjou, just outside Montreal, the Portuguese Community discovered this young, active, kind and a disciplined man.

Luís Miranda was noticed in the firefighting department where he became a professional firefighter. His qualities and honesty led some politicians to notice him and invite him to enter politics since they were looking for someone who could represent the Portuguese community. It was easy for Luís Miranda to conquer a place within his party and the community in general due to his human values and dedication to many causes. He ran for the position of mayor of D'Anjou and was elected. A true Portuguese success! Luís Miranda, the first Portuguese Canadian to become mayor in Canada. He swore in on November 5, 1997.

The young Luís Miranda has been so requested by the Portuguese community to participate in events, after his ascension to politics, to the point that he began speaking Portuguese again, a language long forgotten in his childhood. As well, Luís Miranda decided to go back home every year to visit the places where he spent his childhood.

After the amalgamation process in Montreal, Luís Miranda became city councilor in the city of Montreal, since Ville d'Anjou was one of the amalgamated cities. At the same time, Luís is the president of the municipal and associated council of the department of economical development for Montreal's megacity.

The community lost a firefighter, but won a politician and recovered a Portuguese individual.

JMC - May of 2002

Moniz, José Eliso

Town of Maia, island of S. Miguel,

Azores

Seagulls, skies and sea
As you can see here
It was the name I chose
As title for the book I wrote

Grandparents José and Cremilde proudly
showing granddaughter Michaela.

We have a man who is a popular poet by nature. He is an improviser born in the village of Maia, in the island of S. Miguel, on June 5, 1943. He does not have a lot of schooling, but has much knowledge, and talent to rhyme and to sing. He sang everywhere back home.

In his deambulations in towns and villages, he met Cremilde Pimentel, who was born in Achadinha, on September 9, 1951. They both met and it was love at first sight. José and Cremilde tied the knot on June 19, 1971, at Santa Clara church, in the city of Ponta Delgada. Since he could not provide for his family just by singing, he began considering the option of emigrating. He arrived in Montreal, on October 4, 1967, where he began working in construction. Cremilde arrived in Montreal on October 7, 1971. The couple's first daughter, Sónia, was born in Montreal, and has a degree in business administration. Later on, the family moved to Hull where the two younger daughters were born. Debbye, who also has a business administration degree, is married and has a daughter; and Melanie who is still a student. It was a very difficult journey, but a positive one. After 24 years of construction, José Eliso Moniz hurt himself seriously in 1997. After a slow and not complete recovery, he was sent by the WSIB to do easy jobs. So, life goes on!

Thanks to his ability to write, to rhyme and to sing, José is very popular in the community and, thus, is constantly requested to collaborate in the activities and events of his parish and community. For many years, José collaborated in the TV show "Portugal sem fronteiras" (Portugal without boundaries), where he presented a chronicle about the arts and literature. Once in a while, he would have to present the news of the week.

In 1997, José Elíso Moniz published the poetry book "Gaivotas, Céu e Mar" (Seagulls, Skies and Sea), which was a success in the community. It is a book where José opens his heart about his feelings

José Elíso Moniz, improvising songs, at the Community Centre Amigos Unidos of Hull.

The couple Moniz with granddaughter Michaela and friends Joaquim Medeiros and Carlos Alberto Pacheco at their house in Ottawa.

José Elíso's book "Seagulls, Skies and Sea".

(saudade)* in very simple, but heart-felt verses. It is the soul's voice speaking for itself about the heartland, his ventures and his dream to one day go back to Portugal. At the Holy Spirit Church of Hull, José helps Father António de Sousa in mass, doing the readings and writing for the Parish Bulletin. He also writes for the newspapers "A Voz de Portugal" and "Imigrante", "Diário dos Açores", "Jornal Nacional", "Portuguese Times" and "The Portuguese-American". Even though he has promised his wife not to sing outside Hull, it seems he abused it in the past – he still writes lyrics and sings very often.

In the last event where he was invited to sing, he participated in a "Cantoria ao Desafio" with Gil Rita, Vasco Aguiar and José Fernandes. José sings for pleasure and thus makes no money out of it. Today, with granddaughter Michaella to play with, the couple Moniz lives well with family, friends and the community.

José Elísio, a man with convictions and love for music.

* *Translator's note: Saudade is a Portuguese word for which there is no translation. It indicates homesickness, longing, a sense of loneliness, and all the feelings that are attached to one's distance from his or her homeland, family and surroundings.*

Mother Cremilde with daughters Sónia, Debby and Melanie.

JMC - 2001

Moniz, Marcelino de Almeida

Town of Pico da Pedra, island of S. Miguel, Azores

If there is a well-known individual in the Portuguese community of Toronto, Marcelino Moniz is the person. In December of 1986, He celebrates his 30th anniversary as vice-consul for the Consulate General of Portugal in Toronto.

Vice-Consul Marcelino Moniz in his office at the Consulate of Portugal in Toronto.

- I left Portugal to avoid working in the public services and here I am after thirty years. – he told us, smiling.

- How did that happen? – we asked.

- I was an elementary school teacher at the Pico da Pedra School, in the island of S. Miguel. – To avoid the routine of the public service, I accepted the invitation to emigrate to Canada, sponsored by my brother Antípadro.

- And from here?…

- Well, since my brother was an employee at St. Christopher's House, I lived there for a while. At that time, a group of Portuguese men decided to form a club.

Marcelino Moniz stopped for a while thinking about his past. Then, he continued.

- I think it was the Portuguese Canadian Club. The meeting took place at St. Christopher's House! I still remember some of them: José Menezes – who was the first president of the club – Gaspar Lajes, Benevides and Américo Ferreira. Due to some misunderstandings among them, a smaller group left and decided to form another club. I believe it was called the Portuguese Canadian Association. At that time, they found out about an elementary school teacher who had come from the Azores and invited him to help them. I wrote down the clause and advised them to register the association in the consulate general of Portugal. – he interrupted his narration and began laughing and nodding his head.

- What's so funny? – we asked, half surprised, half curious.

- Because, due to this suggestion, the then consul general – Dr, Armando Nunes de Freitas – invited me to the consulate, alleging he wanted to know me. Armando de Freitas was the first career council in Toronto. He took over on August 1, 1956. Out of courtesy, I paid him a visit and he offered me a job at the consulate since Portuguese immigrants were, at that time, becoming numerous, and there was no one to work at the consulate. I was not interested and I politely declined the offer.

- So, how did you get to work there?

- Armando de Freitas didn't give up on me and sent a letter to Lisbon, asking the government to offer a better position and a better salary. He also requested permission to be replaced by me each time he had to travel or be away. Lisbon accepted all his requests and I didn't have the "guts" to deny the position. This way I was submitted to the fate of being an employee for the public service forever.

We had to laugh with him at this story. Marcelino Moniz continued his story.

- My first salary was $220 a month. I began working in the consulate on December 14, 1956, as a secretary. I was promoted to chanceler on March 30, 1962. On February 3, 1968, I received my last promotion to vice-consul, a position I still hold today.

Marcelino de Almeida Moniz was born on November 1, 1931, in the village of Pico da

Pedra in the island of S. Miguel, Azores. He completed High School and the Public Works. He is married to Nobélia Estrela, also from S. Miguel. Their son, Christopher, was born in Toronto, specialized himself in organic chemistry and is a research engineer at the Shell laboratories. Marcelino arrived in Canada on September 2, 1956, by airplane, via New York.

- I traveled by plane – the clipper from Pan American airlines. The trip "only" took 16 hours.

The thought of this trip was, again, another reason for laughter and for Marcelino to remember old stories, dormant in his subconscious.

- My first job was given to me by the Canadian Immigration Services. I was, temporarily, at the University of Toronto cataloguing books. From here, I went to a company that imported car parts where I had to be in the shipping and receiving section.

- How were things at the consulate?

- It was hard at the beginning - after a pause, he added. – Before this, the honorary consul, Verner Willemsen, had an insurance company of his own and one of his employees – Mrs. Galaka – was also the secretary at the consulate because she spoke Portuguese. So she had been hired by the consulate to help all the Portuguese with their problems. Well, it seems like she was more inclined to help herself than the people who came up to her for help. We found out later on that she was trying to explore every single Portuguese man who came to the consulate by trying to sell them insurance policies, and leaving behind all the consulate matters. So, the first four months I spent to putting everything and put the work up to date.

The old St. Patrick church, when the Patriarch Cardinal of Lisbon D. António Ribeiro visited Toronto in 1968. In the picture we can see, among others, the Consul of Portugal Luís Martins, D. António Ribeiro, Marcelino Moniz, Nobélia Moniz and Alice Ribeiro.

- From here, everything went astray.

- Oh no! – Marcelino interrupted. – We always had a lot of work. You can't imagine the work we had to do when three thousand Portuguese men were hired to work at the sugar factory, in Leamington. It was a big problem… We had complaints from everywhere. They didn't understand the language, didn't like the food, were missing their families, felt ill, wanted to go back, and a list of many other problems. It was a hard period. At that same time, also in Leamington, an individual by the name of Coimbra was fatally run over. He was the second Portuguese men to die in Canada. The first one was Joaquim de Sousa Neves, in Bradford, who was also atropelado. It was a hit and run accident and we never found out who killed him. This was back in 1956. We, at the consulate, served as priests, bosses, friends, advisers to all these people.

- Why did the Portuguese choose Dunas and Spadina as their safe haven?

- One of the reasons was, without any doubt, related to the Unemployment Centre being located there, at that time. So, the unemployed Portuguese men used to gather there to collect their money, to talk to each other, and began spending some time there. On the other hand, a lady from Macau – Ruth – was a Social Worker at St. Christopher's House. She got to know them through many conversations and convinced them to start studying English at St. Christopher's. Thus, more people came to live in the area. The first one to buy a house in this block was Jordão Isidro de Freitas, an individual from Madeira Island. Actually, the people who came from Madeira were the first ones to settle down.

- In this journey that you ended up embracing, in your contact with many consuls, did you ever regret working for the consulate?

- No! I learned something new

Marcelino Moniz holding his son Christopher's hand and accompanying wife Nobélia in the first candlelight procession in Toronto, in 1963.

with each one, I always got along with every single one of them. They were always open-minded people, always worried with the well-being of the community, and nothing else.

- Was there a special moment you remember particularly well?

- Oh yes! – he said, beginning to explain. – The period that began with the revolution of April 25, 1974 until the first constitutional government was a particularly hard one. Both Dr. Melo Gouveia and Ernesto Feu, had many difficulties due to the confusion that was created in the services from constant changes and many incertainties. It was hard, but everything found its path again.

Although Marcelino Moniz was being frequently interrupted by many phone calls, we were still able to ask him, before wrapping up, we asked him if he held some sad moments in his heart, related to his career at the consulate.

- Yes, I do. Personally, I am sad not to be able to have dual citizenship, because my position does not allow it. For me, the Portuguese community is my people, my heartland... I don't know if you understand what I mean. It has been 30 years that I have worked for them, I cannot separate from my people. I also have this volunteer passion... the growth and development of our community is my pride.

- For a moment, a beautiful glare was seen in his eyes. He then smiled and said,

- One of the happiest moments of my life was to see the First Portuguese as champions of the National Soccer League. Of course, when Eusébio also played for our team here in Toronto he contributed to Canada's win in the North American Soccer League... There are things in life which are priceless...

JMC - December of 1986

Monteiro, Francisco da Mota

Carnide Neighbourhood, Lisbon

The pioneer Francisco da Mota Monteiro is a calm individual who, by his own free will, transformed his path in Canada into a very sweet journey. How? Very simple: he went from the shop where he was working to the importation of chocolates. Is it not sweeter?! Let's leave our humour behind and let's get to

Maria Alice and Chico Monteiro on holidays in North Bay beside the first car they purchased in 1959.

the facts. Francisco da Mota Monteiro was born on September 26, 1931, in Carnide, Lisbon.

- I was baptized at the church of Luz. – he said smiling: - I had a twin brother – José – who died three months after being born. According to my parents, the doctor informed them I too would only last a few days. Fortunately, the doctor has already passed away and I'm still here.

Indeed, whoever looks at our pioneer Francisco da Mota Monteiro, cannot imagine him as someone who had to face certain problems when he was born. He is a very tall, strong man with white hair, but not even one is missing. Briefly, he is a healthy man.

- When did you come to Canada?

- I left with my brother Cândido on September 25, 1956, aboard the Saturnia. We arrived in Halifax on October 1. I celebrated my birthday on the Saturnia.

- Did you already have any family in Canada?

- Yes, I did. My brother Avelino was already living here, since 1955. He was the one who sponsored us.

- Were you married when you came to Canada?

- No, I was still single. I married by proxy on April 14, 1957 and my wife came to Toronto, in October of 1957. So, she is also a pioneer.

- And by the logic of things, your children were born in Canada.

- Of course! – he said immediately. – My eldest son, Nelson, was born in Toronto, on October 4, 1960, and Elizabeth, on January 18, 1963. They are still single.

Francisco Mota Monteiro is married to Maria Alice Henriques de Almeida, born in the village of Guarda-Gare, in the district of Guarda, on May 11, 1936.

- How did you end up in Toronto?

- We came to Toronto because Avelino was living in this city. From Halifax, where we had arrived, we took the train on a trip which took two and half days. We arrived in Toronto, on October 3.

The Mota brothers in 1957. From left to right: Cândido, Avelino and Chico.

- What was your first impression of Canada? For someone who was living in Lisbon, this must have been at least strange, right?

- Yes, especially Halifax. It was October. Everything was dark, so sad, the houses were all built from wood, and I found everything really weird. I must confess that I looked at this country with some skepticism, but I adapted fast to this way of life.

- Did you begin working right away?

- Not immediately after arriving. But it didn't take long to find a job. Cândido and I began to work on October 22, at the Frankel & Steel, on Broadview and Queen, a factory specialized in building metal structures. I went to the painting section, but was also responsible for cleaning the steel bars with a metal tooth brush. I was able to manage and at the end of two years I was in charge of the painting section.

- Were you there for a long time?

- I was there until 1963, when I found a job at Ford with a better salary. I went to work at the assembly line. In 1965, I suffered a car accident which forced me to stop for a few weeks. When I went back to work, at Ford, they gave me an easier job to do, even though I was still in the same section. I worked in this section for ten years.

- A decade is a long time. During all those years did you ever think you would be in the import and export business?

- I don't know. I always had this thing for business, perhaps because I was always involved in my father's business. We had a sports bar in Carnide. I was the only one from my brothers who liked working there. I always wanted to help my father.

- So here in Toronto, when did you begin to get involved in the business world?

- It was in 1963. I contacted the firm Eduardo Galrão Jorge Ltd., and began to import marble stones. This is a

Chico and Maria Alice Monteiro with the couple José Correia in a community event.

well known firm in Portugal. However, I was never too successful with the marble business in Toronto because you need to have some knowledge of the product and some people giving you a hand. Nevertheless, I still have some clients who come to me to purchase marble and granite stones. I am actually thinking of expanding this sector of my business.

- How did you get to the chocolate business? – we asked.

- Well! – he began saying, smiling at the same time. – In 1967, I introduced the Regina products because, I remembered very well, they were the chocolates every kid liked in Portugal. The Portuguese community was still small and it took long to introduce the product in the market. In 1972, I was able to begin the regular distribution of the Regina chocolates.

- When you began distributing chocolates, were you still working at Ford?

- No. I left in 1976 to open my own company, the Monteiro Import & Export, a small but self-sufficient company. I am in Mississauga.

- You only have Regina products?

- No! – he said. – Today I have many products from Regina, candies from Lusiteca, cookes from Aliança, products from Compal from Confeitaria Nova Lisboa…

- When you began your import business, was there anyone doing it already?

- If I'm not mistaken, the only ones in the import & export business were the Correia & Sousa and Tércio Dias.

- What about clubs, were you part of any?

- In those old times, I witnessed the birth of the First Portuguese Canadian Centre where I collaborated for a while. I am still a member today of the First Portuguese. The club was founded in September of 1956, around my birthday, that's why I still remember. I was one of the many Portuguese men who pulled a number from a bag to determine my membership number. I think I got number 101.

Francisco da Mota Monteiro, best known as Chico Monteiro, remembered, after this story with the numbers from the bag, the troubles the club had to face at the beginning of its existence. About that, we asked him if he had any interesting moments back in those days that was worth writing about. After thinking for a while, Francisco laughed and said:

- This one happened on the day I traveled from Halifax to Toronto, by train, when I arrived in Canada. The train, besides being very slow, used to stop at every single station. Our only entertainment at that time was to talk to each other and admire the landscape outside the window. At certain time, I looked at my brother and said: Hey! This country must be amazing.

There is a party going on everywhere. My brother asked me: why do you say that. Well, I continued, in every station that we have stopped from Halifax until now, the parking lot is decorated with little flags and lights. When we arrived in Toronto, I asked my brother Avelino about the parties and he told us, laughing all the time, that the illuminated parking lot was a car stand. Oh boy! Did I laugh when I heard that!

Victor Pereira and Chico Monteiro, in 1960, performing for their family when they baptized their children Ana Bela and Nelson.

We were also amused by the story. Really, for someone to arrive at a new country in October and find so many places decorated with flags and lights, it is normal to think that it is a festival. What about sad moments: were there any for Chico Monteiro?

- Fortunately, I never experienced really sad moments that have marked my life. Neither did my brothers, thank God. – His smiling face changed into a sad one. – Of course, we suffered with our mother's passing, in Portugal, in 1966. You know I was here for nine years without going to Portugal. I went in 1965 and my mother passed away a year later. My father also died in Portugal, in 1987. I was there and will never forget this sad moment.

Some rebel tears showed up in our pioneer's eyes. His emotions were stronger than him. To remember is to live, so we respect his tears and his silence. Some moments after, we went back to our conversation, this time focusing on the evolution of our community.

- I would love to see our community continue the prosperous growth it has registered until now, without any troubles, so that our children could be proud. It would be nice to see it growing in harmony and friendship, without any divisions. There are things that could be better, but time will solve them. Still I believe our community knew how to come together and settle well in this strange land.

- What do you think should be done to make things better?

- You know, when our child makes a mistake that's when we should help him! – Our pioneer said almost like a verdict. – So I believe it is our duty to support the community events even when we think things are not being done properly. United we can go very far and can even correct the not so right things.

We took some more time to speak about the Portuguese and the community. Chico Monteiro believes in our community and the potential we have as individuals. We asked him if he had any plans of returning to Portugal.

- That question is an interesting one, but I never thought about it. I like Portugal a lot, I go there whenever I can, but never thought about returning there. – After a long pause, Chico said: - I'm not saying I will never go back because only God knows what tomorrow brings, but I don't think about it. In Canada, I have my life, my children, by brothers… I believe my wife feels the same way as I do. To be honest with you, I don't even think about my retirement yet.

Chico Monteiro with son Nelson in Wasaga Beach in 1961.

With this positive attitude that our pioneer exhibited, we decided to end our dialogue. We feel proud to have this family among us in Canada. We just hope that Chico continues to live his life the same he has always known how to live.

JMC - June of 1988

Monteiro, Manuel Conde Fernandes

City of Setúbal

" **A**ll you want is a night life full of songs", a sentence Fernandes Monteiro heard many times. Manuel Conde Fernandes Monteiro was born in the city of Setúbal, on October 3, 1936. He got to third year at the Commercial School of Setúbal. He began singing and working at a very early age.

The Fernandes family was marked by the dictatorship regime, so the necessity that the family experienced forced every member to work hard to make ends meet. Fernandes Monteiro worked at Cacia, a cellulose factory. At that time, he was the voice of many orchestras in Aveiro, Aloma and Ibéria, the best one at that time. In 1959, when the cellulose factory of Setúbal opened, Fernandes Monteiro returned to his hometown. In Setúbal, he delighted many audiences singing for many bands, among them Júlio Graça, Europa, Rimos and Medolias, and the Blue Star Melodies, the latter the best among the best. Throughout the nights filled with songs, Fernandes Monteiro used to replace the famous António Alvarinho, lead singer of the band "Os 5 de Portugal", a band that performed at the night club of

The Monteiro brothers: Jaime, João Lúcio and Manuel.

the Calçada da Glória, located in Bairro Alto, in Lisbon. His passion for the night and his obligation towards his work forced to go for days without getting any sleep.

In 1969, Fernandes Monteiro's brother Jaime, who had settle down in Toronto a year before after spending some months in Montreal, wrote Manuel and invited him to come to Canada. Sponsored by Jaime, Fernandes Monteiro arrived in Toronto on September 17, 1969. When he arrived in Toronto he told himself he was going to quit singing to dedicate himself entirely to his family and to work. He had since married Fernanda Marques on April 28, 1963, in Setúbal, and a year later on April 28, the daughter Ana Cristina was born. The nights and the songs were causing him some problems at home and he had decided to change the path he had traced for his life. A week later he was singing with Mariano Rego at the famous El Mokambo restaurant, in Toronto. While he was singing in the first floor, he heard a loud rumor coming from upstairs; the scandal between Margareth Trudeau and the rocker Mick Jagger was becoming public.

Thus Fernandes Monteiro was not able to escape his fate in the music world. Not even his family was able to stop him from this passion. After singing with the late Mariano Rego, with whom he recorded two albums, at the El Mokambo, Fernandes Monteiro went to the Império Restaurant where he sang for six months. One night in Império, the Brazilian singer Nilton César heard him sing songs by Nelson Ned, another Brazilian singer, and invited Fernandes Monteiro to perform in Brazil.

The singing life he had chosen was not enough to provide for his family, so he found a job at a factory on Dixie and Queensway where he worked for many years. Fernandes Monteiro also became the master of ceremonies at the Octávio Restaurant whenever there were fado shows. There he worked beside Dina Maria, who had come from Montreal, and with the guitarist Artur Gaipo, with Fátima Ferreira, Mano Belmonte, among others. Fernandes Monteiro joined the guitarist António Amaro and founded the band "Os Cariocas". Back in those days the famous bands of the community were the Boa Esperança, Os Rebeldes, The Lords and the Capas Negras.

In 1976, with António Amaro, Joaquim Machado, Augusto Santos and a guitarist from the town of Nazaré, they founded the band Algarve 76. From here, Fernandes Monteiro went to sing for the band Rio Connection, a band of his preference due to the quality of the musicians and the brass instruments. During the 80s, he was also member of other bands where he worked with Fernando Tavares, Carlitos and Necas Machado. From 1986 to 1992, Fernandes Monteiro joined Herman Paiva (the Portuguese Elvis), Albano, a base player from the island of Pico and an Italian keyboard player to form the band Os Sombras. Meanwhile, in 1982, his wife Maria Fernanda returned to Setúbal taking their daughter Cristina.

Eusébio did not run away from his admiror's hug: Fernandes Monteiro was a true sportsman.

Even though he was doing what he loved, Fernandes Monteiro was an unhappy man. In 1988, tired of being alone, he decided to go back to Portugal to be with his family. Through his friend Francisco Albino, he found a job at Toyota. For three years he fought to be with his family without the night life and the songs he loved so much. On the other hand, Fernandes Monteiro was already too used to the life he was living in Canada. He lost his fight. His wife decided to stay in with their daughter, who was already

Songs and soccer were always part of Fernandes Monteiro's life. Here he is with Fernando Gomes, winner of the Golden Boot.

Fernandes Monteiro with the Consul General of Portugal, Dr. António Montenegro.

Fernandes Monteiro and singer Carlos Rocha.

married. So, Fernandes Monteiro, feeling very lonely, decided to come back to Canada. In 1992, although happy to be a member of the group Os Sombras, Fernandes Monteiro decided to quit his life of songs and music. To live without singing? Don't even think about it! He decided to dedicate himself to the song of Portugal, fado.

Speaking of fado, he remembered one interesting story, a Portuguese professor in Boston asked the Consulate of Portugal to find a fado singer because he wanted to organize a conference about fados for his students. The consul at the time, Dr. Martins, indicated Fernandes Monteiro. Without thinking twice, Fernandes Monteiro told António Amaro and the late Manuel Saldanha and they all took off to Boston. At the university, in the middle of thousands of students, Fernandes Monteiros felt very small, but did not vacillate and sang the best he could. When he finished singing Fado Hilário and saw the crowd in a standing ovation, Fernandes Monteiro felt like it was the happiest day of his life. Just like the old fado song says "It was worth it!" He proudly remembers singing the Canadian National Anthem in Portuguese, with lyrics by José Mário Coelho, at the Varsity Stadium, accompanied by the orchestra from Saint Agnes church, before the soccer game between Benfica and Partizan from Belgrad. Today, after so many years Fernandes Monteiro still lives alone, even though he still keeps in contact with his wife and daughter who has given his two grandchildren: Raquel, who is now 10 years old, and Diogo who is three. He faces his loneliness by keeping contact with his friends and the voice he still has. He sings fado but not his fado (fate).

His friends and the administration of Casa do Alentejo organized an event to celebrate his 45th career anniversary on April 20, 2001.

Unfortunately, his fado has come to an end…

JMC - 2001

Moraes, António Augusto Correia

Beira, Mozambique

António Augusto Correia de Moraes

The pioneer we chose for this story is someone who was born to be successful. To get there though, he had to walk a long path, going through many continents. However, calmly and persistently, he was able to reach the pyramid's top. This is António Augusto Correia Moraes, born in Beira, in Mozambique, on June 2, 1930. His father was from the island of S. Miguel, Azores, and was a director at the Union Castle Line in Beira. So from a very young age, little Tom received an oustanding education in English. Due to a serious illness –suffering from bad circulation – his father had to go on early retirement and decided to return back home where most of his family was living. Tom was 4 years old. In Ponta Delgada, after completing the first four years of school, he went to the then high school Colégio de S. Miguel. From here, Tom went to the Commercial School of Ponta Delgada, where he finished his business degree. Throughout this time, his passion was always music. He used to go to many dances at the Ateneu Comercial of Ponta Delgada where he had more fun just sitting down and listening to the band than actually dancing.

When he turned 16 years old, he began going to the Eden Casino, hiding from his austere family who still thought he was going to the Ateneu Comercial.

At the Eden Casino, Carlos Fernandes, an individual from Madeira Island and owner of the casino's orchestra, began teaching him how to play his first musical notes. Since theory was boring and difficult, Tom used to ask Carlos to teach him only how to play.

- What I wanted was to play, not learn how to read music properly! – Tom Moraes told us with a star in his eyes at his place in Toronto.

- So how do you end up playing in a orchestra in Ponta Delgada?

- The lessons I got from my friend Carlos Fernandes and my musical intuition gave me some knowledge in playing the drums and I was at ease with it. – Tom began telling us laughing at his own story. – I paid him with a shirt. With blood pumping at full

Official document from the first group of men from the Azores who arrived in Halifax, in 1954.

speed on my veins , I went up to the orchestra's conductor, Gualdino Rodrigues, and asked him to let me play drums in the band. To my surprise, shortly after, he called me and invited me to be part of the orchestra. At this orchestra, I met the radio announcer Victor Cruz, who was working at the Emissor Regional in the Azores. We used to play there every Saturday from 8 to 8:30 pm. As a musician, I was making 30 escudos* an hour! – he said laughing. – Good old times!

Before we continued our dialogue, Tom de Moraes looked through the window as if he were looking back in time searching for something. Then he continued:

- With this salary, I was forced to look for another job. I entered the government's public service. I went to work for the agriculture department where I met Fernando Raposo, and from here I was transferred to the Civic Government's department. Because I spoke English, I was hired as the translator in this department.

- How did you get the chance to emigrate to Canada?

- You know, I came with my eyes closed, as we say. I was 23 years old when the chance presented itself. It was the first group of men from the Azores who came to Canadá, in 1954. It was a group of two hundred men, as the documents I still have can prove it. These men were chosen according to physical appearance, good teeth and their schooling – they needed at least the first four years of elementary school. The official from Canada's Immigration who took care of the matter were working in Paris: Odillon Cormier, Charge d'Affaires, Percy Colville, Senior Officer, and Pierre A. Belanger, the Medical Doctor. I was the translator for english and Rui G. de Morais, who is not related to me, was the French translator.

Official letter from the company to António Moraes.

- Who was overseeing the operation from the Portuguese government? – we asked.

- They were the officials from the ministry of Internal Affairs and the emigration council of Lisbon: the inspectors Dr. José F. Neves Belo, the capitain Ferreira da Costa and the doctor José Dias Henriques. The two hundred men from the Azores left Ponta Delgada on April 20, 1954. I left before them, I took the plane directly to Toronto where I arrived on April 16 of that year. I was sent as the translator to establish contact with the Portuguese immigrants who were already living here with the Canadian government and the company that was hiring them. The coordination between the Portuguese and the Canadian emigration department was done by the inspector São Romão through me, in Toronto. I was in charge of everyone's files.

- Which company was hiring them at the time?

- It was R. F. Welsh. I had to verify the way things were going at the rail road where many Portuguese were working and living. When I showed up, they received me as if I were a god. I was the translator and responsible for solving everyone's problems related to food, bad conditions, illness, homesickness, complaints, isolation and some cases of discrimination. Anyways, such a long list of problems I was trained to solve and no condition to be able to solve them. When winter came by, so many of these men were laid-off and I decided to leave my job as well.

- Before leaving the company, where were you working?

- When I left, I was living in Saint Boniface, just outside Winnipeg. It was so cold that I decided to take the train and come straight down to Toronto. This was in November of 1954. Until this date, I was in charge of many job sites, namely in Toronto, Morrisborough, Cardinal Belleville, London, Strathroy, Gravenhurst, Barrie, Allandale, Pale Arthur, among others.

- So when you left you had found another job.

- Yes! In Toronto, I went to work at Eaton's treasury board until 1961, when I decided to go on my own selling insurance until I retired. I was the chefe of the Administration Services of the American Re-Insurance Co. When the company moved to New York I decided to retire. Nobody takes me away from Toronto! – he said very happy.

- What happened to your music?

- I never forgot my music. Living a different life style, I dedicated myself to studying music with a private Canadian teacher, on Bayview Avenue, in Toronto. I began learning music seriously in 1957.

- How did you form the orchestra?

Tom Moraes Orchestra and Choir in Toronto.

- Well, I and a group of fans of the Swing Era, the musical movement that dominated the air waves between 1936 and 1952, decided to record the songs of the biggest orchestras of that time, such as the Banny Goodman, Harry James, Glenn Miller, Tommy Dorsey and others. To put it simpler, I founded the orchestra in September of 1973. We were and still are sixteen members. We used to get together every Thursday to rehearse and play the songs I truly loved. In 1982, when I was told to go to New York to work or to retire, I didn't think twice. I retired and decided to transform the orchestra into a professional one.

- What were your friends, from outside the band, telling you?

- They used to tell us we were playing old music and that we had no future with it. – Tom told us laughing at this comment. – I didn't pay attention to those comments and went to CRJT radio station, in Toronto, and offered the orchestra's services to play in charity concerts. We began performing twice a year. So slowly but surely we began being known. The Lawrence Welk Orchestra, which performed on television, was also giving us a hand in promotion. So we began receiving many invitations, which led to our success.

- Which concerts touched you the most?

- Besides the ones played for charity purposes, I was particularly touched by the concert we played for Jane Fonda, Mickey Rooney, and the opening of "That's Entertainment", at the Royal York Hotel, in Toronto.

- Does the orchestra still have the original members?

- Many are still there. Others have left and new ones have joined in. – Tom confirmed. – Actually, we just began a second phase. From the moment the famous Foster Hewitt – who celebrated the sentence "he shoots, he scores" – sold his radio station, the CJCL Am (The Music of Your Life Station) gave us the opportunity to join the swing era's music to the Maple Leafs and Blue Jays' play by play's. So, our borders were opened to new challenges. For example, the traditional Casa Loma's galas became a reality again. The first Friday of every month we were there playing.

- Is your orchestra unique in Toronto?

- It used to be for many years. Now that our success has been noticed, other bands are trying to follow our footsteps. Fortunately, we were the first ones to arrive and a long time ago.

- Are you planning to take the orchestra to the Azores one day?

Tom was not expecting us to ask him this question. He paused for a moment, and then said:

- I never thought about it. I don't believe it is an easy thing to do. I was once in S. Miguel, but everything was so different. My friends are no longer there. Their children don't know us, and we don't know them.

- Have you ever encounter anybody from the time when you arrived in Canada?

- I saw, in S. Miguel, Dr. Dias Henriques who has a dental office. For reasons not worth mentioning here, Dias Henriques left the emigration services, shortly after being hired. The same fate had capitain Ferreira da Costa.

- Do you remember any funny story from those times?

- Once – he began telling us – I was in Toronto, at the travel agency owned by Zé Aníbal to take care of a certain matter. Zé Anibal was not there, so I decided to wait for him. When he arrived, I got out of my car and heard a man asking Zé whom I was. Joking, Zé told him I was a tourist who had arrived in Canada that week. "Oh!", he replied. "I could swear he was the inspector who took care of my case". Those people thought I was also an emigration inspector.

He laughed again at his own story, as he smoked a cigarette. Tom Moraes is a man who has fulfilled his dreams. He is married to Susan Allison, born in Toronto. The couple has three children, James Edward, 26, Jackline, 25, and Geoffrey, 23. Jackline is married and has already given Tom a beautiful granddaughter, little Zoe. What else can he hope for in life?

- Health and music. Do you know what Mary Griffin did? After selling his television productions and leaving his talk show, he returned to the origins. He was the lead singer for the Freddy Martin's Orchestra. He regrouped the musicians, formed a swing orchestra and is working at the Coconut Grove, for the Ambassador Hotel, in Los Angeles. He is exactly where he began – back to square one. Since he is famous and has money, he will have some impact and will be able to re-launch that beautiful music from 1936-1952. For us, it will be very beneficial.

We left him with this final sentence. Tom Moraes was able to reach success after a long path, and above all, believing in his music, the rhythmic and melodic music from the good old times. It is, afterall, "our" music.

Unfortunately, Tom Moraes has, ever since, left his music forever…

* Old Portuguese currency. It was about 30 cents Canadian.

JMC - November of 1986

Morais, César Alberto Nunes

City of Horta, Faial Island, Azores

César Alberto Nunes Morais was born in the city of Horta, in the island of S. Miguel, one of the nine islands in the Azorean, on February 1, 1942. Among other functions, César was the first Portuguese in Canada to be a manager at the CIBC, on Dundas and Ossignton, in Toronto, from 1974 to 1978. He was also the first Portuguese Canadian to become an immigration judge, a position he held from 1986 to 1992, first at the Immigration Appeal Board, and then at the Immigration and Refugee Board.

Richard de Morais with his father the day César was given the position of the justice of peace.

César was also the first Portuguese Canadian to become justice of peace in Canada, in 2001, working at Toronto's Old City Hall. César Alberto Nunes Morais lived a happy childhood back home, in Horta. When he finished his fourth year at the National High School of Horta (Liceu Nacional), he volunteered at the Portuguese Air Force, where he was a cop at the air base #1 in the town of Sintra. After completing his military service, César de Morais, just like any other dreamer, came to North America in 1965, as a tourist who wanted to know California. On the

César de Morais with Secretary of State of the Portuguese Communities, Dr. Manuela Aguiar.

The Italian ambassador Valerio Brigante giving César the Merit Medal from the Italian Chamber of Commerce of Toronto.

way back, he passed by Toronto, a city he fell in love with, and began thinking about his future here. He came back to Toronto, on December 28, 1965. He went to the Immigration Board to request a permanent resident status and stayed. Since he knew how to speak English, César did not face the challenges that most of our Portuguese people had to live. He went to work for the CIBC, on Eglinton and Yarrow, on January 31, 1966, with a salary of $3600 a year. He stayed at the CIBC for three years where he was promoted to accounting assistant. Through his friend Fernando Silva's invitation, he went to work for an Insurance company between 1969 and 1970. Not feeling very stable at the insurance company, César went back to the CIBC, where he stayed until 1974 as manager of the training section, then moving to the Ossington / Dundas Branch where he became general manager. While working at the CIBC, César was nominated, in 1972, as social assistant and family councilor for the Portuguese Community at the Family Services Association of the Metropolitan Toronto. His job was to help the integration of the Portuguese in the Canadian society and in the job market. At that time, many Portuguese were suffering from psychological depression caused by the problems they had to face in a new country. By his suggestion, the United Way created the Ethnic Speakers Bureau, a department made up of many ethnic groups who spoke English and French who used to go to the factories to speak to the immigrants working there, in their mother tongue, about the laws, rights and responsibilities they had. From 1973 to 1978, César took many courses at the University of Toronto, the Institute of Canadian Banker, the Fellow Institute of Canadian

César de Morais with former consul general of Portugal and wife, the director of the Totta & Açores Bank and wife, and the president of the First Portuguese, and the couple Cardoso.

Bankers, Associate of the Institute of Canadian Bankers and letter of accomplishment from the Institute of Canadian Bankers. He was also a participating member of many conferences and seminars for the Bank, departments of Justice and Immigrantion.

In 1978, César left the CIBC to manage the National Bank, in many branches, until he decided to stay at the Miracle Centre Branch, on College and Crawford, until 1986. He left to start serving Immigration judge. In 1992, César was invited to serve as president and CEO of the Sottomayor Bank of Canada, a position he held until 1996. Still in 1996, he began working as consultant for the Ketchum Canada, a firm specializing in conducting surveys and polls about the Companies Market and Viability, until he accepted the position ofjustice of peace.

Ambassador Luis Navega giving César the insignia.

César Alberto Nunes Morais got married to Débora Maria Cabral da Mota Raposo, from the island of S. Miguel, on December 18, 1971 at the Jarvis and Queen Cathedral in Toronto. They were divorced on September 28, 1990. The couple had two sons: César Manuel, born on November 27, 1974, who passed away on February 27, 1997, after a serious illness. The second one, Richard was born on June 23, 1982, who is still a student.

César has always dedicated much of his time to the Portuguese community and to the Canadian Civic society. From 1981 to 1984, César was president of the community council of Ontário and Manitoba. He was president of the Sport Club Angrense of Toronto from 1984 to 1986. In 1983, he was a member of the Portuguese Relief Fund which raised $137,241 for the Canadian Red Cross. César was elected Delegate of the International Conferences of Portuguese Immigrants Throughout the World, in Portugal, representing Ontario and Manitoba, from 1981 to 1983. Together with Father Nick di Angelis (who is now a bishop) and Father Pires, from S. Sebastian's Church, in Toronto, César asked the Catholic School Board to support the teaching of the Portuguese language in Toronto, which began in the First Portuguese. With Tony Valerio, César tried to form the Portuguese Canadian Chamber of Commerce, but at that time there was not enough commerce in the community to justify the existence of such a chamber. Thus, in conversation with the lawyer Fernando Costa, they decided to form instead the Federation of Portuguese Canadian

Business and Professionals. On January 20, 1982 the FPCBP was founded by Laura Bulger, Fernando Costa, Vasco D'Avillez, César de Morais, Germano Gonçalves, Tina Gabriel, Delkar Maia, Alberto Pereira, Octávio Sampaio, João Santos, Armindo C. Silva e João Gomes. On February 2 of the same year they met to decide about the first board of directors. Thus they decided on the following: Armindo Silva for president, César de Morais for Vice-president, Vasco D'Avillez for Secretary, and Fernando Costa as treasurer.

César de Morais receiving the Medal from the Canadian Red Cross.

César de Morais is also a member of many associations: Association of Professional Executives of Public Service of Canada, Canadian Institute of Administration of Justice, The Canadian Bar Association, Italian Chamber of Commerce of Toronto and Pounding Committee for Cross-Cultural Centre of Toronto. César has received many condecorations in his life namely the Canada's Birthday Achievement Award in 1983, the Order of Henry the Navigator in 1984, the comenda from the Canadian Red Cross in 1985, the Volunteer Services Award from the Minister of Citizenship and Culture in 1985, the Golden Mercury Award and Honour Diploma from the Italian Ambassador and the Italian Chamber of Commerce of Toronto in 1986, the Diploma of Public Recognition from the FPCBP and the Certificate of Recognition from the Canadian Multiculturalism Council from 1985 to 1987.

In the political field, César de Morais is director of the Progressive Conservative Business Association since 1979. He ran for the separate school trustee position, representing Ward 4, in 1980. He organized many community events, conferences and dinners with prime ministers, ministers, premiers, bishops and other dignitaries. He supported the campaigns fo Larry Grossman and Mayor Arthur C. Eggleton. He is a member of the P.C. Metro Policy Committee and vice-president of the Policy in the Progressive Trinity Riding Association. Briefly, César Alberto Nunes de Morais is a man who has always dedicated himself to his Portuguese community and to the country that received him and gave him so many opportunities. The community and the country have known to recognize his efforts.

JMC-2002

Morgado, José Jacinto

Town of Arrifes, island of S. Miguel, Azores

The sensibility people from the islands display is pure. You just have to look at the number of people – young and adults – who participate in bands, orchestras, bands and choirs. José Jacinto Morgado is one of those islanders who is full

José Jacinto Morgado

of sensibility and musical taste.

José Jacinto Morgado was born in the town of Arrifes, in the island of S. Miguel, on June 24, 1954. His parents, Lídia and Miguel Moniz Morgado, arrived in Canada in 1961. José Jacinto Morgado came to live with his parents some years later, on May 2, 1965. Always living in Mississauga, where his family decided to settle down, Joe Morgado

The musical group Os Panteras.

studied at the Gordon Gradon High School. Passionate about music, Joe studied the discipline at the Ontario Conservatory and specialized in guitar, the instrument he loved the most. In 1971, Mário Sousa, João Andrade, Manuel de Sousa and José Braga formed the musical group Panteras and invited Joe Morgado to be part of the group. Since there was already a lead guitarist, Joe was forced to learn bass guitar. At that time, Joe still remembers with longing, the groups that already existed: Boa Esperança, Rebeldes, Capas Negras, Copacabana…

The young Panteras used to rehearse on the Leaver Mushrooms, the same place where the church of São Salvador do Mundo was built. The first performance the group had was arranged by the band Capas Negras for a wedding. They were all so nervous that were forced to take relaxation drugs. "Most of the people at the wedding were from the town of Nazaré. They were so impressed that we were immediately invited to perform at the Nazarenos party in Toronto and Leamington", Joe told us feeling proud. That was the beginning… and since then the band has never stopped. In the summer of 1982, Joe Morgado fell seriously ill. He was submitted to a kidney transplant, which he received from his brother Walter. After that time of crisis, most members of the group left and Os Panteras were just Joe Morgado and Mário Sousa. So, in 1982, the group found new members: Baltazar Silva, Luís Rocha and Gil Gouveia. Already a popular band, the Panteras recorded their first album in 1984 entitled "Minha Aldeia", at the TNT studios with Tony Silva. Up to this day, the Panteras have recorded five albums. After some time of less shows, the band decided to get new members: they got Tony Gouveia and Carlos Caetano. Today the group is made up of Joe Morgado and his brother Walter, Bill Vaz, Carlos Caetano and Tony Silveira because Mário Sousa, the founder, decided to leave the band when they celebrated their silver anniversary. The celebration of the 25 years of the band took place on April 23, 1996, the same day the Portuguese were informed they no longer needed a visa to enter Canada. The Panteras 25th anniversary celebration was one of

the biggest events of our community because they reunited on stage the retired bands: Boa Esperança Capas Negras and Rebeldes, which lead to a trip back in time.

Going back to our original pioneer, Joe Morgado, while dedicating himself to music, worked for the Ruber Made and, in 1983, he opened his video store – Rent-a-Flick Videos – at the Knob Hill Farms at the Dixie Mall. In 1986, he left the video business and began working with Manuel de Paulos at Europa Catering in Toronto and at Europa Convention Hall, in Mississauga.

José Jacinto Morgado married Victória, also a native from the town of Arrifes, where she was born on April 7, 1956. The couple has two daughters: Vicky who was born in Mississauga on August 13, 1977, a university student, and Crystal who was born on May 2, 1984, also in Mississauga.

Victória and Joe Morgado with daughters Vicky and Crystal.

His work load and dedication to the band on weekends are very stressful and Joe needs to take some time off, once in a while. Thus, his favourite hobby is to spend time with his family at his cottage on Niagara Falls. According to Joe Morgado, our community has many more DJs and less musical groups, but there is still enough work for everyone. And since his passion is music, just like it is for his band mates, Joe assured us that the Panteras will continue to work and perform for many more years. All the best Joe! Keep up the good work!

JMC - 1999

Moura, Luís de

Village of Sítio de Piornais, town of

S. Martinho, Madeira Island

Luís and Angelina Moura visiting the Gallery of Portuguese Pioneers in Toronto.

The couple Luís and Angelina Moura is an inter-esting duo. He is tall, calm and is always in a good mood. She is short quite, and kind. Luís was born in the village of Sítio dos Piornais, county of São Martinho, Madeira Island, on Ocober 9, 1926. Just like any child born into a middle class family, Luís completed elementary school and two years of the commercial school. His military service was short, since he was only there for one week due to his father's illness. Angelina was born on February 25, 1930, in the village of Sítio da Ajuda, also in São Martinho. They both got married on September 4, 1954. Luís left Madeira to come to Canada on May 26, 1953, boarding the Nea Healls and arrived in Halifax on June 2 of the same year. From there to London, Ontário it was fast. He arrived in London on June 4. He went to work on a farm where he was responsible for feeding the cows, horses and chickens. He stopped to analyse his situation and thought: "I completed the second year of accounting, was working for the postal services and came to Canada to work in a farm? I don't get it!". About a week later, he decided to come to Toronto with his friend and fellow companion Ramiro Ribeiro. When they arrived at Union Station, in Toronto, always

Luís is cutting his 65th birth-day cake.

thinking positively, Luís laid on the floor close to his luggage and told his friend to do the same, since they had nowhere to go.

- But if we do that the cops will come to get us! – Ribeiro told him.

- That's exactly what I want. The Royal Hotel is too expensive.

And that's what happened. Shortly after, they both fell asleep. Not much longer after falling asleep, the cops woke them up telling them to leave the place. Since they hardly understood each other, the police decided to take them to an Italian church, on McCaul and Dundas, where the priest took them in and gave them food. In exchange for some work at the church, Luís Moura and Ramiro Ribeiro stayed at the church until they found a job. Some days after, one of the Italians that helped in the church gave Luís Moura the contact of another Portuguese man – Sidónio Figueira – who worked in the Scarborough County Club. Sidónio got them a job at the Club's kitchen. Ramiro Ribeiro, before leaving for California where he later settle down, chose construction as his job. A year later, Luís Moura went to work for the Ontario Club, in Toronto, where he was for ten years. Meanwhile, he asked his wife to come to Canada because he did not like living alone.

Angelina arrived in Toronto in February of 1956. The couple has a daughter, Marlene, who was born in Toronto on January 16, 1958, and has a university degree. In 1963, Luís Moura was hired by Northern Electric (today Nortel) where he worked until 1986, the same year he retired. His wife Angelina also decided to retire at the same time as her husband.

Marlene Moura and husband Stanley.

Digging in the past, Luís de Moura remembers helping in the foundation of the Canadian Madeira Club, in 1963. He says it was hard to pull out the roots and weeds so that the Madeira Park would have a nice and welcoming look. He never wanted to be part of the board of directors at the Madeira Club, but was always available to work and contribute in every event. Angelina and Luís love to travel. They have a house in Florida where they spend a lot of time during the year. Luís' mother is still alive – with the enviable age of 98 – which forces him to go back to visit Madeira to be with her. Life is beautiful and simple for Luís and Angelina Moura. We hope it continues to be this way for many more years.

Angelina and Luís during one of their visits to Madeira Island.

JMC-2000

Maria Celina Martins Anjo, a young and beautiful lady, before coming to Canada.

Nóbrega, Maria Celina Martins Anjo

Village of Sítio de Santana, town of São Roque, Madeira Island

W hen we are meant to be hurt by fate there is no escape. Celina Nóbrega is a true example of this saying. Maria Celina Martins Anjo was born in the village of Sítio de

The Nóbrega's with their baby Leslie, who died at the age of 3, in Toronto.

Santana, in the town of São Roque, located in the Madeira, on February 14, 1937. A calm childhood would not prepare her for the sourness of life she would later experience.

She met José de Nobrega, who was from the town of Caniço, in Madeira, where he was born on March 19, 1930. Celina married José by proxy on October 30, 1960. José was a cab driver in Madeira, working for the Taxis' company, owned by his father. José decided to join the first Portuguese group of men from Madeira to come to Canada. He touched the port of Halifax on June 2, 1953. Contrary to his fellow companions, he stayed in Halifax for three years, working as a cook. In 1956, José came to Toronto. Still working as cook, José found a job at the Royal York Hotel and, later on, at the Park Plaza Hotel. When the latter closed down, José went to work for a restaurant for four months, but unfortunately, he mysteriously passed away on February 22, 1983, leaving behind a wife and two daughters aged 17 and 14 without any insurance or pension, since he had been working at the restaurant for less than six months.

Maria Celina came to Toronto on July 14, 1961. In Toronto, the couple saw the birth of three children: Leslie, born on May 15, 1962 who passed away at the age of 3 from a serious illness; Helena, born on August 1, 1965 who has a university degree from York; and Rosemary who was born on October 21, 1968, who is now married and has given Celina a grandson; Kyle. Between the birth of Helena and Rosemany, Celina lost another baby when she was four months pregnant. To help provide for her family, Celina worked for 16 years at the restaurant Flame Pit. With the unexpected death of her husband and the closing down of the Flame Pit, Celina was forced to go on early retirement, sell the house and work harder to provide for her daughters. The widow's pension and the minimal retirement pension was not even enough to survive. With some savings, some extra jobs and the daughters' help, Celina was able to organize a stable life. Celina lives now with her eldest daughter, Helena, who also needs her care.

Celina with daughters Helena and Rosemary and grandson Kyle.

The Nóbregas were founding members of the Madeira Park and Canadian Madeira Club. Celina has visited her brother who lives in Venezuela and her mother, who is 84, in Madeira. Celina helps seniors, specially an elderly lady from Madeira island who was her neighbour and now lives on the Social Centre of Dufferin and Eglinton, in Toronto. The dark clouds that have settled over her head have not darken her kind heart.

JMC - 2000

Celina and José at their garden in Toronto.

Nunes, António

Town of São Roque, city of Funchal, Madeira Island

António Nunes is a man of severe nature. António Nunes was born in the village of São Roque, district of Funchal, in Madeira Island, on December 12, 1924. Working at the family's farm was his first contact with the work force. He completed his military service at the "Quartel de Infantaria" in Funchal and from that time on he began his journey of dreams. He left Funchal, on May 26, 1953 boarding the Nea Healls and touched Halifax on June 1 of the same year, but because customs was closed they could only disembark on the 2nd.

Three years before taking off to Canada, António Nunes got married to his compatriot Conceição de Caires, from Gáua, where she was born on September 12, 1923. The wedding ceremony took place on February 11, 1950. Already living in Toronto,

Conceição Caires and António Nunes.

the young couple witnessed the birth of four children: Tony from who they have three grandchildren; Rosemary who has two children of her own; Elizabeth who has two children; and John who also has two children of his own. These nine grandchildren are now the pride and joy of António Nunes and his wife. However, before getting here, António had to face many challenges in his life. When he arrived in Halifax, António and his fellow companions were places inside a coal train that took them to Montreal. António Nunes was sent to a farm an hour north of Montreal. He was left at the farm's entrance, indicating him to the house where he was supposed to go work. And so he went.

Dressed in a white suit, straw hat and suede shoes, António knocked at the farmer's door to look for a job. And it was dressing this way that António was sent to the ox stall to milk the cows. António still remembers the appearance of his shoes and suit after he was done with the cows. At this farm, António did not have much to eat and was forced to do all the hard jobs. In order not be hungry, António used to drink a lot of milk. Still, he stayed at the farm for about six months. When he decided to come to Toronto, the farmer was so pleased with António's service that he decided to write him a letter of recommendation.

He left for Toronto where he would settle down. His first job in Toronto was at the Scotch Tavern. From here, and for about four years, he worked at the Niagara Falls' slaughterhouse. When the slaughterhouse was sold to another company, António went to work for the Hoster Cleaning Company, a firm owned by a German friend he found at the slaughterhouse. António worked at the Hoster for fifteen years, at which time his friend was in the sulks with António for no particular reason, and António decided to leave and rest for a month. When he thought about going back to work, António went to the Orthopedic Hospital where he was hired to work at the cleaning and maintenance department. This would be his last job, before retirement. After fifteen years at the Orthopedic Hospital, António retired in 1990.

The Nunes family in their first years of Canada.

From left to right: Rosemary, Johny, Conceição, Tony, António and Elizabeth at Tony' wedding.

António Nunes is founding member of the Madeia Park and the Canadian Madeira Club. He was director at the Canadian Madeira Club for one year. Still at the hall rented out by Father Cunha at Santa Maria's Church, António was in charge of the bar. One day he noticed that he had made more money with one bottle of whisky than his partner had made the day before with two bottles. Suspicious and not liking what he had seen, António decided to investigate. The next day, he saw lights in the hall, the money drawer was opened and there was nobody at the hall. He was frightened by the situation and decided to get the money from the drawer to give to the club's treasurer. António wrote a note explaining the situation and left behind. The board of directors did not like what António did. Since António is a man who likes everything to be well explained and crystal clear, he resigned from the executive and has not ever since accepted another invitation to join the board of directors of any club. That's the way António is: honesty above all. Since coming to Canada, António has visited Madeira nineteen times, but his wife has only gone for five times. They have also visited the Portuguese mainland, Boston and New Bedford in the USA and have traveled to many places in Canada. To travel is one of the plans António still has. As a hobby, António likes to go once so often to Niagara Casino. However, as he confesses, he does not spend much money. Since life is a game, it is fine to have such a hobby.

JMC - 2000

Nunes, Conceição Francisco

Town of São Martinho, Madeira Island

Conceição Francisco Nunes

It is hard to find Portuguese women who have been living in Canada for more than thirty years due to the fact that our pioneers – men – used to come to Canada without their families. Still, some of them could not stand living alone and sent a sponsorship letter to their wives, after making the first pay cheque. The late José Nunes was one of them. A short time after arriving in Canada, José Nunes decided to sponsor his wife and son to come and join him. Conceição Francisco was born in the village of São Martinho, in Madeira island, on July 29, 1926. She married José Nunes at the church of São Martinho, in 1951. José arrived in Canada on June 2, 1953 and passed away on March 30, 1989. Conceição went aboard the Saturnia with her son, José Nunes Jr., in August of 1954.

The couple Nunes with elder son José Nunes Jr., days before José Nunes came to Canada.

- A year after arriving in Canada, - Conceição began telling us, still surprised at our interest for her story – I began working for a shoe factory. I was responsible for making the boxes and was getting paid .50 cents an hour.

- What about your husband?

- His job was to pick up balls at a golf field and to cut the grass. He was getting $40 a week.

- Was that the only job he had in Canada?

- No! He changed jobs.

Conceição's son, who was beside her paying attention to every single word of our conversation, added:

Conceição and José Nunes at their house in Toronto, in the early days.

- My father got a job at the mattress factory Sealy Pasterpedic Ltd., on Queensway.

- This was my husband's last job, before dying. – Conceição remembered, unable to hide the tears from her eyes.

Beside us, interested in our conversation, we had Conceição's father, Manuel Francisco, who told us very proud:

- I have been here for twenty years!

Conceição Nunes made use of her father's comment to tell us that her parents came to Canada on February 18, 1968. Her mother has since passed away, and her father is now her company, living with her at home.

- Today I live on my husband's pension and on the widow's pension. – Conceição said, looking proudly at her son: - I must mention that I have a lot of help from my children who are the best.

We decided to go back to our original conversation to dig a little more from our pioneer's past.

- When it comes to jobs, I was tossed up and down, from place to place. I began working in 1957 at the Dr. Ballard, an animal food factory. From here, I went to work for the maintenance department of hydro. Then, I was hired by Torffeco Ltd. to fold bedspreads. At Torffeco, the foreman was my brother Agostinho Martins. In 1976, I underwent surgery and never worked again.

- Do you like living in Canada?

- Even after so much suffering, I like Canada and never thought about going back. My husband and I were here for eleven years without visiting Madeira. We went back for the first time in 1965. I went back there in 1985 and last year. My granddaughter Jennifer is my fellow traveler.

- Did your husband participate in the foundation of the Canadian Madeira Club?

Family picture. José Manuel Nunes, Conceição and José Jr., João Pedro and brother-in-law Alberto Nóbrega.

- Yes! He was always involved in those activities and was founding member.

- My father was one of the members who went knocking from door to door to ask for $20 in order to found the club. – Joe told us.

- During those times, the club meant reuniting those who were away from Madeira and were homesick. Do you still remember anyone from those times?

- Of course! Maria José Camarata, Luísa Camarata, Arlete, Deolinda Ferreira, Augusta de Freitas, Fernanda Belo, Conceição Freitas, Celeste and Zita Pereira, the latter probably my best friend until today. My husband and hers went to school together. Óscar Pereira and my husband were

Cherry farmer owner, José Camacho and José Nunes, in Niagara Falls, in 1953.

Conceição Nunes with father Manuel Francisco and son Joe Nunes.

The late José Nunes with children Joe and John.

always very close.

- We speak about your children with a lot of tenderness. Were they good students?

- Yes they were, thank God! This one here, Joe, studied technological architecture at Humber College and now owns a company…

- A small business company… - Joe explained. – It is Nu-Chair Manufacturing Inc., in Brampton. We make chairs, tables and counters for restaurants, schools and hotels.

- John was a good student, but because of soccer, decided to go to the United States of America…

- My brother got a scholarship in athletics. He used to study and play soccer. He was in the USA for four years where he got a business administration degree.

- I cried so much when he went to the States. John is now at Labatt's where he is sales representative. He is very well in life.

- And it seems you also have some grandchildren…

- Oh yes! – Conceição answered laughing at our insinuation. – John didn't come alone from the USA. He brought with him an American whom he married here. They have a beautiful son, Zacarias. This one here, Joe, has two beautiful children: Aaron and Jennifer.

- So family is now growing…

- It was already big! – she said laughing. – My husband and I sponsored about one hundred people to Canada. My husband alone had eight brothers and I had nine. We sponsored all of them and their families. So, as you can see, we are a huge family!

How many stories – funny or sad – does our pioneer remember? Let's allow her to share some of those.

- When I decided to come to Canada, my husband had told me to sell everything because Canada had everything we could want. So, foolish of me, not even thinking about what I was doing, I sold everything in a low price: clothes, china… really, everything! When I got here I didn't have a place for my son to eat his food. I felt so sad! So, slowly, I had to start buying china – the white dishes – at .25 cents each. My son didn't have a bed. To solve my problem I had arrange his bed on top of my suitcase. Imagine how sad my life was! We were living, together with Oscar and his wife, in a flat we rented from an Italian family. We were only allowed to shower once a week:

one couple on Wednesday and the other on Thursday. It was really hard.

Another time, it was a Sunday, we decided to go to mass. We didn't know anything or anybody, nor did we speak the language. Still we decided to walk until we found a church. We went in and prayed. The priest spoke English and didn't understand anything. When communion came, we were shocked to see bread and wine instead of the Host! That's when we found out the church was not catholic, but Anglican. Joking, my husband used to say he would go back just to drink wine for free. If you don't know the language and traditions of the land, you only have problems.

Conceição Nunes with husband and son Joe.

- When did you buy your first house?

- It was in 1958, located on 9 Wales. It had ten rooms and we paid $14,750. We put $4,000 down payment. Since we rented out the rooms, I had a lot of work with that house. We then moved to a better and bigger house, but when my husband passed away, I had to sell it. Now, I live in this apartment, which I bought for me and my father. It is more than enough.

- And it is about time you rest…

- Absolutely. If I were not so afraid of airplanes, I would travel more often. My granddaughter Jennifer goes with me all the time. My children are the best and I am very happy for them.

We ended our conversation with this comment. We must learn how to keep a happy moment every time we witness one. Our pioneer was living one of those moments. We hope she continues to enjoy the company of her children and grandchildren.

JMC - January 1989

Oliveira, Eduardo Fernandes

Village of Ajuda da Bretanha,

island of S. Miguel, Azores

Maria Ascenção and Eduardo, on their wedding day, in September of 1973.

He was born and lived the first years of his life surrounded by the sea. He loves the sea. Eduardo Fernandes Oliveira was born in the village of Ajuda da Bretanha, in the island of S. Miguel, Azores, on November 15, 1951. As a child Eduardo used to run, whenever possible, to the sea, something that made his mother get upset at him. After completing the primary school years, Eduardo came to Canada, with his brothers and parents. He was 14 when he arrived in Toronto, on October 23, 1966. The family went to live at the house on 56 Montrose Street. Eduardo Fernandes Oliveria went to high school, but for a short period of time. When he turned 16, Eduardo decided to go to work to help out his family. He found his first job on Streetsville working for a firm specializing in bathtubs. In

Maria Rosa Ferreira (singer Jorge Ferreira's mother), Maria José Oliveira, António Oliveira and Diamantina Brasil, in S. Miguel.

Maria Ascenção, Eduardo and daughter Sania.

The Oliveira family when they arrived in Toronto. Sitting: Maria José Fernandes and António Oliveira. Standing: Maria José, Eduardo and Leonilde Oliveira.

1969, he transferred to the Redell Sheet Metal and Roofers, in Hamilton, and from here to Windsor. A year later, he lied about his age in order to work at a transport company, where he began driving trucks at the age of 19. That same year, he found a job at the Airline Cargo, at Toronto's International Airport, to drive trucks between Toronto and Buffalo. From here, he transferred himself to Charterways to drive their buses. In 1975, Eduardo found a job at the Newportfish and for two years he worked for this company driving their trucks between Toronto and New York.

In 1977, Eduardo went back to his old profession – specialist is roofing. He worked for Margven Roofing and Polar Roofing. In 1982, he spent sometime working for Tony Leite Roofing and then went back to Polar until 1984. From here Euduardo went to work for Roman Roofing. In 1984, Eduardo was invited to work for the local union Sheet Metal Workers International – local 30. He accepted and then ran for the Business Representative position. He won that election and since then has been elected every three years to continue representing Local 30.

Eduardo married Maria Ascenção Moniz da Costa Amaral, who was born in the village of Arrifes, in S. Miguel, on June 10, 1954. Maria and Eduardo met in 1968, when she was only 14 years old, and got married in 1973. From a very young age, Maria Ascenção has dedicated herself to work and school. She has taken many courses and is now a student of Art Studies at the Dundas Valley School of Art.

The couple has one daugher, Sania, who was born in Toronto, on February 12, 1977. Sania is still a student and hopes to become a Special Effects Technician for movies.

Eduardo's passion for the sea led him to buy many boats throughout the years. Today he owns a yacht, which he named Ascension, with place for twelve people (42 x 13 feet) where he spends his weekends with family and friends. In 1974, when he bought the Ascension, in Midland, Eduardo sailed for six days with his friends Linda and George Forman, to get to Oakville, where he lives. His favourite "route" is between Oakville and the Toronto island, Port Del Housing, Niagara on the Lake, Fifty Point.

Eduardo has worked hard in his life, but knows how to enjoy the beauties of life… always surrounded by water.

JMC - 1999

Oliveira, João Gabriel

Village of Nordeste, S. Miguel, Azores

To chat with our pioneer João Gabriel Oliveira is not only easy, but also interesting. He is one of those strong Portuguese men who prefer to "break than to bend". This is true of him since 1954, the year he arrived in Canada. Since this time, João has worked hard, has fought and been able to succeed in this enormous land.

Pioneer João Gabriel Oliveira with wife and other family members. Standing: Their friend Medeiros.

- I arrived in Halifax on March 27, 1954. I went aboard the Homeland on March 22. – João began explaining. – In Halifax, we were forced to take the train, which took us to Chatham. From here, we took the bus to Rutheven. You know, I celebrated my birthday aboard the Homeland… What a beautiful gift!

João Gabriel Oliveira was born in the village of Nordeste, in the island of S. Miguel, on March 23, 1930. He is married to Maria de Lurdes Cardoso, from the village of Lomba do Pomar, in the town of Povoação, also in S. Miguel. The wedding ceremony took place at the Saint Michael's church, in Leamington, in 1958.

- It was funny. My wife came to Canada sponsored by her family. – João said. – Back in those days, there were basically no Portuguese girls living here. When I met Maria de Lurdes I said to myself: this one will not get way, she is mine! I was the one that didn't get away. We got married soon after.

- How many children do you have?

- Four girls: Margarida, Denise, Diane and Suzy.

- What was your first job in Canada?

- The first summer, I worked at a farm picking up vegetables. The first winter came along, and

I went to Windsor to work at a bowling place. I worked at the Bowling House for three years. My job description was: to put the pins back on their place. In the summer, while at the Bowling House, I used to work part-time in the farm picking up vegetables as a means of making extra cash.

- At that time, were you living here by yourself?

- At the beginning I was alone. But after, I decided to sponsor my brothers and sisters – three of each – and my parents, who have since passed away.

- Do you still have any family back home?

- Yes! I still have a sister, but I am planning to bring her to Canada. I am taking care of the documents.

- Have you gone back to visit S. Miguel?

- No! I have not gone back to Portugal because I have nothing there. My parents sold everything we had in there. My parents-in-law, the very little they had, distributed it among their children. I don't haveanything from them. My arms are strong enough to provide for my immediate family.

- But… wouldn't you like to see again the place where you were born? – We asked.

- Perhaps… - João said, thinking about our question. – I will perhaps go back one day on holidays. I am sure I will feel awkward. My friends are all gone.

Sunday afternoon card game at the club. Pioneers Liduíno Carvalho, Manuel dos Santos, Manuel Pavão and João Gabriel Oliveira.

To feel a stranger in his own land is a fate the immigrant man must face. To see himself without his friends "who have also left" is another dilemma.

- From those days, do you still remember any friend in particular?

- Yes, I do remember many good friends. – João answered with his voice shaking. – I would love to see again Luís Aragão and António Braga. These two have returned to S. Miguel. Others have already passed away.

- Do you have funny stories to share with us from those early days? – We asked so to change the topic of our conversation.

- You know, back in those days we used to get to Halifax and the Immigration Department had one mission: to place us inside the old trains to go to our destination. The CP employee was "throwing us" outside the train in the stations our cards would indicate. – With a loud laugh, João said: - It was like throwing animals to the pigsty! In Chatham, where I landed, I began making $36 a week. The very few Portuguese that decided to stay here, would join us and we would all cook together the way we knew. I never starved in my life. I worked very hard to pay back the money I was owing in Portugal.

- Speaking of that, who was the first Portuguese man to open business in Leamington?

- It was Mário Rafael! Before that we had a couple of Portuguese guys from Toronto and London who would come to sell us bread and cheese.

- What about a house? Who was the first one to buy one?

- Well, I believe I was the first one to own a house.

Beside us, playing cards, there was a group of João's friends who agreed he has been the first one to buy a house in Leamington. These friends were all pioneers: Liduíno Carvalho, from the town of Povoação, who also came to Canada on March 22, 1954; Manuel Pavão, from S. Miguel, who arrived on April 21, 1956, and is the popular president of the musical band Lira de Nossa Senhora de Fátima of Leamington. During our conversation, someone remembered the famous "Palace of Tears", in Rutheven, where 76 Portuguese men used to live.

- Very sad times, my friend! – Liduíno Carvalho told us. – It was there, in that huge house that we all lived and cried for our loved ones. Thus the reason why we still call it the "Palace of Tears".

- But the hard times are gone, and now you have a better life and a social club where you can spend some time, right? – We asked João.

- Yes! But it was hard to get here. We are all founding members of the Portuguese Community Club of Leamington. We work very hard at this club, but it is needed for all of us. It is worth the troubles.

- Where do you now work?

- I have been working for a long time at the cement factory. I load trucks with cement blocks, using lifts. – João laughed before saying: - You know, my retirement is still far away.

- How do you assess our community's needs?

- I think we have everything we need. We have a good way of living, good jobs, our club, our festivities and traditions… what else can you hope for?

- How do you think the Portuguese are doing in the business and professional fields?

- Very well! We have many Portuguese businesses, in Leamington, and some Portuguese men are very prosperous in the industrial world. Just here, we have Adriano Codinha and Pratas, just to name a few.

- Is there a moment in your life you wish you didn't remember?

- You know, there is this old, Portuguese saying that "sadness does not pay your debts" and I believe it. One day, I decided to go to Toronto with five other friends. When we were getting close to London, we were involved in a very serious car accident. – João stopped for a moment, feeling very emotional, and then said: - One of them, José Pacheco, died instantly. I don't even want to remember it. The other ones, myself included, were all fine.

- So, to forget the sad moments, is there anything happy you remember from those days?

- Back then anything you did was hilarious. When we used to go to church, in Kingsville, we used to get truck that would take at least thirty people. Just going to church was enough to laugh. I just hope God forgives us for what we said and did.

That's how it used to be back then: everything was an adventure and a parody. It was a natural way these men had of forgetting their problems. Time has gone by and each one of them has been able to solve those problems and settle down in the new land. Everything is well when it ends well.

JMC - March of 1988

Oliveira, Maria Leonor

Village of Ribeiras, town of Lajes,

Pico Island, Azores

Maria Leonor Oliveira was born June 2, 1937, in a small place called Pontas Negras located in the village of Ribeiras, the city of Lajes in Pico Island. She completed primary school in Ribeira Seca, in Pico.

Maria Leonor Oliveira

Christmas of 1987: Maria Leonor in Israel in the middle of two military women.

Maria Leonor's daughter-in-law Allison with daughter Meghan on her lap, son Jorge – the day of his graduation – Maria Leonor, daughter-in-law Sidónia, son Carlos and grandchildren Jordan and Britney.

Maria Leonor Oliveira with her entire family, the last family reunion before her father, Augusto, passed away.

Grandchildren Courtney (Carlos' daughter) and Jordan (Jorge's son).

Still living in Pico, she met and married Manuel Machado Madruga, also from her island. They both got married at the church of Ermida das Pontas Negras, on February 4, 1957.

In April of the same year, they embarked for the island of Faial where they settled down in the town of Capelo because her husband was a whaler. It was a summer to forget. In September of 1957, the Capelinhas' volcano erupted constituting a real drama for everyone on the island. Maria Leonor was seven months pregnant and, probably due to the stress of the moment, she lost her baby. They were days of horror! Maria remembers everyone on the island praying for their lives and for things not to get worse. Although pregnant, Maria Leonor was the person encouraging everyone to be strong. The couple, after this double tragedy, decided to go back to Pico. Maria Leonor got pregnant again and gave birth to a son: Carlos Manuel. Carlos was born in the village of Cais do Pico and is now living in Ferguson, Ontário, where he owns CM Renovations.

The Madrugas decided to emigrate to Canada. They arrived in this country on October 15, 1960, when little Carlos was only eight months old. In Toronto, Manuel Madruga began to work at the firm Temperman, a demolishing company. Maria Leonor also began to work, two months after arriving in Toronto. She found a job at a wood factory and her boss was Tony a man from the island of S. Miguel. She began working side by side with two other Portuguese ladies: Maria Zélia and Mariana. A year after arriving, they both decided to go work at a tobacco farm in Strathroy. Maria Leonor always eager to learn and do better, decided to dedicate herself to sewing and babysitting when she got back to Toronto. Without forgetting her duties as a wife and mother, Maria Leonor found time to begin studying English. In 1965, she completed the Early Childhood Education Course at George Brown College and later on, she also obtained the nurse's assistant course. Life was going well for the Madrugas, so they decided to expand their family. Thus the second son of the couple, Jorge, was born in Toronto on March 18, 1963. Jorge is now a high school teacher.

Still back in 1970, she was hired to work at the Runnymeade Hospital. A year later, she was transferred to the senior assistance department, the home care section, a job she still maintains today. Beside her work at the Hospital, she also assists the third age group at St. Christopher's House. The sudden changes of life inspired and forced her to write. She felt a need to open her heart. She began writing simple verses in 1963. In the early 80s, she decided to write a few verses to Rita Pereira to help her understand that everyone faces many different challenges in life and that everyone goes through stormy weather moments. She was able to help her friend and, most importantly, to help herself. The message served as a healing power for her.

In 1987, Maria Leonor and Manuel Madruga divorced. Nevertheless, Maria Leonor did not give up and decided to continue living his life the normal way. She was hired as councilor for Cross Roads, a volunteer house mostly known as 100th Street.

Between 1991 and 1998, in quest of her path, Maria returned to Pico. While in her native island, she published her verses in the newspaper "Dever". Since things did not work out the way she expected, Maria Leonor came back to Toronto.

Maria Leonor with two of her seniors: the famous musician Kushener from New York and jeweler Liberman.

In Toronto, encouraged by her son Jorge, who gave her a beautiful hard cover notebook, Maria Leonor decided to publish her verses. The turning point for her was her son's dedication on the notebook, which read: Mother, poetry is for those who love it. Mother, keep on loving life and writing poetry. This inspired her to publish the book "Emigrante Açoriana" (Azorean Emigrant). Now, she is writing more verses to publish a second book, which has already been "baptized": O Cimo da Montanha (The Top of the Mountain). At the same time, she is recording her verses on CD recited by her. She has also invited the famous community singer Sarah Pacheco to record the song "Mulher Valor Infinito" (Woman, Endless Value) with music by Carlos Caetano, a member of the band Panteras.

From left to right: Helena, son Jorge, godson Herdeberto, ex-husband Manuel Madruga, Maria Leonor, sister Maria Silvina and parents Augusto and Silvina Oliveira.

Maria Leonor loves traveling. She has been to every place in Portugal, North America, Turkey, Israel, Cuba and Italy. Maria Leonor lives with her mother Silvina who is 84 years old. She has decided to dedicate her life helping her neighbour, even if no one recognizes her work. She gives without expecting to receive.

JMC-1999

António Pombeiro Pacheco

Pacheco, António Pombeiro

Town of Ribeirinha, island of S. Miguel,

Azores

António Pombeiro Pacheco was born in the town of Ribeirinha, in the island of S. Miguel, on November 27, 1928. He got married to Maria Cabral Pimentel on September 18, 1956, at the church Conceição da Ribeira Grande. Maria Cabral was also born in Ribeirinha, on

António Pombeiro Pacheco and wife Maria Cabral Pacheco.

October 17, 1934.

António Pacheco emigrated to Canada searching for a better life for his family. He left S. Miguel on March 25, 1960 and arrived in Montreal the day after. His wife and three children, all born in Ribeirinha – Manuel Jeremias, Maria Conceição and Lúcia de Fátima – arrived in Montreal in September of 1961. In Montreal, the couple saw the birth of a fourth child: Helena. When he arrived, António got a job at the airport in the cleaning department. He was there for three months. At the end of this period, he transferred to the kitchen of the Caras Restaurant, also in the airport. He was at the restaurant for two years. Tired of washing dishes he went to work at a fish market. Still unhappy with this job, he went to work for the grocery shop "Casa Estrela da Manhã". António was at this place for five years.

In 1972, António Pacheco decided to buy and open his grocery shop. He bought the one he knew the best: Casa Estrela da Manhã, a house he ran until 1995 the same year he decided to go on retirement. Besides the dedication to his family and work, António was a founding member of the first Portuguese band of Montreal, in 1972 and served as its director for 18 years. He is still a member of the Portuguese Association of Canada, in Montreal, of Casa dos Açores of Quebec and of Casa dos Pais, a social club for seniors. A life of hard work and commitment to the family did not allow the Pachecos to go back to their homeland. They have only traveled for a short period of time, in Canada and the United States. Today, the Pacheco family lives in Laval, Quebec. Mission accomplished!

JMC-2000

Paixão, António Medeiros

Town of Grândola, province of Alentejo

António Medeiros Paixão was born in the town of Grândola, located in the province of Alentejo, on June 15, 1927. Early in his life, António became a professional in the business of stamps and cuttings; he was a locksmith. Early in his life, António decided to be responsible for this family and leave Portugal. The adventure happened on May 13, 1957. Aboard the Pan America flight, which touched down on the island of Santa Maria, Gander and Montreal, António arrived in Canada.

- It was only a seventeen-

A happy family! Grandparents with their children and grandchildren in a family reunion.

hour flight! – Our pioneer began telling us.

- Montreal was your chosen destination. Did you stay there for long?

- No, no! My fellow travelers and I came in the second official group of Portuguese emigrants with specific professions. Logically, we thought we were going to work in our professional field because, according to the instructions we received back home, Canada needed skillful people. – António told us.

- The chancellor Assis, the consul of Portugal's brother-in-law, in Montreal, sent us to Clark City.

- How many people went?

- We were twelve. When we arrived in Clark City, we were surprised to see that our job was to take out huge rolls of mass paper from leather straps and load little carts. It was hard as hell! Mário Nogueira and I was able to do it for a month and half.

- What about the other ones? Did they find another job or decided to go somewhere else?

- Neither! – António said. After, with a beautiful smile, he continued: - As much as we could, we would still get food from the cafeteria for all of them. At night, they would come to sleep at our rooms.

- Do you still remember them?

- Of course! Pedro, Leonel Félix, Armando Albuquerque and others whose names I don't recall at the moment.

- What happened after this adventure?

- We left Clark City and came back to Montreal feeling like killing both the consul and the chancellor. Fortunately, due to diplomatic problems, they were sent off to Tanganica, before we returned to Montreal. – Shaking his head, António laughed at all these adventures, which marked the beginning of a journey in a new country. All the stories he remembers from the past make him laugh now, but when they happened, they were pretty dramatic.

- Did you stay in Montreal for long?

- No, we came to Ontario. In Montreal, there were no jobs available. A group of guys from the Azores we met in Montreal told us to come to Toronto where there were many tobacco farms. And that's what happened.

- Don't tell me that you settle down in Toronto working at the tobacco farms?!

First Portuguese executive thanking the athletes on their NSL championship. Among them, we can see Veiga Nunes, João Ferreira (Banana), A. Paixão, António Vicente and A. Maia. The good old times!

- No way! – António answered laughing at our question. – We found a job in Strathroy. Pedro and Albuquerque were there for only one week. I was able to resist and work there for six years.

- Always in the tobacco fields or did you change jobs?

- I did a bit of everything until I found a job in my field of qualification. In Strathroy, I got a job at the Vampco Aluminum Products, as a welder, a profession that was close to what I knew how to do.

- From Strathroy, where did you go?

- I moved to Toronto. Strathroy was a small town and there weren't too many opportunities. In Toronto, in 1963, I was able to find a job at the Bathurst Tools and Machinery, where I could work doing what I knew best: locksmith. It took time, but I was able to do it.

We could sense in Antónios eyes that as he remembered the past he was proud of his accomplishments. How many sacrifices, self-denials and tears of dissatisfaction did he leave behind?

In 1958, António Medeiros Paixão decided it was time to ask his wife to come and live with him. He sent a sponsor letter to Margarida and their children: José Luís and Carlos Alberto. A year later, they were blessed with the birth of a daughter: Ana Maria. They all have a post-secondary degree and are well in life. Do they know how hard their parents' journey was? Perhaps! But perhaps they will never understand the full extent of such hard work and sacrifices to conquer their goal.

- My children knew how to compensate our sacrifices by studying and living a life without any problems. They are great children!

- Going back to your profession, were you at Bathurst Tools for a long time?

- No, I wasn't there for a long time and it was funny how things went at that place. – António told us with a mysterious smile. – In 1964, the company sent me to Ford to do a certain task. Some time after this, the guys at Ford convinced me to stay at their Oakville plant. I accepted the offer and it is the job I still have today.

The champions party! Martelo on the fans's shoulders and António Paixão on the side holding his jacket and showing tears of joy.

- So you are no longer a locksmith...

- No! I am a Quality Control Inspector and feel fine.

António Paixão was also involved in the First Portuguese Canadian Club for many years and he is still an active member. To spend time at the club is one of António's passions.

- I was a director of the First Portuguese for nine years. When I arrived in Toronto, in 1964, I became a member of the club and soon after became a member of the board of directors. In 1968, Artur Rodrigues, who had been a member of the Portuguese United, convinced me to form a sports section at the club specially dedicated to soccer. He offered his services to form and coach the team. I accepted the challenge and offered to sponsor the team financially. So we went ahead with that idea facing many difficulties because the players of the Portuguese United did not have a very good reputation.

- Were there two Portuguese teams at that time?

- Not in Toronto. There were two soccer teams, but it was one in Toronto, from the First Portuguese club, and one in Oakville, the Arsenal, in 1968.

- Let's go back to the First Portuguese.

- Yes. So, after many challenges to be accepted at the National Soccer League, we were able to accomplish our mission in 1968. A year later, we entered the championships and were victorious. We were the champions of the league. We were extremely happy. In 1968-1969, we also conquered the NSL Cup. Later on, in 1979, with Marinho, we were again champions and conquered the NSL Cup. With Marinho, the First Portuguese team won the championship without any losses. Although there was a good reason to be happy, there was also a reason to be sad.

- Why?

- Because with so many titles conquered, the value of the players went up, which led to expenses the First Portuguese or any club could not support. Bankruptcy was inevitable.

- In your opinion, the First Portuguese should dissolve the soccer team and section? – We asked António with a double intention. First, we wanted to know the personal opinion of a veteran, a man who accepted the challenge of forming a soccer section, assuming the financial responsibility. Secondly, we wanted to know if he did it as to save the club from the financial situation it is in – just like so many other clubs – a situation that the public in general tends to blame on the soccer team.

- In my personal opinion, the First Portuguese should have kept its soccer team if it did not frustrate the finances of the club. Even if soccer is played at the amateur level, it is necessary to have a group of director committed to raise funds and keep the sports section.

The ideal would be to have a team of professionals, which would give the club and the community the acknowledgement they deserve. Unfortunately, that seems impossible to accomplish.

- If you were invited to be part of the executive group of the club, would you still accept it?

- Right now, no! Nine years of responsibilities at the First Portuguese were enough for me. I believe I have done my part in the club and for the community. However, I may still give them a hand once I retire.

- Do you remember any friends from the time you arrived whom you would love to see again?

- Manuel Gonçalves who apparently is now living in Montreal. I would also like to see Júlio Melo, João Rebelo, João Cardoso and many others who are probably back in Portugal.

- Speaking of Portugal, are you planning to return to your country of origin?

- No, I don't even think about it. I feel very well living in Canada. So do my children. I will go to Portugal as often as I can on holidays, but that is it. Specially now, that we have two grandchildren, I don't even think about moving back. Miguel is Carlos' son and Justin is Zé Luís' son. Zé Luís is living in Alberta.

- During these thirty years of Portuguese community, what is the saddest moment you recall?

- The passing of my mother and my mother-in-law. My mother lived with us for ten years and my mother-in-law for twelve.

- What about happy moments, which one has marked you the most?

- I have had many happy moments. My children finished their courses, never gave me any headache and were great. The birth of my grandsons was also a happy moment. Last, but not least, the good life we live in Canada is a reason of joy. Besides, I am healthy, have a job I like, so I cannot really complain.

In 1969, the consul general of Portugal, Luís Augusto Martins and Margaret Campbell, from Toronto's City Hall, paying homage to the folk dance group of Nazaré.

- We sense that your family is perfectly well adapted to the country. It is also noticeable that António Paixão fought very hard at the beginning but is now decided to stay in the country that welcomed him.

- How do you assess the growth and development of the Portuguese community in the past thirty years?

- You now, I developed with it. It has had its good and bad moments, but it has grown. It is still a young community, so I am pleased to see its growth and integration, specially, in the last fifteen years. You know… today my children have Portuguese friends who hold university and college degrees. In the old times, you would not even think about it. Back then, there was only the ambition to work and make money. Today, more and more parents are concerned with their children's education. I am glad it is so because it is the only way to progress in life. Portuguese children must go to universities and must be integrated in all levels of the Canadian society.

We left António Medeiros Paixão with this last thought. We hope his children will continue on the footsteps of their parents and grandparents.

JMC - July of 1987

Pereira, Carlos (da Atouguia) de Jesus

Town of Atouguia da Baleia, city of Peniche

The well-known pioneer Carlos da Atouguia is an extreme nice and simple individual. He has always a smile on his face. Carlos da Atouguia is actually Carlos de Jesus Pereira, born on November 13, 1918, in Atouguia da Baleia, a small town close to Peniche, in the mainland. On May 14, 1953, he embarked for Canada in Lisbon boarding the Saturnia.

- I embarked on the 14th, but actually arrived on the 13th of May. – Carlos told us. – It was already nighttime when we got to Halifax, so we could not embark on that day.

The known Carlos da Atouguia pointing at one of the pictures from the past.

On his side was his wife and pioneer, the happy Odília de Jesus Pereira, also from Atouguia da Baleia. She embarked for Canada on April 18, 1956, boarding the Vulcania, and arrived in New York on April 27 of the same year. From New York, Odília took the train to Toronto, where her husband awaited her.

- We were separated for three long years! – Odília told us. – I stayed in Atouguia with our four daughters.

- Are they now living in Canada? – We asked.

Three pioneers, three good friends! We can see Carlos's smile provoked by the happiness of seeing old friends – particularly Viola – and by the chance of reliving the past.

- Yes, we are all living here. Maria Leonor Barbosa, Maria Teresa Alves, Rosa Lopes and Lena Pereira.

- And we already count a handful of grandchildren. – A happy Carlos told us, interrupting his wife. – They are Rosemary, Emily, Robert, Jenny and Cristina. With a wonderful smile on their face, Carlos and Odília kept quite for a while, as if remembering a sweet moment from the past. We broke the silence with our next question:

- How many men came with you in May of 1953?

- We were about 80, although I don't remember the exact number. There were ten from the Azores and the other ones from the mainland. From Halifax, we all went to Montreal by steam train. The inspector São Romão took us there.

Carlos first job was to milk cows in a farm, in Shelsea, near Hull.

- Since I had no experience in milking cows, the task was so hard that my wrists became swollen. Back home in Atouguia, I was a miller. It had nothing to do with milking cows! I deposited the first 75 dollars I made, in the two and half months I was in Hull, in the local bank.

In one of the visits the inspector São Romão paid him, Carlos was advised to stay in Hull for a year, but Carlos was not willing to obey. Carlos wrote his friend Viola asking him to find him a job where he was living. While waiting for Viola's answer to his letter, Carlos said goodbye to his boss,

Mr. Meredith.

- He got very upset and phoned the consul general. – Carlos told us. – The consul called me and told me off, saying that I was dumber than I looked. I told him that if I were dumb it was not my fault. I told him three doctors, like him, were responsible for my dumbness because they were the ones inspecting me and signing my papers to come to Canada. I left the farm and the owner did not pay me for four days of work because of the consul general.

Meanwhile, Viola answered his letter where he informed Carlos to contact another Portuguese man, Abel Cruz, to find him a job. Through Abel, Carlos went to work for the seven islands where he was making 99 cents an hour.

- Abel Cruz was a crook. He took the $50 I had in the bank. I was left with a dollar, which I kept many years! – Carlos remembered sadly and still hurt. – Still, at the seven islands I made enough money to pay my debts in Portugal. Abel Cruz, who was involved in the Mafia, was assassinated a few years after, in the United States.

Carlos da Atouguia told us many other dramatic stories about Abel Cruz and others who took advantage of the pioneers' simplicity to live at their expense, without working. It is sad, but it happens all the time. Due to the rigorous winter season, Carlos went back to Montreal where, by coincidence, he rented a room where another Portuguese man was living. It was Silva from the town of Vila Franca, in the Azores. Silva knew an employee at the Immigration Services and got Carlos a job in Labrador, as a painter. Feeling homesick and heart broken with the separation from his wife and daughters, Carlos decided to go to Portugal on holidays.

- I embarked in Quebec City and went straight to France. I loved France. From there, I took the train to Lisbon. - Carlos took a deep breath, and continued. – It was the happiest day of my life. After so many hardships, to see my wife

Manuel Alves, Teresa Alves and "dad" Carlos Atouguia participating in an event at the First Portuguese.

and daughters waiting for me, there are no words to explain what I felt! – Carlos could hide a tear that stubbornly came rolling down his face.

- I needed those holidays. When I was in Labrador, I met Salvadinho, from the Algarve. I would love to see him again! Salvadinho advised me to come to Toronto with my family. Thus, I embarked for Canada again, in April of 1955 and in Toronto, João Trindade, from the Madeira island, got me a job at the Seaway Box Springs where I worked for seven years. During our spare time, Duarte – an individual from the Azores – and I used to work at the docks. We were the first Portuguese men to work at the Toronto's docks. When my wife and daughters came over, I decided to rent a house on 110 Lisgar Avenue.

- If that house could speak, it would have many stories to tell! – Otília said, smiling at us.

- It's true! – Carlos agreed. – You cannot imagine what my house was like. At times, it looked like a house for the distressed.

- We had many worries! – Otília said, ending his comment.

- What is past, it is gone! In 1958, I was able to accomplish one of my dreams. I bought a farm, located between Orangeville and Bolton. We lived there for eight years, eight wonderful years! I was known by the nickname "King of the beans". To pick up beans is much worse than to pick up tobacco. My wife and my daughters helped me a lot. Maria Leonor used to drive the truck we used to transport the vegetables to Augusta Avenue where I would then sell them.

- Good old times! – Odília admitted.

- It was on my farm that the group from Madeira Island decided to hold the commemorative festivities that marked the 10th anniversary of the first pioneers' arrival. It was also at this event that they decided to buy the farm, which, later on, became the Madeira Park.

In 1964, the couple from Atouguia da Baleia, decided to sell the farm and buy a supermarket. Pereira Supermercado was very successful. It was sold in 1966 and became known as Craveiro e Costa Supermarket.

- My wife fell ill, my children began looking for a better job, I had a lot of work just for myself, and I decided to sell the supermarket. – Carlos explained. – After selling the supermarket, I did many different things. For four years, I decided to buy and resell houses.

- Today I regret having sold them! – Carlos' wife told us. – We didn't need to do that and it would have been a great source of income.

- In 1970 – Carlos continued – I went to work for the Dixie Fruit Market, where I stayed for twelve years, selling flowers. However, I was only working six months a year. My time to retire arrived and here I am with my wife, happier than ever.

- Happy and the owner of a successful business! – We added, referring to his handmade wooden statues. He has picnic tables, stools, chairs, cages, accessories… and many other items, all done in wood.

- It's true! – He said, laughing at our comment. – I began doing this as a joke. The neighbours saw it and began asking me do similar things for them. So I went from miller to being a carpenter. Not bad! I never imagined I could make such a fortune! Above all, I am healthy, I live in peace and I dedicate myself to a type of work I enjoy. What else can I ask for?

Portuguese Secretary of State, José Cesário, Consul General of Portugal, João Perestrello and Pioneer Carlos da Atouguia having a light-hearted conversation.

We all took a moment to laugh and remember the past in silence. After, in retrospective, we spoke about all the difficulties, deceptions and sacrifices our Portuguese pioneers had to endure when they arrived in Canada. We hope they all can say Carlos' favorite sentence: "It was worth it!"

- How did you get involved in the First Portuguese Canadian Club?

- You know, I am member #11. At that time, when my daughters left the club for the night, the dances would be over, because the men didn't want to dance with other men.

We could not help but laugh at Carlos' stories, not only the one from the dance but other ones he had to share with us.

- I am one of the pioneers of the club and I served as president for two days! This is not even mentioned in the minutes. I signed my name as a businessman so that the club could be incorporated.

- Tell us how you managed to be president for only two days.

- Well, I was designated as president the same day we were preparing the party for the take over of the new executive. We decorated the hall, we prepared everything and decided on the tickets' prices at the door. To my surprise, on the day of the event I found out they had charged more money than we had agreed upon. I was so furious that I decided to resign and didn't want to be president again. That's the way I am.

- And Otília, do you remember any ladies from those times?

- Oh yes! I remember people who used to help at the club and were our friends. – Otília said with a sad look to her face. – I remember Antónia Sousa, Adília Rodrigues, Goia Azevedo, Zeca Vaz and many others whose names I no longer recall. Some of these women I still see once in a while, which helps me remember the good old times.

- And you Carlos, would you like to see anyone in particular?

- I would love to see some old friends: Salvadinho, who is now living in the US, the old Maia, who is now in Kitimat…

- Tell us about the happiest moment you lived in Canada? – We interrupted him.

After reflecting for a while, Carlos took a deep breath and told us:

- I will never forget what my friends did for me. The plaque they gave me as the pioneer from Atouguia da Baleia who helped other Portuguese men come to Canada meant a lot to me. This recognition was probably the moment that touched me the most. I am very proud.

Otília Pereira took the opportunity to show us the plaque in homage to her husband. Does this happy couple, now living a well deserved retirement, think of returning to Portugal?

- No, don't even think about it! To Portugal, I will only go on holidays! – They both said at the same time, sharing the same thought.

- It's in Canada that I have everything: wife, children, grandchildren. - Carlos completed his comment.

We left the Pereira's house happy with their story. This story has a really happy ending, one our pioneer deserves!

JMC - October of 1987

Pereira, Maria Celeste Freitas
Town of Faial do Norte, Madeira Island

Maria Celeste Freitas Pereira

The story of the pioneer Maria Celeste Freitas Pereira is one so tender and full of grace that it can be considered a Christmas carol. At the same time, it is a story filled with the drama of a couple that is separated by the hardness of life, but is able to happily reunite at the end.

Maria Celeste Freitas Pereira was born in the town of Faial do Norte, on Madeira Island, on February 12, 1926. She married Jordão Isidro de Freitas, also from Faial do Norte, on November 12, 1949. Jordão came to Canada as part of the very first group of men from Madeira, who arrived on June 3, 1953. Maria Celeste stayed behind in Madeira with the couple's three children: Eugénio Isidro (who is now 49 years old), Cecília Benvinda (now 48) and the late Orlando José (who died already in Canada, in 1972). Orlando José was the main character of the story we mentioned in the introduction. Maria Celeste arrived at New York's harbour on November 27 and touched down in Toronto on November 28, 1953. Holding the children in her arms with the anxiety of reuniting with her husband, Maria Celeste left the airport leaving behind one member. Blinded by the happiness of seeing her family together again, Celeste and Jordão left the baby Orlando José behind at the airport. Today, it is an episode they remember with a smile, but at the time they almost suffered a heart attack.

- Fortunately, no one stole anything or anybody in Toronto back in the days! – Celeste told us laughing at the story. In Toronto, five other children were born to the couple: Paulo Steven, now 44 years old, Gilberto, 42, Margareth Maria, 41, Raúl, 40, and Gabriel (36). Still today, Maria Celeste is very protective of her children. They will always be her small babies.

This strong woman, besides taking care of her family, found a job, as soon as she got here in 1953, at a cherry company. In 1957, she transferred herself to a sewing factory, working there until 1963, the same year she decided to open, with her husband, the cleaning company New Bright. Before opening the company though, Celeste and her children went to Brazil, in 1960,

because they did not like Canada at all. However, the adventure only lasted six months, and the family returned to Toronto. For the same reasons, they decided to go back to Madeira, in 1971, where they bought a house, but a year later, decided to return to Toronto.

At the request of the children who did not want the mother to work, Celeste and Jordão decided to sell the cleaning company, even though Jordão kept working for it as general manager. Due to the fact that the new owners failed to pay the amount agreed upon at the time the company was sold, the Freitas got back New Bright, even though Celeste and her children were only responsible for cleaning three houses. At that time, an unexpected car accident sent Celeste to the hospital with many scratches and fractures, particularly in her ribs and right knee. The next four years were marked by many operations, a lot of suffering, many therapies and visits to the psychologist. Besides all these problems, Celeste had to live with the pain caused by the passing of her son Orlando José and her husband left her to go live with the nurse that was coming home to take care of Celeste.

Cecília, Miss Cinderela 1969 and third runner up in the Miss Portugal pageant.

Fate can be very cruel! Ill and traumatized by the death of

In the above pictures, we see the entire family reunited. Maria Celeste with her children, children-in-law and grandchildren. True happiness after so much sorrow!

her son and her husband's abandonment, Maria Celeste decided to divide tasks among her children, always supportive of her, and began a small business: she would go door-to-door to sell plastic tumperware. Life was not easy for this woman. Today she is very thankful to her son-in-law, Jack Spadalier, Cecília's husband, who was always ready to help the family by giving her children a job at the hair salons while they were in school. – Jack was the "father" for my children! – She told us, feeling very grateful for everything.

When the Portuguese community celebrated the 25th anniversary with the presence of the president from the Region of Madeira, Alberto João Jardim (in his first official visit outside Portugal), Maria Celeste received the commemorative plaque for being the first Portuguese woman to give birth in Canada. At that time, in 1969, her daughter Cecília conquered

Jordão and Celeste with the couple's first children when they arrived.

the title Miss Cinderela, and was second runner up in the Miss Portugal pageant. According to Maria Celeste, the first Portuguese women to arrive in Canada were Zita do Plácido, now living in Montreal, Mrs. Caires, who lives in Niagara Falls, and Mrs. Nóbrega, from Windsor, besides Celeste. The big distances were the cause of many isolations, at the time, also leading to a huge lack of communication among people in our community.

So to justify Maria Celeste's story as a Christmas carol, in perfect tune with her children, our pioneer allowed her ex-husband (who has since then passed away) to visit her house to see the children. The past is the past…

JMC-1999

Pereira, Óscar Rodrigues

Town of São Martinho, Madeira Island

It would not make sense to spend a day with pioneers and founding members of the Canadian Madeira Club without registering their stories. By accident, we spoke with Óscar Rodrigues Pereira, a native from the town of São Martinho, on Madeira Island, where he was born on September 18, 1926.

Óscar came to Canada integrated in the first group of immigrants from Madeira,

Pereira family

who arrived in Halifax on June 2, 1953. He traveled with other companions to Toronto, by train, but continued until Windsor. He lived in Leamington for three months, where he began working at a vegetables farm, picking up tomatoes, onions and collards. When he found out he was free to go anywhere, Óscar decided to come back to Toronto, with his friend João Gonçalves Teixeira and Franco from Machico. In Toronto, after spending some time looking for a job, Óscar was able to find a job at a factory specializing

Gabriela and Óscar with son José.

in cleaning carpets, then at a carpentry and finally at a chromium-plating factory. After this endeavour, and with some experience in different areas, Óscar found a job at the TTC's publicity departement, but would transfer, shortly after, to a milk factory where he was a truck driver.

In 1962, he bought a garbage truck. A year later, Óscar acquired a taxi and became a taxi driver until his retirement. Today, he owns two taxi cars, which he rented to two drivers. It is a very profitable business one which helps him live well with his family. Back in Madeira Island, he met his better half: Gabriela Fernandes, born in the town of Machico, on October 13, 1927.

Elizabeth Pereira

They were married at the Machico's church by Father Andrade, Óscar's uncle. Just as a curious note, the couple's first son, José, born on May 25, 1953, turned one year old aboard the ship that brought him and his mother to Canada, in 1954.

In Canada, the couple Gabriela and Óscar Pereira saw the birth of another child: daughter Elizabeth, born in Toronto, on September 15, 1964, who is now a teacher in St. Catherines. José also has a bachelor of education, but is a manager at the Laidlaw Corporation, where Óscar found a part-time job to be able to spend some time with his son.

Feeling homesick, missing family and friends from back home were some of the problems our pioneers had to face. Thus, the very active Ângelo Bacalhau decided to celebrate the 10th anniversary of the arrival of the Portuguese in Canada by reuniting all the people from Madeira and organizing an outdoor event, just like they used to do back home. From the beginning, he was able to count with the help from Óscar Pereira, João Camarata and Juvenal de Freitas. They spoke with Carlos da Atouguia, talked about the

Óscar Pereira with Prof. José Carlos Teixeira, Gilberto Araújo, among other pioneers on the day the pioneers from Madeira were honoured.

expenses, and decided to hold the event at Carlos' farm. It was a success. Encouraged by Ângelo Bacalhau, they decided to buy a hall for their events. Thus, they contacted everyone they knew from Madeira to ask them for money to buy the new place. It was hard and many would say no to the idea. They were asking for $20, which was a lot of money back in the days. "But after a few minutes of conversation and two glasses of wine, they would end up giving us the money" – said our pioneer. Once they had the money needed, they bought the farm. After much work and sacrifice, it is still today the pride of every person from Madeira island.

The pioneers who bought and founded the Madeira Park are: João Camarata, Juvenal de Freitas, António Plácido, Óscar Pereira, Eduardo Mendonça and Ângelo Bacalhau. From here, they decided to for the Canadian Madeira Club, which was formed on June 2, 1963. The first hall the club had was the hall at Santa Maria's church, on Adelaide and Bathurst Streets, in Toronto. Óscar Pereira served in the board of directors and was president of the investigation committee the last year he was an active member of the club.

Óscar now spends most of the time in his garden taking care of his roses. On the other hand, he does not lose the opportunity to visit different places. He goes to Madeira island twice a year. Óscar is a happy man who has accomplished all he wanted.

JMC-1999

Pimentel, Eduardo Manuel

Town of Rabo de Peixe, Island of São Miguel, Azores

He is a very simple Portuguese Canadian citizen. He does everything he can to go unnoticed. He is Eduardo Manuel Pimentel, a native from the town of Rabo de Peixe, in the island of S. Miguel, Azores, where he saw the light of day on January 11, 1951. His father, João Pimentel, emigrated to Canada in 1953 and only in 1966 did his wife Maria Angelina and sons – Eduardo, José João and Maria – come to join him.

The young Eduardo Manuel, "Eddy" to his friends, studied in Toronto and has been from a very early age a successful carpenter, specializing in windows. He worked for many years at the Mason Windows' company. In 1989, he successfully founded his company Millennium Installations, a firm specialized in aluminum windows. Eddy Pimentel is a subcontractor and does all the windows assembly

Eduardo and Tracy Pimentel at a Portuguese event.

service in all Ontario schools. Eduardo Manuel Pimentel met, in Toronto, the young and beautiful Tracy Pimentel, a native from Altares, in Terceira island, where she was born on September 9, 1956. Eddy and Tracy got married at St. Helen's church in Toronto, a ceremony presided by Father Libório, on September 24, 1977.

The couple has three children: Jennifer, born in Toronto on July 12, 1978, a student at York University; Darryl, born in

Tracy Pimentel, a happy mother, between her younger children, Melissa and Darryl. A happy and united family!

Toronto on October 26, 1981; and Melissa, who was also born in Toronto on April 14, 1987.

Eddy loves soccer and does not lose an opportunity, during his leisure time, to practice his favourite sport.

When Eddy was younger, he played soccer for the Benfica Açoriano of Toronto, between 1970 and 1978. The most curious thing is that Eduardo Manuel Pimentel has never gone back to his native island, nor has he visited any other part of Portugal. Only his daughter Jennifer was in Lisbon, at Fernando Correia Marques' house and well known author, composer and singer.

However, Eddy has promised to go visit his roots in the near future. Homesickness is responsible for these sudden changes. As a soccer fan, Eddy may be planning to visit Portugal's capital to participate in the Euro Cup 2004, hosted by Portugal. Otherwise, it would be unforgiven...

JMC - 1999

Dressed in Benfica Açoriano's uniform, in the good old times...

The beautiful Jennifer between friends Fernando Correia Marques and Axel, in Lisbon, at a typical restaurant.

Pinheiro, João de Oliveira

Village of Lago, town of Amares, province of Minho

Our pioneer João de Oliveira Pinheiro was born in the small village of Lago, in the county of Amares, a beautiful town in the province of Minho, on February 19, 1942. While attending school, João was also helping his parents in the fields, for agriculture was the only means of survival back in those times.

He completed elementary school in Amares, and when he turned 14 years old, João went to Lisbon. He found a job as a grocer, working at the grocery Mercearia Fernandes, owned by friends of the family, who were from the district of Castelo Branco. João stayed in Lisbon until 1958, the same year he decided to emigrate to Canada. João de Oliveira Pinheiro arrived in Montreal on May 30, 1958, and went to live with his father who had come to the country the year before. João's father, Francisco Veloso Pinheiro, was sponsored to come to Canada by his brother-in-law, António

Maria Júlia Pinheiro with husband João and daughter Irene.

de Oliveira, who is still living in St. Eustacht, Montreal. João and his father went to work for a lumber center in Val d'Or, in northern Quebec, the same year that John G. Diefenbaker became prime minister. Due to the time of crisis and lack of jobs, they were laid off and returned to Montreal. João went to live with his uncle António, in St. Thérèse. After many difficulties, João was able to find a job at a vegetable farm. In the winter, he worked in St. Jerome, living at the farmer's daughter's house, chopping wood and tending the cattle. He remembers having snow until his neck in freezing temperatures. Those were hard times, without any social assistance, as he still remembers. Everyone was basically fighting for a means of survival.

João Pinheiro by his 1957 Ford Mercury, in St. Thérèse, Montreal.

In 1959, António Oliveira (oncle), Joaquina Macedo Oliveira, João Pinheiro, late Francisco Veloso and sister Sameiro Pinheiro.

In 1960, João and his father went to work for an aluminum factory. As a joke, one day João decided to put some glue in a colleague's shoes, but forgot to warn him. When his friend put on the shoes, and hurt himself, João was fired from his job. Through his father, João was able to find a job in Courtland, Ontario. He found a job at a tobacco farm.

In 1962, João asked his parents and brothers to leave Quebec and come to Ontario. João felt that Ontario had a lot more to offer than Quebec. The language, however, continued to be an obstacle for the Pinheiro family. In Quebec, they had to struggle with French and in Ontario with English. Under José Borges' management – who is now living back in Portugal – the Pinheiro family worked in 1964. The family also rented a farm in Strathroy in that same year. At the end of the summer, João decided to try his luck in Toronto, after completing a course as a mechanic for Diesel cars. In Toronto, he found a job at Manuel Rosario's garage. Several months later, José Borges went to work in construction, and since the salary was much higher, João left his job at the garage to also go to construction.

In the winter of 1965, João went to work for a brick factory in Cooksville. In this town, he rented a room from the Fernandes family and ended up marrying the couple's daughter. The

João Pinheiro, Manuel Teixeira and João Dias.

The Pinheiro in Hawaii, celebrating their silver anniversary.

young Maria Júlia da Cunha Fernandes was born in Vila Nova de Cerveria a town in the province of Minho. They got married on July 16, 1966 at Santa Maria's church in Toronto, a ceremony presided by Father Alberto Cunha.

On March 30, 1967, the couple's daughter, Irene, was born at Mississauga General Hospital. Irene is a professional accountant, married and has already presented the couple with a grandson.

Back in 1966, João found a job at Ford Motor, in Oakville, where he worked until 1990, the year he decided to retire. Together with friends Alice and José Pinheiro, the couple participates in many Portuguese events in Mississauga, London and Strathroy, especially in events organized by natives of Minho. They frequently visit the United States of America and other parts of Canada and often visit Portugal and Spain.

To celebrate their 25th wedding anniversary, Maria Júlia and João Pinheiro decided to relive their honeymoon in Maui, Hawaii. This year, they are celebrating their 35th anniversary. Congratulations and all the best!

JMC - 2000

Pires, Virgílio António

Christmas of 1959, in Dawson Creek: Bonza, Larguinho, Pires and Craveiro.

Town of Alverca do Ribatejo

Only those who live and work close to our pioneer Virgílio Pires are able to notice all his skills and qualities. Virgílio Pires likes to help everyone, likes to build new things and, above all, likes to go unnoticed. It is obvious that we respect his way of being in society, but there are times that we cannot just simply ignore his virtues, in part because our community should know this noble man.

Virgílio António Pires was born in the town of Alverca do Ribatejo, on February 15, 1934. He is married to Clara das Neves Pires, a native of Salvaterra de Magos.

- Although her town is near mine, I never met my wife in Portugal – Virgílio told us with a smile. – I met my wife in Toronto! We dated and got married here.

- The world is very small! – we added.

The couple has two children. The older one, Virgílio Junior, was born in Toronto, on May 6, 1963. The younger one, Edward, was also born in Toronto, on June 8, 1965.

- My orlder son has a degree in Industrial Design and is working for Magna parts. Edwar was at U of T for two years, and is now thinking of continuing his studies in painting. He likes it and is good at it. I feel bad that he didn't want to continue in university.

Virgílio Pires left Lisbon by plane on May 13, 1957, heading to Canada. It was a long trip that lasted 16 hours.

- We left Lisbon and landed in the island of Santa Maria, in the Azores. From here, we went to Gander. After a short stop at Gander, I went to Montreal. From here, my companions and I traveled by train to Vancouver.

- Why did you go all the way until Vancouver?

- Because I had some friends from Alverca living there. I was in British Columbia for three years and another year in Quebec, before coming to Toronto. I only came to live in Toronto in 1961.

- What made you come to Toronto?

- It's a long story! – Virgílio began telling us. – It was really hard to find a job at that time. It was the year of the invasion of Hungary, and many Hungarians were coming to Canada as refugees. Because of their condition, they had priority when it came to finding jobs. I was without a job for two months.

- What was your first job?

- Picking apples in Okanagan Valley! – he said, laughing. – I was making ten cents for each box of apples I was picking up. The most I made

Virgílio Pires with brother Armando and one of his employees.

in one day was six dollars! There are still many Portuguese living there and, thank God, they are all doing very well.

- You didn't like to live there?

- It wasn't a case of liking or disliking. It just so happens that I had no style for the job. Curiously, it was one of my friends, a German, who noticing my difficulties at the job asked me if there was anything I knew how to do. I told him that back home I was a mechanic, with a lot of experience. He promised me he would speak to a friend of his, who had a shop and was looking for someone with experience. A few days later, he took me to his friends place and ended up staying there. At this mechanical shop, I began making a dollar an hour. I was responsible for making parts for agriculture machines, just like the ones I was using to pick up apples.

- From here, where did you go?

- I was there for one year. Then, I went to a construction company that was building the railroad. Here, I was making a $1.25 an hour.

- Was it hard?

- Very. It was taking every drop of energy out of me! – Virgílio said. – I am planning to take my family there one of these days, so that they see where I worked and what I had to go through. That job was so hard that one day I got a back injury. When I left the hospital, I decided not to go back to construction. Since I knew how to operate machines, I found a job as a machine operator. Thus, I was an operator for two years. Later on, this company moved to Quebec, and we came with it, to work at the Seven Islands, in 1960.

- So, Toronto still had to wait? – We asked, joking with him.

- Well, we will get there. At that time, still at the Seven Islands, I decided to go to the US, more specifically to New Jersey. I had a friend living there who found me a job. I didn't stay there because I didn't like the place. Since I knew some people who were living in Toronto, I decided to try my luck here in 1961, and never left.

- How were things in Toronto? Was it as hard?

- No! – Virgílio answered, without hesitating. – The day after my arrival, I began working.

I went to work for the Progressiva Food Equipment. I was the first Portuguese to work there. I was working with equipment made of steel. Some time after, the bothers Ferro Silva and Manuel Pereira came to work with us. They now own the Pereira Sheet Metal.

- Did you like it there?

- Oh yes! After five years, the owner opened a new factory and promoted me to manager. It was the Anko Metal Products. I worked with Eddy Kohn for twelve years, and am still good friends with him.

- Why did you leave?

- After twelve years, Eddy decided to sell the companies. I didn't like the new

Virgílio Pires showing the flag he won in the Vela tournament, offered by consul Tânger Correia.

owners, so I decided to leave and open my own company. That's how the Merit Metal Industries was born. I will never forget the opening day. It was December 1st, 1972: I celebrated the opening of my business and the independence of Portugal.

- You are a true Portuguese patriot.

- Yes, I am. Everything that is Portuguese or related to the Portuguese community, I support in every way I can. That's why I am always involved in many events, even though I live far from the community.

- You are now involved as the leader of the committee Sail Portugal-88 and planning the formation of Casa de Lisboa, right?

- Yes! All of that requires a lot of work, it takes too much time from my business, but what can I do? This is the way I am.

- Thank God! – We told him. – If you didn't have people like you, how could our community develop?

- That's also true! But we need more people to work, people who were not concerned in showing off. We need leaders in many groups. Sometimes, I sense we have too many chiefs and not enough Indians.

- Still, you continue to support many community initiatives, specially in sports.

- Yes! Besides supporting Sail Portugal-88, I have also been contributing to the Olympic games, helping the Portuguese in Calgary… You know, I love sports.

- Speaking of sailing, you own a boat in Toronto, don't you?

- Yes! I have a boat with a nice story! – He said, after smiling at us. – It is a canoe I named Feliz Viagem (Good Journey), a typical canoe from the Tagus River, one I found by chance at the Vancouver Expo, in 1986. I bought it to give it to the community museum that we are trying to open. The canoe has become very popular on Lake Ontario because it is different from all the other ones. It is extremely pretty. It was hard to get and to bring to Toronto, but it was worth it. I don't feel sorry for anything I did. I believe life has known how to reward me.

- Going back to the good old times, were you ever involved in any club?

- Yes, I was! - Virgílio remembered, his eyes lost in the horizon, as if searching for the lost memories. – In Toronto, I met Américo, who had played soccer in Caldas da Rainha, and who was involved in the first Portuguese soccer team. It was the Portuguese United Soccer Club, founded on April 5, 1964. I remember the Silva brothers, Artur Rodrigues, Bacalhau, Armando Albuquerque, the Brazilian, Américo from Alenquer... It is hard to remember all of them. I was never a director at the First Portuguese Club, but I am a member and help in everything I can. Nowadays, I am more involved in the community because I am a member of the Federation of Portuguese Canadian Business and professionals, an organization in which I believe and give my best. In the past, I was not too involved in the clubs and associations, because, as I have said before, I lived far from the community.

- Can you tell us any interesting story that happened to you in the past?

- At a certain point, a group of Portuguese and I were all without a job. We heard that in Fort Nelson, they were looking for people to work at the Pipe Line. We got two cars and took off on the Alaska Highway. Back then the Alaska Highway was a stone and dirt road. Due to the dust, we had to drive the cars side by side. When we got to Fort Nelson, still nighttime, we saw a light at a distance. We took the cars there. When we arrived, the light was an enormous campfire, surrounded by immigrants, like us, waiting for the Pipe Line's boss. They wanted to know if there were any jobs available for that day. Well, we decided to wait around the fire. When the man arrived he informed us there was nothing available for anyone. We looked at each other, disappointed, and decided to come back to Dowson Creek. We came back without knowing what to do to find a job. When we were passing by Taylor Flats, in B.C., we were forced to stop because a bridge had fallen and the railroad workers were building a detour for the cars. We took advantage of the delay to look for a job. We were all hired to work in the railroads. After all, it was worth taking the long drive.

- At that time, was your brother already living in Canada?

- No! My brother Armando came to Canada in 1965. He didn't want any partnership in my company, but he is responsible for the management. He is an engineer. He takes care of the management section and I take care of the administration.

- From what I can see, the factory is already too small for so much work.

- It is true! I think I have to move to a bigger place. It appears I will be moving for the third time.

Virgílio Pires, engineer Sarmento, Dr. David Rendeiro, aboard the Tagus Canoe on Lake Ontario.

- Are you considering staying in the same area?

- I hope so because I am now very familiar with this Weston zone.

Virgílio Pires continued his conversation about Weston, the area where he has been living for many years, as well as his interest in staying there. We took the opportunity to ask him how he got involved in the trade of mechanics.

- In Alverca, where I was born, we had two choices, as children: work in the railroad or work in the aviation mechanics. My father worked in the aviation field, so my brother and I went to work there as well.

- Your father is a famous motor specialist, is he?

- Yes, he is! – He said, very proud of his father. – My father was the head person in the trial sector, in the aviation mechanics, in Alverca. Any motor that left the place would need his signature of approval. Master Pires, as he is known, is admired, by most people in Alverca. My father, just like me, was the cover of a magazine, in 1930. My father's picture came in the first page of "Notícias Ilustrado", in 1930, repairing a motor. Both the magazine and the picture are on display at the Air Museum, in Alverca. I have a copy of the picture there.

Behind Virgílio's desk, a big frame displays the old picture, paying a homage to Master Pires.

- You know, my father is still alive, a strong 82 year old man. When he turned 80, I decided to offer him an amplified copy of the picture to give him for his birthday. He loved it!

- Do you remember any other event?

- Many!… When I celebrated 25 years of Canada, I invited all my friends from the good old times. They came from Vancouver, Montreal… It was the best moment we had to remember stories we all lived. Of course, I wasn't able to reunite all my friends, because I was unable to get everyone's address, specially because some went back to Portugal. It was a celebration I will never forget. I would still like to see João Duarte who lives in Montreal, Anselmo Esteves who is now in Lisbon, Carlos Ferreira who is also back in Portugal, in Mem Martins, Tony Martins who is in Vancouver, Rui Mendes who is also in Montreal, Américo from Alenquer who is in California and many others whose names I no longer recall.

The first portuguese soccer club and team in Canada: Portuguese United Soccer Club. In the picture, we can see the Silva brothers, Artur Rodrigues, Bacalhau, Armando Albuquerque, the brazilian and Américo from Alenquer, among others.

- What would you like to see in the community?

- Unity! I really want to see unity. The unity is the key to every success, but very few people live by this. Our community has the potencial to go very far, and it sometimes loses itself in nonsense things.

We left without asking our pioneer which of the two passions gives him more headaches: his community or his company. However, Virgílio, even when he tries to go unnoticed, does not give up. Even if he is alone, he will carry his ideas until the end. Fortunately, according to his own words, life has been treating him well.

We are sure that the Portuguese community, sooner or later, will know how to recognize the efforts done by this pioneer. To the Pires family, we wish all the best.

JMC - September of 1988

Quintal, José de

Village of Sítio das Neves, town of São Gonçalo, Madeira Island

In the city of Funchal, he was a barman at the known Indiana & Baiana house. Since then until today, José de Quintal is an adhrent of the Nacional Madeira soccer team. José de Quintal married Algerina Quintal, a native of the village of Sítio das Neves, in the town of São Gonçalo, where she was born on February 28, 1928. They got married on April 30, 1953, at the church of Socorro de Santa Maria Maior.

José and Algerina de Quintal at the front of their house.

The Quintal's have two children: Rui and Renato. José de Quintal – together with about 101 fellow companions – arrived in Halifax on June 2, 1953. Together with fourteen other men, José was sent to Niagara-on-the-Lake to a peach and cherry farm. He was making .25 cents for each basket of cherries he picked up. When winter arrived, José de Quintal came to Toronto where he found a job at the Greek restaurant Bassels. Because he did not speak English, José began working at the restaurant's pantry. António Plácido, who learned some English back in Portugal, was the Portuguese man responsible for helping those who did not know the language. In 1956, José found a job at the Press Woods Brothers, a meat company where some of his former fellow travelers were working. Later on, the company changed its name to Suifts Eastern, but José Quintal kept working there until 1985, the year the company decided to go out of business. He continued working as a butcher for Bittner's Packers where he worked until he retired, at the age of 65, in 1994.

José de Quintal was one of the Portuguese pioneers from Madeira Island who was raising funds – the famous $20 a household – to buy the farm where today is the Madeira Park. He is also a founding member of the Canadian Madeira Club and one of the members behind the purchase of the place for the club, on College Street, in Toronto. He still remembers with some irony selling – even though illegally – a glass of whisky for .35 cents to

Their house in 1967. José de Quintal always had his mother-in-law following him!

Algerina and José de Quintal saluting Alberto João Jardim during the president's first official visit to Canada. At the back, we can see Fernando Raposo and Jaime Velosa.

José's son Rui with wife Cathy and children Ammy and Ryan, in California.

get money to pay for all the expenses the club had.

José de Quintal served the club as a director for eighteen straight years, almost on a daily basis. Rui, one of José's sons, is now living in California with his wife Cathy and two children: Ammy, 17 years old, and Ryan, 15. Rui owns a pluming company. Renato, the other son, has auto collision shop and lives at home. José de Quintal, now 72 years old, is in excellent health. Since he believes that life is too short, José visits Madeira many times and travels very often to California to see his son and grandchildren. When he celebrated his 25th wedding anniversary, the couple received a cruise as their anniversary gift. As a joke, José plays the lottary every week to see if he can become rich, since he was not able to accomplish that working. Hope is the last one to die.

- Still, I pray that hope dies before me, so that I can still have some more time on this earth. – José said, laughing at this own comment. Politicians often say that Portuguese are good, honest people. José da Quintal is a good example of this saying. All the best to those pioneers who, in 1953, opened the doors to all of us.

* in collaboration with Eugénio Rodrigues

JMC/ Eugénio Rodrigues - 2000

Raposo, João Carlos Botelho

Village of Livramento, City of Ponta Delgada, island of São Miguel, Azores

João and Nídia Raposo – with their dog – at the confort of their home.

The Raposo's have an interesting story to share, one with many "notes". João Carlos Botelho Raposo was born in Livramento, a small village in the district of Ponta Delgada, in S. Miguel, Azores, on June 12, 1933. Soon after completing elementary school, João began working as a carpenter, just like his father.

However, life takes many turns. At the age of 23, João left carpentry and began working in the textile industry, opening his own factory, in the town of Lagoa, until 1967. Before this time, though, he met Nídia Ivone Lima da Ponte, from the town of Rosário da Lagoa, in S. Miguel, where she was born on September 25, 1931. They got married on July 20, 1958, at the church of Rosário da Lagoa. A son was born to the couple: Hernâni Luís, a boy with an outstanding talent for music since the day he was born. Hernâni was born in Rosário da Lagoa, on September 26, in 1960.

Hernâni Raposo with his father thanking artists Mano Belmonte, Mário Marinho and Zé da Vesga, at the end of their performance at Santo Cristo's festivities.

Due to the quality of the work, João's factory grew and won a "merit award" at the S. Miguel's fair, inaugurated by the former minister of corporation, Gonçalves Proença. The award was given to João, in 1964, by the Civil governor, Vasconcelos Raposo. The crisis created by the war Portugal was fighting in Africa was making life very hard in Portugal, and people were paying too many taxes. João decided to leave his wife taking care of the factory and baby Hernâni, and immigrated to Canada, in October of 1965. As soon as he arrived in Toronto, he found a job at the National Knitting Mills. From here, he transferred to Sheridon Nursery.

João Raposo received the Honour Diploma from the Civil Governor of São Miguel.

With life stabilizing in Canada, João Raposo decided it was time to sell his business in Portugal and have his wife and son come to Toronto. They came in 1967, when Hernâni was 6 years old. At this age, Hernâni was already turning any object he found into a musical instrument, even his mother's pans, which served as drum sets. Always wanting to make life better for his

Family Raposo.

family, João went back to his first profession: he became a carpenter and began working in construction. At the same time, João was studying electronics and plumbing, in night school. Much sacrifice, so his family could live better. A few years after arriving in Canada, João decided to open his own company in 1972: the White Eagle Enterprises. His company provided many different services in carpentry, electricity and pluming. Meanwhile, as a good catholic, João

Hernâni Raposo and Father Libório during the celebration of Nídia and João's 25th wedding anniversary.

Nídia Raposo with son Hernâni.

Young Hernâni Raposo at the beginning of his musical career.

helped in church every Sunday at mass and at the Portuguese religious celebrations at Santa Maria's church, in Toronto. He helped fathers Lourenço, Cunha and António and is now helping Father Libório. In 1966, as a devout of Senhor Santo Cristo, he began, with Manuel Arruda, the technical part of the festivities in 1966. Since then, every year João has been responsible for the lights and sound of the festivities at Santa Maria church in Toronto. He was also the carpenter who built the altars where the images of Senhor Santo Cristo, Coração de Jesus and Nosso Senhor Morto are. His son Hernani – today one of the best musicians of the Portuguese community and the owner of one of the best recording studios – has always helped his father in arranging the music for the festivities.

Nídia and João have established their roots in Canada. Now that their son Hernâni and daughter-in-law Edna have given them a grandson, they do not consider the possibility of leaving the country. The only free time he has he dedicates it to church and playing the "Viola da Terra" (the Azorean guitar). His son is also dedicating himself to music.

JMC - 1999

Raposo, Raúl Francisco Lopes

Village of Santa Clara do Loredo,
disctrict of Beja, province of Alentejo

The couple Maria and Raúl Raposo form a respectful duet. They are very active and one of the main reasons the community centre Casa do Alentejo is such a cultural reference. They have been involved in Casa do Alentejo's organization since its foundation. Raúl Francisco Lopes Raposo was born on September 14, 1936, in Santa Clara do Loredo, a village in the district of Beja, in the southern province of Alentejo. Maria de Jesús Faias Raposo was born on October 16, 1938, in Beringel, also a village in the district of Beja.

They got married in the church of Albernoa, on June 4, 1961. Maria and Raúl arrived in Toronto on August 19, 1967, bringing their first son, Jaime Manuel, who was born in Ervides, Beja. Today, Jaime has a degree in Chemistry, owns a cosmetic company, is married and has two children. The couple's second son, Richard, was born in Toronto 29 years ago. He has a degree in Ecology, is single and works with his brother in the cosmetic company.

Raúl and Maria Raposo, dressed up in the traditional clothes from Alentejo, the same ones they use to sing in the "Grupo Coral".

Raúl Francisco, a welder by profession, did not have any difficulty finding a job in Toronto. Bia, the nickname by which Maria is known, kept on doing the job she had in Portugal: a dedicated mother and a seamstress. Just like any good natives of Alentejo, they were both born and will die singing. Thus, as their favourite hobby, they decided to be founding members of Casa do Alentejo Community Centre, in Toronto, on February 20, 1988, and formed the singing group Grupo Coral da Casa do Alentejo. This group could count with the help of Aldina and Manuel Raposo, Milú and António Franco, Guida and Luís

Figueira, Chico Alentejano, Zé Ferro, António Gomes, Ângelo, Boga, Custódio Manguito, Marco Baioa, José Bentes, Joaquim David and Francisco Varela. Unfortunately, some of which have passed away. In 1993, Maria Raposo decided to form the Feminine Singing Group of Casa do Alentejo. These are two groups that make the events at Casa do Alentejo very special and very event where they are requested to sing the Canadian and Portuguese National Anthems.

Richard, Raúl, Maria and Jaime in a family picture.

The "Grupo Coral da Casa do Alentejo" has recorded an album with traditional songs from Alentejo and one song dedicated to Toronto. Maria and Raúl Raposo are the only members who have been part of the executive administration since the foundation of the club. Bia has been particularly involved in the cultural sector.

We wish the best to these two "solo artists" from Alentejo and hope they will always be patient to continue the work they have been doing for Casa do Alentejo and for the Portuguese community in general.

The day Casa do Alentejo organized a surprise event in honour of Raúl Raposo.

JMC-1999

Rebelo, António Cabral

Village of Ribeirinha, island of S. Miguel, Azores

He is a popular man in the Portuguese community of Toronto. He is António Cabral Rebelo, born in the village of Ribeirinha, in the island of S. Miguel, on March 27, 1945. Tony Rebelo, as he is known in the community, com-

pleted elementary school in Ribeirinha and began working in agriculture to help the family.

From a very early age, António began liking music and when he turned 14 years old was already playing the accordeon. On

Portrait of a happy family: Helena and Tony together with daughter Melanie and son Leonel.

February 28, 1964, António Cabral Rebelo arrived in Toronto. For a while, he lived with his sister Filomena, who had come to Canada several years before. Toney Rebelo, just like almost every immigrant, had many jobs and faced many challenges. He worked as carpenter, as waiter at the Park Plaza Hotel, among other things. At the same time, António decided to study at night.

Helena Maria and Tony Rebelo the day of their wedding.

António formed his first band back in the Azores, in the Juventude

Operária Católica. Already in Toronto, Tony decided to form a band – JOC. The group used to rehearse at Santa Maria Church, and later, at the parish of Monte Carmelo. Tony Rebelo – vocals and acordeon, Zé Aguiar – drums, and Manuel Bolhões – guitar, together with two girls from Madeira Island, formed a musical group. This group was nameless until Tony's brother José joined the group with Jacinto Almeida. They formed the first band of the Portuguese community, at the time Mariano Rego and António Amaro were playing in dances and accom-

Good old times: Edmundo Pimentel, José Rebelo, Tony Rebelo, Edmundo Pacheco and Manuel Tavares, the members of "Boa Esperança".

panying artists. They decided to name the band "Boa Esperança! (Good Hope). "Boa Esperança" was a tremendous success and left many good memories. The band began playing songs by the Portuguese group Maria Albertina, but with the "birth" of Rock and Roll and The Beatles, they decided to change their musical study. Tony Rebelo was forced to learn bass guitar and work on his singing skills. The late Eduardo Pacheco came to the band to replace José Aguiar. When Eduardo passed away, "Boa Esperança" decided to invite Helder Freitas to continue the band. The group had twenty years of successes. The farewell party took place in March of 1984 where Helder Freitas, Eduardo Pimentel, Tony Rebelo and José Rebelo played together for the last time.

One last smile as members of "Boa Esperança": the farewell of Helder Freitas, Edmundo Pimentel, Tony and José Rebelo.

Back in the Azores, while integrating the group from Juventude Operária Católica, Tony met and fell in love with Helena Maria Salvador Rodrigues, who was born in the village of Ribeira Seca, on October 30, 1948. They married on July 28, 1969, at the church of Mount Carmel by Father Bernardes. With an expression of sadness, Tony remembers those times at the Juventude Operária Católica where the members began meeting and falling in love with other members. Most of them ended up getting married, just like Tony and Helena. The Rebelos have two children: Melanie, born in Toronto on October 2, 1974, and Leonel, born in Mississauga, on August 8, 1981.

Tony Rebelo as Disc Jockey.

During the festivities of 'Senhor da Pedra' in Toronto, in 2001, Tony Rebelo launched a CD with the songs "Boa Esperança" played. The CD has the title "Relembrar o Passado" (Remembering the Past), a true success in the community.

Nowadays, Tony is still working at a truck parts company and, on weekends, still dedicates his time to the DJ Boa Esperança services, which he formed a year after ending the band. As a DJ, Tony counts on his son Leonel for help. He is still invited to sing for the community in special occasions.

Helena and Tony love traveling. Whenever they can, they visit the Azores, Portuguese mainland, USA, the Caribbean and go across Canada. May they continue to live their dream to the fullest!

JMC - 2001

The couple's 25th wedding anniversary

Rebelo, Fernando Manuel

City of Ponta Delgada, island of S. Miguel, Azores

Fernando Rebelo besides one of his paintings.

He is extremely nice, a true gentleman and a true comedian. He is Fernando Manuel Rebelo, a native of the city of Ponta Delgada, in the island of S. Miguel, Azores, where he was born on September 15, 1917. He is an artist and an athlete. He completed high school in Ponta Delgada. From Antero de Quental's high school, he went to the agriculture school, in Queluz, mainland Portugal, where he completed only the first year. Fernando returned to the Azores to work for the agriculture sector. When he was called to serve in the army, Fernando ended up in the sergeants' course. When he entered the final phase at the army (in Portuguese known as the "peluda"), Fernando applied for the Mail Services in Ponta Delgada. After waiting for a year, he was able to get the job. Curiously enough, his future bride Maria Natália Soeiro, a native of the village of Mosteiros, had also applied for a job at the mail services. Maria Natália was born on March 15, 1920. They married on December 12, 1943, in the church of Nossa Senhora da Saúde, in the village of Arrifes. In Ponta Delgada, he saw the birth of his children: Maria Paula, Luís Manuel, Fernando, Tony, Helena, Margarida and Suzana.

Influenced by his mother who loved theatre, Fernando fell in love with the stage. His mother used to adapt every play she saw and rehearsed at home with her children. She used to say it was the best form of occupying her children during their leisure time. When he was only 8 or 9 years old, Fernando performed his first "solo" play for his grandmother. As he was growing up, Fernando kept on practicing his theatrical skills, at the same time, as he was

The Rebelo brothers, back in the days when they played soccer for the União Micaelense, in the Azores, in 1935

involving himself in sports, mainly volleyball and soccer. At the time, Fernando was practicing his plays with Jovelino Pimentel.

In the village of Fajã de Baixo, where he lived for many years, he performed in many plays and comedy sketches written by José Barbosa. Some of his memorable performances were: Ramo de Hortência, written by Victor Cruz Sr., in 1941; "A Pegureira", by Castanheira Lobo, in 1941; "Manta de Retalhos", by José Barbosa, in 1942; "Moços e Velhos", by José Rocha, in 1948; "A Bisbilhoteira", in 1949. In 1950, Fernando took part in the play "O Eco do Passado e o Presente", to celebrate the first 100th anniversary of the Antero de Quental high school.

Fernando Rebelo among his theatre students from JOC, in 1966.

After so many performances, Fernando decided to come to Canada in 1956. He first lived in Kingston, Ontario, but after a short period of time decided to move to Toronto, where he lived by himself for three years. Fernando had many jobs, from cleaning to construction.

In 1968, his family came to Canada. Also in 1968, he decided to stay at the Modern Building Cleaning services, together with his brother Manuel. He worked for Modern Building until his retirement. Even though, he came to Canada, he did not forget his passion for theatre. In 1966, in Kingston, he created the Portuguese Theatre Group at the Portuguese church hall. The first play they performed was "O exame do menino da escola" (The boy's exam). In Toronto, he began doing plays at St. Patrick's church with young people from the group JOC. In 1969, he performed the comedy "Daqui fala o morto" (Dead man talking), under the supervision of Humberto Carvalho; in 1971-72, he performed "Inês de Castro" and "Botas do Papá", at St. Agnes church; in 1973, with Jovelino Pimentel, he decided to perform again "O menino da Escola" and, for the first time, "O médico brasileiro", at the Harbour Collegiate. In 1977-78, at the First Portuguese Canadian Club, he was the main actor in the comedies "Marido de minha mulher" (My wife's husband) and "Ressonar sem dormir"

Zé Mário, Fernando Rebelo, Rosa Marques, Manuel Marques and Joana in the comedy "Marido da minha mulher", in 1977, at the First Portuguese.

Fernando Rebelo performing "Ceia dos Cardeais", in 1976.

Fernando and Maria Natália Rebelo surrounded by their family during a family celebration.

(To snore without sleeping). In December of 1985, he presented the play "Natal Vivo" (Live Christmas), which earned him the first prize of Portuguese live nativity scenes, initiated by the Portuguese Consulate of Portugal. In 1986, at the First Portuguese, he performed in the

Fernando Rebelo at the S. Pedro swimming pool, in 1934.

Maria Natália and Fernando Manuel Rebelo.

play The Scrooge, based on the work of Charles Dickens.

However, the deceptions he suffered throughout the years in Canada could not be forgotten. Due to a huge lack of interest from the community, Fernando decided to stop his plays. He fought for the love he had for theatre, but was too disappointed to continue. His dream of creating a theatre academy was never accomplished.

Nowadays, Fernando helps in the Casa dos Açores community centre. It was within his family that he found the happiness and fulfillment he was looking for. From his mother Maria Emília da Conceição Furtado Rebelo and his uncles Domingos and José (both painters by profession), Fernando – just like his brother Manuel – fell in love with theatre and passed the passion to his children and grandchildren. Luís Rebelo is also interested in theatre and plays many instruments. Helena has an arts degree and is a professional painter. Margarida is a singer. Tony paints and plays drums. Suzy, the youngest, is a painter. Their cousin Paula Câmara is also a painter. Fernando's grandson Jason is a professional photographer. Briefly, it is a family of artists! Thus, even feeling disappointed at the fact that the was not able to found an academy for the arts, Fernando is a happy man: he still lives in harmony with his family. He is a gentleman and an artist.

JMC-2000

Rebelo, José Cabral

Village of Ribeirinha, island of S. Miguel, Azores

He dreamt about being a carpenter. However, he was born with a talent for music. Slowly, but surely, he was able to accomplish both. José Cabral Rebelo was born in the village of Ribeirinha, in the island of S. Miguel, Azores, on May 19, 1938. In school, José was able to finish all the requirements to enter the Industrial School. The family necessities forced him to start working in the fields with his father, who was a farmer.

His love for music made him want to learn drums, an instrument he played in the Filarmónica

Maria de Lurdes and José Rebelo with granddaughters Alessandra and Simone.

da Ribeirinha, the musical band from his hometown, when he was 14 years old. José Cabral Rebelo arrived in Canada on June 12, 1957, sponsored by his brother Manuel who had come in March of 1954. In Toronto, he began working in construction, together with his brother and living with him at the same house, where they were each paying $10.00 a month.

From 1960 to 1964, he went to work at house parts' factory, where he finally began learning carpentry with a German. In 1963, José married Maria de Lurdes Bernardo, who was also from the village of Ribeirinha, who had come to Toronto in August of 1959. They married in Santa Maria Church on April 20, 1963. Between 1964 and 1968, José went back to construction. Married life was forcing him to work more to be able to provide for his family. From 1968 to 1978, he worked as a carpenter. He bought his first and only house in 1965, on Montrose Avenue, where he still lives after 35 years. In 1978, he got injured. Through his friend Helder Freitas, he found a job at the TD bank where he worked for 20 years, until he decided to go on early retirement.

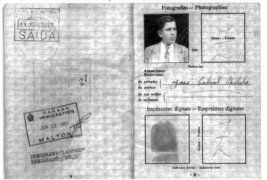

In 1957, José Rebelo and his brother Manuel.

Standing: João Ribau, José Garcia, Paulo, José Rebelo and José Rocha. Bottom row: Rosa Ribau, Filomena Azevedo, Hermínio Azevedo, Rosa Ramos, Alberto Ramos and João Cardoso. They are the band Searas de Portugal.

The Rebelo's have four children: Frances (Frank), born on November 9, 1969, who is a sound technician and an electrician; the late Lucy who was born on April 7, 1970, but passed away in November of the same year due to a severe case of ammonia; Paul, born on July 18, 1972, who has become a teacher; and Lúcia, born on July 24, 1973, a fashion designer. José Cabral Rebelo never forgot his musical talents. In 1964, with the arrival of his brother António in Toronto, he founded the musical band Boa Esperança (Good Hope), with his friends José Aguiar, Manuel Bulhões and Jacinto Almeida. When these three left the band, José invited Edmundo Pimentel, Edmundo Pacheco and Manuel Tavares. The band "Boa Esperança", one of the most famous and popular bands to ever exist in the community, ended in the summer of 1984. All his married, his children have helped the family. At the time "Boa Esperança" was formed, the only band that existed was the one where Mariano Rego was lead singer. After "Boa Esperança's" formation, António Amaro formed the "Cariocas", and other groups such as "Os Rebeldes", "Capas Negras", "Panteras", "Os Lords" and "Copacabana" also appeared in the community. The band "Boa Esperança" performed in every Portuguese community in Canada and in Lincoln Park, USA. They recorded several songs that became hits in the community. Now, to remember the good old times, José Rebelo sings in the church's choir. The first one he joined was at St. Michael's Cathedral (during the first masses celebrated in Portuguese), then, Fernando moved to Santa Maria church, and lately, has been involved in the choir from St. Agnes church. At St. Agnes, together with a few friends from the choir, Fernando decided to form the group "Searas de Portugal", in 1992. José knows how to play the drums, the accordean, and the organ. His brother António is also involved in music, having found the Boa Esperança DJ services.

The Rebelo's with children Lucia, Frank and Paul and granddaughters Alessandra and Simone.

The Rebelo's still go back to their native Azores. In 1999, the entire family decided to visit for the first time mainland Portugal, where they visited Our Lady of Fatima, Nazaré, Cascais, Sintra and Lisbon. They have also been to many places in Canada. José was a member of the First Portuguese Club in 1957, when José Meneses was president and José Rafael secretary. At the time, the Portuguese events had the music of Mariano Rego.

To make up for his early retirement, José – besides traveling – sings, plays his instruments, and still works as a carpenter. José was able to accomplish all his dreams and live well.

JMC - 2000

Rebelo, Norberto Clementino

Village of Lomba da Maia, town of Ribeira Grande,

island of S. Miguel, Azores

Everything in life has a beginning and a beginner. This is the case of our pioneer Norberto Clementino Rebelo who was the first Portuguese man to open a business in Toronto.

Norberto and Olinda Rebelo at home, in Toronto, living their retirement years in peace.

Norberto was born on January 11, 1927, in the village of Lomba da Maia, in the town of Ribeira Grande, in S. Miguel, Azores. He left his native island for Canada on April 23, 1954, boarding the Homeland. Noberto and his fellow travelers arrived in Halifax on April 29, 1954.

At that time, three ships left the Azores archipelago, with three groups of men, all under 35, as was demanded by the Canadian immigration services. With our pioneer, a group of a thousand men left the island of S. Miguel, and another two hundred from the other islands.

We interviewed Norberto at home, located in the Kensington Market. It was interesting to hear his story.

- Our trip lasted six long days. – Norberto began telling us.

- I was luckier! – His wife Olinda interrupted him. Then she explained. – I came by plane. The trip took twelve hours, with a stop in the USA. I arrived on January 27, 1956.

- While you lived here by yourself, how many jobs did you have? – We asked him.

- Many! As soon as I arrived in Halifax, the immigration department sent me to Ontario to work the construction of the railroad. After this, and living in Toronto, I worked in construction, landscaping, roofing, tobacco…

- For a short time, I also worked in the tobacco fields with him. – Olinda remembered with a smile on her face.

- After my wife's arrival, I bought a house. I believe I was the first Portuguese man to buy a house in Toronto. I was fed up with my situation: living in small rooms shared by many people. I bought a house on Adelaide Street, number 699. It was in 1955. Due to the difficulties we all had to share, I ended up renting rooms to those Portuguese men who were coming to Canada and had no place to live. Some of them were in such a bad situation that I was also feeding them. You know, even today when I am walking the streets, some men say hi to me and I do not remember who they are. They are the ones asking me if I remember them from the time they were living in my house.

- He had his job and I was the one taking care of the house. – Olinda told us.

Norberto Sousa may have some doubt about who was the first Portuguese man to buy a house in Toronto, but he is certain he was the first one to own a business. It was in 1956 when he opened Mercado Kensington, in Toronto.

Norberto's first job in the railroad, in 1954. In the picture, we see José Libânio, Manuel de Sá Chadinha, Cabralinho da Lombinha, Norberto Rebelo, the barber, Carlos Baixa and Manuel Cabral.

- That's right! – Norberto told us, always smiling. – The construction company where I was working closed down. I had saved three hundred dollars, and decided to open a small grocery store.

- At that time, it was needed. – Olinda continued. – Every Portuguese person living in Toronto was looking for codfish and Portuguese products. Nobody spoke English at the time. I was the one looking for products, while they were working, even though I didn't speak English myself.

- That's how it was back then! – Norberto said. – It was hard, you know. I didn't know anything about the laws of this country, so I opened the store without paying attention to anything. When, some months later, the government officials knocked at my door, I was petrified. Thanks to the german priests, who were my neighbours, I was able to legalize my business without many headaches. Thank God, those priests helped me a lot. I had helped them many times and never felt sorry I did. They were good people. As we say, "love is paid with love".

- So, you were also the first Portuguese person to import Portuguese products from Portugal?

- I believe so. I began importing olive oil and canned goods from Portugal, in 1963. By that year, I had moved to 50-52 Kensington, where I opened the Rebelo's supermarket.

The circle of life never stops and neither does Norberto Rebelo. His adventurous and business like spirit, made him invest in other enterprises, all of them very successful. We will mention here, the ones that stand out the most. Together with a group of businessmen, Norberto opened the United Portuguese Wholesale, in 1970. In 1975, he inaugurated the restaurant "The Boat", still today the most prestigious Portuguese restaurant. The Boat was, after a few years, sold to two men from Madeira island, Alberto Pereira and the late Gabriel de Freitas. Norberto also opened a fish market, which he rented out to a group of Chinese businessmen.

As he was expanding his business, Norberto never forgot his homeland. In partnership with the business Mar-Peixe from Peniche, from mainland Portugal, and two men from the islands of S. Miguel and Terceira, Norberto opened the "Açor-Peixe", in 1978. This one did not last for too long. To use Norberto's own words, the reason why he steped out of Açor-Peixe was due to Portuguese laws and bureaucracy, which complicates everything.

- Well, I had to sell my part! But, still today, they're owing me some money.

We did not want to remember sad stories, so we decided to change topic.

- Do you miss anyone from those times?

- Oh yes! Manuel Carneiro who is now living in California. Francisco Tavares, known as "Francisquinho da Criação" who is also living in the USA.

- Do you still keep in any friends from those days?

- I don't have time to tell you all of them… - Norberto said, laughing at the comment he made.

- Can you share some of them? – We insisted.

- You know, everyone used to make fun of us because we didn't speak English. One day – I already had my business – I needed to buy mackerels. I didn't know the name in English, so I decided to buy a dictionary to find out the word. I remember writing down in a piece of paper the word "mackerel". I went to White Fish Company to buy what I needed in my English. The employees laughed and made fun of me. The owner heard them laughing and asked what was going on. In my broken English, I told him what had just happened. Instead of laughing at me, he asked me to teach him a hard work in Portuguese. After a few seconds, I remembered that the sound of "lh" was hard to pronounce, so I told him "toalha" (it means towel, in Portuguese). The boss turned to them and asked them to pronounce that word. They were unable to. He turned to them and said: "As you can see, you are not able to pronounce the word he said and he is not laughing at you. Since every client is precious and there are many people looking for jobs, you are fired". I never forgot this incident. The man was tough, but I think he had a point.

Making wine was the portuguese men favourite hobby. Back in the days, Francisquinho da Criação, Manuel Ramos, Norberto Rebelo, Manuel Moleiro (Deolinda's brother), and Manuel Tavares. Picture taken in 1956, in Norberto's first house.

- Is there any other one?

- Oh yeah! There was a funny one that happened to Jaime, a guy from mainland Portugal. Jaime and three other friends went to a Canadian restaurant because they were starving. They looked at the menu many times, but couldn't understand a word. Every time the waitress came to their table, they would ask her to wait a few more minutes. So they decided to order chicken by crowing at her. Jaime called the waitress and when she got to the table, Jaime began saying "Co co ro co co..." The waitress laughed and went to the kitchen. A few minutes later, she returned to the table with a transom dish full of eggs!

We could not avoid laughing at this story. The things a human being needs to do just because a person does not speak a particular language.

- Oh, there was another one. The one with Alfredo Correia, do you remember it, Norberto? – Olinda asked, still laughing.

- Oh yeah! – Norberto answered. – Alfredo Correia was a funny guy. One day, he was at one of the waiting rooms in the immigration services with a few friends to solve some problem. They waited for quite a long time and they felt like going to the washroom. They called one of the employees, but she kept on smiling at them, telling them to wait a little longer. Alfredo walked up to her, very afflicted, and began telling her in sign language, the best he could, he was looking for a washroom. She was still not getting it. So, Alfredo decided to put his pans down and pretended he was sitting down. Feeling very embarrassed, the employee got up and showed him the washroom. Of course, he was the one asking, but the other ones followed him. Oh well, things that happen in life. Telling you these stories isn't nearly as funny as seeing them.

With this story, we finished our interview. All the best to Olinda and Norberto Rebelo!

JMC - April of 1986

Rego, Mariano

Town of Ribeirinha, island of S. Miguel, Azores

Mariano Rego is part of the Portuguese community's history in Canada. "Ribeirinha", nickname by which he is known, celebrated in 1987 60 years of life, 40 years of marriage and 34 of immigration. He was born in the town of Ribeirinha, in the island of S. Miguel, on January 22, 1928.

Mariano Rego arrived in Providence, Rhode Island, on June 24, 1953, boarding the ship Monte Brazil.

- Our trip took 13 days! – Ribeirinha began telling us. – From 1953 to 1957, I lived between the United States and Canada. In 1957, I decided to choose Toronto as my new home.

- How did you come across the opportunity to come to North America?

- I participated in one of those contests launched by the show "Companheiros da Alegria" (Companions in Happiness), and won the first price for playing guitar. That prize gave me a lot of exposure and prestige that I ended up coming to North America. – Mariano told us.

- How old were you when you began playing?

- I was about five years old. Both my parents played guitar and sang fado. That's why I have this passion for fado and for the Portuguese guitar.

Mariano Rego, a native of Ribeirinha, a small town located in the island of S. Miguel, Azores, used to play, from an early age, for the regional radio station – Emissora Regional dos Açores – as well as in the Micaelense theatre, the Micaelense Coliseum, the Ribeiragrandense Theatre, the Vila-Franquense Theatre, to name just a few. In the island of Terceira, Mariano worked in the Angrense Theatre, in the Cine

Mariano Rego and his band. Drums, Augusto Santos; Accordean: Manuel Soares; Lead singer: Arsénio Amaral; guitarist: Mariano Rego.

Azoia, in the American military base and for the radio Clube de Angra. Mariano also performed in the island of Santa Maria. In 1949, Mariano was an artillery soldier in the town of Belém of Ponta Delgada.

- In the early years, I was basically by myself. I worked very hard for the Portuguese and American people. The best memory I have from those times is winning the first prize in the "The New Stars of 1956" television show.

- How did that happen?

- I had this idea of playing two guitars at once. – Mariano explained, laughing at his memories. – Coming to think about it, I am the only person who can play two guitars at once. The Americans were looking at me perplexed.

- Once you decided to settle residence in Toronto, where did you begin your performances?

- I began playing at the Old Spain restaurant with my wife and two daughters.

"Ribeirinha" was the first Portuguese man to form a band in the community. The members were Mariano Rego, Félix Trindade, Carlos Pombo and Orlando Ferreira. Later on, Manuel Soares joined in the accordean, Augusto Santos in the drums and Arsénio Amaral as lead singer.

Mariano Rego and wife surrounded by granddaughters Jennifer, Laura and Amy. A family of musicians!

- When did you form your own band?

- It was in 1961. I played for five years in El Mocambo restaurant, followed by another four at the Stereos Tavern, and another three years at the Heritage Inn, in the airport.

- Why did you decide to go solo?

- The years go by, the times change and we must adapt to the change. – Mariano answered. – When the restaurant Imperio opened I went to play there. I stayed at Imperio for five years.

- Was that where you met Alvarez?

- Yes, it was. It was Frank Alvarez who invited me to play at Imperio. He is a very active man with whom I loved working. – Mariano paused for a second, and then, laughing at his own thoughts, said: - You know, Alvarez was the only boss I had who gave me two salary raises, even though I had never requested them.

Mariano Rego performed with great musicians. He still remembers those times with pride and a sense of longing.

- I remember playing for Hermínia Silva, Rui de Mascarenhas, Maria de Lurdes Resende, Bill Coldel, Shegundo Galarza, among others. I also recorded two compositions with the Toronto's orchestral symphony, where I played the "Viola da Terra", a unique guitar from the Azores.

- Speaking of guitars, you have donated one to a museum in Toronto…

- Yes, I have. It was in 1979. I offered it to the Royal Museum (ROM), in Toronto.

- You loved that guitar. Why did you give it away?

- Yes, I loved that guitar. It was one hundred years old. That guitar had been designed and made by José da Silva, an artist from the island of Madeira. It was beautiful and it had been ornamented by sea shells. I was afraid I would not preserve it well, so I decided to give it to the museum. This way, I was able to preserve the guitar and contribute with an aspect of the Portuguese culture to the enrichment of the Canadian heritage.

One of the biggest religious celebrations in Toronto takes place in the Portuguese community. It is the celebration of Senhor Santo Cristo dos Milagres. This celebration originated in the island of S. Miguel and was brought to Toronto by Mariano Rego, when he decided to offer the image of Santo Cristo to Santa Maria church in Toronto. Mariano still talks about those times.

Good old times… picture taken before the last game Mariano Rego played for the Portuguese United team. Mariano is the last one on the right. Among the pioneers, we can see Zézinho, the goal-tender, Ângelo Bacalhau, Adelino Raposo, Manuel Câmara, Fernando Silva…

- Everything started in 1964. My wife was always very ill. At that time, she was filling so sick that the doctors had told us that there was nothing else to be done. Feeling very desperate, I turned my faith to Senhor Santo Cristo dos Milagres and pleaded him to save my wife. I promised to bring His image to Toronto, if my wife was cured. Well, my wife began feeling

Mariano Rego holding the Portuguese guitar at the Toronto's island airport.

better, she underwent a surgery and has been feeling well since then.

- So, you decided to keep your promise…

- Of course! The image was made in the city of Braga and it took two years to be finished. When the image arrived at the Toronto docks, I went to get it with Felix Trindade, Augusto Santos and other men whose names I don't remember now. We took it directly to Santa Maria church because it was our parish. We were all in tears when we saw the image in the altar. It had been another miracle!

Besides being involved in the organization of the festivities, Mariano Rego was also a collaborator in the television show run by Frank Alvarez at Metro Cable.

- I participated in the shows and "baptized" both of them. The first one we had was the "Lisbon Place Show", and later on, in 1975, we began the "Festival Portuguese". I wish I had participated even more, but I worked at night, especially on weekends.

- You also teach music, don't you?

- Yes, I do. I teach guitar, viola and the "viola da terra", in order to teach our children our musical roots. The Portuguese guitar has a unique sound to it…

- And the Americans, do they like to listen to you?

- Yes, they do. Lately, I have been dividing my time between Florida and Toronto. I usually spend the winter in Florida, where I work at PACS, a local Portuguese association, and at the restaurants Granada, Maurice and Italian Village.

We decided to end our conversation at his point, leaving "Ribeirinha" with his reminiscences from the past. He still remembers his time, back in S. Miguel, when he used to play soccer. Mariano has become a true legend in our Portuguese community.

(Unfortunately, Mariano Rego passed away in 2000).

JMC - May of 1987

Reis, Mercês Resende dos

Island of S. Miguel, Azores

Mercês dos Reis at her atelier.

It is never too late to do what we like and know how to do. Mercês Resende dos Reis was born in the island of S. Miguel, on July 8, 1939. She completed her degree at the Industrial and Commercial School of Ponta Delgada in 1955. From here, Mercês went on to study nursing, still at Ponta Delgada and came to Lisbon to practice at the hospital Santa Maria.

Mercês came to Canada in September of 1967 with husband Manuel dos Reis and son Jaime. When she arrived in Toronto, she did not even have a chance to look at the city because she had to be taken in emergency to the hospital to give birth to her son William. Her second son was named after the former Ontario premier William Davies. After living for several years in Toronto, the Reis family decided to move to Montreal, in 1975. Manuel dos Reis dedicated himself to the profession he had in Portugal – a mechanic – while Mercês began working as a nurse and dedicating herself to painting, a passion she carried with her since she was a child. Due to her mother's opposition to painting, Mercês could never practice what she loved when she was little. When in school, Mercês used to love to draw and to paint. One day, she remembers, the painter Vitor Câmara saw her drawings at the Industrial school and liked them. He advised her to paint, but Mercês's parents were always against it. This way, her parents were proud to announce that their daughters Orlanda and Mercês were nurses and Apolónia was an accountant, and their son Eduardo went to the Air Forces.

Thus, Mercês was only able to start studying and dedicating herself to painting in 1982. From 1982 to 1983, she studied at the atelier Irene Veilleux, in Laval; from 1983 to 1986, she went to the Mireille Forget's Art School, in Laval; in 1986, she became a member of the painters and Sculptures Society in Quebec, and in 1995 and until today, she has been teaching the technique of oil painting and drawing. When we visited Mercês in her own atelier, she was teaching a group of seven students – Portuguese, French and Italian. She also teaches art at the Casa dos Açores of Quebec, a community centre that was formed on July 18, 1978. She has organized more than thirty art exhibits in Lisbon, Azores and Quebec. She is very proud of her sons, both designers working in the movie industry, as well as of her grandson Dilan who, at the age of 3, began drawing.

Mercês Resende dos Reis is a very active member in many Portuguese associations. Besides teaching art at the Casa dos Açores of Quebec, she is art and cultural coordinator in the same centre, she painted a 68 metre squares mural at Nossa Senhora de Fátima Church Hall, in Laval, which

Manuel dos Reis smiles happily at his wife after she completed their grandson's portrait.

she named "A Saudade". She also painted the backdrop of the stage for the first gathering of former Portuguese African soldiers, on November 18, 2000.

Mercês and Manuel dos Reis, today retired from work, have been enjoying the pleasures of life, family and painting. They have also been dedicating a lot of time to the Portuguese community of Quebec. Although delayed, Mercês' talent still came up on time to be recognized.

JMC - 2000

Resende, Eduardo da Costa

Village of Fajã de Baixo, city of Ponta Delgada,

island of S. Miguel, Azores

Whoever was born to be adventurous will not run away from the adventure. Eduardo da Costa Resende impersonates adventure. Eduardo was born in the village of Fajã de Baixo, district of Ponta Delgada, in the island of S. Miguel, Azores, on May 4, 1942. He completed the second year at the Industrial and Commercial School of Ponta Delgada and the third year at the Ferreira Borges' School in Lisbon. In 1959, he applied as volunteer to Portugal's Air Force. He completed in course in the village of Tancos, under the orders of Cornel Alcides and commander Rebelo. The

Eduardo Resende with wife Henriqueta by the frame with his insignias, during the first gathering of combatentes in the Casa dos Açores of Quebec, in 1999.

first commission to be sent to the Portuguese overseas mission in Africa took off from Portugal on March 20, 1961, and arrived in Fortaleza, Angola, when they attacked Nobuangongo, under the operation "Viriato". After nine months of service in Angola, Eduardo came back to Lisbon.

In 1963, Eduardo was sent to Guinea, as part of the biggest operation Portugal had in Africa, in the Como island. In 1975, he went from Guinea to Mozambique, where he took part

Sister Orlanda and brother-in-law Martin, proudly showing Eduardo's insignias.

Eduardo Resende in the military post of Lumbala.

in the "oil war". In the Square of Niassa, Eduardo took part in the War of the Macondos, in the Mocimbo do Revuma, located in the region of Mocimbo da Praia. In 1967, Eduardo came back to Lisbon. Five months after arriving, Eduardo's friend, second lieutenant Celestino sent him back to Angola, where Eduardo would spend the following two years. In this latest mission, Eduardo was severely hurt. As fate's irony, Celestino was also hurt in the mission. They were both sent back to Lisbon, to the military hospital. Eduardo was hurt while fighting. He was hurt on July 11, 1969 and sent to Lisbon the same day, due to the gravity of his wounds. While in the military hospital in Lisbon, Eduardo filled out the application to leave the military service for three times. The difficulty behind the acceptance of his "resignation" was due to the fact that Eduardo was part of the Permanent Department in the army. He was able to receive a positive answer the third time he applied.

Eduardo quit the Air Force and the military life, in November of 1969. Two weeks later, he came to Canada, arriving in Toronto on November 16. He came to live with his parents, Mercês and Jamie, and his sister Mercês who had been in the country for about two years. Accustomed to the hardships of life, working in the farms, in construction and in demolition were not hard tasks for Eduardo. He still remembers working, in 1971, in the demolition of the houses that were standing where Addison on Bay is now located. At the end of 1971, Eduardo went to live in Montreal to work as a truck driver until 1975. Much of Eduardo's family lives in Montreal. In 1975, Eduardo came back to Toronto to work in construction until 1978. Today, he works at Dri-LEC, a company owned by Nuno Aguiar.

Eduardo's love life was also marked by adventure. Still very young and living in Lisbon, Eduardo married Nellie, a girl born in Lisbon. A son, Miguel, was born from this union. The marriage, however, only lasted seven months. After arriving in Canada, Eduardo lived for 19 years with Ermelinda Duarte with whom he has two sons: William and Roy. After the separation, Eduardo met Henriqueta Cota, a native of the island of Terceira, who was divorced and a mother of three: Manuela, Manuel and Joe Coelho. They live in constant happiness and their children get along. After living

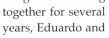

together for several years, Eduardo and Henriqueta married in 2000.

Eduardo Resende jumping from his airplane in Angola.

Eduardo has a passion form hunting and fishing, just like he does for soccer. He is a huge fan of the team Sporting Clube de Portugal and never misses a game. He has installed radios and television sets all over the house I order not to miss a second from the games. Eduardo takes part every year of CIRV's winterfest and has been elected the official fisherman. He only feels sorry he cannot take his boat when he goes on holidays.

The "old" Folkloric group of S. Miguel arriving in Funchal, Madeira Island, in 1957.

Back home, Eduardo was always very active in the social life of his island. He helped fund and danced for the folk group of S. Miguel. Sergeant Eduardo da Costa Resende has received many honours for his courage and loyalty. During the first gathering of "combatentes do Ultra-mar", in 2000, organized in Montreal by the Casa dos Açores of Quebec, Eduardo was the one with the most number of insignias.

Eduardo Resende with son Miguel, in the town of Ericeira, Portugal, in 1995.

In one of the official diplomas he has received, one can read the following: "We honour the sergeant above mentioned for the enthusiasm he has put into every mission he participated. We also honour him for teaching his men a high level of self-sacrifice, always setting the example by taking first

Eduardo Resende practicing his two favourite sports: hunting and fishing.

place in the ranks. Resende, whose motto is 'follow me' is a true leader even in the most critical situations. He is a magnificent commander, one who must be seen as an example of honour to all soldiers from the Air Force". Do we need to say more? Absolutely not!

Eduardo da Costa Resende is now working to make a dream come true: to organize in Toronto a gathering similar to the one that took place in Montreal. He is almost accomplishing what he wants, without any adventures. Now, the fighter should and is able to rest.

JMC-2000

Resendes, António Amaro

Village of Algarvia,

São Miguel island, Azores

António Amaro with son Carlos Resendes.

Music has touched António Amaro Resendes from his childhood. Fado has been his fate. His father used to play the guitar every night and his sister Maria dos Anjos taught him the first chords in the guitar. António fell in love with music immediately and by the age of 17 was already playing at the Regional Radio Station, in the Azores. For each show he was playing live at the radio, António was making fifty

Back in the days, António Amaro performing in the Azores.

escudos (the equivalent to .50 cents), which he had to divide between the two musicians who played with him. However, before we continue with our story, let us find out who our musician is.

António Amaro Resendes was born in Algarvia, a village in the town of Nordeste, in the island of São Miguel, Azores. He was born on January 28, 1926. He completed his high school diploma at the Commercial School of Angra and then obtained the electrician course from a professional school. When he was 16 years of age, António began working as electrician's helper for the company João Soares. In 1950, he went to Terceira island to work at Lajes, the American military base. While there, António Amaro – as he is known among friends – completed two other courses and was promoted to supervisor in the maintenance department. He remained at the Lajes' base until 1964. Meanwhile, not

José Cabral Rasquinha, António's music teacher, with Bento Lima at one of their radio performances.

able to forget his passion for music, António Amaro formed the musical band Insular with Emiliano Santos, Mendonça, and Rosa. During his free time, António Amaro used to play soccer and was a professional player for the Marítimo de Ponta Delgada and Brancos da Praia, in Terceira island.

Back in São Miguel island, António Amaro met Virgínia de Chaves, a native from the island of Santa Maria, with whom he married in 1957, at the church of Corpo Santo, in Angra do Heroísmo, the capita city of Terceira island. The couple has one son, Carlos, who was born in May of 1957.

The group from Terceira island: António Amaro, Gui Fernandes, Ariovalda Maria, Henrique Cordeiro and Hélio Baião.

Looking to expand his horizons, António Amaro decided to leave the island and try his luck in Canada. Never abandoning his guitar, António Amaro arrived in Canada on June 22, 1964. His wife and son were only able to come three months later, due to some demands from the immigration services. In Toronto, António Amaro found a job in his field of expertise, working as electrician for a private company. At the end of a six-month period, he found a job as a welder,

António Amaro, Fernando Silva, Fontes Rocha, Isabel Santos, Fernando Farinha and Nuno at the end of a performance.

on Streetsville. In 1966, he was hired to work at Douglas Aircraft where he worked until 1985. Due to an unexpected stroke, in 1986, António Amaro was forced to retire. The sad end to his professional life brought a light to his passion: António Amaro decided to dedicate himself full-time to music.

António Amaro remembers arriving in Canada and, the following day, being asked to play at a tavern on Spadina Avenue for Isabel Santos, the first Portuguese singer in Canada. In 1964, António Amaro founded the group Os Toureiros with his friend Arsénio. Some years later, the pair decided to expand the group and with lead singer Fernandes Monteiro formed the band Os Cariocas. This band played for 16 years. The last band he formed was the Apolo 73 with Tony Gouveia and Albano Ferrão. However dedicated he was to his bands, António Amaro had always a special place on his heart for fado. He has played in the Azores, in mainland Portugal and everywhere in North America where there is a Portuguese com-

Fontes Rocha and António Amaro playing for Fernando Farinha.

munity. António played for 20 years with Tony Melo and Manuel Maurício and is now playing with Leonardo Medeiros and Hernâni Raposo whenever possible.

Throughout his life as a Portuguese guitar player, António Amaro played for many famous "fadistas" (fado singer): Maria Madeira, João Fernandes (from Madeira island), Hermínio Silva, Manuel Quieto, Gui Fernandes, Henrique Cordeiro, Ariovalda Maria, Izalino Santos, Patrícia

Augusto and António Amaro playing for Isabel Santos.

Rodrigues (from the Azores), Rui de Mascarenhas, Rodrigo, Manuel de Almeida, Fernando Maurício, Ada de Castro, Simone de Oliveira, Maria Armanda, Anita Guerreiro, Maria Valejo, Luís Braga, Filipe Duarte, Júlio Peres, Carlos Macedo, Esmeralda Amoedo, Lídia Ribeiro, Lenita Gentil, Vasco Rafael, among others, all from the mainland Portugal.

Nowadays, when he is not playing, António Amaro dedicates his time to building and creating instruments specially guitars. In 1993, he created the instrument "Guita", which is a combination of the Portuguese guitar with the "Viola da Terra" (the Azorean guitar). This Guita is now at the Gallery of Portuguese Pioneers. He is an honorary member of the Angrense Club of Toronto and member of the Portuguese Cultural Centre of Mississauga.

António Amaro is a reference in the Portuguese community. He has had a fulfilling life, with some dramas but many successes. When he is happy, he plays his fados. When he misses his homeland, he plays fado. António Amaro lives fado to the fullest.

JMC - 2002

The president of Casa do Alentejo Community Centre of Toronto paying homage to António Amaro.

Monsigneur Eduardo Resendes, in Ottawa, the day he received the Order of the Infante D. Henrique from the Portuguese government.

Resendes, Monsignor Eduardo

Village of Faial da Terra, town of Povoação, island of S. Miguel, Azores

He is a great man and a great priest. Eduardo Resendes was born in the village of Faial da Terra, Povoação, a town in the island of S. Miguel, Azores. When he was only 11 years old, Eduardo decided to enter de seminary. At the Diocesan Seminary of Angra do Heroísmo, in the island of Terceira, Eduardo was an outstanding student and athlete.

The young Eduardo Resendes was ordained at the cathedral of Angra do Heroísmo, on June 15, 1958. In October of the same year, he began working in the same cathedral where he had been ordained. Eduardo was there for three years. From 1961 to 1965, he was the private secretary to Manuel Afonso de Carvalho, bishop of the Azores. In November of 1965, Eduardo was nominated chaplain in the Portuguese Air Force, serving in Guinea, Mozambique and in Portugal's mainland.

Homage to Monsigneur Resendes at the Portuguese Cultural Centre of Mississauga: the misses from the club, Raimundo Favas, Jack Prazeres, monsigneur Resendes, Mayor Hazel McCallion, consul general Artur de Magalhães and Gilberto Moniz.

Eduardo Resendes came to Canada in 1975, and began his service in Mississauga. Since there was not a Portuguese church, Eduardo Resende began celebrating mass in the Portuguese club. From his arrival, Father Eduardo Resende has dedicated himself to the development of the Portuguese community. He organized the catechesis, the youth, and the Theatre groups.

On October 8, 1978, he blessed the first stone announcing the construction of the Santíssimo Salvador do Mundo church, in Mississauga. This church, the first built in the archdiocese of Toronto under the leadership of a Portuguese priest was a symbol of Portuguese pride in the community. Everyone volunteered to help Father Eduardo Resendes build the first Portuguese church in Mississauga. The church was inaugurated on November 25, 1979, with the participation of Portuguese and Canadian individualities both from the catholic and civic life.

In 1980, Father Eduardo Resendes was recognized by the Portuguese government with the Order of Infante D. Henrique for the work he had done. The Order was presented by the former president of the republic, General Ramalho Eanes.

Due to the expansion of the Portuguese community in Mississauga, Father Resendes began expanding his dreams: he decided to build a new and bigger church. In March of 1995, Father Resendes and his parishioners saw the dream transformed into reality when they inaugurated the church Christ the King. On February 27, 1996, by a decree signed by His Holiness Pope John Paul II, Father Eduardo Resendes was given the title of Monsignor.

Monsignor Resendes has been an active member of the Portuguese Club of Mississauga and was one of the members who helped raise funds for the purchase of the premises where the Portuguese Cultural Centre of Mississauga is now located. This cultural center recognized, in 2003, all the work monsignor Resender has done

Monsigneur Eduardo Resendes, on holidays with Manuel da Silva, Frank Alvarez, Tony Melo and Albertino Domingues.

for the Portuguese community, especially in Mississauga.

Monsignor Eduardo Resendes is a good priest who knows how to serve his parishioners. Let his dreams continue!

JMC-2004

Ribau, Zália Anita Lopes

Village of Glória, district of Aveiro

She was born for the arts and lives for the arts. Zália Anita Lopes Ribau was born in the village of Glória, in the district of Aveiro, on November 25, 1956. When she was seven years old, she came to Canada with her parents, Calisto and Anunciação Ribau, and with her brother Calisto and sister Cristina. Zália arrived in Toronto on May 17, 1964. From a very early age, she was in love with the arts. At Sheridan College, Zália finished her Fashion and Knitting diploma and went on to York University to complete a business and manufacturing degree.

Zália Ribau showing one of many prizes she has received.

Zália is married to musician Agostinho Teotónio – from the bands Zip Zip, Quo Vadis, and others. They married on August 20, 1977. Agostinho Teotónio is still in love with music – he plays the saxophone and the flute – but works for Toronto's city hall. The couple has two children: Paco Ruben, born August 25, 1978, and Nicole Anita, born March 29, 1983. Both children seem to take after their mother, since they both love the arts.

Zália addressing the public at the City of Toronto Awards for excellence in fashion design. On Zália's right, former Toronto mayor Barbara Hall.

As a student, Zália decided to start her own business, in 1979, as a designer. At school, she always won the first prizes. In 1975, Zália presented her first collection in the television show Festival Portuguese. In 1982, Zália opened The Nest boutique, on college, for children. Due to her many trips to the United States and all over Canada, Zália was forced to close her boutique on July 31, 1988. She decided to keep her warehouse, where she was

Paco Ruben and girlfriend.

creating and making her line of clothing.

The first international order Zália received was in 1964 for London, England. In 1994, she was able to break the barriers in Paris, a city known to be difficult to conquer. Zália has also been receiving orders from Saudi Arabia and Kuwait. Slowly, but surely, her line of children's clothing – MOKA – became known.

Success had been side by side with Zália. The famous Spanish store "El Corte Inglés" loved her creations. In 1995, Zália traveled to Madrid to sign a contract to work for El Corte Inglés. Two years later, Zália conquered two more important markets: Italy and Taiwan.

Zália Ribau between her daughter Mónica and her son's girlfriend.

Zália admits she was always lucky to find the help she needed from the Canadian embassies and consulates in every country she has been to. Zália has been working with great international names from the world of the arts, politics and fashion. She began appearing in the best fashion magazines. Zália Ribau is a successful woman, happy with what she does and what she creates.

Zália has a stable family who is very supportive of her. She is a very dedicated wife and mother. She tries to spend as much time with her family as she can. Zália is happy to say that her MOKA collection has been chosen by Mila Mulroney – wife of former Canadian prime minister Brian Mulroney –, by the Rockfeller family, Michael Jackson. To explain the name MOKA for her collection, Zália said that she created two clothing collections: one for men and another one for women, which received a prize. This collection was all in brown tones. Since she is a coffee lover, Zália decided to adapt the name from coffee and the colour brown (which in Portuguese is "castanho").

Zália has received many national and international destinctions: Vogue Bambino, in 1996; Sanyo Best Design & Best Quality 1987, City of Toronto Awards For Excellence in Fashion Design, 1997. Nowadays, tired of traveling, Zália decided to send most of her orders to specialized places, instead of keeping her factory.

To sell all items from her collections,

Zália and Agostinho Teotónio: a happy couple!

Models Monica and her cousin.

Zália Ribau decided to open another boutique, located on 1448 Dundas Street West. The Moka Collection Boutique marks, at the same time, Zália's return to the Portuguese community. Zália now hopes that her children continue walking the path she has laid out for them.

JMC-2001

Moka Collection Boutique.

Ribeiro, Américo Martins

Campo d'Ourique neighbourhood, Lisbon

Américo Martins Ribeiro

Américo Martins Ribeiro is an artist in every sense of the word. Born in Campo d'Ourique, a small neighbourhood, in Lisbon, on November 12, 1925, Américo began learning the art of ceramics when he was still very young. Américo began working as an apprentice at the ceramic factory Viúva Ferrão, near Lisbon, and then went to the factory Santana, where he worked for many years.

Américo Ribeiro is married to Estrela Ribeiro, who is also a native from Lisbon, and has a daughter, Maria Helena. Américo is a proud father, grandfather, and great-grandfather.

In August of 1960, the Ribeiro family came to Canada. Even though working a different job, until his retirement, Américo never gave up his love for ceramics. He has organized many exhibits at the Consulate General of Portugal, in Toronto, at Toronto's City Hall, at the Howard Johnson Hotel, among others. He has also exposed his work at the Portuguese Club of Mississauga, at the Canadian Madeira Club, at the First Portuguese Canadian Club, and at Casa do Alentejo.

Due to his natural talent, Américo was asked to teach ceramics at Humber College, and throughout the years he has given many workshops. In 1998, he received an invitation from the Academy of Arts in São Paulo, Brazil, to present his work. Unfortunately, due to some setbacks, he has not been able to travel to Brazil.

Joe Eustáquio giving Américo Ribeiro the Merit Award from the community in 1999.

Américo Ribeiro has also been invited to write a book about ceramics, when he was teaching at Humber College, a project he was happy to work on. With the help of professor Betty James, Américo published two important books about the art of ceramics. Américo is a very active man, never stopping his work and exhibits. He is a reference in the Portuguese community in Canada.

JMC - 1999

Ribeiro, Daniel Bernardes

Santa Catarina neighbourhood, Lisbon

Maria do Céu and Daniel Bernardes Ribeiro are a very nice, outgoing couple who never miss a chance to participate in as many portuguese events as they can.

Daniel was born in Santa Catarina, a small neighbourhood in Lisbon, on October 19, 1940. Since his childhood, Daniel got used to immigrating because his father was a marine sergeant, in Portugal, who was sent to Africa on many missions.

Daniel Ribeiro and Maria do Céu.

Thus, Daniel was brought up in Luanda and Moçâmedes, in Angola. When he turned 20 years old, Daniel moved to France where he lived and studied French for four years, before returning to Portugal. Back in Portugal, Daniel found a job as a French teacher. While in Angola, Daniel met Maria do Céu dos Santos, who was born in Luanda on May 30, 1945. They married at Mosterios dos Jerónimos in Lisbon, on December 24, 1966.

A short time after his marriage, Daniel went back to France to apply for the Canadian immigration services. Daniel arrived in Canada on May 17, 1968. Maria do Céu came to live with her husband two months after his arrival. She brought with her the couple's first son, Paulo Alexandre, born in France, in January of 1968. The couple's second son, Charles Richard,

Daniel and Maria do Céu as part of a religious procession at Santa Maria Church, in Hamilton.

Daniel and Maria do Céu surrounded by their two sons Charles Richard and Paulo Alexandre.

was already born in Toronto, in July of 1974.

Daniel Ribeiro began his life in Toronto by finding a job in construction: he was working for a tunnel building company. Due to the fact that he spoke English and French, he soon found a job at the Universal Workers Union, local 183, as a worker's representative and interpreter for the Portuguese and Italian immigrants. In 1975, Daniel, in partnership with António Santos, opened a garage in Hamilton. He has now sub-leased the garage to one of his mechanics. He is now dedicating himself to the Real Estate business. Daniel decided to open the Jamesville Real Estate Inc., in Hamilton, with his son Paul Alexandre, who has a bachelor in geography. In 1997, Daniel also decided to open the travel agency "Canada Travel". Simultaneously, Maria do Céu owns the Mary's Clothing & Gift Store, in Hamilton, a store she has been managing for the past eighteen years.

Maria do Céu has a bachelor in chemistry, but has never dedicated any time to her profession. On the other hand, Daniel is an active member of the Portuguese community, participating in a great number of social and cultural activities. He is also a member of the Liberal Party in Hamilton and is a close friend of many politicians. Daniel is also a founding member of the Portuguese Canadian National Congress and its director for the region of Central Ontario. Besides being founding member, Daniel has also served as president of Lusofest, the organization responsible for the Portugal Day festivities in Hamilton. Finally, Daniel has been the president of the Hamilton Portuguese Community Centre, since 1994.

Wherever there is a Portuguese event, one is sure to find the couple Maria do Céu and Daniel Ribeiro.

JMC - 2000

Ribeiro, Rui

Village of Serro Ventoso, Town of

Porto de Mós

Rui and Belmira Ribeiro.

The pioneer Rui Ribeiro has an interesting story to tell. Officially, he was the only Portuguese man from the mainland Portugal to arrive in Canada among the first group of men from Madeira island. The reason behind this is very simple: Rui Ribeiro, a truck driver by profession, went to work for Casa Singer, in Funchal, Madeira Island. There, he found out about Canada's request for immigrants. Not thinking twice, Rui decided to apply. This way, even though there were also recruitments taking place in mainland Portugal, Rui had to board the boat from Madeira with the first group of men who came to Canada from that island.

Rui Ribeiro was born in the village of Serro Ventoso, in Porto de Mós, on October 29, 1925. He was the first one in his town to get a truck driver's license. He went to Madeira Island, and from there, Rui came to Canada. He boarded the ship Nea Healls and touched the port of Halifax on June 2, 1953, but was only able to "enter" Canada the following day, due to the late arrival of the ship.

The first week in Canada was not a very pleasant one for Rui. Without a fixed place where he could work, Rui had to travel, by train, from Halifax to Montreal, from there to Toronto, then to London and ended up in Strathroy. In Strathroy, Rui worked at a tobacco farm for one week. From there, he was sent to Niagara Falls to work at the building of the hydro tunnel for about a year. In May of 1955, due to the crisis that was affecting southern Ontario, Rui came back to Toronto, where he found a job at construction.

Meanwhile, Rui Ribeiro decided to marry Belmira Ferreira, at the church of São Pedro of Porto de Mós, on June 21, 1952. Belmira was also a native of Porto de Mós. The couple's daughter – Eva – was also born in Porto de Mós, on February 3, 1954. In Canada, the couple saw the birth of two sons: Adolfo, born in Niagara Falls, on October 16, 1954, and Dennis, born in Toronto, on January 31, 1956.

Belmira and Rui Ribeiro with children Eva, Adolfo and Dennis.

The couple Ribeiro at their son Adolfo's wedding.

In 1964, together with brother-in-law Guilherme Rodrigues, Rui Ribeiro acquired a dump truck and began successfully running their own company. For many years, the company grew, Rui and Guilherme were able to buy more trucks and employ many people. However, in 1989, due to the Free Trade Agreement signed between former prime minister Brian Mulroney and the United States, Rui and Guilherme were forced to close

Rui and Belmira's wedding anniversary.

the business, due in part to lack of work. In 1990, Rui decided to go back to construction, working again for somebody else. A year later, due to his age, Rui decided to retire and decided to dedicate his time to the things he enjoyed doing.

From the time he arrived in Canada, Rui has helped found the First Portuguese Canadian Club and was one of its members for many years. Because he loves hunting, Rui was a member of the Luso-Trap Association.

The couple Rui Ribeiro lives in Toronto with daughter Eva. The sons are now married and have already given the couple a few grandchildren, for their delight. Rui Ribeiro still lives a happy, modest life. All the best.

JMC - 1999

Rui exhibits the pair of boots he used when he traveled to Canada. Rui has donated these boots to the Galery of Portuguese Pioneers.

Rocha, Tibério Pimentel Paulo da

Village of São Sebastião, city of Ponta Delgada,

island of S. Miguel, Azores

L ife's setbacks were never a reason to make Tibério Rocha enter in despair. Tibério Pimentel Paulo da Rocha was born in São Sebastião, in the district of Ponta Delgada, in the island of S. Miguel, Azores, on August 10, 1929. He finished elementary school in Ponta Delgada, in 1940. As time went by, Tibério began working and studying English at the same time. In 1948, the then young Tibério Rocha fell very ill

Fernanda and Tibério Rocha.

and was sent to a special clinic in Parede, a town near Lisbon. While he was hospitalized, Tibério fell in love with one of the employees. Back in the Azores, Tibério decided to marry by proxy Carminda Dias, who was born in the town of Vila Rei, in the province of Beira Baixa, in mainland Portugal. Carminda was born on April 27, 1924.

When Tibério's wife arrived in the Azores, the couple decided to marry at the church of São Sebastião, in Ponta Delgada, on January 10, 1951. The couple's son, Vitor Manuel Dias da Rocha, was born in Ponta Delgada. Vitor is former member of the Real Estate and is now operating his own company as computer technician. Vanda Maria, the couple's daughter, was born in the village of Vila do Porto, in the island of Santa Maria. For 12 years, Vanda worked for the government of Ontario, in Toronto. However, a serious illness sent Vanda to the hospital where she has been for twelve years.

Tibério Rocha and friends working at a farm in 1957.

Tibério tells his life's tale this way: "I always wanted to immigrate and to know new places. In 1956, I was working for the Terra Nostra society, located at Santa Maria's airport, in the Azores. I had a good job, a stable family and life. Still, when I had the opportunity to register myself to come to Canada, I didn't think twice. I was not too excited about this, because I had previously tried to go to Brazil and Africa, and was never accepted. In order to impress the Canadian immigration officials, I had to learn a few things about agriculture. On April 27, 1957, I arrived in Montreal, at the airport Dorval, after a long air-

Tibério's "gang" at the railroad.

plane trip. All eighty passengers on board were sent to the train station, where they were united to other groups of men traveling to different parts in Ontario. We slept on wooden benches. When the number of passengers reached 400, the train took us to Lethbridge, in the province of Alberta. Three long days and three long nights of suffering. When we left the train, our faces and clothes were so durty, we looked black. We were then divided in groups of two, three or four people according to the farm where we were supposed to go work. Interestingly enough, my groups were made up of four men and we were all office employees sent to work in a farm.

In 1958, Tibério Rocha, the cook and two friends at Morisburg, in Ontario.

We used to see many men pass by on the road, carrying their luggage to an unknown place. It gave us the idea to do the same. We worked very hard, did not eat well and slept in a wooden hut with no conditions and snakes for company. We had a Portuguese flag at our hut's door, and many Portuguese men came to see us – even a priest from a place called Picture Butte, north of Lethbridge, came to speak to us. We hung on to our posts, until we were free to go. That happened when our original contract was cancelled and we decided to come to Toronto, this time traveling by train on the people's department, instead of the animal's carriage. In Toronto, we met a few Portuguese men and found a place to live on Augusta and Kensington. It took us some time to find one of the few jobs that were available back then. One day, and tipped off by one of my friends, I went to Union Station and looked for a fellow who worked for the R.F. Welch Ltd.

Vitor Rocha the day of his first communion in Caolbourg, in 1959.

I was hired immediately, and with me António Gonçalves, Aristides de Melo Gambôa, the latter was already giving up on Canada and was planning to return to the Azores where he had a good job at Ribeira Grande's city hall. At the railway, we were working sixteen hours a day. I was so frustrated that I used to cry and, for a while, thought about returning to my hometown. With much sacrifice, mixed with pride, I decided to stay and got used to the situation".

One day, still at the railroad, Tibério and a group of friends asked a french-canadian worker to go to the bank for them because they needed money orders. The French-Canadian, who was not an honest man, took their money and disappeared. Some time after, and still not trusting anybody, Tibério and friends asked the boss to let them leave earlier so they could go themselves to the bank. Dressed very poorly and looking very filthy, the group went to the bank. To their surprise, when one of the employees saw them, called the police thinking they were going to rob the bank. Tibério and friends were taken to prison. Stories that our pioneers have to share with us that only now, many years later, can we begin to laugh at them.

Tibério's children, Vanda and Vitor, in 1959.

After working at the railroads, Tibério found a job at the factory General Wire & Cable, in Cobourg, where he lived for four years. It was during this time that Tibério decided to ask his family to come to Canada. Thus, in October of 1958, his wife Carminda and children Vanda and Vitor, arrived in Canada.

In 1961, Tibério moved back to Toronto where he found a job at the Dosco Steel, a factory which produced Chain Lynk Fences for Hollywood. Accepting an invitation by his friend Manuel Câmara, Tibério entered the Real Estate, after completing his course in 1967. In 1971, Tibério became a broker. Between 1976 and 178, Tibério Rocha founded the T. Rocha Real Estate, becoming one of the brokers with the biggest number of agents working for him. Tibério was also the first Portuguese man to work for A.E. Le Page Real Estate.

Being a workaholic did not bring any happiness to Tibério. Spending long hours at the office and lacking a lot of time from his family created a situation of loneliness in his wife, Carminda Dias, leading to their divorce.

In 1988, Tibério remarried for the second time with Fernanda Costa, a native of Ponta Delgada, in the island of S. Miguel, Azores. Tibério was submitted to a tri-bypass in 1992, which forced him to go on early retirement.

Socially speaking, Tibério has been a member of the First Portuguese Canadian Club, Casa do Benfica, Lusitânia and Casa dos Açores. He now spends a lot of time with Cidália and Arminda Rego, the daughters of the late Mariano Rego, and with community singer Avelino Teixeira working on the establishment of the Mariano do Rego Memorial Fund, an organization which will give scholarships to music students, specially to those studying Portuguese guitar.

Tibério has been and continues to be a very active member of our community.

JMC - 2001

The Irish-Canadian couple that received Tibério Rocha, António Gonçalves, Carlos Ponte and Aristides Melo Gamboa in 1957.

Santos, Abílio Seabra dos

Village of Avelãs de Cima, County of Anadia, district of Aveiro

A bílio Seabra dos Santos is a small, happy man. The years have gone by and left certain marks on his face, but have never taken away the will to live. Abílio Seabra dos Santos was born in Avelãs de Cima, a village located in the county of Anadia, in the district of Aveiro, on January 1, 1918. When he finished primary school, Abílio began working at Sapec, selling agriculture products.

Abílio completed the military service in the city of Coimbra and in Terceira Island. In 1940, during World

The Seabra couple.

War II, he was again called back to the army, as part of the first contingent that went the military base of Lajes, in Terceira, to support the English troops. Even though Portugal was neutral in this war, the government, pressed by Winston Churchill, decided to let the allies use the base at Terceira Island in their fight against Germany. It was the same year the Japonese entered East Timor. After the war, Abílio stayed in Terceira working at the base. Due to a best salary offer, Abílio decided to abandon the English side and began working for the Americans.

During the first phase of his military life, Abílio met and fell in love in Helena Borges Dinis, a native of Terceira Island, where she was born on August 18, 1926. Abílio and Helena married on February 18, 1944 at the church of Fonte Bastardo, in the city of Praia da Vitória, in Terceira. On April 3, 1945, the couple's daughter, Célia, was born in Fonte Bastardo, in Terceira Island. On May 2, 1946, in Avelãs de Cima, was born the son Joaquim.

Three friends, one adventure.

Abílio first immigrated to the United States where he spent five years. Back in Portugal, Abílio was always tormented by the spirit of adventure and the will of having a better life. He signed up to go to Australia. He was called to the medical inspec-

Abílio's citizenship card.

tion, but failed due to an unknown "shadow" on his lungs. Meanwhile, Abílio read an ad on the newspaper asking for men to work in Canada. Not thinking twice, Abílio went to sign himself up. The day he received the authorization to come to Canada, he was also called to go to Australia. He chose Canada. Abílio boarded the Saturnia, in Lisbon, on May 8, and arrived in Halifax on May 13, 1953. He was part of the very first official group to arrive in Canada. The entire group was sent to Montreal where each one received different tasks and was assigned a different place to work. Abílio stayed in Montreal, in a Religious Institution, to milk cows in the farm of the Christians brothers. Since he knew how to speak English fairly well, from the years he has spent in the USA, Abílio decided to move to Vancouver. It was a really bad move, as he later confessed.

In Vancouver, he had no friends and did not find a job. Forced to go ask for shelter at a local Salvation Army, Abílio met a Portuguese man from the island of

The Seabra's with children, Clélia and Joaquim.

Madeira who had come to Canada with his family, after spending many years in England. They were both surprised to see each other – two Portuguese men – in Vancouver. The old man could not find him a job, but offered him a house to stay. Abílio looked for a job in Prince George, Whitehorse, among other places, but was never successful in finding a job. He went back to Vancouver and to the Salvation Army. He was finally able to find a job at the railroad, north of Vancouver, but it was not for long. At the Salvation Army, Abílio wrote a letter to his friend António Heleno, who was back in Montreal, to ask him for money so he could move to Toronto.

Abílio arrived in Toronto in 1954. His first job was at a restaurant, washing dishes. He was making $25 a week. Unhappy with poor salary he was making, Abílio went on to look for another job and was hired by the CBM where he remained for many years. As a sign of gratitude, he made plans for this friend Heleno to come to Toronto and found him a job. In 1955, Abílio bought his first house – perhaps the first Portuguese man to buy a

house in Canada – on 222/224 Bellwoods Avenue, for twelve thousand dollars. In 1956, he decided it was time to bring his wife and children to Canada. For $4 a week, Abílio rented his place to many Portuguese men who were arriving in Toronto in the early years.

In 1969, due to family problems, Abílio decided to go back to Portugal. Back in Anadia, he was taking care of his parents and close siblings. Applying the knowledge he has acquired in Canada, Abílio bought an historical farm, without much money, and resold it shortly after for double the money. After his parents' death, Abílio decided to move with his wife to Terceira Island dividing, from that moment on, his life between Terceira Island and Toronto.

Abílio Seabra receiving the Certificate of Honour from former premier Bob Rae for being the first Portuguese to become a Canadian citizen.

His dream is to return to Canada to live with his children and grandchildren. His son, Joaquim, has a painting company, and his daughter Clélia, has been working for 36 years at the Citizenship and Immigration bureau and is the mother of Cristina Lebre. Abílio believes he was the first Portuguese man to become a Canadian citizen, on August 25, 1958. When the community celebrated its 40th anniversary of the official arrival, Abílio received a certificate of honour from the former premier Bob Rae.

Abílio is a man with much will and strength to continue his life, a life full of tales to tell his children and grandchildren.

JMC - 2000

Silva, Carlos Barbosa da

Town of Lagoa, island of S. Miguel, Azores

Carlos Barbosa da Silva was born in the town of Lagoa, in the island of S. Miguel, Azores, on January 27, 1929. From his childhood, Carlos' life has been marked by the fields and by agriculture. Carlos married Maria da Glória de Almeida at the church of Santa Cruz da Lagoa, in S. Miguel, on October 25, 1953. Maria Glória was also born in Lagoa on July 19, 1933.

Carlos Barbosa da Silva arrived in Canada on March 27, 1954, aboard the Homeland, with six hundred other men from the Azores. The same day he arrived, he was put on a train to Montreal, and from here went to Hamilton, in Ontario. The farmer's owner took him to Winnona to another fruit farm he had. From Winnona, Carlos transferred to Windsor and Harrow where he worked in the tobacco fields. In the winter, very rough in Windsor, he was living in Rhutevin where he was making $1 a week. Good old times…

The Barbosas.

Top row, from left to right: Jaime Euleutério, Carlos Silva, António Correia, José Marcolino and João Luis Moisés. Bottom row: Miguel, Eduardo Massinha and a canadian student.

Back in the days, news would not travel fast and our pioneers would only find out about job opportunities through other mates. It was this way Carlos found out about a Mr. Cabral, from Galt, who used to find work for other Portuguese men. Carlos went to Galt, but was very unlucky, since Mr. Cabral was not able to find anything for him.

In May of 1955, Carlos found a job at the railroad where he stayed until the beginning of winter. He spent the winter season working at a restaurant, although

he was already receiving money from the Unemployment Center. In the summer, Carlos decided to stay in construction, while working – whenever he could – at the tobacco farms. In December of 1956, Carlos' wife, Glória, arrived in Toronto from Portugal. The couple's daughters were already born in Toronto: Tina and Glória Maria. They are both married and have each two children. In 1957, Carlos da Silva went to work for Concrete Pipe where he stayed for 13 years.

Between 1969 and 1970, Carlos da Silva fell very ill. Advised

Top row, from left to right: Manuel da Lagoa with a group of friends from Povoação. Bottom row: Carlos da Silva with two friends from Povoação and Faial.

by his doctor, Carlos decided to quit his job – where he used to do the night shift – and went back to construction. His health was getting worse by the day and Carlos decided to find a better job. He sent many applications to the Peel Board of Education and was finally hired in 1971 to the maintenance department. Carlos Barbosa da Silva would stay at the Board of Education for 23 years, having left in 1993 to retire.

Carlos da Silva and wife were never involved in clubs or associations. The couple likes to travel. They have been to Cuba, Israel, Spain, France, West Canada, mainland Portugal and the Azores and Madeira Islands. We wish them a long life in order to be able to continue their journey.

JMC - 1999

Carlos da Silva and wife with daughters Glória Maria and Tina.

Silva, Fernando da

Madragoa neighbourhood, Lisbon

He has "fate written on the palm of his hand".* He was born in the heart of Madragoa, a neighbourhood in the outskirts of Lisbon, on October 3, 1931. He is Fernando da Silva, the first fado singer in Canada, according to most of our pioneers. Fernando da Silva arrived in Canada on August 10, 1956. He began singing fado with the late Mariano Rego and

Fernando da Silva.

273

Fernando Silva singing with António Tabico.
The good old times...

At the restaurant, El Chico, owned by Chico Alentejano
until 1967, Fernando with António Amaro.

Orlando. Later on, he teamed up with Frederico Bulhões, António Amaro, Gabriel Teves and others to sing fado. The First Portuguese Canadian Club was the first place where he performed in Toronto. Besides singing fado, Fernando worked in a factory as furniture polisher.

Fernando da Silva married Cristina Silva. The couple had two children, both born in Toronto: Fernando and Elizabeth da Silva. A short man, with a big heart and provocative attitude towards life, Fernando was always a well liked and respected person. Together with other fado singers, such as Chico Aletejano, Zé Gomes and Maria Gomes, Fernando da Silva formed the group "Alegres do Fado" participated in many fund raising initiatives for institutions.

Health problems and an unexpected stroke forced Fernando to retire and to stop singing. Fate did not choose a happy ending for Fernando. He retired in 1997. He had always been ready to help his neighbour and ended up living stuck to a wheel chair at the Maynard Nursing Home, in Toronto. He has everything in life, but he is not a happy man. He is surrounded by people, but feels lonely. It is his fate, a fate he sang throughout his life time, but which has not left a happy spot for him. Still, when talking about fado, Fernando smiles with "saudade". After all, saudade is the only thing left for him.

The late Fernando da Silva and his friend,
the late Chico Alentejano.

Fernando da Silva passed away in 2003.

The title of a Portuguese fado song.

JMC - 2001

Zé Gomes and Fernando da Silva.

Silva, Hildebrando Borges da

Village of Sé, city of Angra do Heroísmo, Terceira island, Azores

Have you ever had the chance to visit the Hildebrando's Gallery, on 1078 Dundas Street West, in Toronto? If you haven't, you should. At the Gallery, you will find many reasons to go back for a visit and to redecorate your house. The gallery belongs to the artist Hildebrando Silva, a native of the Terceira Island. Hildebrando Borges da Silva was born in Sé, a village in the outskirts of Angra do Heroísmo, the capital

At an exhibition, Hildebrando stands by his paintings.

city of Terceira Island. He was born on October 24, 1922. He completed a commerce degree at Dr. Oliveira Salazar School, in Terceira.

- I have been drawing and painting since I can remember – Hildebrando confessed. – Until the age of 12, I studied with my aunt where she was teaching. So I never had a set school.

Sponsored by his brother-in-law, Abílio Santos, Hildebrando arrived in Toronto on September 15, 1966, bringing all the family with him: wife, Guiomar, and six children – four girls and two boys. He already has eight grandchildren.

- Why did you decide to come to Canada?

- Well, I had a good job, but it was enough to provide a good life for my children. I do not regret having come to Canada.

Hildebrando is our Portuguese pioneer in the art of painting letters, landscapes, canvases… Since he arrived in Canada, he has dedicated himself to an art that is present at residential and commercial houses, the Portuguese consulate, among other places.

- I don't think there is a Portuguese club or restaurant in Toronto that does not have one, or more, of my paintings. I have always been helped by our community – Hildebrando confessed.

Hildebrando and wife Guiomar at one of his exhibitions.

- Where have you worked?

- Back in Terceira, I worked for the ministry of commerce and in 1947, I began working at the military base of Lajes until 1966, the year I came to Canada.

- You were well respected at Lajes...

Hildebrando, at his gallery, in Toronto.

- Yes, thank God. I was recognized by the American military with a diploma for the good services I performed for them. I painted letters, canvas, landscapes and military scenes with sergeants and soldiers. I even held two exhibitions at Lajes.

- Did you paint outside the military base?

- Yes, I used to paint for cultural events in Terceira. I painted the murals and scenarios for more than 100 plays.

- In Toronto, how has it been?

- In here, my life took a more professional aspect, even though I never refused to help the Portuguese clubs. But in a country like this, with a wife and six children, I had to begin taking my painting life very serious. Fortunately, the Portuguese community has always been there to help me. I could always count on churches, clubs, restaurants, any other business people and individuals. In order to pay them a homage, I am planning to organize an exhibit at a hotel honoring the Portuguese Community.

Hildebrando is one of those pioneers who know how to recognize all the help he has received.

- Among your children, is there one who has your vocation?

- Only Liger does. He is the only one of my six children who paints. He is self-employed and is doing very well. – Hildebrando continued, with a smile on his face. – They are all talented, especially Fátima, but their family lives prevent them from practicing their talents.

- Have you won many awards?

- I have especially in Terceira. Here, I have won many contests, which have opened many doors for me in the Canadian market. Fortunately, I have many assignments.

- What do you prefer: painting or drawing?

- I prefer painting both in oil and acrylic. When time allows, I love painting.

Hildebrando was born a true artist. We pay homage to the man and the artist whom we respect and admire.

JMC - July of 1987

Silva, João Domigos da

Town of Lagoa, island of S. Miguel, Azores

For our Portuguese community, Canada is such a small country! One only needs to travel to another city to find an old friend. I went to Winnipeg and found a former friend who used to live in Galt-Cambridge and who is now living in Calgary. At Mário Pontes' home, I found João Domingos da Silva, a big activist for the Portuguese community in Canada who, for many years, served as director and president of the Oriental Sport Club of Galt-Cambridge. Now, in Calgary, he continues his activism. So, who is this man?

João Domingos da Silva was born in the Lagoa, a town in the island of S. Miguel, in the Azores. He married Natália da Conceição in the island of Terceira. The couple has one daughter: Ana Cristina who is an elementary school teacher in Calgary and is married to Francisco Ávila. João Domingos arrived in Canada on June 10, 1972. He lived in Toronto before moving to Galt. In Galt, now Cambridge, João was a very active member at the Oriental Club, as a secretary and later as a president.

João Silva still remembers the time when they bought the soccer field – where the Portuguese team "Os Belenenses" played once. Many Portuguese people lent money to the Oriental Club for the purchase of the field. Somehow, some members understood it had been a donation. Many used the situation to create problems. Tired of all the comments, João decided, in 1977, to speak to the president Artur Escobar to pay all the debts. Together with Artur Escobar, João

A happy family. Standing: Ana Cristina and husband Francisco Ávila. Sitting down: Natália da Conceição and João Domingos da Silva, in Winnipeg at Mário Pontes' place.

went from door to door to pay the loans. Many people decided not to accept the money and turned the loan into a donation. Others accepted the money, and all the debts were paid.

In Calgary, where he has been living since

April 23, 1999: João wins the Immigrants of Distinction Awards.

1979, his own a drywall company – the Skyline Drywall. According to João, the Portuguese community of Calgary is made up of 3500 members approximately. There are many social centers, such as the one by the church of Nossa Senhora de Fátima, the Portuguese Society of Calgary and the Portuguese School.

Lately, João's drywall company has been sponsoring the Carlgary Stampede. João Domingos da Silva is now fighting to keep the Portuguese church opened, which he helped to build, since Father António Magalhães decided not to stay there. According to João, Father Magalhães was not very friendly to the parishioners, which led to many Portuguese deciding not to attend mass on Sundays or even participate in any service. With an empty church, the priest decided to move to Ontario.

João will always be an active member of the Portuguese community wherever he goes. We wish him all the best.

JMC - 1999

Silva, Manuel da

Village of Ribeira Seca, town of Ribeira Grande, island of S. Miguel, Azores

O ne of the positive aspects we find as we write the history of our community is the way they were able to succeed after so much sacrifice and hard work. Manuel da Silva is one of those successful individuals. He was born in the village of Ribeira Seca, in Ribeira Grande, a county in the island of S. Miguel, on May 20, 1927.

- When I arrived in Canada, I was received by a huge snowstorm – Manuel da Silva began telling us. – I ship I boarded took off from the island of S. Miguel to the island of Santa Maria, on April 27, 1956. In Santa

The Silva's with daughter Marcia at their Toronto home.

Maria, I took the airplane from Air France to Montreal, on April 29. When I arrived there was so much snow that I was scared.

- Did you stay in Montreal?

- Yes, but only for ten days! – He continued. – I was at a farm sawing lettuce seeds. One of my brothers-in-law invited me to go work with him at the railroad.

- Who was your brother-in-law?

- It was Jacinto Requema who, unfortunately, has already died.

- Did you stay at the railroad for a long time?

- More or less. When I got there and saw so many duty carriages, people with long beards and bad temper I was very afraid and decided not to stay. Since I had my brother, José da Silva, living in British Columbia, I took the train and headed there.

- Alone?

- No. I went with my friend, the late Manuel Barbosa. It was a hard trip. We got there so pale we thought we were going to die.

- Why?

- Since we did not know how to speak English or French, we did not know how to ask for food. The only thing we could see at the display was pears and coke. That's what we had. Back then, not speaking the language was the greatest obstacle we encountered.

One of our pioneer's favourite hobbies: the traditional slaughter of pigs. In the picture, Dinis da Silva, Manuel Simé, Manuel Silva, Floriano Borges, Manuel Machado and Manuel Moniz.

- Did your brother find a job for you and your friend right away?

- Yes. A short time after arriving we began working in construction. I was making $2.80/hour. In one year, I made more money than my brother who came to Canada before me. He didn't work in construction and was making less money.

- Were you always in construction?

- No. In British Columbia, everyone wanted to go work for Alcan, an aluminum factory. I applied to work there, but was not very lucky. There were too many applications and very few positions available. One day, Mr. Bruno, one of the supervisors at Alcan, asked us to go clean a local church. Luís Souca and I accepted the proposal and went to clean the church for two days. When we finished, Mr. Bruno gave us $40 for the work we had done. Since it was a service for a church, we did not accept the money. Mr. Bruno thought it was a nice gesture from our part and offered us a job at Alcan. That's what we wanted.

- Did you stay there for a long time?

- No! I was only there until 1959.

- What happened after?

- That year, I decided to go back to Portugal to get married. I had had enough of living alone.

- We dated for 15 years! – Irene Silva began saying. Irene, our pioneer's wife, was also born in the village of Ribeira Seca. – We got married at the church of São Pedro da Riberia Seca, on October 18, 1959.

- And then we came together to Canada? – We asked.

- No! – Manuel da Silva continued his story. – I came back in February of 1960 and in April I got a job at the Seven Islands, in construction.

    - I only came to Canada on June 16, 1961. – Irene said.

    - So you met in Montreal?

    - Yes! – Manuel da Silva continued.

    - So your children were all born in Montreal...

    - No, oh no! They were all born in Toronto. Durval was born on March 5, 1963. Victor was born on September 11, 1966; and Marcia on May 28, 1971. They were all born in Toronto.

Durval's baptism at the church of Santa Maria. Godparents: Luis Rego and Maria de Jesus.

Manuel da Silva at the Santa Maria's choir during Santo Cristo's festivities.

    - How did that happen?

    - In 1961, when I was still at the Seven Islands, I got a back injury. I had to undergo surgery and could not work for one year. After much suffering and having stopped working for so long, the compensation board decided to give me $2,000 and advised me to move to another place. At the same time, there was not much left to do at the Seven Islands, so I decided to move to Toronto.

    - Since you had a back injury, what job did you find when you got to Toronto?

    - I was lucky. I got a job at the cleaning and maintenance department at City Hall. It's the job I still have. I have been there for more than 25 years. – Manuel said proudly.

    - His many years of service have been recognized by City Hall. – Irene told us.

    - Yes! I received a commemorative watch from the Municipality of Metropolitan Toronto. The party took place at the Sherato Hotel. It was wonderful.

    Going back to the early years, we asked our pioneer if he had any interesting or funny stories to share with us. Thinking a while, searching for the best stories, Manuel da Silva began his narrative:

    - When I was in British Columbia, one day a boss asked me to help him dig a hole. That's what I did. It was such a hot day! Once in a while, I heard the boss talking to me, but since I did not speak English, I was nodding my head, sort of agreeing with everything he was saying. And I kept working like a donkey. The more he spoke to me, the harder I worked. I was sweating like a pig. All of a sudden, the boss came to me, grabbed me by the arms and forced me to sit down. Using his arms to communicate, even though I did not understand much of the sign language, he was telling me to rest. Only then did I understand he had been trying to tell me to take a break. It was actually the coffee break! Back then we worked very hard because we did not want to loose our jobs. When I tell my children this story, they all laugh… They have no idea how much we suffered!

- Were you a member of any club in those old times?

- No! I only sang for a few years at the Santa Maria's choir. I was going to that church, and since I liked singing, I ended up joining the choir.

- But you didn't stay there for too long?

- No! I moved to the east side of the city and was a little far for me to go to the church downtown. I feel sad, though, because I love singing.

- When you retire, are you planning to go back to Portugal?

- I don't know! I always thought about going back to the island of S. Miguel, but years have gone by and here I am. When I was there, recently, I found everything so different. Most of my friends and family members are no longer there. So, I don't know. I will probably stay here with my wife, children and grandchildren.

- Does your wife want to go back?

- Yes! – Irene answered instantly. – When I retire, I am planning to go back. I have never forgotten my childhood in the island, where I was born. I want to go back to my place, across the church where I used to go to pray. Here, everything is so far. But, as my husband says, God knows what the future may hold.

JMC - November of 1988

Silva, Manuel da

Village of Sítio da Serra D'Água,
town of Machico, Madeira island

Manuel da Silva was born on June 19, 1920, in the Sítio da Serra D'Água, a village in the town of Machico, on Madeira island. When he was 5 years old, he left his hometown and came to the city of Funchal.

In Funchal, he lived at his oncle's house, his mother's brother. At school, Manuel studied with Father Laureano, at Socorro. He used to pray more than he studied. When he turned 17 years old, he went work at the docks, in Funchal, where he took his license. In 1941, he began his military service in Mafra, a town in the outskirts of Lisbon. Coming back to Madeira island, Manuel continued his military service as part of the 4th Batallion in Ponte Nova. In 1944, after finishing his military service, Manuel da Silva began working at the Hotel Bela Vista. The hotel's boss, an Italian, taught him landscaping. From here, Manuel went to the Agrarian Station, a place where he had to take care of fruit trees. Manuel worked here from 1945 to 1948.

Still back in Madeira, Manuel da Silva married to Maria Manuela in 1946. They were divorced in 1980. The couple had eight children: Maria Manuela, Emanuel Humberto, Rita

Manuel da Silva with the docks uniform in Funchal.

First group of men from the Madeira island to arrive in Toronto. Standing, from left to right: Manuel da Silva, Aleixo Jardim, João Camarata, José Sabino, Manuel Camacho, José Camacho, Luís Mora, Manuel Firmino Gouveia, Manuel Gomes, Eduardo Mendonça, António Nunes, late Manuel Frias, Fernando Belo, Elias Gonçalves, Mário Nóbrega, late António Nunes, late Juvenal de Freitas, António Plácido, Silvino Vieira, Juvenal Gomes, José de Freitas, José Patrício, Óscar Pereira, José Quintal, late Ângelo Bacalhau, a canadian pilot instructor and Santa Clara Gomes.

Maria, Fátima Maria – who was born in 1948 and passed away in 1949 – and José Adriano were all born in Madeira island. José Adriano was only 19 months when he arrived in Canada. In Toronto, three more children were born: Margarida, John and Ana Maria. Manuel da Silva has seven grandchildren and two great-grandchildren.

In 1953, Juvenal de Freitas, a close friend of Manuel, told him about the chance of coming to Canada. From the time he heard about Canada to actually immigrating was a very short time. A group of 102 men from Madeira Island – Manuel included – and one man from mainland Portugal boarded the Nea Healls in Funchal on May 26, 1953, and arrived at Pier 21, in Halifax, on June 1, 1953. From Halifax, the group of men took the train to Montreal. Since Manuel da Silva spoke some English, he was nominated the official translator for his friends at the immigration office. Manuel da Silva still remembers that, at the train station, a group of about 30 men were chosen by the farmers who were there looking for manpower. Manuel da Silva, who

Manuel da Silva planting trees at Madeira Park.

had been chosen by the tallest farmer there, was fired on the second day because he did not know how to milk cows. After moving from Montreal to Quebec City, from one farm to another, Manuel da Silva decided to go to the Consulate of Portugal and asked for help to come to Toronto.

Manuel da Silva arrived in Toronto on July 5, 1953, and went right away to Niagara-on-the-Lake where his friends Álvaro Ferreira and Juvenal de

Freitas were living. He came back to Toronto and worked for a few months as busboy at the El Mocambo Club. From here, he applied and was hired to work at the Dr. Ballard, a factory specialized in animal food products. Manuel da Silva worked at Dr. Ballard for 32 years and only left in 1985 when he retired.

Manuel da Silva has always been an active member of our community. He was part of the group of men who tried to have a club to socialize at the end of hard week of work, suffering and loneliness. They founded the Portuguese United – today the First Portuguese Canadian Club – a club that was hard to found because each person wanted to represent his own region in Portugal. Together with Juvenal de Freitas, Camarate, Júlio Pinto, João Tiago, and others raised funds - $4,500 in total – and bought a farm where they founded the Madeira Park and, at the same time, the Canadian Madeira Club. Father Cunha helped him get the space for the club, right across from Santa Maria church. Until today, Manuel da Silva has been the only founding member to be part of every executive. In 1966, Manuel da Silva was appointed the director responsible for Madeira Park for his knowledge of plants and trees.

Age does not forgive anything. Thus, Manuel da Silva is thinking of "retiring" from the park when he turns 80. However, most people believe that being 80 years old will not be a good excuse to take him away from Madeira Park.

JMC

MADEIRA
PARK
RECORDACAO
FESTA
PORTUGUESA
DE - 1965

Silva, Mário

Island of S. Miguel,

Azores

Mário Silva has a Bachelor of Arts in Political Science from the University of Toronto and a Language Certificate from the Sorbone University, in Paris. Mário Silva was the special assistant to the Ontario minister of health and in 1994 was elected, for the first time, as Toronto's city councilor. His election represented his first victory

Consul General of Portugal, Artur Magalhães, imposing the Merit Medal to Mario Silva, in the presence of the president of the Portuguese Assembly of the Republic, Mota Amaral.

in trying to enter the world of politics when he defeated Tony O'Donohue, a politician who had served as councilor for 30 years.

When he was first elected into City Hall, Mário Silva was nominated chair of the Economic Development Committee and member of the executive, public works and municipality affairs committees. Later on, he was also chosen to be deputy mayor. In November of 1997, he was re-elected as city councilor of the now Mega City of Toronto and nominated for the Urban Development Committee. At the same time, Mario was nominated to be part of the Economic Development committee, the group responsible for coordinating efforts that attract more business to the city and develops the existing companies and industries. In 1999, Mario was nominated director of Toronto Hydro.

In 2000, Mario Silva runs for the third time to the Toronto City Council and is once again re-elected. This time, Mario takes the responsibility of vice-chair for the Toronto's Transport Commission and for the Development and Planning Committee, and became president for the Exhibition Place. Maria Silva has also been a member of the Canadian Association "Feed the Children", an association that works both nationally and internationally.

Mario Silva with Canada's Prime Minister Paul Martin.

In 2004, Mario Silva realized one his biggest dreams, as he ran for the federal election. Mario Silva became the first Portuguese Canadian to be elected Member of Parliament in Ottawa. He was re-elected in January of 2006.

JMC - 2006

Mario Silva with the late pope John Paul II, in Toronto, in 2002.

A group of individuals from the Portuguese community after the imposing of insignias in Toronto: Laurentino Esteves, Chef Albino Dias, Mário Silva, President of the Portuguese Assembly of the Republic Mota Amaral, Professor Manuela Marujo, Judge Arlindo Frazão, Ambassador José Luiz Gomes, José Eustáquio, Chef José Carlos Ferreira and Ermídio Alves.

Silva, Martinho Henriques

Town Sever do Vouga,

District of Aveiro

Martinho da Silva at one of his favourite places: a radio studio.

Martinho Henriques Silva was born in Silva Escura, a small village in Sever do Vouga, a town in the district of Aveiro, in northern Portugal. Martinho Henriques Silva was born on September 4, 1952. With his family, Martinho arrived in Canada on August 15, 1968, with five years of high school done in Portugal. He was 15 years old. After completing the then Grade 13, Martinho applied to York University. However, an invitation by Father Cunha to join the morning radio show "Ecos de Portugal" on CHIN, made him change his mind. This was November of 1973. His radio experience lasted until 1974. He came back to CHIN in January of 1982 with the show "Wake-up Portuguese Style" with a lot of success.

Courageous, leftist, and ambitious enough, Martinho conquered many friends and enemies. At CHIN, his ironic criticism to individuals and institutions made him a person with many followers, but just as many enemies. A member of the NDP party (Neo-Democrats) in Ontario, since 1985, Martinho Silva was elected as trustee in 1985. This experience inspired him to search a career in politics.

In 1988, Martinho Silva was elected as Toronto City Councilor, a position he held until 1997. Martinho Silva was the first Portuguese Canadian to be elected trustee and city councilor in Toronto.

Martinho Silva and Rosa Sousa inaugurating the sign "Rua do Alentejo" at the previous Casa do Alentejo headquarters, on Dufferin Street, in Toronto.

Martinho Silva has the perfect profile for politics. An unfortunate moment in his career caused him a rupture with the voters who did not elect him the third time.

Mario Silva and Martinho Silva, the two Silvas who served simultaneously as councilors for Toronto's City Hall.

Martinho Henriques Silva is married to Cerília Perna Ministro, a native from the province of Algarve and is the father of Décio Ministro Silva, born in Toronto.

Today, Martinho Silva divides his days between Canada and Portugal, working for CHIN Radio and the directory phone book Blue Pages. He is finally living the life he has so hard worked for.

JMC - February of 2004

Simas, Leonel Alberto Silva

Town of São Mateus do Pico,

island of Pico, Azores

Leonel Alberto Silva Simas has a history worth registering. Leonel Alberto was born in the town of São
Mateus do Pico, in the island of Pico, on August 1, 1946. He left
his island two weeks after completing elementary school, when
he was 12 years old.

*Leo and Maria do Carmo Simas at
one of their trips.*

With his parents – Rosa Silvina and Leonel Simas Sr.
–, Leonel came to Canada on June 24, 1959. They decided to
choose West Lorne, in Ontario, as their place of residence. When he was only 16 years of age,
Leonel found a job in New Brunswich where his uncle Manuel Garcia was working as boss of a
construction site. Leonel first began working in a military base. Although he was earning a lot
of money - .75 cents/hour, a good salary back in the days – Leonel could not handle the cold
temperatures and the physical effort he had to make. Leonel missed his parents. The company's
owner, Laurino Rocca, liked Leonel and sent him to Toronto to a job site he had in the city. At
the time, the Simas family moved to Oakville.

*A rare moment: Leo leaves the presidency
of the Portuguese Club of London and his
wife becomes president. The two commemorative cakes that will never be forgotten!*

In 1965, Rocca's uncle needed workers at his
London site and Leo Simas was chosen to go with a group
of other men. This assignment in London only lasted
six months. Coming back to Oakville, Leo spoke to his
father about the possibility of the family forming their
own construction company. His plan went into action. In
1967, they founded Simas Constructions, a company in
partnership with Leo, his father, his cousin José Silva and
Vasco Bettencourt. They successfully began their work in
London. In 1970, they sold the company to Mateo's Group
of London. Leo Simas stayed in the new company as
supervisor. Between London and Toronto, Leo Simas was
responsible for a group of 180 men. Leonel Simas Senior
retired and went back to Pico in 1972, dedicating himself
to agriculture until his death.

*As president of the Portuguese
Club of London, Leo always
helped everyone, even at the
bar.*

In 1975, Leo left the Mateo's Group and founded
his second company with two Italian friends: Mario Libertori and
nephew Joe Libertori. It was the birth of Alwel Forming and Colony
Investments, a firm responsible for building and selling houses and
apartments. From one place to another, Leo Simas met the young
Maria do Carmo Ribau, a native from the town of Gafanha da
Encarnação, in the district of Aveiro. Maria do Carmo was born on
September 15, 1951. They both got married at St. James Church, in
Oakville, in a ceremony presided by the late Father Lima Esteves, on
June 23, 1973. In London, the couple saw the birth of three daugh-
ters: Lisa Lee, a student at Guelph University who wants to be a

teacher; Katherine Maria, who studies Business & Marketing at Sheridan College, in Oakville; and Jennifer Ann, who is still in high school and wantsto be a teacher.

Tired of so many job sites, so much traveling in Ontario, of the snow and cold, Leo decided to sell his share of the company to his partners. In 1984, he went back to Pico with his family. Back home, he felt a stranger, a true "immigrant" in his homeland. Seven months later, disappointed with everything, Leo decided to come back to London, Ontario.

In 1986, Leo decided to get back into business and founded the Forest City Forming Ltd with his german friend Eugene Drewll. The company has been successfully growing until this date.

Family portrait: Maria do Carmo and Leo Simas with daughters Lisa Lee, Katherine Marie and Jennifer Ann.

The Simas' family have been very active in the Portuguese community, specially in the Portuguese Club of London. Leo was its president in 1979-80, 1993-94 and in 1995. Curiously, his wife was also president from 1995 to 1997.

As their favorite hobby, the Simas love to travel. They have been to mainland Portugal and all the Azores' islands and is planning to go Madeira. They have also been to the USA, Mexico, the Bahamas… They also know Canada from coast to coast.

Leo also loves to play golf. On weekends, Leo is lost and found at the golf courts. Family and business are Leo's both passions. He has been rewarded for so many years of hard work.

JMC - 2001

Sousa, António Santos e

City of
Nazaré

The sacrifices of the early years have not affected our pioneer António Sousa, a native of Nazaré, a beautiful coastal city in mainland Portugal. He is known for his great sense of humour. António Santos e Sousa was born on June 3, 1925, in Nazaré, a land known for its connection to the sea. He left his homeland in 1953 to come to Canada. António was part of the first group of official

Family portrait.

Portuguese men to arrive in Halifax, aboard the Saturnia, on May 13, 1953.

The day he arrived in Canada, António was sent right away to Sarnia to a chicken farm. Disliking his job, António decided to move to Montreal with his friend Fernando Ramalho who helped him fill out the application to go to Labrador as the main helper to the Chef José Ramalho, who was Fernando's father. After a few months in Labrador and always dreaming of having his own business, António Sousa moved to Toronto where he opened and managed, from 1955 to 1958, the first Portuguese restaurant in Canada: "The Portuguese Restaurant", located on Nassau and Bellview streets. Curiously, António Sousa sold his restaurant to Fernando Ramalho. This restaurant represented the first of many businesses to come.

António Santos e Sousa married to Maria Antónia Rocha at the church of Nossa Senhora da Nazaré on December 14, 1949. Just like António, Maria Antónia was also born in Nazaré on May 7, 1924. Maria Antónia came to Canada in 1954 and passed away on October 25, 1997. The couple's first son José Júlio was born in Nazaré on February 19, 1951. He has a Bachelor of Education and is now vice principal at Saint Luigi's Catholic School, in Toronto. José Júlio has three children, all born in Toronto: Jorge, born on August 3, 1977, Tanja Maria, born on July 2, 1988 and Isacc, born on December 17, 1989.

António Sousa and Maria Antónia had a second son – Anthony Charles – already born in Toronto, on September 27, 1958. Charles works for the Royal Bank where he is senior manager of accounting. Charles is the father of three children: Cristine, born on June 30, 1989; Justin, born on April 15, 1992; and Jessica, born August 15, 1996. A happy family!

Between the years of 1955 and 1980, António Sousa opened many businesses, besides the restaurant described above. In 1956, in partnership with José Correia, he founded the "Correia & Sousa Portuguese Importers" and several fish markets in Toronto and one in Winnipeg to sell the fish the company was importing. In 1958, he joined Delkar Maia

The first group of Portuguese men from mainland Portugal who left for Canada on May 8, 1953.

to open the Portuguese bakery and pastry Ibéria, a business he kept for five years. In the 70's, together with Raúl Costa, António opened the "Toronto Advertising Co.", a designing company. In the late 70's and early 80's, together with his two sons, António opened the Lift Finance Inc and the A. Sousa Enterprises, a company specializing in the building, remodeling and selling of houses.

Nazaré's folkloric group, 1st prize at the International Festival of Folklores, in 1964, the year António Sousa was its director.

António retired in 1991 and now enjoys life with his family and many friends, even though he deeply misses his late wife. António always told his family and friends that "if someone spends twelve dollars when they only make ten dollars, there is no way this person will make it in life".

António Sousa was always a defendant of the Portuguese culture and education. When he was a member of the Board of Directors at the First Portuguese School, in 1971, he designed and printed the logo "Education is our weapon". António Sousa is founding member #1 of the First Portuguese Canadian Club, a club that was founded on September 23, 1956. He served twice as its president: in 1960 and 1975. He is still an active member of the club. António Sousa is also one of the founding members – and holds the card #12 – of the now extinct Nazaré

Sousa family at community gathering.

Recreative Club that had been founded on March 21, 1968. Still, the folkloric group has survived until today.

Whenever feeling tired from his busy life, António Sousa would pack and travel with his inseparable wife. He now has a house in Nazaré and one in Florida. He has been the Portuguese pioneer to travel everywhere in Canada: Halifax, Sarnia, Bun, Winnipeg, Calgary, Labrador, Kitimat, Newfoundland, Prince Edward Island, Nova Scotia, Quebec City, Montreal, Toronto, Ottawa... Now, in his retirement, he enjoys swimming every morning, goes for a walk with old friends spends time with his family and is still involved in many community activities.

He is proud of what he has accomplished and what he has done. Those who came after him are also proud and thankful for what he has done.

JMC - 1999

Sousa, Conceição Gouveia de

Town of Porto da Cruz, Madeira Island

The pleasant Conceição Gouveia de Sousa was born in the town of Porto da Cruz, in Madeira Island, on October 12, 1924. From a very early age, she moved to the city of Funchal where she lived with her godmother. She married the late pioneer José Linhares de Sousa at the church of São Pedro, in October of 1947. José Linhares de Sousa was born in the town of Santa Luzia, in the district of Funchal, on June 18, 1925. The couple had two children both born in Funchal. The first was José Manuel, born on June 7, 1948, and who now has two children of his own: Christopher and Lisa. The second one was Maria Teresa, born on September 20, 1949, who became

Conceição Gouveia de Sousa

the first Portuguese Canadian lawyer, and probably the first Portuguese Canadian judge, working now in Ottawa. Madame Maria Teresa is married and a mother of three children: Sarah, Patrick and Daniel. Maria Teresa got her Bachelor of Arts at the University of Toronto and went to law school from the University of Ottawa. She is now living in Ottawa.

The pioneer José Linhares arrived in Halifax on June 2, 1953.

- I almost died aboard the Saturnia because I got seasick. – Conceição told us. – And when I came to Toronto by train I also felt very sick.

José de Sousa decided to live near Toronto where he found a job at a mushroom farm. Two months later, unhappy with his job, he came back to Toronto. He found a job at the kitchen of the Hotel St. Riche, today the German Club.

Conceição and José de Sousa on their daughter's wedding day

Meanwhile, Conceição arrived in Canada on August 15, 1954, with her children José Manuel, who was 7 years old, and Maria Teresa, who was 4 years old. It was a hard, long trip. By boat, they went from Funchal to Lisbon and from there to New York. Then, from New York, she came to Toronto by train.

A month after arriving in Canada, Conceição found a job at a laundry where she was

José Linhares de Sousa with friends and boss' in the first Christmas in Toronto.

José de Sousa with brothers Francisco, Claudio and Fernando.

making $10 a week. She was there for four years. José de Sousa, fed up with his job at the hotel's kitchen, decided to look for another job, was else he was determined to go back to Madeira. He applied at Toronto's Hydro. He waited for three months and... nothing! A friend of his advised him to call Hydro every week. He decided to follow his friend's advice and several weeks later got the job. José worked there for 32 years until his retirement. Unfortunately, José Linhares passed away on October 25, 1996, victim of cancer.

José and Conceição Sousa with children José Manuel and Maria Teresa in 1955.

Back in the days, José Linhares was one of the founding members of the Madeira Park and the Canadian Madeira Club. He loved taking care of his home, reading and going out with his family. He went back to visit Madeira almost every year. On the other hand, the fear of airplanes only allowed Conceição to go back twice.

After leaving the laundry, Conceição went to work at the Princess Margaret Hospital in the food and diet department. At the end, she was the manager of the diet section for patients with diabetes. She worked in the hospital for 31 years and retired in 1989.

Today, Conceição still lives at her house by herself, but often visits or is visited by her children and grandchildren. At the Saudade Museum in Halifax, and at the Gallery of Portuguese Pioneers, in Toronto, Conceição Gouveia de Sousa left many of her and her husband's belongings so that they may tell a story to future generations. She goes out with her friends many of which are pioneer Portuguese women.

Judge Maria Teresa Linhares de Sousa.

She is proud of her past and present, and is sure that the future will be even better for her family.

JMC - 1999

Sousa, Elvino Silveira Medina de

Graciosa Island, Azores

Prof. Elvino Sousa with wife Ana Maria and Prof. Irena Blayer from Brock University.

Elvino Silveira Medina de Sousa was born in Graciosa Island, in the Azores archipelago, on December 28, 1956. He immigrated to Canada with his parents in 1970 when he was only 13 years old. A dreamer and an outstanding student, Elvino found in school and books the right path to follow. An honour student since the beginning, Elvino completed a Bachelor and a Masters Degree at the University of Toronto and obtained his Ph.D. from the University of Southern California, in the United States of America.

Elvino Sousa and wife Ana Maria at the Academia do Bacalhau's event, in Toronto. In the picture we can see Ivo and Mia Azevedo, Connie Lino, consul general Artur Magalhães and Rui Gomes.

Luis Louro, Connie Freitas and Victor Sousa giving Prof. Kim Vicente the merit diploma from the Federation of Portuguese Canadian Business and Professionals.

Professor Elvino S. Sousa, Ph.D., P. Eng., began his academic career at the University of Toronto in 1986. Today, besides his teaching career, Elvino dedicates time to the Bell University Labs in Computer Engineering where he is the chair. Professor Elvino was the first Portuguese Canadian to teach at the University of Toronto, and probably the first Portuguese Canadian professor in Canada. At the moment, Elvino Sousa is also the Older Endowed Chair of the University of Toronto.

Together with Kim J. Vicente (B.A. Sc., M.S., Ph.D.), Elvino is one of the references in the university of Toronto's academia.

Elvino is married to Ana Maria Pancada, a psychologist in the Portuguese community who has also obtained her degree from the University of Toronto. The couple has two children – Michael and Sandra – both born in Toronto and presently studying in university.

Professor Elvino S. Sousa is a calm, quite individual. He displays the natural characteristic of a scientist and a researcher. Elvino is an individual who knows how to honour both his country of birth and his country of choice.

Prof. Elvino Sousa (Science and Technology) receiving the new Pioneers Award from Ian Bandeen, Trustee from the S. M. Blair Family Foundation.

JMC - 2004

Sousa, José Eduardo dos Santos e

City of Nazaré

To leave one's homeland is not an easy task. However, when that individual is determined to fight and to conquer, no obstacle is too big to stop him. This is the case of our pioneer José Eduardo dos Santos e Sousa who was able to fight and conquer one of the highest positions within Varig, the Brazilian airline.

José Eduardo dos Santos e Sousa – Jess for his friends – was born in the town of Nazaré, in the mainland Portugal, on November 18, 1935. He left Portugal to immigrate to Canada on October 29, 1954

From left to right: Iam Hills, Marisa Lynne, Nina Sousa, José Eduardo de Sousa and Eduarda Lee.

and arrived in New York on November 7. That same day, Jess took the train from New York to Toronto.

- Did you travel by boat? – We asked, beginning our dialogue.

- Yes. I boarded the Vulcania. I felt like I had a very important mission to accomplish because I was accompanying my sister-in-law Maria Antónia and my nephew José Júlio. The reason for this was very simple: my older brother António had already immigrated to Canada in the spring of 1953. I came to this country sponsored by my brother who paved the way for me.

- Does that mean that the immigration experience was easier for you?

- At first, yes! Obviously, it is much easier to come to a new country where your older brother is awaiting you. However, that doesn't mean my life was easy. To the very contrary!

- What were some of the hardships you had to face?

- I came to this country when I was only 18 years of age. Back in Portugal, I had just finished completing my diploma from the Commercial School. I turned 19 years old a few days after arriving in Canada. I remember that I spent New Year's Eve of 1954 sitting by a lamp on the corner of Bathurst and Dundas looking at traffic and crying. I shed many tears that night...

How many pioneers – just like Jess – spent New Year's Eve crying? How many more evenings? Loneliness, tears, frustration, hard work and "saudade" will always be part of our pioneers' memoirs.

- As soon as I arrived in Canada – and after sleeping for just a few hours against my brother's will – I went to work. I still remember seeing my brother making me corn flakes breakfast at 5 in the morning. – Jess continued his tale, now having a bitter sweet laugh over his stories. – So I went to my first job in Canada. I was taken there by this nice, young man from the Azores. I regret not remembering his name.

- Where did you work?

- I had to unload grass rolls from trucks and place them in the golf courts. I was there for ten days.

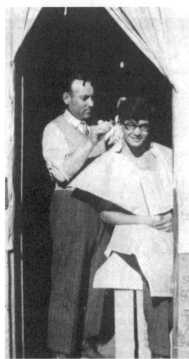

In 1955, in Kitimat, Jess Sousa at Gil's barber shop.

And so began the tale of a young boy in a strange land where everything was different. Due to the hardships and sacrifices he had to face and make in life, Jess wrote the following poem:

"Saudade is a something we feel without seeing;

It is a tear, it is a yes, it is a no;

It is everything! It is willing something without wanting it;

It the worst, it is the best memory of life".

- My best friend from those times was Fernando Ramalho! – Jess told us. – With him I shared many laughs, wrote many verses to the Chinese man who served us rice and chicken by old City Hall. Due to lack of money, we used to walk everywhere.

- How did you end up getting the nickname Jess?

- Well, that one was for self-defence. I hated when people called me Joe. Canadians used to call every immigrant man Joe. So, I began telling them that my name was Jess. It is an acronym for my name: J for José, E for Eduardo, S for Santos and the second S for Sousa. Thus, Jess was born...

For all sharing a laugh with him about the origin of Jess, we spoke about the time he spent in Kitimat in the early years.

- It was all Fernando Ramalho's idea. Myself, Fernando, Alberto and Manuel decided to go to Kitimat. Fernando spoke English well, so he got a job right away. We took a little longer. Still, we met Delkar Maia's father – whom I consider the Portuguese ambassador in Kitimat. He got me a job at Alcan. My first task was to dig a trench, under

In Kitimat: Fernando Ramalho, António Gonçalves and José Eduardo Sousa.

the supervision of a foreman, a superintendent and a plumber. They were all bossing me around. I was never afraid of work, but to be submitted to extremely hard work and having people making fun of me on top of that was too much for me to handle. I was so furious that I decided to go to the local union to complain – in my broken English – to the boss. I told him what was happening. Not forgetting my business instincts, I presented him a deal: that I would get him ten votes for every Portuguese man he could hire. Obviously, the boss used me for his interests! I was hired as jobstwart and there were plenty of jobs for the Portuguese men. I was able to survive and was able to help my fellow countrymen. Many wanted to pay me, but I never wanted a cent for helping my people.

- That way, you were a union member with benefits?

- Yes. I remember it was I who showed the job site to inspector São Romão when he went to Kitimat. After some time, I was working more for the local union (AFL) than I was for the company.

- What else do you remember from the time you spent in Kitimat?

- Good question! I have many stories that touched me. For example, having to take shifts to use the bed to sleep. That bed was always warm. I slept from midnight to 8 in the morning, another friend of mine from 8 in the morning to 4 in the afternoon and the third one from 4 in the afternoon to midnight. Another thing that touched me profoundly was the psychological trauma I observed in several men. They were honest men, well married, had children, but due to the loneliness, isolation, and sacrifices in general, they were behaving like homosexuals. Unbelievable! I was very young, so my experience in Kitimat marked me deeply. That is the reason I did not stay there very long.

- So what did you do?

- Due to all those stories and to my youth, I

A true portuguese party: Fernando Ramalho, Jess Sousa, Coutinho and António Gonçalves.

decided to head off to Toronto and to visit Portugal.

- When did that happen?

- It was in October of 1956. I boarded the Saturnia with Zé Júlio, Zé Correia, Júlio Batalha, among others. It was during that trip that I met Nina, a young woman I ended up marrying.

- Well, the Saturnia was something like the Love Boat, then!

- Oh, you can say that again. It was a trip I will never forget. I had fun, I forgot what I had suffered in Kitimat and I met Nina.

- Did you get married in Portugal?

- No! I came back to Canada in April of 1957, via New York, to meet Nina's family. We got married on May 18 of that year, in Brooklin. However, I was once again alone with my wife, without family or friends. So, once again I decided to come to Toronto.

José Eduardo Sousa married Nina Maria Lombardo, born in the United States of America, but from an Italian background. The couple has two children: Eduardo Lee, married and living in Italy, and Marisa Lynne, single. However, before the birth of Jess' daughters, many things still happened to him.

- In Toronto, I decided to open a contractors company in partnership with Folgado and Alves. We began building pre-built homes in the fields by the lake. Nina was part of the team: she was the one cooking for us. Before having the houses ready, we were sleeping in the car. I used to carry the material, and my partners were the carpenters.

- How did you step out of the partnership?

- Nina got pregnant and insisted she wanted the baby to be born in the United States. So, in November of 1957, I went back to the States.

Although happy with their daughter's birth, Jess and Nina were not very successful in the United States. Life was hard everywhere!

Jess and Nina Sousa with fado diva Amália Rodrigues when she celebrated her career's 50th anniversary.

- After spending many days looking for a job I was only able to be hired by a car factory, the Yonkers. I was living in Brooklin, an hour and a half to two hours away from my workplace. A short time after, I was laid-off. I spent some time unemployed, and then was able to find a job at the Warendorf and Kaufman Flower Shop, in New York. Delivering flowers had a positive outcome: I met and spoke with many celebrities such as Marilyn Monroe, Joanne Woodward, Arthur Godfrey...

- So it was worth it!

- Yes, it was. After applying for over one hundred jobs in one day, I received a call from two places. One was from the UN's Portuguese Department of Statistics and the other one to work for Varig. It was a hard decision to make! I decided to accept Varig's position. Now, I am glad I did. I have been working there for 29 years.

- But you have been promoted.

- Yes! Now, I am the business manager, in Toronto. Actually, this was the position I was offered to come back to Toronto. I came back on May 20, 1968.

Changing the subject, we decided to ask Jess about the impact the negative news about Brazil has had on Varig.

- It was very negative. The weather, the news about how unsafe it is to be in Brazil, especially in Rio de Janeiro, have greatly affected the company.

- How did you try to solve this problem?

- We tried to show the truth about Brazil, especially to those who were calling us to cancel their trips. Reality is, the floods in Brazil did not affect the tourist sites, such as Copacabana and Leblon.

We also tried to find out if Jess has dedicated in time to the Portuguese community.

- As soon as I arrived in Toronto, I was invited to be part of the Nazaré Recreative Club, since I am from Nazaré. I have also been a member of the First Portuguese Canadian Club and in 1972 I was invited to be the vice-president of the National Soccer League.

- After so many years of Canada, what lesson did you learn?

- The best lesson is the one we learn with life, that is to value every-thing we do and we have. But we

Years went by, but Jess Sousa kept his friendship with Roberto Carlos. They met again, in 1988, at the Roy Thompson Hall, in Toronto.

should value these things at the right time, not when it is too late. We tend to take things for granted.

- At a point in your life, we were also invited to be the master of ceremonies for some shows...

- Oh boy! It was Amadeu Vaz's idea. I presented the brazilian singer Roberto Carlos, the first time he was in Toronto. Good old times!

We left Jess with this memory. Jess Sousa was the first Portuguese man to conquer the top of Varig airlines in Toronto. He is a role model in the community. We wish him all the best.

JMC - May of 1988

(Tabico), Maria de Lourdes Faria Câmara

Town of Capelas, island of São Miguel, Azores

It is a happy and a united family. They all sing different styles of music, but are all very talented for music. They are the Tabico's. Maria de Lurdes Faria was born on February 21, 1947. She began singing fado when she was only 14 years old, at the religious festivities in her hometown. She arrived in Canada in June of 1970, to live with António de Freitas Câmara, a native of the town Santo António Além Capelas, in the island of São Miguel. António de

Tabico, son Tony Tabico, and wife Lurdes Faria.

Freitas Câmara, best known by the nickname Tabico, was born on January 3, 1941 and began singing at the Holy Spirit festivities when he was only 13 years of age. He is a natural joker, an improviser. We can best appreciate his talent and humour when he is asked to improvise when singing.

António Tabico arrived in Canada on March 2, 1970, with a contract to sing in Montreal. He sang, and enchanted those who heard him sing. Lurdes and António married on October 14, 1985, in Toronto.

António Tabico improvising one of his songs.

António has two daughters from his first marriage. With Lurdes, António Tabico had son Anthony Steve Faria da Câmara, on February 25, 1977. Just like his parents, Anthony Steve is an outstanding singer and a fado lover, specially the fado from the city of Coimbra, which he sings passionately everywhere he goes. Anthony – known as Toninho Tabico – was an outstanding student. Besides singing, Lurdes and António Tabico founded the enterprise Tabico Catering, in 1978, and opened the family restaurant "O Tabico", in Toronto, in 1996.

Back in 1971, António Tabico, Lurdes Faria, Mariano Rego and Gabriel Teves founded the group Caravana Açores, an artistic group, which made many tours in North America and in the Azores. For 14 years, António Tabico was also the chair of the committee responsible for the festivities of Senhor da Pedra, at St. Agnes church, in Toronto, with Father Antero de Melo. Lately, António Tabico was one of the founders of the festivities of Nossa Senhora da Luz at St. Mathew's church.

Master Tabico and son Tony Câmara during a pilgrimage to the Azores.

From a very early age, António Tabico has been a pilgrim involved in the Holy Week religious pilgrimages. He is the founding member of the Portuguese Canadian Association of Pilgrims of São Miguel. Tabico's son joined the group when he was very little and has since been an active pilgrim going with his father and a group of Portuguese Canadian pilgrims to the Azores.

From left to right: the bishop of the Azores, Monsigneur Resendes, Consul geral João Perestrello, António Tabico, Professor José Carlos Teixeira, Mrs and Mr. Lamartine Silva during the Conference of Azorean Culture.

António Tabico, while a member of Caravana Açores, recorded eight LPs and four singles and launched two videos about the Azores and about São Miguel island. Recently, he wrote a book about the pilgrimages to the Azores titled "Pilgrims, the faith of a people". Tony Câmara Jr. has also recorded two CDs, one with fados from Coimbra and another one with ballads.

The Tabico's: a family marked by success and happiness.

JMC - 1999

Tavares, Afonso Maria

Town of Rabo de Peixe, Island of São Miguel, Azores

Afonso Tavares in his garden.

Afonso Maria Tavares was born in the town of Rabo de Peixe, in the island of São Miguel, Azores, on March 13, 1929. His life is full of drama, difficulties and many victories. Tired of his life as a farmer, Afonso decided to try his fate in Canada, as soon as he finished his military service in São Miguel. After passing all the inspections in Lisbon, Afonso boarded the Saturnia to immigrate to Canada. He arrived in Halifax on May 4, 1953, with eighteen other fellow travelers.

From Halifax, Afonso traveled to Montreal, and was taken to St. Michèlle, in the northern part of the city, where he worked until October of that year. Afonso spent the winter in Montreal and, in April, he went to work at the Seven Islands, in Labrador, with other friends from Rabo de Peixe who traveled with him. In 1955, Afonso decided to move to Toronto, choosing Brampton as his place to settle down. He believes he was the first Portuguese person to live in Brampton which at the time was a city of ten thousand people.

For two years, Afonso worked in green-houses. He fell sick and had to be hospitalized in Brampton and then moved to Toronto's General Hospital. The doctor's diagnosed him with tuberculosis, a diagnosis which proved, later on, to be wrong. Still in 1957, CNR invited him to go to Montreal to work as translator for a group of one hundred and some Portuguese men who had come from the Azores. Afonso left the hospital and went to Montreal. At the end of his appointment as translator, Afonso decided to try his luck in Vancouver where he lived for six months. Due to his critical illness, Afonso returned to Toronto and went again to the hospital to find out if he was still suffering from tuberculosis. Unable to come with a conclusive diagnosis, the doctors suggested and sent him to a mental institute in

In Lisbon, a group of men from São Miguel island who came to Canada aboard the Saturnia on May 8, 1953. Top row: Evaristo Almeida, José da Silva, José Bento, António do Couto, Constantino da Silva, Manuel Machado, Guilherme Rodrigues and Jaime Pacheco. Middle row: Armando Vieira, Afonso Maria Tavares, Hélio Vasconcelos, João Martins, Manuel Arruda and Manuel Vieira. Bottom row: Moreira, José Martins, Mário Ferreira da Costa, José Martins and Várzea.

Milton. At the end of six months, feeling depressed with his situation, Afonso decided to return to Portugal. It was May of 1958. At that time, he was already building the movie theatre Cine Mira Mar, with the money he has saved while working in Canada and decided to conclude it. Back home, Afonso thought about his illness and consulted with a german doctor who told him that his illness was caused by loneliness. The doctor's prescription was "work and get married".

In Montreal, at the S. Joseph's Oratory: Hélio Vasconcelos, José da Silva, Evaristo Almeida, José Branco, Jaime Pacheco, Afonso Maria Tavares among others.

So it was done. Afonso was dating Natália de Jesus Gonçalves, a native from his hometown and decided to marry her. The ceremony took place in 1959. With Natália, Afonso has son Nuno and daughter Helena do Rosário. Pregnant with the third child, Natália passed away, in 1969, from labour complications before getting to the hospital.

Having to provide for this family and in debt due to the construction of Cine Mira Mar, which was not as successful as he thought it would be, Afonso was forced to emigrate. Back in 1960, soon after his son's birth, Afonso went to Bermuda, sponsored by his late brother Filipe Maria, avoiding Canada due to the "tuberculosis case" which forced him to leave the country.

In Bermuda, where he lived for four years, he worked for a good boss, Peter Rego, who was the son of an Azorean couple. Although illegal, Afonso was able to work at a vegetable farm, with the help of Peter Rego.

Still unhappy with his situation, Afonso decided to return to the country he was trying to avoid. He landed in Montreal. He was caught by the Immigration Department, but after one day he received the application to become a landed immigrant. A year later, Afonso became a Canadian citizen. He returned to the Azores and lived there until his wife passed way while in labour.

After the Carnation Revolution, which took place on April 25, 1974, Afonso Maria Tavares was elected the political representative for Rabo de Peixe, a position he had for two years. After several months, Afonso decided to marry a second time. Still in Rabo de Peixe, Afonso married Inês do Espírito Santo, the sister of the bishop of Macau, Paulo José Tavares. Married a second time and the theatre sold to another company, Afonso Tavares decided to emigrate definitely to Canada with

In Bermuda, Afonso at the vegetable farm where he is used to work.

his wife and children. Afonso returned to Brampton. His first job was in construction, but some months later found a job in the cleaning departament of Termoelectric, where he worked for 18 years until he retired in 1994.

Afonso is now a dedicated landscaper. While in Bermuda, he learned how to work with plants and flowers. Now, his Brampton home shows how much he learned. Afonso is growing more than 1,500 plants a year, which he sells in the spring. The money he makes he gives to charity.

Afonso was one of the members who raised money and helped in the construction of

José, Helena, Ana, Nuno, Mrs and Mr Afonso Tavares on Nuno's wedding day.

Nossa Senhora da Fátima church, in Brampton. He is also founding member of the Portuguese Community Centre of Brampton. The club was formed in 1980. He was also founding member of the Association "Friends from Rabo de Peixe" in 1998, today known as "Association of the Friends from Rabo de Peixe". At the Malta Parket, in Brampton, there is a sign with Afonso's name in recognition for what he has done in maintaining it.

Since he has retired, Afonso has been dedicating himself to social causes. He helped his nephew, Father José Domingos Tavares, raise funds for a church in Mozambique. Afonso has been going to jails to bring some words of comfort to the prisoners. He is a short, but active man.

Afonso has recently donated many of his works and souvenirs to the Gallery of Portuguese Pioneers.

JMC - 2000

Teixeira, Manuel

Town of Celorico de Basto, province of Minho

He has faced many hardships in life. He has always been truthful to his values. He is Manuel Teixeira, born in the village of Ribas, in Celorico de Basto, a town located in the province of Minho. Manuel was born on June 1, 1927. He is a very active man. Manuel went to the Freião Seminary, in the northern city of Braga, until the age of 18. Not finding his vocation to become a priest, Manuel decided to leave the seminary and went to the city of Santarém, north of Lisbon, where he completed his degree on Agronomy.

John Dias, Rosalina Teixeira and Manuel Teixeira at CIRV Fm, in Toronto.

When he finished his degree, Manuel returned home and found a job in Braga, in the Agrarian Society. During this time, he met Rosalina de Fátima da Costa Machado and fell immediately in love with her. The couple got married on November 29, 1953. The couple's oldest daughter, Maria de Fátima, was born in the small northern town of Amares. As a good catholic, and because he spoke French and English well, he worked for some time in the sanctuary of Fatima, the town where the Virgin Mary appeared to the three shepard children in 1917. Together with friends Joaquim Tavares de Matos and Manuel Lourenço, Manuel Teixeira worked as translator for the tourists who visited Fatima.

While practicing his language skills, Manuel met Father Raul Gagnon, from Montreal, with whom he became friends. Since he could not become a priest, as he thought he could as a child, Manuel thought about the possibility of immigrating to another country. With the same friends he worked with in Fatima, Manuel took off to Canada aboard the Greek ship Arosa Star.

Manuel arrived in Quebec on April 20, 1955. Manuel stayed in Montreal, his late friend Joaquim went to Quebec city and the late Manuel Lourenço went to Vancouver. A true devout of our lady of Fatima, Manuel – who still had Father Gagnon's contact – went to Notre Dame cathedral, in Montreal, to speak to his friend Father Gagnon. On the way to Notre Dame, he

In 1966, at Maria do Sameiro de Sá's tobacco farm, in Strathroy. Manuel Teixeira, João Pinheiro and wife Maria Júlia, Maria do Sameiro Sá, José Pinheiro and the Teixeira's children: Fátima, Francisco and Filomena.

encountered two Portuguese men from the Azores who helped him find a room to stay. Back then, people in Montreal knew little about Portugal. Actually, most of them only knew Our Lady of Fatima and dictator Salazar.

His knowledge of agronomy together with Father Gagnon's help allowed Manuel to find a job easily at the city's botanic garden where he had to look after the treatment and preservation of trees. While working, Manuel went to the University of Montreal to get his degree in agronomy from Portugal recognized. The process took six months. He decided to continue his studies.

From left to right: the friends Pinheiro, Manuel Teixeira, John Dias and consul general João Perestrello.

At the University of Montreal he studied Humanities and science. Between 1960 and 1970, Manuel worked as a teacher for the Montreal Catholic Board teaching English and French. Manuel Teixeira worked for the city's botanic garden until 1960, the same year he transferred to the Rothmans, Benson & Hedges where he worked until July 1, 1987.

Manuel retired when he was 60 years, but he chose to keep himself active as a volunteer in many social initiatives.

Back in 1959, Manuel was nominated immigration councilor for Quebec's immigration department. In 1960, he was a trustee for the Quebec's ministry of education. Manuel Teixeira served as president of the Ethnic Association of Quebec. His many years of volunteer work earned him, in the 70s, the queen's merit medal. The former prime-minister Pierre Trudeau gave him the Order of Canada medal in 1983. Together with Manuel Mota, Carlos Sousa, Serafim Teixeira, Domingos Reis and António Galego, Manuel Teixeira founded the Portuguese Catholic Union of Canada. From here, Manuel was behind the creation of many other initiatives, like the creation of the newspaper "Voz de Portugal" (Portugal's Voice), the newspaper "Jornal do Emigrante" – Manuel being its owner – and the Federation of Portuguese Organizations of Quebec. In 1960, he created the radio show "Hora Portuguesa" on CKS.

In 1997, Manuel Teixeira decided to go back to Portugal. He lives in the town of Amares, in the district of Braga. Due to his condition and life experience, Manuel was invited to be the vice-president of the Firefighters of Amares and has been an honorary member of many associations. He is now actively writing for many magazines and newspapers.

JMC - 2000

In 1983, at the Floral Clock in Niagara Falls: Maria Júlia Pinheiro, Rosalina and Manuel Teixeira.

Teixeira, Professor José Carlos

Town of Ribeira Grande, São Miguel island, Azores

José Carlos Teixeira was born in the town of Ribeira Grande, in the island of São Miguel, Azores, in 1959. When he was 18 years old, José Carlos emigrated to Canadá and settled down in Montreal. There, he studied French in high school and went to the University of Quebec

where he got a B. Sc. in 1983 and a M. Sc. in 1986. For his master's dissertation, José Carlos defended a thesis on the Portuguese community. From here, José Carlos decided to move to Toronto to continue his studies at York University. In 1993, José Carlos finished his Ph.D. in Geography, one of the few students of Portuguese descent to obtain a Ph.D. While studying, Carlos Teixeira kept his interest in the Portuguese community. From 1994 to 1996 he was hired by York University and in September of 1996 he was hired by the University of Toronto to teach geography at the Scarborough and St. George campus.

The founders of the Gallery of Portuguese Pioneers Manuel da Costa, José Mário Coelho and Bernardete Gouveia awarding Professor José Carlos Teixeira the honorary membership. In the picture, we also see professor Teixeira's wife, Maria.

Professor José Carlos Teixeira is the director of the American Ethnic Geographer, a magazine which focuses on the study of urban populations, social geography and community migrations. This magazine has been an ethnic entrepreneurial initiative in North America which studies with particular interest the Portuguese communities of Toronto and Montreal.

Professor José Carlos Teixeira also writes for the Canadian Geographer, the Urban Geography, the Great Lakes Geographer, the Professional Geographer, the Portuguese Studies Review, the Canadart, the Revue Européene des Migrations Internationales. He has collaborated with the Encyclopedia of Canada's Peoples, edited in 1999, by the University of Toronto Press.

Prof. José Carlos Teixeira with Professor Aida Baptista at the Azorean Cultural Week, in Toronto.

Professor José Carlos Teixeira, the pioneer Afonso Tavares, the regional director of Portuguese communities Alzira Silva listening to the President of the Azores', Carlos César, homage to the Portuguese pioneers.

He is the co-author, with Gilles Lavigne, of "The Portuguese in Canada: From Cod Fishers to Urban Islanders", published in 2000 by the University of Toronto Press.

Professor Teixeira is an enthusiast of the Gallery of Portuguese Pioneers, in Toronto and is its Honorary Member since 2003. He has also been an active member of the committee, which is trying to open the Immigrants Museum in the town of Ribeira Grande, in the Azores.

His love for the Azores and the Portuguese communities in Canada has made him get involved in many projects. Professor Teixeira has also participated in many symposiums, conferences and cultural weeks. From 2003, Professor Carlos Teixeira has been teaching at the University of Okanagan, in British Columbia. He keeps researching the Portuguese community and helping many colleagues from different universities in Canada and the United States.

Professor Carlos Teixeira was recently awarded the Merit Medal from the Portuguese Government for his outstanding work in the universities and about the Portuguese community.

JMC-2005

Professor José Carlos Teixeira and Professor Vitor Pereira da Rosa, from Ottawa, at the Portuguese Consulate in Toronto.

President of the University of the Azores, Vasco Garcia, Professor Onésimo Teotónio de Almeida and Professor José Carlos Teixeira.

Tomás, Mário Coelho

Lisbon

We should always remember those who contributed to the development and expansion of the Portuguese community in Canada. It is the case of the late Mário Coelho Tomás who dedicated his life to family and the community. Mário Coelho Tomás was born in Lisbon, on September 20, 1931. After completing his elementary school, he went to a professional school where he became a welder. This course and a will to have a better life took Mário to France. He did not like it in France and decided to come back to Lisbon.

Maria Beatriz Tomás at the First Portuguese Canadian Club receiving from Walter Lopes and Lucy Cardoso the silver platter honouring the late Mário Coelho Tomás, in 1991.

In 1973, the Tomás family with grandmother Dulce Henriques Rego.

In 1955, he emigrated to Canada with his friend – and later an entrepreneur – Amadeu Vaz.

In 1956, Mário Tomás decided to go to Portugal on holidays. During this time, he met Maria Beatriz Henriques Rego who was born in the town of Bombarral, north of Lisbon, on June 17, 1930. It was love at first sight and they married months after meeting each other. In 1957, Mário and Maria Beatriz decided to move to Canada. They began their new life in Ottawa, where the couple's oldest daughter was born. Mary Betty was born on July 19, 1958. Before becoming a professional welder, Mário Tomás worked many different jobs, both in Ottawa and in Toronto. In Toronto, the couple saw the birth of Mary Jenny, on July 25, 1960 and José Luís, on March 9, 1967. Not happy with his life, Mário Tomás decided to start importing newspapers from Portugal. He was able to get the exclusive to the soccer newspaper A Bola. He began his business at home where he sold the newspapers and magazines from Portugal.

Businesses were growing and Mário decided to ask the owner of Lisbon Bakery to let him sell the newspapers there. From there, the couple decided to open their own place on March 5, 1965. Thus was born the Portuguese Book Store, on Nassau Street, in Toronto. In the early days of the business, Mário Tomás decided to keep his job as welder while his wife looked after the business. Although some people criticized the fact that someone was selling records and newspapers from Portugal, Tomás never gave up and his business was one of the most successful ones of our community. Some time later, Mário was forced to quit his job at the Havilland to help his wife in the bookstore. He was above all a dedicated father and husband. Mário was also an active member of our community and never said no to any initiative.

Fate is sometimes very cruel to human beings. During a trip to Portugal, where he was spending holidays, on October 9, 1986, he was the victim of fateful car accident near the town

Mary Betty Tomás with daughter Charlotte, welcoming the President of Portugal, Jorge Sampaio and Portugal's First Lady, Maria José Ritta, at the Portuguese Book Store.

Nelly Furtado in the Portuguese Book Store among her fans.

In 1956, Maria Beatriz Tomás signing the book the day of her wedding.

of Castro Verde, in the province of Alentejo. Mário Tomás Coelho and his cousin Felicidade de Jesus both died at the scene. Maria Beatriz was saved by a bystander who took her from the burning car. It was a drama for the family and for the Portuguese community of Toronto. Still life goes on.

Maria Beatriz decided to take care of her family and the family's business. The children were helping their mother in the store after school. In February of 1996, they closed the store on Nassau Street and moved it to a bigger and better place on Dundas Street where it still is today.

Today, the Portuguese Book Store is administered by Maria and Mário's children. Maria Beatriz is a proud woman, a happy mother and an accomplished grand-mother of six. Betty is married to Gino Ciavarrella and has two daughters; Jenny married to António Coimbra and has two children; José Luís is married to Ana and has also two daughters.

After so many setbacks, the family is now a happy one. The business is still successful just like the late Mário Tomás had envisioned. We wish them all the best!

JMC - 2000

1956: wedding picture.

Trindade, Augusto Felix

Santos-o-Velho neighbourhood, Lisbon

Augusto Felix Trindade shows the natural features of someone born in one of Lisbon's many neighbourhoods. He is a joker and someone with a great sense of humour. Augusto Felix Trindade was born on January 29, 1931.

- When I left Lisbon I had no idea what was awaiting me. It was one of those adventures we do not come to understand how they happen in the first place. – Felix began

Felix Trindade today. A man with a happy and successful life.

telling us. – I met Bernardino on the way to Canada and became close friends while sharing our life stories aboard the Britania from the Canadian Pacific airlines.

- Did you arrive in Canada that same day?

- Yes! On May 28, 1960. We got in trouble as soon as we landed. – Felix told us laughing at his own stories. At Durval's airport, in Montreal, we saw a restaurant and decided to enter because we were very hungry. An employee from CP took us to a motel and the following day we took off to Toronto. In Toronto, we went to Alberto's place, a friend of Bernardino's. That same day, I rented a room from a Yugoslavian woman for $5 a week. Bernardino stayed at Alberto's place.

- Did you find a job right away?

From left to right: Felix Trindade, Vince Monticelo, Carlos Pombo and Augusto, the members of the band 4 Pesos.

- No! For a week I could not find anything. One of those days, I met a Portuguese who told me about the Ramalho's restaurant. I went there and met the Ramalhos, Mimi and António Sousa.

- Did you speak English when you came to Canada?

- No! Not even a word! But I resolved my problem easily. I used to go to the dances at the International Institute on College and Crawford. With the girls I met there I began managing my English skills. I still feel sorry that the International Institute closed down. Well, now that we are talking about speaking English, I just remembered. The first week we arrived in Toronto, Bernardino and I went to the immigration department to look for a job. It used to be on Bloor near the Varsity Stadium. Once there, we could not find the door. Bernardino knew a few words in English and asked a man that was passing by the whereabouts of the door. The guy pointed and said "over there". Since none of us knew what "over there" meant, we decided to ask another man. When he heard us asking for the "over there", the man looked at us with a strange face and left without even saying a word. When we found out the meaning of "over there", we couldn't stop laughing.

- Did you at least get a job?

- Yes! I went to the woods. I had to operate a woodchopper machine. It was so dusty I thought I was going to die. But I needed a job, so I stayed there. I was working for the Zelacto Co. for .95 cents an hour.

- Were you there for a long time?

- For a year and half. A friend of mine from the Azores knew I had worked in the naval states in Portugal and tried to find me a job at the Leavins & Brothers. They built boat and airplane parts. I got the job and worked there for about three years. I began making $1.70 an hour and was making $2.75 when I left. It was a good job. They used to lay off people in the winter time, but always kept me there.

- Why did you leave this company?

- I got a job, making more money, at the Gran Piane Marine, in Oakville. I was there for six months working in the making of yachts. I left because of the music.

- Does that mean that you began dedicating yourself to an artistic life?

- Yes! Still, for some time, while singing at the El Mocambo, I sold houses. I worked in the Real Estate business with Ilídio Caires who was from Madeira Island.

- So you were the man who could play the seven instruments, as we usually say...

- Yes, more or less. I entered the entertainment life in 1961. Maria do Rego, most commonly known as Ribeirinha, and I formed a duet and went to perform at the Old Spain, on Bloor Street. At the end of two weeks we left and decided to form a quartet. Mariano contacted Orlando Ferreira, a guy from Madeira island, who played the accordion and I contacted Carlos Pombo, a drummer from Lisbon. We rehearsed and played a few shows for free at the International Institute. From there, we were hired to play at the El Mocambo.

- Were you together, as a quartet, for a long time?

- Yes! The first one to leave the group of Orlando, but he was replaced by Manuel Soares. I still miss those times when I was singing and playing. I loved singing great hits such as Granada, Malagana, Cucurucucu, Paloma, and many others.

- Did you record any album?

- Yes! Mariano Rego had the idea and we went along. Two of those songs were my own: Any and Emigrante. The record sold well, but I never saw an penny from it.

- Did you do any tours?

- Yes! We obviously sang in Toronto, but went also to Montreal, New York, New Jersey, Boston, Cambridge, Waterbury, Denabury, Norther, New Bedford, Providence and Fall River.

- Did you sing with anyone famous?

- I met Rui Mascarenhas with whom we had dinner at the Radio City. There I spoke with Tony Curtis and Sammy Davis Junior. I even have a picture with them.

- At a certain point in your life, you decided to form your own band...

- Yes, that was around 1967. The best musician in the group of Mariano Rego, but he never liked to change. I began feeling the need to change our repertoire if you wanted to continue being successful. So I decided to form my own band with an Italian guy Vince Monticelo, with Augusto and Carlos Pombo. Vince ended up marrying Fernanda, the group's lead singer.

- Did you record any albums with your group?

- Of course! I recorded an LP and one single. I counted with the help of pianist Claudio Medeiros, with Judy Evans and Carrie Romo. Both the LP and the single sold well.

- 4 pesos, the name of your band, was known for the number of female singers it had.

- Yes! You know, young men like admiring young women. So we decided to even have dancers and Carrie Romo, Fernanda, the Hermanas Mexicanas and Carmen were the lead singers. Our band was full of life.

- You are now a businessman?

- Not exactly now. From 1980 to 1982, my wife and I ran a model school. It was called the Barbizone Modeling School. I had many Portuguese students. The school had nine teachers.

- Why did you leave music?

- In 1974 I found myself to tired. I went to the doctor who recommended some rest and a different job. I decided to rest because I love my life too much. So, I began going early to bed and my health got better. Music was good but it had to come to an end. To sleep only three to four hours a night was not very healthy.

- Do you remember any particular story you want to share with us?

Carmen, Felix Trindade, Carrie Romo, Caló and Augusto performing. The good old times!

- I have many stories to share... One day, still in the band with Mariano Rego, we went to play in Massachussets. That area is known for the many restaurants it has. At the party, in a ranch owned by a rich man from Madeira, we met this guy who owned a construction company in the United States. He invited us to eat at his place. When I arrived, he kept on telling me he wanted his daughters to marry a Portuguese guy. That's when I realized he wanted me to flirt with one of his daughters. They were actually good looking, but what the hell?!!!

- And now?

- Now? I am keeping myself busy. I work for myself. I dedicate myself to photography, just for pleasure. I went to the University of Toronto where I got a degree in Graphic Designing. Now I am a freelancer and own the MHW Wilkie and Associates. I am also dedicating myself to the business of importing different objects from other countries, which I then sell to the public.

This is the way Felix Trindade is. He was the pioneer among Portuguese lead singers, in Canada. Still today, Felix keeps the smile and the attitude of a native from Lisbon. He misses the good old times, but lives his life with the same care-free spirit he always had. The community owes a lot to him.

JMC - January of 1989

Vaz, Amadeu Caria

City of Nazaré

To interview our pioneers is always a chance to remember the past dramas and glories, which marked the life of each person who came from Portugal and who helped form our Portuguese community. It is a way to remember the times that passed.

One of the pioneers who made a difference was Amadeu Caria Vaz. Amadeu was born in the beautiful town of Nazaré, on October 20, 1928. He is married to Maria Albertina Duarte Mafra, who is also from Nazaré. The couple has two daughters: Júlia Rosa, born in Nazaré, and Elizabeth, born in Toronto. Amadeu left Lisbon aboard the Vulcania, on May 1, 1955, arriving in Halifax on May 6.

After a tiring train trip, Amadeu arrived in Toronto on May 7, 1955.

- I traveled with 250 other Portuguese men. I don't even remember any of their names. It has been 32 years. – Amadeu began telling us. – I remember the late Mário Tomás, Júlio Batalha, Justino Vinagre and brother Joel, Luís Francisco and his late brother, Carlos Moreira…

- Did you all come to Toronto? – We asked him.

- Not all of us. As soon as we arrived in Toronto, we saw ourselves getting into adventures. Since we had a contract to work at different farms, the late Mário Tomás and I went to Windsor to pick up potatoes. When we got there, we noticed that we had to pick up the potatoes with our hands. We did not like it and left right away. We arrived in Windsor at 11 am and went back twelve hours later. We didn't change our clothes. We were in deep trouble. Because we didn't accept the job, the return ticket had to be paid by us. So, carrying our own luggage and not knowing a word of English, much less the way back to Toronto, we were lost for a while. At a certain point, we met a guy who indicated us the way to the station and we took the bus back to Toronto. Because I

Rosa Maria, Roberto Carlos and Amadeu Vaz at the Imperio Restaurant, in Toronto.

didn't speak English, I kept telling the guys at the ticket booth "yes" to every single question. All I know is that two tickets cost me $7, a fortune back then. When we got to Toronto, we went to Isabel Gomes' place and told her our adventure. Ramalho heard our story and asked us for the tickets. He looked at the tickets and couldn't stop laughing. I had bought two-way tickets. The following day we went to the station and they reimbursed the difference.

- You mentioned Isabel Gomes. Who is she?

- Isabel Gomes is married to Manuel Gomes. They are a couple from Madeira Island who helped the Portuguese men with meals and a place to stay. Their home was one of the meeting points for the Portuguese pioneers.

- What was your first job in Canada?

- For three weeks I was looking for a job but never got anything. After this time, I got a job at the railroad, where I worked from May to October. When the cold winter arrived, I came back to Toronto and went to work for the Benvenut Hotel, on Avenue Road. In 1957, I went to Kitimat to work in construction. In October of 1958, I came to Toronto and for the following ten years I kept on working in construction. That's the life of an immigrant. It is perhaps the best school in life.

In July of 1968, Amadeu decided to leave construction and began selling records. A decision that changed his life.

Amadeu's first show as a businessman. From left to right: Armando Viegas, Natalina José, Artur Garcia, Amadeu Vaz and Manuel Mira, in 1986.

- I have always been fascinated by business and the artists' world. So, with my brother Luis, I opened the first record store. It was called Portugal Records Co, on Augusta Avenue. Mário Tomás had already opened his bookstore. In collaboration with the company Penha, from the United States, I organized the first tour of Raul Solnado in North America.* The very first tour I organized outside Canada was with the group of Natalina José, Artur Garcia and Mário Simões, in March of 1968. This was my first step and it has been a never ending story until today.

- As an entrepreneur, which tour pleased you the most?

- The biggest and the one I enjoyed the most was with the brazilian music king Roberto Carlos, in 1972 and again in 1973.

- Of all the artists you worked with, which one left you the best impression?

- I believe they are all my friends. I cannot complain about any of them. However, I need to single out the admirable Roberto Carlos and ultimately Nicolau Breyner.

- Besides organizing shows, you have also been involved in the radio business.

- That's right! I was the first one to open a closed-circuit radio station in Portuguese.

It was called Portugal Radio Club, located on College Street, right beside Imperio Restaurant. Luis and I had the radio show for about six years.

Amadeu was also one of the founding members of the First Portuguese Canadian Club, as he remembers.

- The Portuguese club was born in 1956, on Nassau Street. When I came to Toronto from Kitimat, the club was born. I tried to get a committee to get the club running and to change its location to Augusta Avenue. The members of the committee were Américo Carvalho, Jordão the carpenter, Chico Alentejano, António Alentejano, Luís Francisco, Ricardo, myself and many others. We organized many shows to raise funds, many of which with Mariano Rego.

- Who was the "old Alves"? – We asked trying to solve a mystery many people were curious to find out.

- "Old Alves" was the chair of the commission where I was also a member. He was a good man. Back then, he had already been in Canada for at least 20 years. He lived close to Niagara Falls and no longer spoke Portuguese well. He heard that there was a group of Portuguese men living in Toronto and took off trying to find our whereabouts. Old Alves was from Lisbon. He was a good friend of the men and the club.

- What was your function at the club?

- I was a director and was responsible for the organization of the soccer commission with Ricardo Francisco.

- We know you left the club because you didn't agree with certain things...

- Yes! At the time there was the attack on the Santa Maria ship, some members began making the club a political gathering and I left.

After 32 years of Canada, Amadeu is a happy, successful man. Is he thinking of returning to his native Portugal?

- No! I am staying here. I will always go to Portugal on holidays or on business.

We wish Amadeu the continuation of much success and many other tours to come. We must also thank him for everything he has done for our community, specially in the promotion of Portuguese artists.

* Raul Solnado is one of the most famous comedy actors in Portugal.

JMC - November of 1987

Velosa, Jaime Fernandes

Town of Santa Luzia, city of Funchal, Madeira Island

Many years after the first encounter, Jaime Velosa and José António Gonçalves meet again at the Tropical Nights, in Mississauga.

Jaime Fernandes Velosa has an interesting life story to share. He was born in Santa Luzia, a small town in the city of Funchal, on Madeira Island, on May 21, 1933. His love for soccer took him to the Azores. After playing a few seasons for the team Nacional da Madeira, Jaime got a contract to play for the Clube Desportivo Praiense, the team from Terceira island. Jaime played for the Praiense for three seasons, leaving this team to join the rival Lusitânia for another two seasons.

While in the Azores, Jaime met Olga Maria Furtado da Costa, a native from the city of Ponta Delgada, in the island of São Miguel, where she was born on November 28, 1940. Jaime and Olga Maria married in Terceira island in 1958. The hardships of life forced Jaime Velosa to consider emigrating to Canada. Without his wife, Jaime tried his luck in the new country where he arrived on April 18, 1966. His first job was at Reagal Toy. Jaime also worked in cleaning and sales. As a retail salesman, Jaime had the chance to travel all over Canada and the United States. In 1969, he got a job at an Aluminum factory. Later in 1974, Jaime decided to open his own company, the Madeira Azores Aluminum, specializing in home and commercial repairs.

Jaime and Olga Maria have six children. The seventh one, Maria Dulce, died in

An historic picture. Standing: Juvenal Belo, Tiago Alves, António Pereira, Manuel Branco and father Mendes. Sitting: J. Patrício, José Manuel Quintal, Juvenal de Freitas, Jaime Velosa, António Pontes and Martinho Vasconcelos.

1960 when she was only four years old. Four of his children were born in Terceira: Ricardo, born on August 14, 1963; Maria da Graça, born March 13, 1959; Ana Paula, born November 8, 1961; and Helena, born March 6, 1968. Jaime's youngest son was already born in Toronto: Kimmy, born April 14, 1971.

Jaime has always been a dedicated individual to all the cultural events related to his native Madeira island. He never misses any event organized by the Canadian Madeira Club, specially at the Madeira Park. Since 1966, Jaime has been an active member of the Canadian Madeira Club, and has also served as a director. From 1974 to 1978, Jaime also served as president of the club.

Always creative and trying to help his neighbour, Jaime was the first one to create a Christmas party for children, in 1970, where the Canadian Madeira Club decided to give toys to all the children of the club. He was also the organizer of the first New Year's Eve party at the club.

At The Boat restaurant, Jaime Velosa talks to Ângela and Alberto João Jardim during the 25th anniversary of the Portuguese community.

Jaime and Olga Velosa with children, children-in-law and grandchildren.

In 1975, Jaime decided to bring new blood to the Canadian Madeira Club and organized the first Miss Madeira pageant.

During the celebrations of the 25th anniversary of the Portuguese Community, Jaime Velosa was one of the people responsible for the visit of the President of Madeira, Alberto João Jardim, to Canada. Jaime also invited the poet José António Gonçalves to participate in the club's anniversary. As he now confesses, Jaime lost a lot of money and business when working for the club, but does not regret any aspect.

Nowadays, Jaime Velosa still has his business and spends a lot of his time in Florida. He is planning to spend a lot more time in Florida with his wife, when he retires. Jaime is also planning to visit Madeira more often. After a life of hard work and dedication to the community, Jaime deserves to enjoy the beauties life has to offer.

(Jamie Velosa passed away in 2004).

JMC - 1999

Veloso, Carlos Manuel da Silva

Town São Pedro, island of São Miguel, Azores

He was touched by the passion of electronics at a very young age and has never left it since then. Carlos Manuel da Silva Veloso, owner of Advanced Electronics, felt he had a vocation for electronics when he was only 8 years old. After taking a professional course about radio electronics, when he was 14 years old, Carlos began building electric circuits.

Carlos Manuel da Silva Veloso was born in São Pedro, a town in the island of São Miguel, in the Azores, on October 29, 1938. In 1965, he moved to the town of São Sebastião. Carlos began getting noticed in the city of Ponta Delgada, already in 1959, when he

The Veloso couple.

began arranging emissions in churches to transmit the mass for the ill, and the sound services for the entire island. Carlos participated in the first television experiences in the Azores. At the time, Carlos was member of the firm Sonar. Due to the natural limitations and isolation imposed by the island, Carlos began thinking bigger and convinced himself that he needed to leave the island. He had the

The Velosos with children. A happy family!

Carlos Veloso presenting the Videophone.

Electronics course from the Commercial and Industrial School and had completed another one by correspondence from the National School of California, in 1963. With these two courses in hand, Carlos did not hesitate when opportunity presented itself to immigrate to Canada. For six months, Carlos visited eleven different cities in Canada to choose the one he felt was the most adequate to settle down. He went back to São Miguel and while living there decided that Toronto would be his destination. Meanwhile, Carlos opened an electronics repair store known as Pereira & Pereira. Carlos also decided to marry his long time girlfriend Élia Maria Lourenço Couto, a native from the island of São Miguel. The wedding took place on June 13, 1965 and the honeymoon was in Toronto.

As soon as he arrived in Toronto, Carlos began working immediately in electronics, going from home to home to fix appliances. While working,

Carlos decided to go back to school. He went to Centennial College and later on to the Radio College of Canada. In 1968/69, when he graduated from college, Carlos got a job as inspector at an electronics factory. He was also working part-time at Speedy Auto-Radio & TV. Later on, Speedy Auto-Radio & TV hired him full time as technical supervisor for seven years.

At the end of seven years at Speedy Auto-Radio & TV, Carlos had many Portuguese clients and decided to open his own store. In 1973, Carlos opened his store on Dundas, near the intersection with Dovercourt. At the end of seven years, and with the business expanding, Carlos felt the need to move to a bigger and wider store. That's when he moved a block to the west to open Advanced Electronics.

Brian's graduation day from York University.

The Velosos have three children, all born in Toronto and all with degrees from the university: Dori Linda, born on November 22, 1970 and a graduate from the University of Guelph; Nancy, born on July 11, 1972 and a graduate from the University of London; and Brian, born on August 8, 1976 and graduate in economics from York University.

In 1998, the family Veloso celebrated the 25th anniversary of Advanced Electronics. Carlos has received many awards and recognitions: Qualified Dealer, 100% Guarantee Service, Medal of Excellence for 25 years of service for the RCA, among others. In the 70s, Carlos Veloso founded the Proculture Society with friends Manuel Mira, António Sousa and Humberto Carvalho.

One of Carlos' biggest successes was the presentation of Videophone, a televised communication device that expanded throughout Canada and Portugal. Carlos is above all a great individual always ready to help his neighbour.

JMC-1999

Vesga, Zé da

Town of Santa Maria

de Lamas

Zé da Vesga, the artistic name of José Ferreira Soares, is a native of the town of Santa Maria de Lamas, where he was born on March 21, 1939. From a very young age, Zé da Vesga moved to the town of Ovar, in mainland Portugal – where he still has a home. Zé da Vesga is considered the best songwriter and composer of

Zé da Vesga receiving the Merit Medal from Ovar's City Hall, in Portugal.

all the Portuguese communities of North America. Zé da Vesga is a poet with a fine sensitivity, a natural melody to his lyrics and a composer of great value.

When he was only 8 years old, Zé da Vesga went to the musical schools of Ovar and Boa União. By the age of 10, Zé was integrating a musical band. He studied saxophone, among other instruments. By the age of 14, Zé became the Sax and soprano player for the Ovarense musical band.

While doing his military service, Zé da Vesga played in the infantry 6, in the city of Porto, while studying music at

Zé da Vesga and Catarina Cardeal in one Song Festival organized by CIRV, after conquering the first place. In the picture we also see the singer Emanuel from Portugal, Frank Alvarez and José Mário Coelho.

the Oporto's conservatory. He was elected to play for the police's musical band of Oporto, directed by Sergeant Gomes.

Throughout his life, Zé da Vesga has played in many bands and groups, such as the Banda Marcial 1º de Agosto de Coimbrões, Vila Nova de Gaia, Filarmónica de Matosinhos, Satélite, Pop 6, Tony Biscaia, The Lords, Muje among many others. He also founded the musical school of A. Dias Simões, in Ovar.

Nowadays, Zé da Vesga is a member of the Portuguese Society of Authors – SPA. He has also won many song festivals: CIRV's song festival in 1992 with the song Amante d'Alma Inteira; in 1993, he won first place with the song "Pecado de Amar". From 1993 to 2000, Zé da Vesga always won one of the three top places in the CIRV's song festival with the songs Balada Proíbida, Por te querer, Desta Vez, Canto Magoado, Bluff de Mim (lyrics of Rui Balsemão), Quero ver-te, Se quiseres, Um Pouquinho de Espaço, Nas Margens do Tempo. All these songs were performed by different artists from the Portuguese community.

In Newark, USA, Zé won third place in the Foundation Bernardino Coutinho's song festival, in 1995 and 1996 with the songs Meditação and Porquê, Porquê. In 1997, he won first place with the song Chuva de Amor, interpreted by Sónia Mara and second place with the song Amor é o teu nome. In 1998, Zé da Vesga won third place with the song Aconteceu. In 1999, Isabel Sinde con-

Zé da Vesga singing one of his songs.

quered the first place with Zé's song Romance Colorido. Finally, in 2000, Zé da Vesga chose the Portuguese community diva Sarah Pacheco to interpret his song "Eu sou" at the first Portuguese Youth Festival, organized by the television station RTP-Porto, in the town of Matosinhos.

Zé da Vesga has dedicated most of his life to music and he has always tasted success. Zé da Vesga is a poet and musician in the Portuguese community from whom we come to expect much more.

JMC-2004

Vieira, Manuel

Town of Água de Pau, island of São Miguel, Azores

Our pioneer Manuel Vieira was born in Água de Pau, in the island of São Miguel, in the Azores, on March 4, 1929. Still as a child, Manuel began working in the fields and farming was his profession. Tired of his life as a farmer, Manuel Vieira tried to search for new horizons and a better way of life. Canada seemed to be the perfect choice for change. He boarded the Saturnia and took off to Canada on May 13, 1953, traveling with eighteen other men from São Miguel and another group from mainland Portugal.

Manuel Vieira married Maria Manuela, a native from the city of Ponta Delgada, in the island of São Miguel, where she was born on February 19, 1942. Manuel married her by proxy on February 19, 1953. Maria Manuela, who is also a pioneer, came to Canada to live with her husband in October of 1953, in Toronto. The Vieira's have a daughter, Isaura, now Mrs. Brott. Isaura is now the proud mother of two girls.

Standing: José Bento, Afonso Maria Tavares, Armando Vieira, two german friends, Manuel Vieira. Sitting: a romanian friend and João Martins.

As soon as he arrived in Halifax, Manuel Vieira was sent to Quebec to work on a vegetable and a tobacco farm. Manuel was there for six months. When the first contract ended, Manuel decided to go to Montreal where he found a job to work in the construction of tunnels just north of the city. In 1955, Manuel decided to move to Toronto. By March of 1956, unable to find a job, Manuel went to Winnipeg. There he found a job in construction. At the end of nine months in Winnipeg, Manuel moved to Kanora, Ontário, and stayed there until February of 1957. By this time, Manuel chose Toronto as the place to settle down. He got a job

The couple Vieira with daughter, son-in-law and granddaughter on Manuel's 65th birthday.

Maria Manuela and Manuel Vieira with granddaughters Isaura and Júlia.

as a supervisor for the Mac Eachern Ltd. For 16 years, Manuel hired many Portuguese men who came knocking at the door looking for a job. Mac Eachern closed down and Manuel Vieira got a job at the Mississauga Board of Education in the maintenance department. Manuel stayed at the Board of Education until he decided to retire.

Manuel Vieira, just like many of his fellow travelers, searched for a place where he could spend a few hours with friends to talk about the hardships they all faced when arriving in Canada. Thus, when the First Portuguese Canadian Club was formed, Manuel Vieira served as treasurer for six months. Later on, in 1986, Manuel Vieira became member and served as director of the Portuguese Club of Mississauga. After many years of dedication and hard work to the community, Manuel Vieira decided to quit the clubs and associations to spend more time with his family.

Manuel Vieira is now traveling with his wife getting to know Canada better and visiting Portugal, specially the Azores, more often.

JMC - 1999

Viola, António Faria

Village of Nossa Senhora da

Conceição, town of Peniche

O n January 20, 1986, the Portuguese community of Toronto had the opportunity to be at the Consulate General of Portugal where many pioneers received merit medals to celebrate the 30th anniversary of their official arrival in Canada. Among these pioneers, there was the oldest of them all: António Faria Viola.

António was born on August 25, 1920, in Nossa Senhora da Conceição, a village in the town of Peniche, in mainland Portugal. He arrived in Canada on June 7, 1952, aboard the Vulcania from Lisbon to Halifax. He is a professional carpenter. His wife, Maria, joined him in 1963. Now that he is retired, António Viola would like

António and Maria Viola.

to see old friends, such as João Silva who is now living in Prince George and who had come to Canada in March of 1952, a year before the first official group of Portuguese men had arrived in Canada with working contracts. He also misses Gilberto, who was from the town of Vila Franca de Xira, in mainland Portugal, the Silveira and Ribeiro friends who are living in Kitimat and Frederico Gomes Guerra and Norberto Mota who helped António when he arrived in Canada. These two had arrived six months before António Viola.

- When I arrived in Canada, I traveled by myself. I mean I was the only Portuguese man from Peniche aboard the Vulcania traveling to Canada. – António began telling us. – There were a few others, but they were all going to the United States. I still remember two other guys – Salvadinho and Zé Batata who later became my first colleague at work – who traveled as tourists, but obtained the landed immigrant status six months after. Back then, it was very hard to survive in a country like this.

- How did you communicate with the Canadian people?

- I don't even know how I understood them. I used gestures, pointed my fingers to different things... I don't know. You know, because I didn't speak English, I spent the first three weeks in Canada eating pork chops.

This is the way our pioneers began their new life in a new, strange and cold country with people speaking a different language and having different customs. How does one communicate with them? How can you find a job and adapt yourself to the new situation?

António Faria Viola receiving the merit medal from consul general of Portugal, Tânger Correia.

- It is hard to explain! We feel lonely and there is huge emptiness in our hearts. When people used to explain things to us, we didn't understand them, but tried to guess what their saying by their gestures and by what we see. We tend to imitate others. You know, it is the survivor's law.

- Where did you find your first job?

- I began working on Seven Islands, in the Quebec. I was there for nine months working on the railroads. From here, I went to Goose Base, the American-Canadian military base in Labardor where I worked for three years. From here, I spent another six month period in Bafim Island. Then I worked in Vancouver, Kitimat and many other locations which I no longer remember. I then took some time to go back to Portugal to visit my family. When I returned to Canada, I decided to live in Toronto.

- After working in so many different places in Canada, we must have some funny stories to share with us. Do you recall one in particular which has touched you in a special away?

- I often remember the five days I spent aboard the Vulcania when I came to Canada. Back then, when you left your country you would have an inspector traveling with you to help you with the bureaucratic situations you faced. As I said, there were two other Portuguese guys traveling on the same boat, and the inspector decided to introduce us to make the trip more pleasant. When you have someone to talk to, time goes by faster. When we were introduced, I found them to be very rude, but they promised to keep me company. As soon as the inspector left, they looked at me and disappeared. I never spoke to them during the trip because they pretended they did not know me and ran away from me every time they spotted me. I was very intrigued by this. When we arrived in Halifax, I asked them if I could take a taxi with them to the address I had with me. I told them that my friend would perhaps be able to help them too. They didn't accept my offer and went alone. I took a taxi and followed them. When they stopped in front of their friend's house, I did the same. At this point, they were looking at me with very angry eyes. I asked their friend if he knew my friend to which he said yes. They had even been talking about me. So I entered the house with those two angry guys looking at me. I couldn't resist it anymore and asked them why they were acting so strangely. To my surprise, they began laughing and told me they thought I was from PIDE* because I had been introduced by the immigration inspector. Then I found out that they actually had a reason to fear me. They had tried boarding another ship a day before we left Lisbon and were kicked out last minute due to an anonymous tip. So they were afraid of me. That's how it was with Salazar.

- Did you become friends after this incident?

- Yes! When we took the train in Halifax to come to Montreal we were already good friends. I opened a Port wine bottle to celebrate our new friendship.

- How was work like in an environment where people only spoke English or French?

- Well, at the beginning, I lived a few funny situations. When I was working at the Seven Islands, in Quebec, I used to enter and leave my job without saying a word because I didn't speak English, nor French. The other Portuguese who was working at the Seven Islands was located 40 miles from my job site. He was also from Peniche. So during the week I was basically deaf, but then on weekends, when my friend from Peniche came down to visit me, we sounded like a pair of parrots. I just couldn't keep my mouth shut.

António Viola showing his 1952 passport with his friend and pioneer Carlos da Autoguia at the 50th anniversary of the Portuguese community in 2003.

Today, when we hear these funny, but dramatic stories, it is still difficult to imagine the hardships and sacrifices our pioneers made among people they did not understand and who, in return, would make fun of their efforts. Perhaps the biggest frustration is to have the will to do something, but be unable to do it because of a language barrier.

- And the fear we had of losing our jobs. – Viola continued. – When I was at the Seven Islands, my colleagues were French Canadian men from Nova Scotia. They spoke both English and French with a strange accent. When they spoke English to me, I used to answer "No parle French". Other times, they would speak French to me and I say "me no speak English". I was always confused by their accent. Now, I laugh at the situation, but back then it was pretty dramatic.

Beside António Viola, his wife Maria was laughing at his stories and admiring proudly her husband. We asked her what she thought of Canada when she first arrived.

- I found Canada a very strange country. When I left the airplane, in Montreal, I almost fell on the stupid snow. I still don't know how I found my balance. I was astonished with the snow. When I got home, my husband had already purchased a pair of boots for me.

- She landed in Montreal and came to Toronto by bus. – António Viola told us.

- Did you ever fear you would lose your husband, that he would forget about you?

- No! I didn't even think about it. Just like I never thought that I would come to live in Canada one day. We had decided that he would come to Canada for a few years to make some money and then return to Portugal.

- That's right! – António told us. – Back in Peniche, I had a shop and a furniture store. In 1952, things were difficult in Portugal and I thought about emigrating to Venezuela. Then, I gave up on that idea, and ended up choosing Canada. I only wanted to make some money and return home. In 1958, I actually went back to Portugal and stayed there until 1963.

- However, fate had decided something else for you.

- True! In 1963, my son was almost reaching the age to go into the military service and there were talks that he could be sent to Angola or Mozambique to fight in the war. So I decided to come back to Canada and to bring my family with me.

- Do you regret that decision?

- No, absolutely not! I would probably be well living there, since the furniture industry prospered very well, but things here are different. Thank God, my children are also very well in life.

- And you, Mrs. Viola, do you regret coming to Canada?

- Never! I like Canada a lot. When I go to Portugal on holidays, I am always waiting to come back.

- She likes Canada more than I do. – António interrupted.

- It is true! – Maria continued. – Besides, here I have my two children and four grand-children. Canada is beautiful both in the winter and in the summer time.

After some many years in Canada and so many sacrifices, António Viola still prefers in hometown in Portugal.

- I have a house there, my children are well in life, so I would definitely be better there. I could fish, talk to my old friends, I don't know… there are so many nice things to do there. Oh well! Maria needs medical attention and I know that here she will be looked after in a special away.

- Did you ever suffer any setback in Canada?

- No, not really! Life was always beautiful for me. I was always a healthy person, always had a job…

What better ending can you have for a story and for a life of adventure in a different country? We hope that the Violas continue enjoying life to its fullest with their family.

* PIDE was the Portuguese police with an international mandate under the dictatorship run by António de Oliveira Salazar.

JMC - February of 1986

The first Portuguese dog to travel to Canada brought by António Viola. In the picture we also see Michelle Ribeiro playing with the dog.

Viveiros, Henrique da Ponte

Town of Santa Bárbara da Ribeira Grande,

island of São Miguel, Azores

Henrique da Ponte Viveiros is a fighter. He was born in the town of Santa Bárbara da Ribeira Grande, in the island of São Miguel, Azores, on September 22, 1943. After completing the mandatory schooling, Henrique went to work in the fields with his family. He also completed his military service in São Miguel between 1964 and 1966. Henrique was also trained to go to Africa to fight the war on Portugal's side, but never went.

Always hoping to reach new horizons and to find a better way of life, Henrique da Ponte Viveiros decided to emigrate to Canada. He arrived on January 6, 1967 and chose Brampton, in Ontario, as his place

Henrique, a proud grandfather, with his grandson.

to live. At that time, the city had a population of approximately 17 400 people, but very few Portuguese. Henrique decided to go to Brampton because his father was already living there since 1965. His first job in Brampton was at the Tender Fresh chicken factory. He remembers giving the boss José Carvalho, a Portuguese man from Portugal's mainland, two bottles to see if he could find him a job because things were really hard at that time.

From here, Henrique had many jobs, including picking up tobacco in the summer.

Family picture: Maria da Conceição, Sandy, Kevin, Debbie and Henrique Viveiros.

The Viveiros family at a portuguese event.

Sometime after, he found a job at Dexi Cup where he worked for seven and half years. Meanwhile, on October 18, 1968, Henrique married Maria da Conceição Jácome da Costa by proxy. Maria was born on April 18, 1944, in the town of Ribeira Grande. In June of 1969, the couple blessed their union at Santa Maria church in Toronto. In December of 1973, Henrique decided to quit his job at Dexi Cup and returned to Portugal. There, he bought a taxi and worked as a taxi driver for one year. Unhappy with his situation, Henrique decided to return to Canada. He came back on December 24, 1974, several months after the carnation revolution in Lisbon.

The couple has three children, all born in Brampton: Sandy, born in 1970; Kevin, born in 1972; and Debbie, born in 1975. Sandy is married and is the proud mother of one boy and Kevin is also the proud father of a girl. When Henrique returned to Canada in 1974, he was unable to find the job he had left. He came during the time of crisis in Ontario. The only job he found was in construction where he worked for seven months. From here, he went to Mississauga to work at a metal factory. At the end of 1975, his friend João Felício invited João to work with him in home delivery of bread. At the end of a three month period, Henrique took over the entire business, even with his wife's fear it would not work out. So for the next four and half years, Henrique

Maria and Henrique Viveiros on holidays... whenever they can take a break from their busy life.

worked six days a week, delivering bread to 120 homes. While buying his bread and delivering it to people's homes, Henrique saw the Nelson Food Store for sale. The store was owned by João Farias. Still with his wife's fears, Henrique decided to purchase the store in 1985. It has been fifteen long but successful years. The now Viveiro's Supermarket is a reference in the Portuguese community in Brampton. When he purchased the supermarket, Henrique began making Azorean, Madeira and mainland style sausages, which proved to be a success.

Although a busy businessman, Henrique Viveiros never forgot the social aspect of the Portuguese community. He was one of the founding members of the Portuguese Community Centre of Brampton and served as its director for many years. Together with his brother Emanuel, Henrique was the first one to organize the Holy Spirit festivities in Brampton and the celebration of Our Lady of Fatima.

To be involved in his community is for Henrique a therapy which helps him relax from his daily life, while helping him forget the sacrifices he made to come to Canada, the sacrifices he made while living in Canada and the feeling of constantly missing his homeland. Henrique da Ponte Viveiros is a fighter and true conquer.

JMC - 1999

Viveiros, Manuel Nunes de

Town of Machico, Madeira island

W ith much work and sacrifice, he came and conquered. Manuel Nunes de Viveiros was born in Machico, a small town in Madeira island, on October 7, 1935. He

Manuel and Anneliese Viveiros.

studied at the Industrial School of Funchal, in Madeira. At the end of his studies, he volunteered to join the Portuguese Air Force where he took an electronics course. While at the Air Forces, Manuel traveled to Portugal's mainland and then, in 1960, to Guinea, during the war between the Portuguese colonies in Africa and Portugal.

On April 1, 1963, Manuel decided to try his fate in Canada. Since he had an electronics course, it was not too difficult for him to find a job. For eleven years, Manuel worked as an electronic technician at Solacanada. When he noticed the opportunities Canada offered to business people, Manuel Viveiros decided to open his own company. Thus, in 1973, he began operating a shop of electric transformers and adapters from his home's basement. Due to the high number of demands, his business quickly expanded. Manuel was making high quality adapters and selling them for lower prices.

In 1974, he decided to rent a store on Tornbram Road, in Brampton, and opened his factory of adapters and electric trans-

The Viveiros at the Madeira Park.

Manuel Viveiros serves a Madeira-style Kebab to his wife and friends at the Madeira Park.

formers. Sales reached the highest peak in a very short period of time. Ten years later, in 1984, he bought a 90 squared-feet property where he now has his factory – REX Manufacturer, in Rexdale. Nowadays, Manuel employs 180 people.

When he arrived in Canada, Manuel decided to study English at night. While going to school, he met the young Anneliese, a beautiful lady from Austria, who was also a recent immigrant in Canada. Manuel and Anneliese married on July 31, 1969. Anneliese works with her husband and is the company's treasurer.

The Medeiros' are honorary members of the Canadian Madeira Club of Toronto. They frequently visit Portugal's mainland, Madeira island and Austria. They love traveling and have

been to USA, all over Canada, Hong Kong, Macau, China, Thailand, Malasia, Singapore, Bali, Egypt, Israel and most countries in Europe. They have an apartment in Florida where they spend eight weeks every year, taking two weeks each time. Rex Manufacturer is the most advanced electronics company in Canada and it possesses the best electronic technicians in the country. Thus, they provide parts to big companies, such as the Toronto's Transit Commission.

Anneliese and Manuel Viveiros were made for one another. They even share a passion for hunting. They hunted each other and are now a happy, successful couple.

Manuel Viveiros welcoming to his factory the president of the Madeira Autonomous Government, Alberto João Jardim.

JMC - 1999